4th Edition

English Bus H[

Smaller Groups

C000161062

British Bus Publishing

Body codes used in the Bus Handbook series:

Type:
A	Articulated vehicle
B	Bus, either single-deck or double-deck
BC	Interurban - high-back seated bus
C	Coach
M	Minibus with design capacity of 16 seats or less
N	Low-floor bus (Niederflur), either single-deck or double-deck
O	Open-top bus (CO = convertible - PO = partial open-top)

Seating capacity is then shown. For double-decks the upper deck quantity is followed by the lower deck.

Please note that seating capacities shown are generally those provided by the operator. It is common practice, however, for some vehicles to operate at different capacities when on certain duties.

Door position:-
C	Centre entrance/exit
D	Dual doorway.
F	Front entrance/exit
R	Rear entrance/exit (no distinction between doored and open)
T	Three or more access points

Equipment:-
T	Toilet	TV	Training vehicle.
M	Mail compartment	RV	Used as tow bus or engineers' vehicle.

Allocation:-
s	Ancillary vehicle
t	Training bus
u	out of service or strategic reserve; refurbishment or seasonal requirement
w	Vehicle is withdrawn and awaiting disposal.

e.g. - B32/28F is a double-deck bus with thirty-two seats upstairs, twenty-eight down and a front entrance/exit., N43D is a low-floor bus with two or more doorways.

Re-registrations:-
Where a vehicle has gained new index marks the details are listed at the end of each fleet showing the current mark, followed in sequence by those previously carried starting with the original mark.

Annual books are produced for the major groups:
The Stagecoach Bus Handbook
The First Bus Handbook
The Arriva Bus Handbook
The Go-Ahead Bus Handbook
The National Express Coach Handbook (bi-annual)

Regional books in the series:
The Scottish Bus Handbook
The Welsh Bus Handbook
The Ireland & Islands Bus Handbook
English Bus Handbook: Smaller Groups
English Bus Handbook: Notable Independents
English Bus Handbook: Coaches

Associated series:
The Hong Kong Bus Handbook
The Malta Bus Handbook
The Leyland Lynx Handbook
The Postbus Handbook
The Mailvan Handbook
The Toy & Model Bus Handbook - Volume 1 - Early Diecasts
The Fire Brigade Handbook (fleet list of each local authority fire brigade)
The Police Range Rover Handbook

Some earlier editions of these books are still available. Please contact the publisher on 01952 255669.

English Bus Handbook: Smaller Groups

This fourth edition of the English Bus Handbook: Smaller Groups is part of a series that details the fleets of certain bus and express coach operators throughout Britain. A list of current editions is shown on page 2. The operators included here are more of those who provide tendered and commercial services, primarily in England. They are the smaller groups which have not featured in their own dedicated volume. There are two other parts to the English Bus Handbook set; Notable Independents includes the former municipal fleets and a large selection of independent operators which meet the criteria for inclusion, while the third caters for the coach and touring fleets. Information and suggestions that will help us to develop these titles would be welcome.

Quality photographs for inclusion in the series are welcome, for which a fee is payable. Unfortunately the publishers cannot accept responsibility for any loss and they require that you show your name on each picture or slide. High-resolution digital images of six megapixels or higher are also welcome on CD or DVD.

To keep the fleet information up-to-date, the publishers recommend Key Publishing's magazine Buses published monthly, or for more detailed information, the PSV Circle monthly news sheets.

The writer and publisher would be glad to hear from readers should any information be available which corrects or enhances that given in this publication.

Principal Editors: Stuart Martin and Bill Potter

Acknowledgments: We are grateful to the operating companies, Tony Hunter, Tom Johnson, Andy Rigby and Michael Sanderson for their assistance in the compilation of this book. The cover photograph is by John Young; the frontispiece and rear cover views are by Richard Godfrey.

1st Edition (2008) - ISBN 1 904875 60 2

2nd Edition (2009) - ISBN 9781904875 63 5

3rd Edition (2011) - ISBN 9781904875 66 6

ISBN 9781904875 72 7

Published by British Bus Publishing Ltd

16 St Margaret's Drive, Wellington, Telford, TF1 3PH

© British Bus Publishing Ltd, September 2013

e-mail: Orders@britishbuspublishing.co.uk

www.britishbuspublishing.co.uk

Contents

Centrebus	5		Rotala	83	
Centrebus-Bowes			Central Connect		
High Peak Buses			Diamond		
Huddersfield Bus Co			Flights		
K-Line			Hallmark Coaches		
Kimes			Preston Bus		
Paul James Coaches			Wessex Connect		
White Rose					
			Transdev	97	
			Blazefield		
EYMS Group	19		London Sovereign		
East Yorkshire					
Finglands			Wellglade	110	
Whittle			Kinchbus		
			Midland General		
			Notts & Derby		
National Express Group	33		TM Buses		
National Express			Trent-Barton		
King's Ferry					
West Midands			YourBus	119	
Dundee					
			Vehicle index	122	
Le Group RATP	63				
Bath Bus Co					
Epsom Bus & Coach					
London United					
Manchester Metrolink					
Selwyn's, Hayton's					
Yellow Buses					

Frontispiece: **From RATP's Yellow Buses fleet, 416, Y416CFX, a Volvo B7TL with East Lancs bodywork, is seen in the Bournemouth.** *Richard Godfrey*
Below: **Remaining with Veolia Transdev are the Blazefield services in Lancashire and Yorkshire. Representing this fleet is 1108, YJ60ADV.** *Richard Godfrey*

CENTREBUS

Bowers - Centrebus - Huddersfield Bus Co - K-Line - Kimes - West End Travel

Centrebus Ltd, 102 Cannock St, Leicester, LE4 9HRP

Centrebus Holdings, Penistone Road, Waterloo, Huddersfield,

High Peak Buses Ltd, Aspincroft Garage, Town End, Chapel-en-le-Frith, SK23 0NU

107	w	P27MLE	Dennis Dart 10.2m	Plaxton Pointer	B37F	1996	Armchair, Brentford, 2002
113	w	L713JUD	Dennis Dart 9.8m	Plaxton Pointer	B37D	1994	MK Metro, 2004
116	w	N431CHL	Dennis Dart 9.8m	Norther Counties Paladin	B40F	1995	Stagecoach, 2008
117	w	N432CHL	Dennis Dart 9.8m	Norther Counties Paladin	B40F	1995	Stagecoach, 2008
128	HI	K828NKH	Dennis Dart 9m	Plaxton Pointer	B34F	1992	Tim's, Sheerness, 2003
129	DU	M829RCP	Dennis Dart 9.8m	Northern Counties Paladin	B39F	1995	Countryman, Ibstock, 2003
132	HI	N132XND	Dennis Dart 9.8m	Plaxton Pointer	B40F	1995	MK Metro, 2004
158	HI	P158MLE	Dennis Dart 9.8m	Plaxton Pointer	B37F	1996	Armchair, Brentford, 2002
160	DU	P160MLE	Dennis Dart 9.8m	Plaxton Pointer	B37F	1996	Armchair, Brentford, 2002
181	HI	XIL6081	Dennis Dart 9m	Plaxton Pointer	B34F	1992	London General, 2003
182	HI	XIL6082	Dennis Dart 9m	Plaxton Pointer	B34F	1992	London General, 2003
189	DU	M389KVR	Dennis Dart 9.8m	Northern Counties Paladin	B37F	1995	Countryman, Ibstock, 2003
205	CO	YN55UTA	Volkswagen Transporter	Bluebird Tucana	M16	2005	Judges, Corby, 2010
207	CO	YX05FFY	Volkswagen Transporter	Bluebird Tucana	M10	2005	Judges, Corby, 2010
208	CO	YX05FNT	Volkswagen Transporter	Bluebird Tucana	M10	2005	Judges, Corby, 2010
209	SA	T1WET	Mercedes-Benz Sprinter	Mercedes-Benz	N16F	2007	
217	CO	YX12CGV	Volkswagen Transporter	Bluebird Tucana	M10	2012	
218	CO	YX12CGY	Volkswagen Transporter	Bluebird Tucana	M10	2012	
219	CO	YX12CGZ	Volkswagen Transporter	Bluebird Tucana	M10	2012	
220	CO	KX06APV	Optare Solo M850	Optare	N28F	2006	First, 2010
221	CO	KX06APY	Optare Solo M850	Optare	N28F	2006	First, 2010
222	CO	KX06APZ	Optare Solo M850	Optare	N28F	2006	First, 2010
223	ST	PJZ9451	Optare Solo M850	Optare	N27F	2002	Bennetts, Warrington, 2010
224	ST	PJZ9452	Optare Solo M850	Optare	N27F	2002	Bennetts, Warrington, 2010
225	CO	YJ51XSO	Optare Solo M920	Optare	N27F	2002	Horsburgh, Pumpherston
226	DH	V261HEC	Optare Solo M850	Optare	N27F	1999	Metro, Blackpool, 2010
227	EL	V262HEC	Optare Solo M850	Optare	N27F	1999	Metro, Blackpool, 2010
228	HO	V264HEC	Optare Solo M850	Optare	N27F	1999	Metro, Blackpool, 2010
229	CO	KX55PFD	Optare Solo M850	Optare	N27F	2006	Northamptonshire CC
230	CO	KX55PFF	Optare Solo M850	Optare	N27F	2006	Northamptonshire CC
231	CO	KX55PFO	Optare Solo M850	Optare	N27F	2006	Northamptonshire CC
232	CO	KX03KYW	Optare Solo M920	Optare	N33F	2003	

Centrebus comprises several small operations mostly adjacent to a line following that of the M1/M6 motorways. Central operations and administration are based in Leicester. Seen in Hemel Hempstead is 160, P160MLE. *Dave Heath*

The Optare Solo has found favour with Centrebus and is to be seen on many of its rural services. One of many acquired from Veolia is 245, W50PJC, seen in Peterborough. *Mark Doggett*

233	HU	YJ51XSH	Optare Solo M920	Optare	N31F	2001	
234	HO	YJ51XSL	Optare Solo M920	Optare	N31F	2001	
235	CO	YJ07EFY	Optare Solo M710	Optare	N22F	2007	
236	CO	YJ07EFZ	Optare Solo M710	Optare	N22F	2007	
237	CO	YJ07VRV	Optare Solo M710	Optare	N27F	2007	
238	CO	YJ07VRW	Optare Solo M710	Optare	N22F	2007	
239	SA	YC51HAA	Optare Solo M920	Optare	N33F	2001	
240	SA	PJZ9450	Optare Solo M920	Optare	N33F	2003	
241	SA	W654PUT	Optare Solo M920	Optare	N35F	2000	Veolia, 2011
242	SA	S20PJC	Optare Solo M920	Optare	N30F	2002	Veolia, 2011
243	SA	W30PJC	Optare Solo M920	Optare	N34F	2001	Veolia, 2011
244	SA	W40PJC	Optare Solo M920	Optare	N34F	2001	Veolia, 2011
245	SA	W50PJC	Optare Solo M920	Optare	N34F	2001	Veolia, 2011
246	SA	W60PJC	Optare Solo M920	Optare	N34F	2001	Veolia, 2011
247	SA	CE52UWX	Optare Solo M850	Optare	N32F	2002	Veolia, 2011
248	SA	CE52UWY	Optare Solo M850	Optare	N32F	2002	Veolia, 2011
249	SA	YJ06YPT	Optare Solo M990	Optare	N37F	2006	Veolia, 2011
250	LE	MX05ELO	Optare Solo M920	Optare	N34F	2005	Veolia, 2011
251	SA	YJ56AUN	Optare Solo M990	Optare	N37F	2006	Veolia, 2011
252	SA	YJ56AUO	Optare Solo M990	Optare	N37F	2006	Veolia, 2011
253	SA	YJ56WVO	Optare Solo M990	Optare	N37F	2006	Veolia, 2011
254	SA	YJ56YRX	Optare Solo M920	Optare	N33F	2006	Veolia, 2011
255	SA	YN03ZXB	Optare Solo M920	Optare	N34F	2003	Veolia, 2011
256	SA	YN03ZXC	Optare Solo M920	Optare	N34F	2003	Veolia, 2011
257	SA	YN03ZXD	Optare Solo M920	Optare	N34F	2003	Veolia, 2011
258	LE	YJ54BTV	Optare Solo M850	Optare	N27F	2004	Veolia, 2011
259	DU	YJ05WDD	Optare Solo M850 SL	Optare	N27F	2005	Grant Palmer, Dunstable
260	DU	YJ05WDE	Optare Solo M850 SL	Optare	N27F	2005	Grant Palmer, Dunstable
261	DH	B8WER	Optare Solo M850	Optare	N27F	1999	Holmeswood Coaches
262	DH	W301EYG	Optare Solo M850	Optare	N23F	2000	Holmeswood Coaches
263	DH	B6WER	Optare Solo M850	Optare	N23F	2000	Holmeswood Coaches
264	CO	KX55PGE	Optare Solo M850 SL	Optare	N25F	2006	Northamptonshire CC
265	DH	YN03ZXA	Optare Solo M920	Optare	N33F	2003	Veolia
266	DH	V266HEC	Optare Solo M850	Optare	N27F	1999	Holmeswood Coaches
267	DH	V265HEC	Optare Solo M850	Optare	N27F	1999	Holmeswood Coaches

English Bus Handbook: Smaller Groups

Optare Solo 302, FJ08MBV, is one of ten based in Dunstable and is seen in the Marlowes area of Hemel Hempstead while working route H4. *Mark Lyons*

268	SA	D1WET	Optare Solo M920	Optare	N29F	2005	Veolia
269	DH	MX04VLV	Optare Solo M920	Optare	N33F	2004	Littles, Ilketon
270	DH	YN04LWU	Optare Solo M920	Optare	N33F	2004	Veolia
271	LE	W606PTO	Optare Solo M920	Optare	N33F	2000	Nottingham CT
272	LE	W607PTO	Optare Solo M920	Optare	N33F	2000	Nottingham CT
273	LE	W608PTO	Optare Solo M920	Optare	N33F	2000	Nottingham CT
274	LS	YN53SVE	Optare Solo M850	Optare	N29F	2003	Transdev
275	ST	YN04LWT	Optare Solo M920	Optare	N33F	2004	Veolia
276	SA	YJ51ZVX	Optare Solo M920	Optare	N33F	2002	City of Nottingham, 2013
277	HI	YJ51ZVZ	Optare Solo M920	Optare	N33F	2002	City of Nottingham, 2013
278	HI	YN54CFF	Optare Solo M850	Optare	N29F	2004	
300	LS	YN03NDU	Optare Solo M920	Optare	N34F	2003	Ipswich Buses, 2010
301	DU	FJ08MBU	Optare Solo M950	Optare	N33F	2008	
302	DU	FJ08MBV	Optare Solo M950	Optare	N33F	2008	
303	DU	FJ08MBO	Optare Solo M950	Optare	N33F	2008	
304	ST	FJ08MBF	Optare Solo M880	Optare	N29F	2008	
305	ST	FN08CHH	Optare Solo M880	Optare	N29F	2008	
306	DU	FN08CHG	Optare Solo M880	Optare	N29F	2008	
307	LE	MX08DJJ	Optare Solo M850	Optare	N28F	2008	
308	HU	YJ09MJO	Optare Solo M950	Optare	N29F	2009	
309	KL	YJ09MJU	Optare Solo M950	Optare	N30F	2009	
310	EL	YJ59NPF	Optare Solo M950	Optare	N33F	2009	
311	EL	YJ59NPG	Optare Solo M950	Optare	N33F	2009	
312	EL	YJ59NPK	Optare Solo M880 SL	Optare	N28F	2009	
313	EL	YJ59NPN	Optare Solo M880 SL	Optare	N28F	2009	
314	EL	YJ59NPO	Optare Solo M880 SL	Optare	N28F	2009	
315	EL	YJ59NPP	Optare Solo M950	Optare	N28F	2009	
316	EL	YJ59NPU	Optare Solo M880 SL	Optare	N28F	2009	
317	EL	YJ59NPV	Optare Solo M880 SL	Optare	N28F	2009	
318	GR	YJ59NPA	Optare Solo M950	Optare	N33F	2009	
319	GR	YJ59NPC	Optare Solo M950	Optare	N33F	2009	
320	GR	YJ59NPD	Optare Solo M950	Optare	N33F	2009	
321	GR	YJ59NPE	Optare Solo M950	Optare	N33F	2009	
322	ST	YJ10EYO	Optare Solo M950	Optare	N28F	2010	
323	ST	YJ10EYP	Optare Solo M950	Optare	N28F	2010	

324	EL	S624JRU	Optare Solo M850	Optare	N30F	1998	Go-South Coast, 2010	
325	EL	S625JRU	Optare Solo M850	Optare	N30F	1998	Go-South Coast, 2010	
326	HO	S626JRU	Optare Solo M850	Optare	N30F	1998	Go-South Coast, 2010	
327	EL	S627JRU	Optare Solo M850	Optare	N30F	1998	Go-South Coast, 2010	
328	HO	YG02FVZ	Optare Solo M920	Optare	N33F	2002	Ipswich Buses, 2010	
329	EL	S629JRU	Optare Solo M850	Optare	N30F	1998	Go-South Coast, 2010	
330	EL	S630JRU	Optare Solo M850	Optare	N30F	1998	Go-South Coast, 2010	
331	DH	S276AOX	Optare Solo M850	Optare	N27F	1999	National Express WM, 2010	
332	DH	X232MBJ	Optare Solo M920	Optare	N33F	2001	Ipswich Buses, 2010	
333	DH	X233MBJ	Optare Solo M920	Optare	N33F	2001	Ipswich Buses, 2010	
334	DU	X234MBJ	Optare Solo M920	Optare	N33F	2001	Ipswich Buses, 2010	
335	HU	X235MBJ	Optare Solo M920	Optare	N33F	2001	Ipswich Buses, 2010	
336	HU	X236MBJ	Optare Solo M920	Optare	N33F	2001	Ipswich Buses, 2010	
337	HO	NY03PUV	Optare Solo M920	Optare	N33F	2003	Abbots of Leeming, 2010	
338	HO	MX06BTE	Optare Solo M920	Optare	N33F	2006	BAA, Glasgow, 2010	
339	ST	MX08MYW	Optare Solo M880	Optare	N28F	2008	Britannia Parking, 2010	
340	EL	MX09TDG	Optare Solo M920	Optare	N33F	2003	Peoplesbus, 2010	
341	EL	R606NFX	Optare Solo M850	Optare	N30F	1998	Go-South Coast, 2010	
342	EL	R607NFX	Optare Solo M850	Optare	N30F	1998	Go-South Coast, 2010	
343	EL	R608NFX	Optare Solo M850	Optare	N31F	1998	Go-South Coast, 2010	
344	EL	R613NFX	Optare Solo M850	Optare	N31F	1998	Go-South Coast, 2010	
345	LE	W6JPT	Optare Solo M920	Optare	N34F	1998	JPT, Middleton, 2010	
346	LE	VU52UEA	Optare Solo M920	Optare	N33F	2002	Munro, Jedburgh, 2010	
347	DH	VU52UEC	Optare Solo M920	Optare	N33F	2002	Munro, Jedburgh, 2010	
348	ST	YJ05XMZ	Optare Solo M850	Optare	N28F	2005	Richmond, Barley, 2010	
349	DU	YN53ENL	Optare Solo M920	Optare	N33F	2003	Anglia, Beccles, 2010	
350	HI	MX03YCT	Optare Solo M920	Optare	N29F	2008	Woods, Wigston, 2008	
351	ST	MX05ENF	Optare Solo M920	Optare	N29F	2008	Britannia, Bournemouth, 08	
352	ST	MX05EKT	Optare Solo M920	Optare	N29F	2008		
353	ST	MX05EKV	Optare Solo M920	Optare	N29F	2008		
354	HO	MW52PZE	Optare Solo M850	Optare	N30F	2003	FairRider, Huddersfield, '07	
355	HO	MX03YCZ	Optare Solo M850	Optare	N27F	2003	FairRider, Huddersfield, '07	
356	HO	MX04VMG	Optare Solo M920	Optare	N33F	2004	Mistral, Knutsford, 2006	
357	HO	MX55BYK	Optare Solo M850	Optare	N28F	2005		
358	HO	YJ56WFH	Optare Solo M920 SL	Optare	N32F	2006	Operated for Metro (Yorks)	
359	HO	YJ56WFK	Optare Solo M920 SL	Optare	N32F	2006	Operated for Metro (Yorks)	
360	HO	MX56NLP	Optare Solo M920 SL	Optare	N31F	2006		
361	HO	MX07BCO	Optare Solo M780	Optare	N24F	2007		
362	HO	YJ57UFH	Optare Solo M710 SL	Optare	N24F	2007		
363	ST	S285NRB	Optare Solo M920	Optare	N33F	1998	City of Nottingham, 2008	
364	ST	T297BNN	Optare Solo M920	Optare	N33F	1998	City of Nottingham, 2008	
365	ST	T298BNN	Optare Solo M920	Optare	N33F	1998	City of Nottingham, 2008	
366	CO	YG52DFX	Optare Solo M920	Optare	N32F	2002	Eve, Dunbar, 2011	
367	CO	V110LVH	Optare Solo M920	Optare	N31F	1999		
368	LE	K2YCL	Optare Solo M920	Optare	N31F	1999		
369	HI	X938NUB	Optare Solo M920	Optare	N33F	2000	Richmond, Barley, 2008	
370	DH	X942NUB	Optare Solo M920	Optare	N34F	2000		
371	DH	X944NUB	Optare Solo M920	Optare	N34F	2000		
372	HI	CE52UXF	Optare Solo M920	Optare	N31F	2003		
373	SA	CE52UWZ	Optare Solo M920	Optare	N31F	2003		
374	DH	MX53FDG	Optare Solo M920	Optare	N31F	2003		
375	DH	YJ54UBH	Optare Solo M920	Optare	N31F	2005		
376	DH	YJ05WDA	Optare Solo M920	Optare	N31F	2005		
377	DH	YJ05XMU	Optare Solo M920	Optare	N31F	2005		
378	DH	YJ06FXP	Optare Solo M780	Optare	N27F	2006		
379	DH	YJ06FXR	Optare Solo M920	Optare	N31F	2006		
380	HU	MX04VMC	Optare Solo M920	Optare	N33F	2004	Stringer, Pontefract, 2010	
381	HU	MX55WCW	Optare Solo M920	Optare	N33F	2005	Tyrerbus, Nelson, 2010	
382	ST	MX53FEG	Optare Solo M850	Optare	N29F	2004	Bromyard Omnibus, 2006	
383	ST	MX53FEH	Optare Solo M850	Optare	N29F	2004	Ambassador, 2006	
384	HI	FN56BWV	Optare Solo M750 SL	Optare	N27F	2006		
385	LE	MX06BPO	Optare Solo M850	Optare	N33F	2006	Huyton, Liverpool, 2007	
386	HI	FN56CZS	Optare Solo M750 SL	Optare	N27F	2007		
387	ST	MX03YCM	Optare Solo M850	Optare	N29F	2003	Henderson, Hamilton, 2007	
388	ST	Y38HBT	Optare Solo M850	Optare	N29F	2001	NE Somerset UA, 2007	
389	ST	Y39HBT	Optare Solo M850	Optare	N29F	2001	NE Somerset UA, 2007	
390	ST	MX03YDA	Optare Solo M850	Optare	N29F	2003	Comfybus, 2007	
391	ST	VU02TSV	Optare Solo M920	Optare	N33F	2002	Irvine, Law, 2007	
392	ST	VU02TSX	Optare Solo M920	Optare	N33F	2002	Irvine, Law, 2007	
393	ST	MX07JNL	Optare Solo M780 SE	Optare	N22F	2007		

Grantham is the location for this picture of 559, R559UOT, a full-length Dennis Dart with UVG UrbanStar bodywork. The UrbanStar model developed into the Compass, a type also operated by Centrebus.
John Young

394	CO	MX07JNN	Optare Solo M780 SE	Optare	N23F	2007	
395	ST	MX07BCF	Optare Solo M950	Optare	N33F	2007	
396	DU	YJ60LRA	Optare Solo M950	Optare	N33F	2010	
397	DU	YJ60LRE	Optare Solo M950	Optare	N33F	2010	
398	SA	YJ60LPY	Optare Solo M950	Optare	N33F	2010	
399	SA	YJ60LPZ	Optare Solo M950	Optare	N33F	2010	
428	ME	AV51AVA	Mercedes-Benz Vario O810	Plaxton Beaver 2	B27F	2002	
433	HI	R149UAL	Mercedes-Benz Vario 0814	Alexander ALX100	B27F	1998	Arriva Midlands, 2008
434	HI	R151UAL	Mercedes-Benz Vario 0814	Alexander ALX100	B27F	1998	Arriva Midlands, 2008
438	HI	R161UAL	Mercedes-Benz Vario 0814	Alexander ALX100	B27F	1998	Arriva Midlands, 2008
439	HI	R162UAL	Mercedes-Benz Vario 0814	Alexander ALX100	B27F	1998	Arriva Midlands, 2008
440	GR	R164UAL	Mercedes-Benz Vario 0814	Alexander ALX100	B27F	1998	Arriva Midlands, 2008
441	HI	R166UAL	Mercedes-Benz Vario 0814	Alexander ALX100	B27F	1998	Arriva Midlands, 2008
445	BO	YN54WCO	Mercedes-Benz Vario 0814	Plaxton Beaver 2	B29F	2004	
446	BO	YN54WCP	Mercedes-Benz Vario 0814	Plaxton Beaver 2	B29F	2004	
447	HI	YN54WCY	Mercedes-Benz Vario 0814	Plaxton Beaver 2	B29F	2004	
449	HI	YN54WCZ	Mercedes-Benz Vario 0814	Plaxton Beaver 2	B29F	2004	
450	DU	YN55YSG	Mercedes-Benz Vario 0814	Plaxton Beaver 2	B29F	2005	
451	CO	YN55YSH	Mercedes-Benz Vario 0814	Plaxton Beaver 2	B29F	2005	
452	HI	YN54DCU	Mercedes-Benz Vario 0814	Plaxton Beaver 2	B29F	2004	County Links, Solihull, 2013
500	LE	Y534XAG	Dennis Dart SLF 10.1m	Plaxton Pointer 2	N30D	2001	London United, 2012
501	SA	YX13EJA	ADL E20D	ADL Enviro 200	N41F	2013	
502	DU	S502APP	Dennis Dart SLF 10.7m	Plaxton Pointer 2	N39F	1998	Sovereign, 2004
503	DU	KUI6564	Dennis Dart SLF	Plaxton Pointer	N41F	1998	K-Line, Honley, 2007
504	ST	HJZ9928	Dennis Dart SLF 8.8m	Plaxton Pointer MPD	N29F	2000	Woods, Leicester, 2008
505	ST	HJZ9929	Dennis Dart SLF 8.8m	Plaxton Pointer MPD	N29F	2000	Woods, Leicester, 2008
506	SA	YX13EJC	ADL E20D	ADL Enviro 200	N41F	2013	
507	LE	W617YBN	Dennis Dart SLF 8.8m	Plaxton Pointer MPD	N28F	2000	
508	SA	W618YBN	Dennis Dart SLF 8.8m	Plaxton Pointer MPD	N28F	2000	
510	LE	R141RLY	Dennis Dart SLF 10.1m	Plaxton Pointer 2	N30D	1997	Trustybus, Harlow, 2009
511	DU	T411LGP	Dennis Dart SLF 10.1m	Caetano Compass	N30D	1999	Connex, 2004
512	DU	S462LGN	Dennis Dart SLF 8.8m	Plaxton Pointer MPD	N29F	1999	Epsom Buses, 2004
513	HU	S522KFL	Dennis Dart SLF 9.3m	Marshall Capital	N32F	1998	Trustybus, Harlow, 2009
514	DH	T949BNN	Dennis Dart SLF 10.7m	Plaxton Pointer 2	N40F	1999	TrentBarton, 2012
516	DU	S466LGN	Dennis Dart SLF 8.8m	Plaxton Pointer MPD	N29F	1999	Epsom Buses, 2004

518	HI	V400CBC	Dennis Dart SLF 10.7m	Plaxton Pointer 2	N39F	1999	Midland Classic, 2010
519	DU	T419LGP	Dennis Dart SLF 10.1m	Caetano Compass	N30D	1999	Connex, 2004
521	DU	Y451TBF	Dennis Dart SLF 8.8m	Plaxton Pointer MPD	N29F	2001	
522	DU	W922JNF	Dennis Dart SLF 8.8m	Plaxton Pointer MPD	N29F	2000	Liskeard & District, 2002
523	SA	Y242FJN	Dennis Dart SLF 8.8m	Alexander ALX200	N28F	2001	Stagecoach, 2012
524	LE	Y246FJN	Dennis Dart SLF 8.8m	Alexander ALX200	N28F	2001	Stagecoach, 2012
525	HU	Y247FJN	Dennis Dart SLF 8.8m	Alexander ALX200	N28F	2001	Stagecoach, 2012
526	u	R459LGH	Dennis Dart SLF 10.1m	Plaxton Pointer	N36F	1997	Go-Ahead London, 2010
527	LE	R460LGH	Dennis Dart SLF 10.1m	Plaxton Pointer	N36F	1997	Go-Ahead London, 2010
528	HU	Y254FJN	Dennis Dart SLF 10.1m	Alexander ALX200	N31F	2001	Stagecoach, 2010
529	LE	LX51FHE	Dennis Dart SLF 10.1m	Alexander ALX200	N35F	2001	Stagecoach, 2010
530	ST	P130PPV	Dennis Dart SLF 10.7m	East Lancs Spryte	N42F	1997	Ipswich Buses, 2010
531	DU	P132PPV	Dennis Dart SLF 10.7m	East Lancs Spryte	N42F	1997	Ipswich Buses, 2010
533	ST	Y256NLK	Dennis Dart SLF 8.8m	Plaxton Pointer MPD	N29F	2001	Ensignbus, 2012
534	CO	Y259NLK	Dennis Dart SLF 8.8m	Plaxton Pointer MPD	N29F	2001	Ensignbus, 2012
535	DH	S939UAL	Dennis Dart SLF 10.7m	Plaxton Pointer 2	N41F	1998	Trentbarton, 2011
537	ST	Y257NLK	Dennis Dart SLF 8.8m	Plaxton Pointer MPD	N29F	2001	Ensignbus, 2012
538	LE	V508EFR	Volvo B6LE	East Lancs Spryte	N37F	2000	Stagecoach, 2008
539	LE	R319NGM	Dennis Dart SLF 10.1m	Plaxton Pointer	N33F	1997	Thamesdown, 2010
540	HU	NK53TJV	Bluebird LMB LFCC9	Plaxton Pointer 2	N29F	2003	Go North East, 2010
541	ST	LN03AYL	TransBus Dart 10.7m	TransBus Pointer	N37F	2003	Trustybus. 2009
542	DU	LN03AYM	TransBus Dart 10.7m	TransBus Pointer	N37F	2003	Trustybus. 2009
543	GR	AE55MVL	ADL Dart 10.7m	MCV Evolution	N40F	2006	Trustybus. 2009
544	LE	EU04BZY	TransBus Dart 10.7m	TransBus Mini Pointer	N29F	2004	Trustybus. 2009
545	HU	AE55VGD	ADL Dart 10.7m	MCV Evolution	N27F	2006	Trustybus. 2009
546	LE	Y976TGH	Dennis Dart SLF 9.3m	Plaxton Pointer 2	N29F	2006	Go-Ahead London, 2012
547	LS	AE06HBU	ADL Dart 10.7m	MCV Evolution	N27F	2006	Trustybus. 2009
548	LS	AE06HBX	ADL Dart 10.7m	MCV Evolution	N27F	2006	Trustybus. 2009
549	LE	LK07GTF	ADL Dart 4	ADL Enviro 200	N29F	2007	Trustybus. 2009
550	DU	Y263FJN	Dennis Dart SLF 10.1m	Alexander ALX200	N35F	2001	Stagecoach, 2010
551	w	LX51FHE	Dennis Dart SLF 10.1m	Alexander ALX200	N34F	2001	Stagecoach, 2010
552	GR	R552UOT	Dennis Dart SLF 10.7m	UVG Urban-Star	N44F	1997	Marchwood Motorways, 03
553	DU	Y301FJN	Dennis Dart SLF 10.1m	Alexander ALX200	N35F	2001	Stagecoach, 2010
554	DU	Y302FJN	Dennis Dart SLF 10.1m	Alexander ALX200	N35F	2001	Stagecoach, 2010
555	GR	SN55DVC	ADL Dart	ADL Pointer	N38F	2005	
556	ST	Y297FJN	Dennis Dart SLF 10.1m	Alexander ALX200	N35F	2001	Stagecoach, 2010
557	GR	Y298FJN	Dennis Dart SLF 10.1m	Alexander ALX200	N35F	2001	Stagecoach, 2010
558	SA	Y299FJN	Dennis Dart SLF 10.1m	Alexander ALX200	N35F	2001	Stagecoach, 2010
559	GR	R559UOT	Dennis Dart SLF 11.3m	UVG UrbanStar	N44F	1997	Marchwood Motorways, 03
560	LE	Y968TGH	Dennis Dart SLF 9.3m	Plaxton Pointer 2	N29F	2006	Go-Ahead London, 2012
561	LE	Y972TGH	Dennis Dart SLF 9.3m	Plaxton Pointer 2	N29F	2006	Go-Ahead London, 2012
562	DU	R462LGH	Dennis Dart SLF 10.1m	Plaxton Pointer	N36F	1997	Go-Ahead London, 2010
563	DU	Y352FJN	Dennis Dart SLF 10.1m	Alexander ALX200	N35F	2001	Stagecoach, 2010
564	ST	Y261FJN	Dennis Dart SLF 10.1m	Alexander ALX200	N35F	2001	Stagecoach, 2010
565	CO	Y264FJN	Dennis Dart SLF 10.1m	Alexander ALX200	N31F	2001	Stagecoach, 2010
566	DU	W566XRO	Dennis Dart SLF	Plaxton Pointer 2	N40F	2000	Sovereign, Stevenage, 2004
567	LS	Y256FJN	Dennis Dart SLF 10.1m	Alexander ALX200	N31F	2001	Stagecoach, 2010
568	LS	Y257FJN	Dennis Dart SLF 10.1m	Alexander ALX200	N31F	2001	Stagecoach, 2010
569	LS	Y258FJN	Dennis Dart SLF 10.1m	Alexander ALX200	N35F	2001	Stagecoach, 2010
570	GR	Y259FJN	Dennis Dart SLF 10.1m	Alexander ALX200	N35F	2001	Stagecoach, 2010
571	LS	LX51FGP	Dennis Dart SLF 10.1m	Alexander ALX200	N35F	2001	Stagecoach, 2010
572	GR	LX51FGZ	Dennis Dart SLF 10.1m	Alexander ALX200	N35F	2001	Stagecoach, 2010
573	DU	LX51FHD	Dennis Dart SLF 10.1m	Alexander ALX200	N35F	2001	Stagecoach, 2010
574	CO	LX51FPJ	Dennis Dart SLF 10.1m	Alexander ALX200	N35F	2001	Stagecoach, 2010
575	HU	LX51FHC	Dennis Dart SLF 10.1m	Alexander ALX200	N31F	2001	Stagecoach, 2010
576	LE	Y276FJN	Dennis Dart SLF 10.1m	Alexander ALX200	N35F	2001	Stagecoach, 2010
577	SA	FE52KNS	TransBus Dart 8.8m	TransBus Mini Pointer	N30F	2002	West End, Melton Mowbray
578	SA	VU52UEK	TransBus Dart 8.8m	TransBus Mini Pointer	N29F	2002	West End, Melton Mowbray
579	SA	EU03EUD	TransBus Dart 8.8m	TransBus Mini Pointer	N29F	2003	West End, Melton Mowbray
581	DU	R314NGM	Dennis Dart SLF 10.1m	Plaxton Pointer	N33F	1997	Thamesdown, 2010
582	w	R315NGM	Dennis Dart SLF 10.1m	Plaxton Pointer	N33F	1997	Thamesdown, 2010
583	GR	R317NGM	Dennis Dart SLF 10.1m	Plaxton Pointer	N33F	1997	Thamesdown, 2010
584	SA	R484LGH	Dennis Dart SLF 10.1m	Plaxton Pointer	N36F	1997	Go-Ahead London, 2010
585	DU	W985WDS	Dennis Dart SLF	Caetano Nimbus	N44F	2000	Gibson & Dist, Renfrew, 03
586	LE	V559JBH	Dennis Dart SLF 9.3m	Plaxton Pointer 2	N26F	1999	Judges, Corby, 2010
587	HU	V355DLH	Dennis Dart SLF 8.8m	Marshall Capital	N25F	1999	Judges, Corby, 2010
588	w	R309NGM	Dennis Dart SLF 9.3m	Plaxton Pointer	N34F	1997	Judges, Corby, 2010
590	GR	R155VLA	Dennis Dart SLF 10.1m	Plaxton Pointer 2	N34F	1998	Central Connect, 2009
591	HI	R132RLY	Dennis Dart SLF 10.1m	Plaxton Pointer	N34F	1997	Central Connect, 2009
593	LE	T163RMR	Dennis Dart SLF 10.7m	Plaxton Pointer 2	N38F	1999	Thamesdown, 2010

In 2006, eight Plaxton Centro-bodied VDL SB120s joined the fleet and are now working in Dunstable and Stevenage. One allocated to Stevenage is 607, FJ56ZWC. *John Young*

594	DU	X194FOR	Dennis Dart SLF	Caetano Compass	N42F	2000	Burton's, Haverhill, 2006
595	CO	T165RMR	Dennis Dart SLF 10.7m	Plaxton Pointer 2	N38F	1999	Thamesdown, 2010
596	CO	T164RMR	Dennis Dart SLF 10.7m	Plaxton Pointer 2	N38F	1999	Thamesdown, 2010
597	w	P749HND	Dennis Dart SLF 10.7m	Plaxton Pointer 2	N38F	1999	Stephensons, Rochford, '13
598	LE	Y978TGH	Dennis Dart SLF 10.7m	Plaxton Pointer 2	N38F	1999	Go-Ahead London, 2013
599	KI	V159EFS	Dennis Dart SLF 11.3m	Plaxton Pointer SPD	N42F	1998	Central Connect, 2009
601	DU	FH06KGK	VDL Bus SB120	Plaxton Centro	N40F	2006	
602	DU	KE06NZW	VDL Bus SB120	Plaxton Centro	N40F	2006	
603	DU	KE06NZX	VDL Bus SB120	Plaxton Centro	N40F	2006	
604	DU	KE06RXL	VDL Bus SB120	Plaxton Centro	N40F	2006	
605	ST	FJ56YBV	VDL Bus SB120	Plaxton Centro	N40F	2006	
606	ST	FJ56YBW	VDL Bus SB120	Plaxton Centro	N40F	2006	
607	ST	FJ56ZWC	VDL Bus SB120	Plaxton Centro	N40F	2006	
608	ST	YJ56JYB	VDL Bus SB120	Plaxton Centro	N40F	2007	
613	HO	KUI9266	DAF SB200	Wrightbus Commander	N44F	2003	
614	HO	JUI9268	DAF SB200	Wrightbus Commander	N44F	2004	
615	HO	YJ05PVO	VDL Bus SB120	Wrightbus Cadet 2	N39F	2005	
616	HO	YJ55WTD	VDL Bus SB200	Wrightbus Commander	N44F	2005	
617	HO	YJ06LFO	VDL Bus SB120	Wrightbus Cadet 2	N39F	2006	
618	HO	YE06HRX	VDL Bus SB120	Plaxton Centro	N40F	2006	
619	HO	YJ07JWC	VDL Bus SB120	Wrightbus Cadet 2	N39F	2007	
620	HO	YJ07JVL	VDL Bus SB120	Wrightbus Cadet 2	N39F	2007	
621	HO	YJ07JVM	VDL Bus SB120	Wrightbus Cadet 2	N39F	2007	
622	HO	YJ07JLU	VDL Bus SB120	Wrightbus Cadet 2	N39F	2007	Ludlows, Halesowen, 2007
623	HO	YJ56BSU	VDL Bus SB120	Wrightbus Cadet 2	N39F	2007	
624	HO	YD02RBX	DAF SB120	Wrightbus Cadet	N39F	2002	Smith, Coupar Angus, 2010
625	HO	YD02RBZ	DAF SB120	Wrightbus Cadet	N39F	2002	Smith, Coupar Angus, 2010
626	KI	Y284HUA	DAF SB120	Wrightbus Cadet	N39F	2001	Ludlows, Halesowen, 2009
627	HU	YJ07JSZ	DAF SB120	Plaxton Centro	N40F	2007	Arriva Scotland, 20
648	DH	B5WER	MAN 12.240	Plaxton Centro	N45F	2009	
649	DU	FJ59FYS	MAN 12.240	Plaxton Centro	N37F	2009	
650	DH	FJ59FYT	MAN 12.240	Plaxton Centro	N37F	2009	
652	HU	BC05JHO	MAN 14.220	MCV Evolution	N29F	2005	Airparks, Birmingham, '10

Joining the fleet in 2011 were ten VDL SB180s that carry MCV Evolution bodywork, a model for which Arriva Bus and Coach are the distributors. Pictured near Leeds is 661, YJ60GFO. *Tony Greaves*

660	LS	YJ60GFE	VDL SB180	MCV Evolution	N40F	2011	
661	LS	YJ60GFO	VDL SB180	MCV Evolution	N40F	2011	
662	LS	YJ60GFU	VDL SB180	MCV Evolution	N40F	2011	
663	LS	YJ60GFV	VDL SB180	MCV Evolution	N40F	2011	
664	LS	YJ60GFX	VDL SB180	MCV Evolution	N40F	2011	
665	LS	YJ60GFY	VDL SB180	MCV Evolution	N40F	2011	
666	LS	YJ10DFA	VDL SB180	MCV Evolution	N40F	2010	Arriva demonstrator, 2011
667	LS	YJ10DFC	VDL SB180	MCV Evolution	N40F	2010	Arriva demonstrator, 2011
668	LS	YJ60GGP	VDL SB180	MCV Evolution	N40F	2011	
669	LS	YJ60GGU	VDL SB180	MCV Evolution	N40F	2011	
679	DH	L103LRA	Volvo B10B	Northern Counties Paladin	B49F	1993	TrentBarton, 2011
680	DH	L104LRA	Volvo B10B	Northern Counties Paladin	B49F	1993	TrentBarton, 2011
681	DH	L102LRA	Volvo B10B	Northern Counties Paladin	B49F	1993	TrentBarton, 2011
682	DH	X233WRA	Optare Excel L1180	Optare	N45F	2000	TrentBarton, 2011
685	DH	W224PRB	Optare Excel L1180	Optare	N45F	2000	TrentBarton, 2011
687	HI	X227WRA	Optare Excel L1180	Optare	N45F	2000	TrentBarton, 2011
688	DH	X231WRA	Optare Excel L1180	Optare	N45F	2000	TrentBarton, 2011
689	DH	X232WRA	Optare Excel L1180	Optare	N45F	2000	TrentBarton, 2011
690	DH	FN04HSK	Scania L94 UB	Wrightbus Solar	N44F	2004	TrentBarton, 2011
691	DH	FN04HSV	Scania L94 UB	Wrightbus Solar	N44F	2004	TrentBarton, 2011
692	DH	FN04HTP	Scania L94 UB	Wrightbus Solar	N44F	2004	TrentBarton, 2011
693	DH	FN04HTU	Scania L94 UB	Wrightbus Solar	N44F	2004	TrentBarton, 2011
694	DH	FN04HSC	Scania L94 UB	Wrightbus Solar	N44F	2004	TrentBarton, 2011
695	DH	FN04HSL	Scania L94 UB	Wrightbus Solar	N44F	2004	TrentBarton, 2011
696	DH	FN04HSX	Scania L94 UB	Wrightbus Solar	N44F	2004	TrentBarton, 2011
697	DH	FN04HTC	Scania L94 UB	Wrightbus Solar	N44F	2004	TrentBarton, 2011
698	DH	FN04HTT	Scania L94 UB	Wrightbus Solar	N44F	2004	TrentBarton, 2011
701	LE	DAZ4302	Optare Excel L1150	Optare	N43F	1996	Trent Barton, 2005
702	HU	Y2DRM	Scania L94UB	Wrightbus Solar	N43F	2001	DRM, Bromyard, 2005
703	KI	YN51MJE	Scania L94 UB	Wrightbus Solar	N43F	2001	Fowlers, Holbeach Drove
704	DH	YN08AOJ	Scania OmniTown N230 UB	Wrightbus Solar	N36F	2008	
705	LE	YN07LDC	Scania OmniTown N230 UB	East Lancs Esteem	N34F	2007	
706	LE	K3YCL	Scania OmniTown N230 UB	East Lancs Esteem	N34F	2007	
707	LE	YN07LDE	Scania OmniTown N230 UB	East Lancs Esteem	N34F	2007	
708	DU	K5YCL	Scania OmniTown N230 UB	East Lancs Esteem	N34F	2007	
709	DU	K6YCL	Scania OmniTown N230 UB	East Lancs Esteem	N33F	2006	

English Bus Handbook: Smaller Groups

Seen in Leeds, Scania OmniCity 785, YN03UWR, carries lettering for the main link between the city and Leeds/Bradford airport which is located near Yeadon. These buses were new to Menzies who provide internal transport at London Heathrow, and many of the features for luggage remain. *Steve Rice*

710	DU	L170EKG	Scania N113 DRB	Alexander Strider	N48F	1994	Newport Buses, 2007
711	DU	L71EKG	Scania N113 DRB	Alexander Strider	N48F	1994	Newport Buses, 2007
712	DU	L172EKG	Scania N113 DRB	Alexander Strider	N48F	1994	Newport Buses, 2007
713	LE	M113SLS	Scania L113 CRL	Wright Endurance	N47F	1995	
714	LE	M521UTV	Scania L113 CRL	Wright Endurance	N47F	1995	
715	HI	FD02SFE	Optare Excel L1180	Optare	N41F	2002	Nottingham CT, 20
716	HI	FD02SFF	Optare Excel L1180	Optare	N41F	2002	Nottingham CT, 20
717	DU	N632XBU	Scania L113 CRL	Wright Endurance	N42F	1995	
719	HU	YJ08DWK	VDL Bus SB200	Plaxton Centro	N45F	2008	
720	HU	YJ08DWL	VDL Bus SB200	Plaxton Centro	N45F	2008	
721	HU	YJ08DWM	VDL Bus SB200	Plaxton Centro	N45F	2008	
722	HU	YJ08DWN	VDL Bus SB200	Plaxton Centro	N45F	2008	
723	HU	YJ08DWO	VDL Bus SB200	Plaxton Centro	N45F	2008	
724	HU	YJ08DWP	VDL Bus SB200	Plaxton Centro	N45F	2008	
725	HU	YJ58FFP	VDL Bus SB200	Plaxton Centro	N44F	2008	Arriva demonstrator, 2011
726	LE	YT09FME	Scania OmniLink K230 UB	Scania	N45F	2009	
727	LE	YT09FMF	Scania OmniLink K230 UB	Scania	N45F	2009	
728	KI	W178CDN	DAF SB220	Ikarus Polaris	N44F	2000	GM North, 2008
730	DH	L108VDM	Scania N113 CRB	Alexander Strider	BC50F	1994	Avon, Prenton, 2010

731-735		DAF SB220	East Lancs Myllennium	N46F		2000-01	Stagecoach, 2008
731	HU	X211HHE	**733**	HU	X213HHE	**734**	HU X214HHE	**735**	HU X215HHE
732	HU	X212HHE					

736	HO	R11WAL	DAF SB220	Ikarus Citibus	B49F	1997	Millport Motors, 2002
737	HO	M844RCP	DAF SB220	Northern Counties Paladin	B49F	1995	Arriva Bus & Coach, 2000
739	LE	YN53CHC	Scania OmnCity CN94 UB	Scania	N24D	2004	Airport Parking, 2009
740	LE	YN53CHD	Scania OmnCity CN94 UB	Scania	N24D	2004	Airport Parking, 2009
742	DH	YAZ4142	DAF SB220	Northern Counties Paladin	B49F	1996	North Kent Express, 2001
743	SA	M850RCP	DAF SB220	Northern Counties Paladin	B49F	1995	K-Line, Honley, 2001
744	LE	PAZ9346	DAF SB220	Northern Counties Paladin	B49F	1995	Go Coastline, 2002
745	LE	YJ58FFE	VDL Bus SB200	Plaxton Centro	N45F	2008	
746	LE	YJ58FFH	VDL Bus SB200	Plaxton Centro	N45F	2008	
747	LE	YJ58FFK	VDL Bus SB200	Plaxton Centro	N45F	2008	
748	DH	YN08MRO	Scania K230 UB	Wrightbus Solar	N44F	2008	Wrightbus, 2010

Crossing the Lancashire and Yorkshire borders is Optare Tempo 774, YJ10EZG, from the Elland depot near Leeds. It is seen at Lydgate on the scenic route to Rochdale. *John Young*

749	SA	YR59NNT	Scania K230 UB	Wrightbus Solar	N44F	2010	
750	SA	YR59NNU	Scania K230 UB	Wrightbus Solar	N44F	2010	
751	SA	YR59NNV	Scania K230 UB	Wrightbus Solar	N44F	2010	
754	w	TIL4051	Scania N113 CRB	Alexander Strider	BC50F	1994	Northern Blue, 2010
756	DU	K106YTX	Scania N113 CRB	Alexander Strider	BC50F	1994	Northern Blue, 2010
758	KI	KB10BUS	VDL Bus SB200	Wrightbus Pulsar 2	N44F	2010	
759	KI	AN09BUS	VDL Bus SB200	Wrightbus Pulsar 2	N44F	2009	
760	HU	YT60YYM	Scania OmniLink K230 UB	Scania	N42F	2011	
761	HU	YT60YYN	Scania OmniLink K230 UB	Scania	N42F	2011	
762	HU	YT60YYO	Scania OmniLink K230 UB	Scania	N42F	2011	
764	KI	FX04TJY	VDL Bus SB200	Wrightbus Commander	N44F	2004	
765	GR	YJ04BMV	VDL Bus SB200	Wrightbus Commander	N44F	2004	
766	KI	YJ55KZZ	VDL Bus SB200	Wrightbus Commander	N44F	2005	
770	HU	YJ05XOO	Optare Tempo X1200	Optare	N36F	2005	Wilfreda, Adwick-le-Street
771	LE	YAZ4143	Optare Excel L1180	Optare	N41F	2002	Nottingham CT, 2012
772	SA	FD51EYY	Optare Excel L1180	Optare	N41F	2002	Nottingham CT, 2012
773	EL	YJ10EZF	Optare Tempo X1130	Optare	N38F	2010	
774	EL	YJ10EZG	Optare Tempo X1130	Optare	N38F	2010	
775	EL	YJ10EZH	Optare Tempo X1130	Optare	N38F	2010	
776	EL	YJ10EZK	Optare Tempo X1130	Optare	N38F	2010	
777	GR	YJ10EZC	Optare Tempo X1130	Optare	N38F	2010	
778	GR	YJ10EZD	Optare Tempo X1130	Optare	N38F	2010	
779	GR	YJ10EZE	Optare Tempo X1130	Optare	N38F	2010	
780	LS	YN03UVS	Scania OmniCity CN94 UB	Scania	N42F	2003	Menzies, Heathrow, 2010
781	LS	YN03UVW	Scania OmniCity CN94 UB	Scania	N42F	2003	Menzies, Heathrow, 2010
782	LS	YN03UVZ	Scania OmniCity CN94 UB	Scania	N42F	2003	Menzies, Heathrow, 2010
783	LS	YN03UWA	Scania OmniCity CN94 UB	Scania	N42F	2003	Menzies, Heathrow, 2010
784	LS	YN03UWP	Scania OmniCity CN94 UB	Scania	N42F	2003	Menzies, Heathrow, 2010
785	LS	YN03UWR	Scania OmniCity CN94 UB	Scania	N42F	2003	Menzies, Heathrow, 2010
786	LS	YN03UWS	Scania OmniCity CN94 UB	Scania	N42F	2003	Menzies, Heathrow, 2010
787	LS	YN03UWT	Scania OmniCity CN94 UB	Scania	N42F	2003	Menzies, Heathrow, 2010
788	DH	YN06CJE	Scania OmniCity CN94 UB	Scania	N42F	2006	Beestons, Hadleigh, 2011
789	DH	YN07WXP	Scania OmniCity CN230 UB	Scania	N42F	2007	Beestons, Hadleigh, 2011
790	DU	R220HCD	Volvo B10BLE	Wright Renown	B46F	1998	Oxford Bus Company, 2011
791	DU	R322HCD	Volvo B10BLE	Wright Renown	B46F	1998	Oxford Bus Company, 2011

English Bus Handbook: Smaller Groups

792	SA	KIW8606	Volvo B10M-60	Van Hool Alizée	C49FT	1991	West End, Melton Mowbray
793	SA	PJI6431	Volvo B10M-60	Macedonian Motor CI (2001)	B46F	1990	Veolia, 2012
794	SA	LIL9666	Volvo B10M-60	Joncheere Deauville	C49FT	1989	West End, Melton Mowbray
795	SA	UYF463	Volvo B10M-60	Van Hool Alizée	C49FT	1991	West End, Melton Mowbray
796	SA	WET1K	Volvo B10M-60	Plaxton Excalibur	C49FT	1992	West End, Melton Mowbray
798	SA	K728DAO	Volvo B10M-55	Alexander PS	BC49F	1993	West End, Melton Mowbray
801	CR	MRY1W	Leyland Olympian ON2R56G13Z4	Leyland	B43/29F	1992	Stagecoach, 2008
803	HU	K3YCL	Leyland Olympian ON2R50C13Z4	Northern Counties Palatine	BC43/27F	1992	Stagecoach, 2008
812	GR	G622OTV	Volvo Citybus B10M-55	Alexander RV	B47/37F	1990	Trent Barton, 2008
814	LE	H474CEG	Leyland Olympian ON2R50G13Z4	Leyland	B47/31F	1990	Stagecoach, 2008
818	KI	PAZ3184	Leyland Olympian ON2R50C13Z4	Alexander RH	B47/31F	1990	Dublin Bus, 2002
819	KI	TAZ4064	Leyland Olympian ON2R50C13Z4	Alexander RH	B47/34F	1990	Dublin Bus, 2002
820	KI	YAZ8774	Leyland Olympian ON2R50C13Z4	Alexander RH	B47/33F	1990	Dublin Bus, 2002
821	KI	YAZ8773	Leyland Olympian ON2R50C13Z4	Alexander RH	B47/33F	1990	Dublin Bus, 2003
822	KI	TAZ4062	Leyland Olympian ON2R50C13Z4	Alexander RH	B47/31F	1990	Dublin Bus, 2004
823	KI	TAZ4063	Leyland Olympian ON2R50C13Z4	Alexander RH	B47/31F	1990	Dublin Bus, 2004
827	GR	G127NGN	Volvo Citybus B10M-55	Northern Counties	B45/35F	1989	Irvine, Law, 2008
873	GR	V415KMY	Dennis Trident	East Lancs Lolyne	N45/26F	1999	Stephensons, Rochford, '12
874	GR	T148CLO	Dennis Trident	Plaxton President	N45/26F	1999	Metroline, Harrow, 2012
875	LS	T421XVO	Dennis Trident	East Lancs Lolyne	N53/34F	1999	Nottingham CT, 2012
876	LE	T422XVO	Dennis Trident	East Lancs Lolyne	N53/34F	1999	Nottingham CT, 2012
877	GR	T415BNN	Dennis Trident	East Lancs Lolyne	N45/26F	1999	Nottingham CT, 2012
878	GR	K7YCL	Dennis Trident	East Lancs Lolyne	N45/26F	1999	Nottingham CT, 2012
879	LE	T419XVO	Dennis Trident	East Lancs Lolyne	N49/34F	1999	Nottingham CT, 2012
880	LE	YAZ8827	Dennis Trident	East Lancs Lolyne	N51/35F	1999	Nottingham CT, 2012
881	KI	V929FMS	Dennis Trident	Alexander ALX400	N47/27F	1999	Portsmouth University, '06
882	KI	PO51WNN	Dennis Trident	Plaxton President	N47/29F	2001	GHA, New Broughton, 2006
883	KI	T648KPU	Dennis Trident	Alexander ALX400	N51/26F	1999	Red Route, Northfleet, 2008
885	KI	PO51UNS	Dennis Trident	East Lancs Lolyne	N46/24F	2001	Go-Ahead London, 2011
886	KI	PO51UNW	Dennis Trident	East Lancs Lolyne	N46/24F	2001	Go-Ahead London, 2011
892	LS	X267NNO	Dennis Trident	Alexander ALX400	B47/24D	2000	Stagecoach, 2011
893	LS	V313GLB	Dennis Trident	Alexander ALX400	B45/19D	1999	Metroline, Harrow, 2011
894	LS	V315GLB	Dennis Trident	Alexander ALX400	B45/19D	1999	Metroline, Harrow, 2011
895	LE	V317GLB	Dennis Trident	Alexander ALX400	B45/19D	1999	Metroline, Harrow, 2011
896	LS	V906FEC	Dennis Trident 9.9m	East Lancs Lolyne	B45/27F	1999	AtBus Staines, Leeds, 2010
897	LS	V907FEC	Dennis Trident 9.9m	East Lancs Lolyne	B45/27F	1999	AtBus Staines, Leeds, 2010
904	LE	YN07LHT	Scania OmniDekka N230 UD	East Lancs Olympus	NC45/27F	2007	TransDev London, 2010
905	HU	YN07LHW	Scania OmniDekka N230 UD	East Lancs Olympus	NC45/27F	2007	TransDev London, 2010
906	HU	YN07LHZ	Scania OmniDekka N230 UD	East Lancs Olympus	NC45/27F	2007	TransDev London, 2010
920	KI	GK04NZU	VDL Bus DB250	East Lancs Lowlander	N47/27F	2004	Dublin Bus, 2008
924	KI	GX06AOE	Volvo B7TL	East Lancs Olympus	N45/27F	2006	Southdown PSV, 2011
925	LE	Y366GKR	Volvo B7TL	East Lancs Vyking	N47/32F	2000	
926	GR	PO51UMF	Dennis Trident	East Lancs Lolyne	N46/24F	2001	Go-Ahead London, 2011
931	HO	H231LOM	Scania N113DRB	Alexander RH	B45/31F	1990	Travel West Midlands, 2002
942	LE	H242LOM	Scania N113DRB	Alexander RH	B45/31F	1990	Travel West Midlands, 2002

Grantham-based Dennis Trident 926, PO51UMF, arrived at Centrebus from Go-Ahead London. Since then, two similar buses from the same batch have joined the fleet with the acquisition of Kimes. *John Young*

Previous registrations:

AV51AVA	AJ51REP	NY03PUV	XL03AOL
B5WER	FJ09ZKC	PAZ3184	90D1037, H690PTW
B6WER	W293EYG, K4HWD	PAZ9346	M848RCP
B8WER	V263HEC	PJI6431	G533LWU
BC05JHO	W444APS	PJZ9451	YC51GZW
D1WET	CN05ARO	PJZ9452	YC51GZW
DAZ4302	V394KVY	PJZ9456	MK03EJY
EU03EUD	C11WET	S20PJC	YG52DHA
FE52UNS	Y1WET	T1WET	MX59KNJ
GK04NZU	04D34671	TAZ4061	X234MRJ
HJZ9928	W871VGT	TAZ4062	90D1039, H960PTW
HJZ9929	W872VGT	TAZ4063	90D1043, H961PTW
K2YCL	V120LVH	TAZ4064	90D1056, H664PTW
K3YCL	YN07LDP	UYF463	H199DVM
K4YCL	PO51UMF	VU52UEA	VU52UEA, K6YCL
K5YCL	YN07LDF	VU52VGK	J7WET
K6YCL	YN06TGE	W301EYG	L301EYG, L6HWD
K7YCL	T416BNN	W617YNB	B1JYM
KIW8606	H177DVM	W618YNB	BUS1S
KUI6564	S782ENE, 98D70567	WET1K	YJ06YPT
KUI9266	YJ03PDY	XIL6081	K860LGN
KUI9268	YJ04HUP	XIL6082	K854LGN
LIL9666	F771OJH	Y366GKR	01D46496
M844RCP	M844RCP, KUI9266	YAZ4142	P904TWW
MRY1W	J114KCW	YAZ4143	FD51EYV
MX03YPG	MX03YPG, X10BUS	YAZ8773	90D1047, H950PTW
MX06BPO	MX06BPO, K5YCL	YAZ8774	90D1053, H808PTW
N19FUG	N614DWY	YAZ8827	T405BNN

Depots and allocations:

Corby (5 South Folds Road, NN18 9EU) - CO

Volkswagen Transporter	205	207	208	217	218	219		
Mercedes-Benz	430							
Optare Solo	220	221	222	225	229	230	231	232
	235	236	237	238	264	366	394	
Dart	534	565	574	595	596			

Doveholes (Hallsteads) - DH

Mercedes-Benz	440	445						
Optare Solo	226	261	262	263	265	266	267	269
	270	331	332	333	347	374	375	376
	377	378	379					
Dart	514	535						
Optare Excel	682	685	688	689				
Volvo B10B	679	680	681					
MAN 12.240	648	650						
Scania L94	690	691	692	693	694	695	696	697
	698							
Scania N113	730							
Scania K230	704	748						
Scanoa OmniCity	788	789						
DAF SB220	742							

Dunstable (Humphrys Rd, LU5 4TP) - DU

Mercedes-Benz	450						
Optare Solo	259	260	301	302	303	306	334	349
	396	397					
Dart	113	129	160	189	502	503	511	512
	516	519	521	522	531	542	550	553
	554	562	563	566	573	581	585	594
VDL SB120	601	602	603	604			
MAN 12.240	649						
Scania N113	708	709	710	711	712	756	
Volvo B10BLE	790	791					

Elland (Lock View, HX5 9HD) - EL

Optare Solo	227	228	310	311	312	313	314	315
	316	317	324	325	327	329	330	340
	341	342	343	344			
Optare Tempo	773	774	775	776			

Folkingham (Sleaford Road, NG34 0SB) - KI

Dart	599		
DAF SB120	626		
Scania sd	703		
DAF SB220	728	764	766
VDL SB200	758	759	
Olympian	818	819	820	821	822	823
Trident	880	881	882	883	885	886
DAF DB250	920		
Volvo B7TL	924		

Grantham (Tollemache Road South) - GR

Optare Solo	318	319	320	321			
Dart	543	552	555	557	559	570	572	583
	590						
VDL SB200	765						
Optare Tempo	777	778	779				
Volvo Citybus	812	827					
Olympian	801						
Trident	873	874	877	878	926		

Hinkley (Jacknell Road) - HI

Dart	128	132	158	181	182	518	591	
Optare Solo	350	369	372	384	386			
Mercedes-Benz	428	433	438	439	446	447	449	451
	452							
Optare Excel	687	715	716					

Huddersfield (Penistone Road, HD5 8QU) - HU

Optare Solo	233	308	335	336	380	381		
Dart	513	528	545	575				
Bluebird	540							
SB120	627							
MAN	652							
VDL SB200	719	720	721	722	723	724	725	731
	732	733	734	735				
Scania	702	760	761	762				
Tempo	770							
Olympian	803							
Trident	895							
Scania dd	905	906						

Honley (Station Road) - HO

Optare Solo	234	309	326	328	337	338	354	355
	356	357	358	359	360	361	362	
VDL SB120	613	614	615	617	618	619	620	621
	622	623	624	625				
VDL SB200/220	736	737						
Scania N113	942							

Leeds (Washington Street) - LS

Optare Solo	274	300	345					
Dart	547	548	567	568	569	571		
VDL SB180	660	661	662	663	664	665	666	667
	668	669						
Scania Omnicity	739	740	769	769	780	781	782	783
	784	785	786	787				
Trident	875	879	892	893	894	896	897	

Leicester (Humberstone Lane) and (Wenlock Way, LE4 9HU) - LE

Optare Solo	250	258	271	272	273	307	346	368
	385							
Dart	500	507	510	524	526	527	529	539
	544	546	549	560	561	578	586	593
	598							
Volvo B6	538							
Optare Excel	701	771						
Scania sd	705	706	707	713	714	726	727	
VDL SB200	744	745	746	747				
Olympian	814							
Trident	876							
Volvo B7TL	925							
Scania N230	904							
Scania N113	931							

Saxby (Old Station Drive) - SA

Iveco Daily	209							
Optare Solo	239	240	242	243	244	245	246	247
	248	249	251	252	253	254	255	256
	257	268	373	398	399			
Dart	508	523	558	577	578	579	584	
Enviro 200	501	506						
VDL SB220	743							
Scania K230	749	750	751					
Optare Excel	772							
Volvo B10M	792	793	794	795	796	797	798	

Stevenage (Whitworth Road) - ST

Optare Solo	223	224	275	304	305	322	323	339
	348	351	352	353	363	364	365	382
	383	387	388	389	390	391	392	393
	395							
Dart	504	505	530	533	537	541	546	564
VDL SB120	605	606	607	608				

Stored, Withdrawn - u/w

Remainder

EYMS GROUP

East Yorkshire - Scarborough & District - Whittle

East Yorkshire Motor Services Ltd; Finglands Coachways Ltd; Whittle Coach & Bus Ltd, 252 Anlaby Road, Hull, HU3 2RS

No.	Depot	Reg	Chassis	Body	Layout	Year	Notes
20	HL	A20EYC	Mercedes-Benz Vario O816	Plaxton Cheetah	C33F	2010	
52	HL	39EYD	Volvo B10M-62	Berkhof Axial 50	C53F	1999	Yellow Buses, 2004
55	HL	A8EYC	Volvo B12B	Plaxton Panther	C49FT	2006	
56	HL	A6EYC	Volvo B12B	Plaxton Panther	C49FT	2006	
57	HL	A7EYC	Volvo B12B	Plaxton Panther	C49FT	2006	

61-68   Volvo B12B   Caetano Levanté   C49FT   2007-08

61	HL	A1EYD	**63**	HL	YX07HJE	**67**	HL	YX07HJK	**68**	HL	YX08FYP
62	HL	A15EYC	**65**	HL	YX07HJG						

No.	Depot	Reg	Chassis	Body	Layout	Year	Notes
70	HL	A10EYC	Volvo B12B	Plaxton Panther Centenary	C49FT	2007	
71	HL	A14EYC	Volvo B12B	Plaxton Panther Centenary	C49FT	2007	
72	HL	A9EYC	Volvo B12B	Plaxton Panther	C49FT	2007	
73	HL	787EYC	Volvo B12B 13.5m	Volvo 9700 Prestige Plus	C53FT	2010	
74	HL	FN62CEA	Volvo B9R	Caetano Levanté	C49FT	2012	
75	HL	FN62CEU	Volvo B9R	Caetano Levanté	C49FT	2012	
76	HL	FN62CGX	Volvo B9R	Caetano Levanté	C49FT	2012	
77	HL	YX62FLL	Volvo B9R	Plaxton Elite	C49FT	2012	

78-83   Volvo B9B   Caetano Levanté   C48FT   On order for 2013

78	HL	-	**80**	HL	-	**82**	HL	-	**83**	HL	-
79	HL	-	**81**	HL	-						

No.	Depot	Reg	Chassis	Body	Layout	Year	Notes
85	HL	-	Dennis Trident	Alexander ALX400	NC(72)F	2003	*in build*
122	HL	FH05URN	Volvo B12B	Caetano Levanté	C49FT	2005	National Express, 2013
123	HL	FH05URP	Volvo B12B	Caetano Levanté	C49FT	2005	National Express, 2013
124	HL	FH05URR	Volvo B12B	Caetano Levanté	C49FT	2005	National Express, 2013
244	HL	BU03RTX	DAF SB120	Wrightbus Cadet	N39F	2003	
245	SH	FJ53LZW	VDL Bus SB120	Wrightbus Cadet	N39F	2004	
246	HL	MK53BLU	MAN 14.220	East Lancs Myllennium	N40F	2003	Veolia England, 2009

East Yorkshire in Hull, along with the Worcestershire operation, provide several coaches on National Express work as well as their own coaching activities. Now in East Yorkshire colours is Caetano Levanté 61, A1EYD.
Mark Doggett

Carrying the Scarborough & District fleetname is Dennis Dart 333, T284PVM, which was acquired from Prosper during 2004. Currently, some twenty Darts operate from the depot in this famous Yorkshire resort. *John Young*

250-254

			Optare Excel L1070		Optare		N36F	1998		
250	SH	R250PRH	252	SH	R252PRH	253	SH	A16EYC	254	SH	A17EYC

283-286

			Mercedes-Benz O405		Optare Prisma		BC47F*	1997	* 285/6 are B49F	
283	u	R283EKH	284	HL	EYC73	285	SH	P285WAT	286	BN	P286WAT

287-296

			Optare Excel L1150		Optare		N40F	1998		
287	HL	S287RAG	290	HL	S290RAG	293	HL	S293RAG	295	SH	S295RAG
288	BN	S288RAG	292	HL	S292RAG	294	HL	S294RAG	296	SH	S296RAG

298	u	S298PKH	Mercedes-Benz O405		Optare Prisma		B49F	1998	
299	DD	S299PKH	Mercedes-Benz O405		Optare Prisma		B49F	1998	
300	SH	S330PKH	Mercedes-Benz O405		Optare Prisma		B49F	1998	
302	HL	W817UAG	Dennis Dart SLF 8.8m		Plaxton Pointer MPD		N29F	2000	Whittle, 2011

303-307

			Dennis Dart SLF 10.7m		Plaxton Pointer 2		N39F	1999		
303	BN	T303JRH	304	BN	T304JRH	306	BY	T306JRH	307	BD	T307JRH

308-313

			Volvo B10BLE		Alexander ALX300		N44F	2000		
308	DD	W408JAT	310	SH	W410JAT	312	PN	W412JAT	313	HL	W413JAT
309	HL	W409JAT	311	HL	W411JAT						

318	SH	S789NRV	Dennis Dart SLF		Caetano Compass		N40F	1999	Frodingham Coaches, 2001
319	SH	T701APX	Dennis Dart SLF		Caetano Compass		N38F	1999	Frodingham Coaches, 2001

320-329

			MAN 18.220		Alexander ALX300		NC42F	2002		
320	HL	YX02LFK	323	HL	YX02LFN	326	HL	YX02LFR	328	HA	YX02LFT
321	HL	YX02LFL	324	HA	YX02LFO	327	HL	YX02LFS	329	HL	YX02LFU
322	HL	YX02LFM	325	HL	YX02LFP						

330	HL	WU51LBE	MAN 18.220		Alexander ALX300		N42F	2002	Neoman, 2002
333	SH	T284PVM	Dennis Dart SLF 10.7m		Plaxton Pointer 2		N38F	1999	Prosper, Manchester, 2004

The Petuaria Express was launched in April 2010 and links Gilberdyke, Newport, Elloughton and Brough with the heart of Hull. This weekday service, X57, features ten return journeys a day and terminates in the city centre. Vehicles carry a special livery as shown by 367, YX10EYS. *Richard Godfrey*

338-342

338-342			Volvo B7RLE			Wrightbus Eclipse Urban	N44F	2004		
338	EL	YX54FWL	**340**	WA	YX54FWN	**341**	HL	YX54FWO	**342**	HL	YX54FWP
339	EL	YX54FWM								

343-348

343-348			Volvo B7RLE			Wrightbus Eclipse Urban	N43F	2006		
343	HL	YX56FHL	**345**	HL	YX56FHN	**347**	HL	YX56FHP	**348**	EL	YX56FHR
344	HL	YX56FHM	**346**	HL	YX56FHO					

353-360

353-360			ADL Dart 4 10.7m			ADL Enviro 200	N37F	2007		
353	SH	YX57BXA	**355**	SH	YX57BXC	**357**	SH	YX57BXE	**359**	SH	YX57BXG
354	SH	YX57BXB	**356**	SH	YX57BXD	**358**	SH	YX57BXF	**360**	SH	YX57BXH

361-366

361-366			Volvo B7RLE			Plaxton Centro	N44F	2008		
361	SH	YX58CWA	**363**	SH	YX58CWD	**365**	SH	YX58DCE	**366**	SH	YX58DCF
362	SH	YX58CWC	**364**	SH	YX58CWE					

367-372

367-372			Volvo B7RLE			Wrightbus Eclipse Urban	N45F	2010		
367	EL	YX10EYS	**369**	HL	YX10EYU	**371**	HL	YX10EYW	**372**	HL	YX10EYY
368	EL	YX10EYT	**370**	BY	YX10EYV					

418	KD	YX51MUO	Mercedes-Benz Vario 0814	Plaxton Beaver 2	B31F	2002	
419	DD	YX51MUP	Mercedes-Benz Vario 0814	Plaxton Beaver 2	B31F	2002	
420	EL	X147JWP	Optare Solo M850	Optare	N29F	2001	Whittle, 2007
421	SH	Y351DAB	Optare Solo M850	Optare	N29F	2001	Whittle, 2007
422	SH	Y352DAB	Optare Solo M850	Optare	N29F	2001	Whittle, 2010
423	HA	VX05LKM	Optare Solo M850	Optare	N29F	2005	Whittle, 2010

461-481

461-481			Dennis Dart SLF 8.8m			Plaxton Pointer MPD	N29F	2000		
461	HL	W461UAG	**471**	SH	W471UAG	**477**	HA	W477UAG	**480**	HA	W80EYM
464	SH	W464UAG	**476**	SH	W476UAG	**478**	SH	W478UAG	**481**	BN	W481UAG
470	SH	W70EYM								

482-490

482-490			Dennis Dart SLF 8.8m			Plaxton Pointer MPD	N29F	2001		
482	BN	Y482VRH	**485**	SH	Y485VRH	**487**	BY	Y487VRH	**490**	BY	Y49VRH
483	HL	Y483VRH	**486**	BY	Y486VRH	**489**	SH	Y489VRH			

Displaying the pre-National Bus livery of East Yorkshire is Volvo B7TL 706, YX55DHN, currently allocated to Elloughton. Bodywork is Wrightbus' Eclipse Gemini model. *Mark Lyons*

| 491 | HL | YY52KXJ | Dennis Dart SLF 8.8m | Plaxton Pointer MPD | N29F | 2002 | |
| 495 | BY | YX04JVY | TransBus Dart 8.8m | TransBus Mini Pointer | N29F | 2004 | |

496-501			Enterprise Plasma EB01	Plaxton Primo	N28F	2006	
496	BN	YX06HVJ	**498**	BN	YX06HVL	**500**	HL	YX06HVN	**501**	HL	YX06HVO
497	BN	YX06HVK	**499**	HL	YX06HVM						

604-611			Volvo Olympian	Northern Counties Palatine	B47/30F	1996	
604	HL	P604SAT	**606**	DD	P606SAT	**608**	BY	P608SAT	**610**	BY	P610SAT
605	PN	P605SAT	**607**	PN	P607SAT	**609**	DD	P609SAT	**611**	SH	P611SAT

614	HL	N746ANE	Volvo Olympian	Northern Counties Palatine II	B47/30F	1996	Finglands, 2010
616	BN	N748ANE	Volvo Olympian	Northern Counties Palatine II	B47/30F	1996	Finglands, 2010
617	HL	R417SOY	Volvo Olympian	Northern Counties Palatine II	B47/29F	1997	Finglands, 2013
619	HL	R419SOY	Volvo Olympian	Northern Counties Palatine II	B47/29F	1997	Finglands, 2013
620	HL	R420SOY	Volvo Olympian	Northern Counties Palatine II	B47/29F	1997	Finglands, 2013

622-636			Volvo Olympian	Northern Counties Palatine	B47/29F	1998	
622	SH	S622MKH	**626**	SH	S626MKH	**630**	WA	S630MKH	**634**	BY	S634MKH
623	HL	S623MKH	**627**	BY	S627MKH	**631**	WA	S631MKH	**635**	SH	S635MKH
624	EL	S624MKH	**628**	EL	S628MKH	**632**	PN	S632MKH	**636**	SH	S636MKH
625	EL	S625MKH	**629**	PN	S629MKH	**633**	SH	S633MKH			

| 637 | BN | R782SOY | Volvo Olympian | Northern Counties Palatine II | B47/29F | 1998 | Armchair, Brentford, 2003 |

646-657			Volvo B7TL 10m	Plaxton President	N41/25F8	2000	*650-7 are N41/27F
646	SH	W439WGH	**649**	SH	W499WGH	**652**	HL	X508EGK	**655**	PN	PL51LDV
647	HL	W448WGH	**650**	HL	X584EGK	**653**	u	PL51LDJ	**656**	PN	PL51LDZ
648	HL	W544WGH	**651**	HL	X592EGK	**654**	EL	PL51LDU	**657**	DD	PL51LEF

658	HL	8225KH	Volvo B7TL	Plaxton President	N45/28F	2000	
659	WA	W659WKH	Volvo B7TL	Plaxton President	N45/28F	2000	
662	HL	YX51AYA	Volvo B7TL	Plaxton President 4.1m	N47/28F	2001	
663	HL	YX51AYB	Volvo B7TL	Plaxton President 4.1m	N47/28F	2001	

English Bus Handbook: Smaller Groups

Seen arriving at Filey bus station is 710, YX06CXL, one of six Volvo B7TLs which joined the fleet in 2006.
Mark Lyons

664-667		Volvo B7TL 10m			Plaxton President		N41/25F	2000	Go-Ahead London, 20
664	DD	PN02XBH	**665**	BN	PN02XBP	**666**	BN	PN02XBS	**667**	HL	PN02XBU

668	HL	PN02XBR	Volvo B7TL			Plaxton President		N47/28F	2002	JPT, Middleton, 2011
669	HL	PJ02RBY	Volvo B7TL			Plaxton President		N47/28F	2002	JPT, Middleton, 2011

670-677		Volvo B7TL			Plaxton President 4.1m		N47/28F	2001-02	
670	HL	80EYC	**672**	EL	YY52LCM	**674**	HL	YY52LCO	**677**	HL	YY52LCU
671	HL	YY52LCL	**673**	PN	YY52LCN	**676**	HL	YY52LCT			

678-689		Volvo B7TL			TransBus President 4.1m		N46/28F	2003	
678	HL	YX53AOD	**681**	HL	YX53AOG	**684**	SH	YX53AOK	**687**	HL	YX53AON
679	HL	YX53AOE	**682**	HL	YX53AOH	**685**	SH	YX53AOL	**688**	HL	YX53AOO
680	HL	YX53AOF	**683**	BN	YX53AOJ	**686**	HL	YX53AOM	**689**	BN	YX53AOP

690-695		Volvo Olympian			Northern Counties Palatine		B49/33F	1996	Stagecoach, 2004
690	BY	P549EFL	**692**	HL	P558EFL	**694**	HL	P574EFL	**695**	EL	P577EFL
691	HL	P557EFL	**693**	HL	P565EFL						

696-707		Volvo B7TL			Wrightbus Eclipse Gemini		N45/29F	2005	
696	BY	834EYD	**699**	PN	YX05EOS	**702**	BN	YX55DHJ	**705**	HL	YX55DHM
697	PN	YX05EOP	**700**	HL	YX05EOT	**703**	HL	YX55DHK	**706**	EL	YX55DHN
698	HL	YX05EOR	**701**	PN	YX05EOU	**704**	HL	YX55DHL	**707**	WA	YX55DHO

708-713		Volvo B7TL			Wrightbus Eclipse Gemini		N45/29F	2006	
708	HA	YX06CXJ	**710**	DD	YX06CXL	**712**	HA	YX06CXN	**713**	PN	YX06CXO
709	HA	YX06CXK	**711**	SH	YX06CXM						

714-721		Volvo B9TL			Wrightbus Eclipse Gemini		N45/29F	2007	
714	HL	YX07HKA	**716**	HL	YX07HKC	**718**	HL	YX07HKE	**720**	HL	YX07HKG
715	DD	YX07HKB	**717**	DD	YX07HKD	**719**	HL	YX07HKF	**721**	HL	A18EYC

722-726		Volvo B9TL			ADL Enviro 400		N45/32F	2007	
722	SH	YX57BWD	**724**	BN	YX57BWF	**725**	BN	YX57BWG	**726**	HL	YX57BWH
723	SH	YX57BWE									

East Yorkshire, like many of the larger operators, has taken hybrid vehicles having been awarded Green bus funding. Its choice has been the Enviro 400 with ten being placed in service in 2011. Showing the promotional lettering that has been applied to the batch is 908, YX11DVP, which was pictured in Longhill.
Richard Godfrey

727-746 — Volvo B9TL — Wrightbus Eclipse Gemini — N45/29F — 2008

No		Reg	No		Reg	No		Reg	No		Reg
727	BY	YX08FYA	732	HA	YX08FYF	737	WA	YX08FYL	742	SH	YX08FXD
728	WA	YX08FYB	733	HA	YX08FYG	738	WA	YX08FYM	743	HL	YX08FXE
729	HA	YX08FYC	734	WA	YX08FYH	739	SH	YX08FXA	744	HL	YX08FXF
730	HA	YX08FYD	735	WA	YX08FYJ	740	SH	YX08FXB	745	HL	YX08FXG
731	HA	YX08FYE	736	WA	YX08FYK	741	SH	YX08FXC	746	HL	YX08FXH

747-756 — Volvo B9TL — Wrightbus Eclipse Gemini — N45/29F — 2009

No		Reg	No		Reg	No		Reg	No		Reg
747	DD	YX09BKA	750	EL	YX09BKF	753	WA	YX09BKK	755	HA	YX09BKN
748	DD	YX09BKD	751	EL	YX09BKG	754	HA	YX09BKL	756	HA	YX09BKO
749	EL	YX09BKE	752	HA	YX09BKJ						

757-777 — Volvo B9TL — Wrightbus Eclipse Gemini 2 — N45/29F — 2009-10

No		Reg	No		Reg	No		Reg	No		Reg
757	HL	YX09GWA	763	DD	YX09GWJ	768	HL	YX59FGN	773	WA	YX59FGZ
758	HA	YX09GWC	764	DD	YX09GWK	769	HL	YX59FGO	774	WA	YX59FHA
759	HL	YX09GWD	765	DD	YX09GWL	770	HL	YX59FGP	775	WA	YX59FHB
760	BY	YX09GWE	766	DD	YX09GWM	771	HL	YX59FGU	776	WA	YX59FHC
761	HL	YX09GWF	767	HA	YX59FGM	772	WA	YX59FGV	777	HL	YX60DWK
762	DD	YX09GWG									

| 778 | EL | A19EYC | ADL Trident 2 12m | | ADL Enviro 400 | | | N47/33F | | 2010 | |

881-885 — Volvo B7TL 10m — Plaxton President — PO45/19F — 2000 — Go-Ahead London, 2012

No		Reg	No		Reg	No		Reg	No		Reg
881	SH	A10EYD	883	SH	897EYX	884	SH	794EYD	885	SH	165DKH
882	SH	152FRH									

901-910 — ADL E400H — ADL Enviro 400 — N45/32F — 2011

No		Reg	No		Reg	No		Reg	No		Reg
901	HL	EYH876	904	HL	YX11DVL	907	HL	YX11DVO	909	HL	YX11DVV
902	HL	YX11DVJ	905	HL	YX11DVM	908	HL	YX11DVP	910	HL	YX11DVW
903	HL	YX11DVK	906	HL	YX11DVN						

Special event vehicles (showing original owner):

100	HL	SS7376	Bedford OB	Duple Vista	C29F	1949	McKinley, Prestonpans
202	HL	202YTE	Leyland Titan PD2/37	East Lancs	O37/28F	1963	Lancaster City Transport
644	HL	VKH44	AEC Regent V MD3RV	Willowbrook	B30/26R	1956	East Yorkshire

Scarborough would not be complete without its open-top service that plies between The Spa and the Sands. Six former Go-Ahead London Volvo B7TLs with Plaxton President bodywork are currently used, represented here by 884, 794EYD. *Richard Godfrey*

Ancillary vehicles:

9910	HL	46EYB	Volvo B10M-55	Alexander PS	TV	1994	Finglands, 1997
9911	HL	546EYB	Volvo B10M-55	Alexander PS	TV	1994	Finglands, 1997
9912	HL	665EYL	Volvo B10M-55	Alexander PS	TV	1994	Finglands, 1997
9913	HL	334EYL	LDV Convoy	LDV	TV	2002	Hertz-ScotHire, 2004
9914	HL	95EYM	Volvo B10M-55	Alexander PS	TV	1994	Finglands, 2004

Previous registrations:

39EYD	T335AFX	A10EYC	YK07HKN
46EYB	-	A10EYD	X579EGK
80EYC	YY52LCK	A14EYC	YK07HKO
95EYM	-	A15EYC	YX07HJD
152FRH	X588EGK	A16EYC	R253PRH
165DKH	X594EGK	A17EYC	R254PRH
334EYL	-	A18EYC	YX07HKH
546EYB	-	A19EYC	YX60DWL
665EYL	-	A20EYC	YX59FSD
696EYC	YX05EOO		
787EYC	YX59FSE		
794EYD	X593EGK		
834EYD	-	EYC73	R284EKH
897EYX	X591EGK	EYH876	from new
8225KH	W658WKH	SS7376	SS7376, 1949MN, KSU381
A1EYD	YX07HJC	W70EYM	from new
A6EYC	YX55FVB	W659WKH	W659WKH, WLT694
A7EYC	YX55FVC	WU51LBE	EYH876
A8EYC	YX55FVA	YX06CXJ	YX06FET
A9EYC	YX57BWJ		

Springtime at the Crows Nest Holiday Park in Gristhorpe and Alexander Dennis-bodied Volvo B9TL 724, YX57BWF is seen heading for Scarborough. In addition to the Volvo, the Enviro 400 has also been built on Scania units. *Richard Godfrey*

Depots and allocations:

Beverley (Sow Hill Station) - BY

Dart	306	486	487	490	495
Volvo B10BLE	370				
Olympian	608	627	634	690	
Volvo B7TL	696				
Volvo B9TL	727	760			

Bridlington (Bessingby Lane Industrial Estate) - BN

Primo	496	497	498	
Dart	303	307	481	482
MB Prisma	286			
Optare Excel	288			
Olympian	606	616	637	
Volvo B7TL	665	666	689	702
Volvo B9TL	724	725		

Driffield (Middle Street South) - DD

Mercedes-Benz Vario	419							
Mercedes-Benz O405	299							
Volvo B10BLE	308							
Volvo B7TL	657	664	710					
Volvo B9TL	714	715	716	717	747	748	762	763
	764	765	766					

Another view of the Hybrid Enviro 400, this time of the off-side of 908, YX11DVP, as it heads back to Hull on route 56. *Richard Godfrey*

Elloughton (Stockbridge Road) - EL

Optare Solo	420				
Volvo B7RLE	338	339	348	367	368
Olympian	624	625	695		
Volvo B7TL	654	672	706		
Volvo B9TL	749	750	751		
Trident	778				

Hornsea (Cliffe Road) - HA

Optare Solo	423							
MAN 18.220	324	328						
Volvo B7TL	712							
Volvo B9TL	729	730	731	732	733	752	754	756
	757	758						

Hull (Anlaby Road, HU3 2RS) - HL

MB Vario	20							
Primo	499	500	501					
Volvo B10M	52							
Volvo B12B	55	56	57	61	62	63	65	67
	68	70	71	72	73	122	123	124
Volvo B9R	74	75	76	77				
DAF SB120	244							
MAN 14.220	246							
MAN 18-220	320	321	322	323	325	326	327	329
	330							
Volvo B10BLE	311	313						
Mercedes-Benz O405	284							
Excel	287	290	292	293	294			

Dart	302	461	483	489	491			
Volvo B7RLE	341	342	343	344	345	346	347	369
	371	372						

Olympian	604	614	617	619	620	691	692	693
	694							
Volvo B7TL	647	648	650	651	652	658	662	663
	667	668	669	670	671	674	676	677
	678	679	680	681	682	683	686	687
	688	698	700	703	704	705	708	709
Volvo B9TL	714	716	718	719	720	721	726	743
	744	745	746	757	759	761	769	770
	771	777						
Enviro 400 Hybrid	901	902	903	904	905	906	907	908
	909	910						
Heritage	100	202	812	644				

Pocklington (Railway Street) - PN

Volvo B10BLE	312						
Olympian	605	607	628	629	632		
Volvo B7TL	655	656	673	697	699	701	713

Scarborough (Barry's Lane) - SH

Optare Solo	421	422						
Excel	250	252	253	254				
SB120	245							
Optare Excel	296							
Mercedes-Benz O405	285	300						
Volvo B10BLE	310							
Volvo B7RLE	361	362	363	364	365	366		
Dart	304	318	319	333	464	470	471	476
	477	478	480	485				
Enviro 200	353	354	355	356	357	358	359	360
Olympian	610	611	622	623	626	633	635	636
Volvo B7TL	646	649	684	685	711	881	882	883
	884	885						
Volvo B9TL	722	723	739	740	741	742		

Withernsea (Bannister Street) - WA

Volvo B7RLE	340							
Olympian	630	631						
Volvo B7TL	659	707						
Volvo B9TL	728	734	735	736	737	738	752	753
	772	773	774	775	776			

Unallocated and stored - u

| Kidderminster (loan) | 418 |
| Remainder | |

As we go to press, it has been announced that the Finglands operation will be sold to First with an anticipated completion date of October 2013. No vehicles will be involved and those listed below will initially move to Hull for evaluation. The coach operation is being sold separately. Charles Finland worked for Rolls Royce as a test driver until 1907 when he started Finglands Hire Cars and Bookings. He originally ran luxury limousines and demand gave him the opportunity to expand into coach hire. Scheduled coach services followed and Finglands became the first coach company to run a scheduled service between Manchester and London. Recently the principal services have plied between Manchester city centre and Didsbury, a service which provides a link between the university buildings and the many student halls of residence. Seen in Fallowfield is 1709, W417JAT, one of four moved from Hull in 2010.
John Young

Finglands

374	MA	RYV77	Volvo B10M-62	Plaxton Paragon	C49FT	2002	
375	MA	HIL7745	Volvo B10M-62	Plaxton Panther	C49FT	2002	Dorset Queen, 2004
376	MA	10RU	Volvo B12B	Plaxton Paragon	C49FT	2006	
377	MA	YN55WTP	Volvo B12B	Plaxton Paragon	C49FT	2005	
378	MA	YX56HYM	Volvo B12B	Plaxton Panther	C49FT	2007	
379	MA	FC07MFC	Volvo B12B 13.8m	Volvo 9700	C32FT	2007	
380	MA	647JOE	Volvo B12B	Plaxton Paragon	C53F	2006	Whittle, 2009
381	MA	YX09FUO	Volvo B12B 13.8m	Volvo 9700	C53FT	2010	
382	MA	YX02JFY	Volvo B12M	Plaxton Paragon	C49FT	2002	
1601	MA	YY52KXK	Dennis Dart SLF 8.8m	Plaxton Mini Pointer	N29F	2002	East Yorkshire, 2013
1602	MA	YY52KXL	Dennis Dart SLF 8.8m	Plaxton Mini Pointer	N29F	2002	East Yorkshire, 2013
1603	MA	YY52KXM	Dennis Dart SLF 8.8m	Plaxton Mini Pointer	N29F	2002	East Yorkshire, 2013

1701-1705

		ADL E300 11.8m		ADL Enviro300	N44F	2006	
1701	MA	YX56DZJ	**1703**	MA	YX56DZL	**1704**	MA	YX56DZM	**1705**	MA	YX56DZO
1702	MA	YX56DZK									

1706-1709

		Volvo B10BLE		Alexander ALX300	N44F	2000	East Yorkshire, 2010
1706	MA	W414JAT	**1707**	MA	W415JAT	**1708**	MA	W416JAT	**1709**	MA	W417JAT

1759	MA	X585XKH	Dennis Trident	Alexander ALX400	N45/29F	2000	East Yorkshire, 2006
1760	MA	X584XKH	Dennis Trident	Alexander ALX400	N45/29F	2000	East Yorkshire, 2006
1761	MA	X761ABU	Volvo B7TL	Plaxton President	N45/28F	2000	
1762	MA	X762ABU	Volvo B7TL	Plaxton President	N45/28F	2000	
1763	MA	X763ABU	Dennis Trident	Alexander ALX400	N45/29F	2000	
1764	MA	X764ABU	Dennis Trident	Alexander ALX400	N45/29F	2000	

1765-1768

		Volvo B7TL		Plaxton President	N45/28F	2001	
1765	MA	MF51LZW	**1766**	MA	MF51LZX	**1767**	MA	MF51MBV	**1768**	MA	MF51MBX

1792-1795

		Volvo B9TL		Wrightbus Eclipse Gemini	N45/29F	2008	
1792	MA	YX08FWE	**1793**	MA	YX08FWF	**1794**	MA	YX08FWG	**1795**	MA	YX08FWH

Bramhall Green provides the background to this view of Finglands' 1801, YX51AYH, one of twenty Volvo B7TL operated, this example having Plaxton President bodywork. *John Young*

1796-1801			Volvo B7TL			Plaxton President 4.1m		N47/28F	2001-02	East Yorkshire 2009-10
1796	MA	YX51AYC	**1798**	MA	YX51AYE	**1800**	MA	YX51AYG	**1801**	MA	YX51AYH
1797	MA	YX51AYD	**1799**	MA	YX51AYF					

1802-1805			Volvo B7TL			Plaxton President 4.4m		N47/27F	2002	Go-Ahead London, 2012
1802	MA	PJ02RAU	**1803**	MA	PJ02RAU	**1804**	MA	PJ02RAU	**1805**	MA	PJ02RAU

Previous registrations:

10RU	YN55WTO		RYV77	YR52MDZ
647JOE	VX55OBW		X584XKH	46EYB
HIL7745	HJ02HCG		X585XKH	546EYB

Depot:

Wilmslow Road, Manchester, M14 5LJ (MA)

Volvo B10M	374	375				
Volvo B12B	376	377	378	379	380	381
Volvo B12M	382					
Dart	1601	162	1603			
Enviro 300	1701	1702	1703	1704	1705	
Volvo B10BLE	1706	1707	1708	1709		
Dennis Trident	1759	1760	1763	1764		
Volvo B7TL	1761	1762	1765	1766	1767	1768	1792	1793
	1794	1795	1796	1797	1798	1799	1800	1801
	1802	1803	1804	1805				

EYMS' other operation is Whittle, based in Kidderminster, which now uses a green and cream livery applied in a similar style to the main fleet. Recent additions have seen several Darts transferred from East Yorkshire, and from 2011, Whittle gained National Express contracts. One of four Enviro 200s is 159, YX56HVH. *Mark Doggett*

Whittle

11	KD	RUI2116	Dennis Javelin 12m	Plaxton Première 320	C57F	2000	
12	KD	W119PNP	Dennis Javelin 12m	Plaxton Première 320	C57F	2000	
14	KD	T638XNP	Dennis Javelin GX 12m	Plaxton Première 350	C48FT	1999	
15	KD	XKH455	Volvo B12B	Plaxton Paragon	C57F	2006	
16	KD	RCE510	Volvo B12B	Plaxton Paragon	C53F	2006	
17	KD	YX07HKJ	Volvo B12B	Plaxton Paragon	C53F	2007	
18	KD	YX07HKK	Volvo B12B	Plaxton Paragon	C53F	2007	
19	KD	YX07HKL	Volvo B12B	Plaxton Panther	C49FT	2007	
20	KD	YX07HKM	Volvo B12B	Plaxton Panther	C49FT	2007	
21	KD	YX60FLR	Volvo B9R	Plaxton Panther	C53FT	2011	
22	KD	YX07HJJ	Volvo B12B	Plaxton Panther	C49FT	2007	
23	KD	YX62FLC	Volvo B9R	Plaxton Elite	C51FT	2012	
64	KD	YX07HJF	Volvo B12B	Caetano Levanté	C48FT	2007	
127	KD	VX55OBU	Volvo B12B	Plaxton Panther	C49FT	2006	Whittle, Kidderminster, '13
84	KD	FJ11GJX	Volvo B9R	Caetano Levanté	C48FT	2011	
85	KD	FJ11GJY	Volvo B9R	Caetano Levanté	C48FT	2011	
86	KD	FJ11GJZ	Volvo B9R	Caetano Levanté	C48FT	2011	
87	KD	FJ11GKA	Volvo B9R	Caetano Levanté	C48FT	2011	
88	KD	FJ11GKC	Volvo B9R	Caetano Levanté	C48FT	2011	
89	KD	FJ11GLV	Volvo B9R	Caetano Levanté	C48FT	2011	
152	KD	V428DND	Mercedes-Benz O405 N2	Mercedes-Benz	N40F	1999	
153	KD	V429DND	Mercedes-Benz O405 N2	Mercedes-Benz	N40F	1999	
154	KD	YX03MWG	Dennis Dart SLF 10.7m	Plaxton Pointer 2	N41F	2003	
155	KD	YX03MWJ	Dennis Dart SLF 10.7m	Plaxton Pointer 2	N41F	2003	
156	KD	YX03MWK	Dennis Dart SLF 10.7m	Plaxton Pointer 2	N41F	2003	
157	KD	YX56HVF	ADL Dart 4	ADL Enviro 200	N37F	2006	
158	KD	YX56HVG	ADL Dart 4	ADL Enviro 200	N37F	2006	
159	KD	YX56HVH	ADL Dart 4	ADL Enviro 200	N37F	2006	

Whittle's northern terminus is in the Shropshire town of Bridgnorth. Here, 170, YX04JVW, a TransBus Dart is seen preparing for the return journey south. *John Young*

160	KD	YX56HVJ	ADL Dart 4	ADL Enviro 200	N37F	2006	
161	KD	R409FFC	Dennis Dart SLF 10.1m	Wrightbus Crusader	N35F	1998	Rotala, 2012
162	KD	Y213HWJ	Dennis Dart SLF 10.7m	Plaxton Pointer 2	N37F	2001	Central Parking, 2005
163	KD	Y214HWJ	Dennis Dart SLF 10.7m	Plaxton Pointer 2	N37F	2001	Central Parking, 2005
164	KD	GK03NFT	TransBus Dart 10.7m	TransBus Pointer	N37F	2003	Crosskeys, Hythe, 2005
165	KD	W462WAG	Dennis Dart SLF 8.8m	Plaxton Pointer MPD	N29F	2000	
166	KD	W466UAG	Dennis Dart SLF 8.8m	Plaxton Pointer MPD	N29F	2000	
167	KD	W468WAG	Dennis Dart SLF 8.8m	Plaxton Pointer MPD	N29F	2000	
168	KD	W469WAG	Dennis Dart SLF 8.8m	Plaxton Pointer MPD	N29F	2000	
169	KD	W494EOP	Dennis Dart SLF 8.8m	Plaxton Pointer MPD	N29F	2000	
170	KD	YX04JVW	TransBus Dart 10.7m	TransBus Pointer	N37F	2004	

Previous registrations:

RCE510	VX55OBY	XKH455	VX55OBV
RUI2116	V616FWP	Y214HWJ	99D80584
T638XNP	T638XNP, RCE510		

Depot:

Stourport Road, Kidderminster, DY11 7QL (KD)

Javelin	11	12	14					
Volvo B12B	15	16	17	18	19	20	64	
Volvo B9R	23	84	85	86	87	88	89	
Mercedes-Bez O405	152	153						
Dart	154	155	156	161	162	163	164	165
	166	167	168	169	170			
Enviro 200	157	158	159	160				

NATIONAL EXPRESS GROUP

National Express Ltd, 1 Hagley Road, Birmingham, B16 8TG

West Midlands Travel Ltd, 51 Bordesley Green, Birmingham, B94QS

Tayside Public Transport Co Ltd, 44-48 East Dock Street, Dundee, DD1 3JS

The Kings Ferry Ltd, The Travel Centre, 199 Eastcourt Lane, Gillingham, ME8 6HW

National Express & Hotel Hopper

1	SH	FJ56PFE	Scania K340 EB4			Caetano Levanté		C49FT	2006		
2	SH	FJ56PFF	Scania K340 EB4			Caetano Levanté		C49FT	2006		

3-21			Scania K340 EB6			Caetano Levanté		C61FT	2007		
3	SH	FJ07DVH	8	SH	FJ07DVO	13	SH	FN07BYX	18	SH	FJ57KHX
4	SH	FJ07DVK	9	SH	FJ07DVP	14	SH	FN07BYZ	19	SH	FJ57KHY
5	RP	FJ07DVL	10	SH	FJ07DVR	15	SH	FJ07BZA	20	SH	FJ57KHZ
6	SH	FJ07DVM	11	SH	FN07BYV	16	SH	FJ07BZB	21	RP	FJ57KJA
7	SH	FJ07DVN	12	SH	FN07BYW	17	SH	FJ07BZC			

22	SR	FJ57KHM	Scania K340 EB4			Caetano Levanté		C49FT	2007		
23	SH	FJ57KHK	Scania K340 EB4			Caetano Levanté		C49FT	2007		

24-39			Scania K340 EB6			Caetano Levanté		C61FT	2007		
24	SH	FJ57KHL	32	SH	FJ57KGZ	36	SH	FJ57KHD	38	SH	FJ57KHF
25	SH	FJ57KJE	33	SH	FJ57KHA	37	SH	FJ57KHE	39	SH	FJ57KHG
26	SH	FJ57KHT	35	SH	FJ57KHC						

51	SR	FJ57KJU	Scania K340 EB4			Caetano Levanté		C49FT	2007		
52	SR	FJ57KJO	Scania K340 EB4			Caetano Levanté		C49FT	2007		
53	SR	FJ57KHO	Scania K340 EB4			Caetano Levanté		C49FT	2007		
58	SR	YN55NDZ	Scania K114EB4			Irizar PB		C49FT	2006		

National Express currently has an extensive fleet of coaches, many working on airport contracts as well as its own services. In addition most vehicles used on National Express services are contracted to other operators. Details of these are in the *National Express Coach Handbook* that is part of this series. From the 2007 intake of Scania K340s with Caetano Levanté bodywork is 6, FJ07DVM. *Mark Bailey*

60-72 · Volvo B12B · Caetano Levanté · C49FT · 2006-07

No	Op	Reg	No	Op	Reg	No	Op	Reg	No	Op	Reg
60	SR	FJ06URH	64	SH	FH06EAW	67	RP	FH06EAX	70	RP	FH06EBL
61	SR	FJ06GGK	65	RP	FN06FLH	68	RP	FH06EBM	71	RP	FJ06URO
62	SR	FJ06URG	66	SR	FH06FMA	69	RP	FH06EBN	72	SH	FJ07DWN
63	RP	FN06FMC									

No	Op	Reg	Chassis	Body	Code	Year
95	SH	FJ57KHP	Scania K340 EB4	Caetano Levanté	C49FT	2008
96	SH	FJ57KHR	Scania K340 EB4	Caetano Levanté	C49FT	2008
102	SR	FJ10EZV	Scania K340 EB4	Caetano Levanté	C49FT	2010

110-135 · Volvo B9R · Caetano Levanté · C48FT · 2010-11

No	Op	Reg	No	Op	Reg	No	Op	Reg	No	Op	Reg
110	SR	FJ60HXS	117	SR	FJ11MKL	124	SR	FJ11MKF	130	SR	FJ11MJK
111	SR	FJ60HXT	118	SR	FJ11MKE	125	SR	FJ11MKG	131	SR	FJ11MJO
112	SR	FJ60HXU	119	SR	FJ11MKK	126	SR	FJ11MKM	132	SR	FJ11MJU
113	SR	FJ60HXV	120	SR	FJ11RDO	127	SR	FJ11MKN	133	SR	FJ11MJV
114	SR	FJ60HXX	121	SR	FJ11RDU	128	SR	FJ11MKU	134	SR	FJ11MJX
115	SR	FJ60HXY	122	SR	FJ11RDV	129	SR	FJ11MKV	135	SR	FJ11MJY
116	SR	FJ60KVS	123	SR	FJ11MKD						

136-143 · Volvo B9R · Caetano Levanté · C48FT · 2012

No	Op	Reg	No	Op	Reg	No	Op	Reg	No	Op	Reg
136	SH	FJ12FYL	138	SH	FJ12FYN	140	LA	FJ12FYR	142	LA	FJ12FYO
137	SH	FJ12FYM	139	SH	FJ12FYP	141	LA	FJ12FYH	143	LA	FJ12FXD

144-161 · Volvo B9R · Caetano Levanté · C48FT · 2013

No	Op	Reg	No	Op	Reg	No	Op	Reg	No	Op	Reg
144	SR	FJ13EBG	149	LA	FJ13EBO	154	LA	FJ13EBZ	158	LA	FJ13ECE
145	LA	FJ13EBK	150	LA	FJ13EBP	155	LA	FJ13ECA	159	LA	FJ13ECF
146	LA	FJ13EBL	151	LA	FJ13EBU	156	LA	FJ13ECC	160	LA	FJ13ECN
147	LA	FJ13EBM	152	LA	FJ13EBV	157	LA	FJ13ECD	161	LA	FJ13ECT
148	LA	FJ13EBN	153	LA	FJ13EBX						

No	Op	Reg	Chassis	Body	Code	Year
A801	WD	X162ENJ	Mercedes-Benz Sprinter 311D	Frank Guy	M8	2001
A802	WD	X164ENJ	Mercedes-Benz Sprinter 311D	Frank Guy	M8	2001
A803	WD	Y228NLF	Mercedes-Benz Sprinter 311D	Frank Guy	M8	2002

8321-8352 · ADL Dart 4 9.5m · ADL Enviro 200 · N22F · 2008

No	Op	Reg	No	Op	Reg	No	Op	Reg	No	Op	Reg
8321	WD	SN08AAU	8329	WD	SN08ABU	8337	WD	SN08ACV	8345	WD	SN08ADZ
8322	WD	SN08AAV	8330	WD	SN08ABV	8338	WD	SN08ACX	8346	WD	SN08AEA
8323	WD	SN08AAX	8331	WD	SN08ABX	8339	WD	SN08ACY	8347	WD	SN08AEB
8324	WD	SN08AAY	8332	WD	SN08ABZ	8340	WD	SN08ACZ	8348	WD	SN08AEC
8325	WD	SN08AAZ	8333	WD	SN08ACF	8341	WD	SN08ADO	8349	WD	SN08AED
8326	WD	SN08ABF	8334	WD	SN08ACJ	8342	WD	SN08ADU	8350	WD	SN08AEE
8327	WD	SN08ABK	8335	WD	SN08ACO	8343	WD	SN08ADV	8351	WD	SN08AEF
8328	WD	SN08ABO	8336	WD	SN08ACU	8344	WD	SN08ADX	8352	WD	SN08AEG

No	Op	Reg	Chassis	Body	Code	Year
8353	SH	T503TOL	Volvo B6BLE	Wright Crusader	N35F	1999

8354-8358 · ADL E20D · ADL Enviro 200 · N29F · 2011

No	Op	Reg	No	Op	Reg	No	Op	Reg	No	Op	Reg
8354	WD	MX61BBE	8356	WD	MX61BBJ	8357	WD	MX61BBK	8358	WD	MX61BBN
8355	WD	MX61BBF									

8541-8547 · Mercedes-Benz Citaro O530 · AN30D · 2008

No	Op	Reg	No	Op	Reg	No	Op	Reg	No	Op	Reg
8541	WD	KX58GUA	8543	WD	KX58GUD	8545	WD	KX58GUF	8547	WD	KX58GUH
8542	WD	KX58GUC	8544	WD	KX58GUE	8546	WD	KX58GUG			

8548-8553 · Mercedes-Benz Citaro O530 · AN30D · 2003 · Quality Line, 2008

No	Op	Reg	No	Op	Reg	No	Op	Reg	No	Op	Reg
8548	WD	BU53AXN	8550	WD	BU53AXP	8552	WD	BU53AXT	8553	WD	BU53AXV
8549	WD	BU53AXO	8551	WD	BU53AXR						

8554-8560 · Mercedes-Benz Citaro O530 LE · N21 · 2008

No	Op	Reg	No	Op	Reg	No	Op	Reg	No	Op	Reg
8554	WD	KX58GCJ	8556	WD	KX58GCL	8558	WD	KX58GTU	8560	WD	KX58GTZ
8555	WD	KX58GCK	8557	WD	KX58GCM	8559	WD	KX58GTY			

No	Op	Reg	Chassis	Body	Code	Year
8561	WD	KX58GUJ	ADL Dart 4	ADL Enviro 200	N25F	2008
8562	WD	KX58GUK	ADL Dart 4	ADL Enviro 200	N25F	2008
8563	WD	KX58GUO	ADL Dart 4	ADL Enviro 200	N25F	2008

8564-8573 · Mercedes-Benz Sprinter 515cdi · KVC · M9 · 2009

No	Op	Reg	No	Op	Reg	No	Op	Reg	No	Op	Reg
8564	WD	KX58BJK	8567	WD	KX58BJO	8570	WD	KX58BFA	8572	WD	KX09CJO
8565	WD	KX58BJV	8568	WD	KX58BKA	8571	WD	KX58BJY	8573	WD	KX09CJU
8566	WD	KX58BJU	8569	WD	KX58BJZ						

National Express operates the Hotel Hopper service that links the principal hotels around Heathrow Airport with the terminals. The initial fleet was replaced in 2008 by twenty-nine Alexander Dennis Dart 4s with Enviro 200 bodywork. Illustrating the type is 8325, SN08AAZ, seen at Hatton Cross. *Mark Lyons*

8574-8579
Mercedes-Benz Citaro O530   AN30D   2003-04   Arriva London, 2011

| 8574 | WD | BX04MXR | 8576 | WD | LX03HCG | 8578 | WD | LX03HCU | 8579 | WD | LX03HDE |
| 8575 | WD | LX03HCE | 8577 | WD | LX03HCL | | | | | | |

8600-8605
NAW Cobus 2700s   Cobus   N15T

| 8600 | WD | 8600 | 8602 | WD | 8602 | 8604 | WD | 8604 | 8605 | WD | 8605 |
| 8601 | WD | 8601 | 8603 | WD | 8603 | | | | | | |

8606-8622
DAF SB220   East Lancs Myllennium   N29D   2000   Aviation Defence, 2009

8606	WD	X831NWX	8611	WD	X836NWX	8615	WD	X840NWX	8619	WD	X844NWX
8607	WD	X832NWX	8612	WD	X837NWX	8616	WD	X841NWX	8620	WD	X845NWX
8608	WD	X833NWX	8613	WD	X838NWX	8617	WD	X842NWX	8621	WD	X846NWX
8609	WD	X834NWX	8614	WD	X839NWX	8618	WD	X843NWX	8622	WD	X847NWX
8610	WD	X835NWX									

| 8623 | WD | R425AOR | Denis Dart SLF | | UVG UrbanStar | N25D | 1998 | Aviation Defence, 2009 |
| 8624 | WD | R426AOR | Denis Dart SLF | | UVG UrbanStar | N25D | 1998 | Aviation Defence, 2009 |

8625-8629
Volvo B6LE   Wrightbus Crusader   N21F   1996   Aviation Defence, 2009

| 8625 | WD | N241WRW | 8627 | WD | N244WRW | 8628 | WD | N245WRW | 8629 | WD | N246WRW |
| 8626 | WD | N243WRW | | | | | | | | | |

8637-8640
MAN 14.220   MCV   N28D   2006   Aviation Defence, 2009

| 8637 | WD | AE55MVF | 8638 | WD | AE55MVG | 8639 | WD | AE55MVH | 8640 | WD | AE55MVJ |

8641-8645
NAW Cobus 2700s   Cobus   N15T   2009

| 8641 | WD | 8641 | 8643 | WD | 8643 | 8644 | WD | 8645 | 8645 | WD | 8645 |
| 8642 | WD | 8642 | | | | | | | | | |

8646-8657
Mercedes-Benz Citaro O530   AN30D   2010

8646	WD	BK10EHT	8649	WD	BK10EHW	8652	WD	BK10EHZ	8655	WD	BK10EJX
8647	WD	BK10EHU	8650	WD	BK10EHX	8653	WD	BK10EJU	8656	WD	BK10EJY
8648	WD	BK10EHV	8651	WD	BK10EHY	8654	WD	BK10EJV	8657	WD	BK10EJZ

National Express was instrumental in the design of the Caetano Levanté coach which incorporates an internal lift for access that met the provisions of the then new Disability Discrimination Act. The product is exclusive to National Express and while originally available only on the Volvo B12B chassis, it is now also supplied on Scania, MAN products as well as the later Volvo chassis. Volvo B9R 134, FJ11MJX is seen in Cambridge. *John Young*

8658-8663 — NAW Cobus 2700s — Cobus — N15T — 2012

8658	WD	8658	**8660**	WD	8660	**8662**	WD	8662	**8663**	WD	8663
8659	WD	8659	**8661**	WD	8661						

8664	-	-	Mercedes-Benz Sprinter 811
8665	-	-	Mercedes-Benz Sprinter 811
8666	-	-	Mercedes-Benz Sprinter 811

Ancillary vehices:

TR1	LU	LK53KWD	Volvo B12B	TransBus Panther	TV	2003
TR2	LU	LK53KWE	Volvo B12B	TransBus Panther	TV	2003
TR3	LU	LK53KWF	Volvo B12B	TransBus Panther	TV	2003

Depots and codes: Bishops Stortford (Start Hill, Great Hollingbury) - SH; Luton Airport (LA); West Drayton (Sipson Road) - WD (buses) and SR (coaches); reserve coaches are shown as RP. Details of the other National Express fleets may be found in the *English Bus Handbook : Groups Handbook*.

Five of the Optare Solo buses from 1999 now reside in Scotland. Representing them is 298, T298UOX, seen on a local city service in Dundee. *Richard Godfrey*

West Midlands - Coventry - Tayside

01-16			Ansaldo Tram			Ansaldo		AB58T	1998-99		
01	03	05	07	09	11	13	15				
02	04	06	08	10	12	14	16				
241	t	R241XDA	Mercedes-Benz Vario 0814			Alexander ALX100		B27F	1998		
244	WA	P244AAP	Volvo B6BLE			Wright Crusader		N35F	1997		

277-320			Optare Solo M850			Optare		B27F	1999		
277	u	S277AOX	292	u	T292UOX	298	DD	T298UOX	303	PB	T303UOX
281	u	S281AOX	293	u	T293UOX	300	DD	T130UOX	319	PB	T319UOX
286	PB	S286AOX	295	DD	T295UOX	301	DD	T301UOX	320	PB	T320UOX
287	PB	S287AOX									

321	DD	YT51EBC	Optare Solo M850		Optare		B27F	1999	
322	DD	YT51EBD	Optare Solo M850		Optare		B27F	1999	

502-547			Volvo B6LE			Wright Crusader		N37F	1996		
502	u	P502EJW	516	u	P516EJW	524	WB	P524EJW	544	u	P544EJW
508	WN	P508EJW	517	u	P517EJW	533	WB	P533EJW	547	WA	P547EJW
510	u	P510EJW	519	WB	P519EJW	534	WB	P534EJW			

554-581			Volvo B6LE			Wright Crusader		N37F	1997		
554	WN	P554LDA	564	WB	P564MDA	568	WB	R568XDA	581	WN	R581XDA
555	WN	P955LDA	566	WB	P566MDA	569	WB	R569XDA			

582-606			Volvo B6LE			Wright Crusader		N37F	1998		
582	PE	R582YON	586	CV	R586YON	598	WN	R598YON	601	WN	R601YON
584	WB	R584YON	591	WA	R591YON	600	WN	R160YON	606	u	R606YON

620-681			Volvo B6LE			Wright Crusader		N37F	1998-99		
620	WN	S620VOA	638	WN	S638VOA	650	u	S650VOA	674	u	S674VOA
626	WN	S626VOA	639	WN	S639VOA	662	WN	S662VOA	677	WA	S677VOA
632	WN	S632VOA	640	WN	S640VOA	669	WA	S669VOA	680	WB	S680VOA
633	WN	S633VOA	648	WA	S648VOA	673	WA	S673VOA	681	u	S681VOA
634	WN	S634VOA									

Thirty Enviro 200s replaced for early Darts and Optare Excels during the spring of 2013. Illustrating the type is 802, BX62SCV, seen passing the Queen Elizabeth Hospital in Birmingham. *Richard Godfrey*

687-711

		Optare Excel L1070		Optare			N38F	1999	
687	u	S687YOL	693	u	S693YOL	708	u	S708YOL	711	u	S711YOL

687	u	S687YOL	693	u	S693YOL	708	u	S708YOL	711	u	S711YOL

801-830

ADL E20D · ADL Enviro 200 · N37F · 2013

801	BC	BX62SBY	809	BC	BX62SKV	817	WB	BX62SVP	824	PE	BX62SYW
802	BC	BX62SCV	810	WB	BX62SLV	818	WB	BX62SVU	825	PE	BX62SYZ
803	BC	BX62SEY	811	WB	BX62SNF	819	WB	BX62SXD	826	PE	BX62SZC
804	BC	BX62SFJ	812	WB	BX62SNK	820	WB	BX62SXH	827	PE	BX62SZD
805	BC	BX62SFY	813	WB	BX62SNU	821	WB	BX62SXR	828	PE	BX62SZE
806	BC	BX62SJU	814	WB	BX62SOH	822	WB	BX62SYA	829	PE	BX62SZJ
807	BC	BX62SKJ	815	WB	BX62SUA	823	PE	BX62SYC	830	PE	BX62SZR
808	BC	BX62SKU	816	WB	BX62SUG						

1344-1386

Volvo B10B · Wright Endurance · B48F · 1995-96

1344	t	N344WOH	1350	t	N350WOH	1368	t	N368WOH	1385	t	N385BOV
1345	t	N345WOH	1355	t	N355WOH	1377	t	N377WOH	1386	t	N386BOV
1349	t	N349WOH	1366	DDt	N366WOH	1384	t	N384BOV			

1401-1430

Volvo B10L · Wright Liberator · N43F · 1997

1401	u	P401EJW	1408	YW	P408EJW	1416	u	P416EJW	1423	u	P423EJW
1402	u	P402EJW	1409	u	P409EJW	1417	u	P417EJW	1424	u	P424EJW
1403	u	P403EJW	1411	YW	P411EJW	1418	u	P418EJW	1426	u	P426EJW
1404	u	P404EJW	1412	u	P412EJW	1419	WA	P419EJW	1427	u	P427EJW
1405	u	P405EJW	1413	YW	P413EJW	1420	u	P420EJW	1428	u	P428EJW
1406	YW	P406EJW	1414	u	P414EJW	1421	WA	P421EJW	1429	u	P429EJW
1407	YW	P407EJW	1415	u	P415EJW	1422	u	P422EJW	1430	PB	P430EJW

1431-1460

Volvo B10L · Wright Liberator · N43F · 1997

1431	WA	P431JJW	1438	WA	P438JJW	1446	WA	P446JOX	1453	WA	P453JOX
1432	YW	P432JJW	1439	WA	P439JJW	1447	YW	P447JOX	1454	WA	P454JOX
1433	WA	P433JJW	1440	WA	P440JJW	1448	u	P448JOX	1455	u	P455JOX
1434	WA	P434JJW	1441	u	P441JOX	1449	u	P449JOX	1456	u	P456JOX
1435	u	P435JJW	1442	u	P442JOX	1450	YW	P450JOX	1457	YW	P457JOX
1436	WA	P436JJW	1443	u	P443JOX	1451	u	P451JOX	1459	WA	P459JOX
1437	u	P437JJW	1445	u	P445JOX	1452	u	P452JOX	1460	u	P460JOX

Vehicles allocated to Coventry carry a pale blue livery. Showing the scheme as it leaves Corporation Street is Mercedes-Benz O405 1625, S625VUK. Several of the type have been placed in the reserve pool as they are now some fifteen years old. *Richard Godfrey*

1461-1480   Volvo B10L   Wright Liberator   N43F   1997

1461	u	R461XDA	1467	u	R467XDA	1472	u	R472XDA	1477	WA	R477XDA
1462	u	R462XDA	1468	u	R468XDA	1474	WA	R474XDA	1478	u	R478XDA
1463	u	R463XDA	1470	u	R470XDA	1475	WA	R475XDA	1479	WA	R479XDA
1464	u	R464XDA	1471	u	R471XDA	1476	u	R476XDA	1480	u	R480XDA
1465	u	R465XDA									

1501-1514   Volvo B10L   Alexander Ultra   N43F   1997

1501	t	P501KOX	1505	t	P505KOX	1509	t	P509KOX	1512	t	P512KOX
1503	u	P503KOX	1507	u	P507KOX	1510	u	P510KOX	1514	t	P514KOX
1504	u	P504KOX	1508	t	P508KOX						

1515-1522   Mercedes-Benz O405N   Mercedes-Benz/UVG   N43F   1998

1515	PE	R515XOB	1517	u	R517XOB	1520	PE	R120XOB	1522	u	R522XOB
1516	PE	R516XOB	1518	PE	R518XOB	1521	PE	R521XOB			

1525-1627   Mercedes-Benz O405N   Mercedes-Benz   N43F   1998

1525	PE	R125XOB	1552	u	R552XOB	1578	u	S578VUK	1604	u	R604XOB
1526	u	R526XOB	1553	PE	R553XOB	1579	CV	S579VUK	1605	u	R165XOB
1527	u	R127XOB	1554	PE	R554XOB	1580	u	S580VUK	1606	u	R606XOB
1528	u	R128XOB	1555	u	R155XOB	1581	u	S581VUK	1607	WB	S607VUK
1529	u	R529XOB	1556	WB	R556XOB	1582	WB	S582VUK	1608	CV	R608XOB
1533	u	R533XOB	1557	u	R557XOB	1585	WB	S585VUK	1609	u	S609VUK
1534	u	R534XOB	1558	CV	R558XOB	1586	WB	S586VUK	1610	CV	S610VUK
1536	PE	R536XOB	1560	WB	S160VUK	1589	WB	S589VUK	1611	u	R611XOB
1537	u	R537XOB	1561	WB	S561VUK	1590	u	S590VUK	1612	CV	S612VUK
1538	u	R538XOB	1563	CV	S563VUK	1591	CV	S591VUK	1613	WB	S613VUK
1539	u	R539XOB	1564	CV	S564VUK	1592	WB	S592VUK	1614	PE	S614VUK
1540	PE	R140XOB	1565	u	S565VUK	1593	PE	S593VUK	1616	PE	S616VUK
1541	PE	R541XOB	1566	CV	S566VUK	1594	CV	S594VUK	1618	WB	S618VUK
1542	u	R542XOB	1568	CV	S568VUK	1595	u	R595XOB	1619	u	S619VUK
1543	PE	R543XOB	1569	CV	S569VUK	1596	u	R596XOB	1620	PE	S620VUK
1545	PE	R545XOB	1570	CV	S570VUK	1597	u	R597XOB	1621	PE	S621VUK
1546	PE	R546XOB	1571	CV	S571VUK	1598	u	R598XOB	1622	u	S622VUK
1547	CV	R547XOB	1572	CV	S572VUK	1599	WB	R599XOB	1624	u	S624VUK
1548	CV	R548XOB	1573	PE	S573VUK	1600	u	R160XOB	1625	CV	S625VUK
1549	PE	R549XOB	1574	u	S574VUK	1601	u	R601XOB	1626	u	S626VUK
1550	CV	R550XOB	1576	u	S576VUK	1602	u	R602XOB	1627	PE	S627VUK
1551	u	R551XOB	1577	WB	S577VUK	1603	u	R603XOB			

2006 saw the arrival of a batch of Volvo B7RLEs with Wrightbus Eclipse Urban bodywork, all of which are now allocated to Walsall. Seen heading out to Brownshill along Lichfield Street 1769, BX56XCN, illustrates the Wrightbus Urban design. Further examples of this model have subsequently been taken into stock. *Mark Lyons*

1628-1700

												Mercedes-Benz O405N			Mercedes-Benz			N43F		1998		

1628	PE	T628FOB	1647	PE	T647FOB	1665	PE	T665FOB	1683	WN	T683FOB
1629	PE	T629FOB	1648	PE	T648FOB	1666	WB	T266POC	1684	WN	T684FOB
1630	PE	T630FOB	1649	PE	T649FOB	1667	WB	T667FOB	1685	WN	T685FOB
1631	PE	T631FOB	1650	WN	T650FOB	1668	WB	T668FOB	1686	WN	T686FOB
1632	PE	T632FOB	1651	WB	T651FOB	1669	WN	T669FOB	1687	t	T687FOB
1633	PE	T633FOB	1652	WB	T652FOB	1670	WN	T670FOB	1688	t	T688FOB
1634	CV	T634FOB	1653	WB	T653FOB	1671	WN	T671FOB	1689	t	T689FOB
1635	CV	T635FOB	1654	WN	T654FOB	1672	WN	T672FOB	1690	u	T690FOB
1636	CV	T636FOB	1655	CV	T655FOB	1673	WN	T673FOB	1691	u	V691MOA
1637	PE	T637FOB	1656	CV	T656FOB	1674	WN	T674FOB	1692	u	V692MOA
1638	PE	T638FOB	1657	PE	T657FOB	1675	WN	T675FOB	1693	w	V693MOA
1639	PE	T639FOB	1658	PE	T658FOB	1676	WN	T676FOB	1694	WB	V694MOA
1640	PE	T640FOB	1659	CV	T659FOB	1677	WN	T677FOB	1695	WB	V695MOA
1641	PE	T641FOB	1660	WN	T660FOB	1678	CV	T678FOB	1696	WB	V696MOA
1642	PE	T642FOB	1661	WN	T661FOB	1679	WN	T679FOB	1697	WB	V697MOA
1643	PE	T643FOB	1662	WN	T662FOB	1680	CV	T680FOB	1698	WB	V698MOA
1644	u	T644FOB	1663	u	T663FOB	1681	WN	T681FOB	1699	WB	V699MOA
1645	PE	T645FOB	1664	u	T664FOB	1682	WN	T682FOB	1700	WB	V170MOA
1646	PE	T646FOB									

1701-1707

			Mercedes-Benz O405N			Mercedes-Benz			N43F		2000		

1701	WB	V701MOA	1703	CV	V703MOA	1705	PE	V705MOA	1707	PE	V177MOA
1702	WB	V702MOA	1704	PE	V704MOA	1706	PE	V706MOA			

1743	PE	S343MOJ	Mercedes-Benz O405N	Mercedes-Benz/UVG	N43F	1997	Mercedes-Benz, 1999

1750-1787

			Volvo B7RLE			Wrightbus Eclipse Urban			N42F		2006		

1750	WA	BX56XBS	1760	WA	BX56XCD	1770	WA	BX56XCO	1779	WA	BX56XCZ
1751	WA	BX56XBT	1761	WA	BX56XCE	1771	WA	BX56XCP	1780	WA	BX56XDA
1752	WA	BX56XBU	1762	WA	BX56XCF	1772	WA	BX56XCR	1781	WA	BX56XDB
1753	WA	BX56XBV	1763	WA	BX56XCG	1773	WA	BX56XCS	1782	WA	BX56XDC
1754	WA	BX56XBW	1764	WA	BX56XCH	1774	WA	BX56XCT	1783	WA	BX56XDD
1755	WA	BX56XBY	1765	WA	BX56XCJ	1775	WA	BX56XCU	1784	WA	BX56XDE
1756	WA	BX56XBZ	1766	WA	BX56XCK	1776	WA	BX56XCV	1785	WA	BX56XDG
1757	WA	BX56XCA	1767	WA	BX56XCL	1777	WA	BX56XCW	1786	WA	BX56XDH
1758	WA	BX56XCB	1768	WA	BX56XCM	1778	WA	BX56XCY	1787	WA	BX56XDJ
1759	WA	BX56XCC	1769	WA	BX56XCN						

The Scania OmniLink integral buses are frequently seen in the centre of Birmingham. Pictured in Queensgate while heading out to Perry Beeches is 1847, BV57XHP, from Perry Barr depot. The OmniLink is promoted as a dual-purpose solution for city and suburban operations, incorporating a high-capacity bus on city and suburban routes with low initial cost and exceptional operating efficiency. Further batches arrived in 2009 and 2010. *Richard Godfrey*

1788-1847
Scania OmniLink CK230 UB   Scania   N43F   2007

1788	BY	BV57XFB	1803	BY	BV57XFS	1818	BY	BV57XGJ	1833	BY	BV57XHA
1789	BY	BV57XFC	1804	BY	BV57XFT	1819	BY	BV57XGK	1834	BY	BV57XHB
1790	BY	BV57XFD	1805	BY	BV57XFU	1820	BY	BV57XGL	1835	BY	BV57XHC
1791	BY	BV57XFE	1806	BY	BV57XFW	1821	BY	BV57XGM	1836	BY	BV57XHD
1792	BY	BV57XFF	1807	BY	BV57XFX	1822	BY	BV57XGN	1837	PB	BV57XHE
1793	BY	BV57XFG	1808	BY	BV57XFY	1823	BY	BV57XGO	1838	PB	BV57XHF
1794	BY	BV57XFH	1809	BY	BV57XFZ	1824	BY	BV57XGP	1839	PB	BV57XHG
1795	BY	BV57XFJ	1810	BY	BV57XGA	1825	BY	BV57XGR	1840	PB	BV57XHH
1796	BY	BV57XFK	1811	BY	BV57XGB	1826	BY	BV57XGS	1841	PB	BV57XHJ
1797	BY	BV57XFL	1812	BY	BV57XGC	1827	BY	BV57XGT	1842	PB	BV57XHK
1798	BY	BV57XFM	1813	BY	BV57XGD	1828	BY	BV57XGU	1843	PB	BV57XHL
1799	BY	BV57XFN	1814	BY	BV57XGE	1829	BY	BV57XGW	1844	PB	BV57XHM
1800	BY	BV57XFO	1815	BY	BV57XGF	1830	BY	BV57XGX	1845	PB	BV57XHN
1801	BY	BV57XFP	1816	BY	BV57XGG	1831	BY	BV57XGY	1846	PB	BV57XHO
1802	BY	BV57XFR	1817	BY	BV57XGH	1832	BY	BV57XGZ	1847	PB	BV57XHP

1848-1907
Scania OmniLink CK230 UB   Scania   N43F   2009

1848	WA	BX58SXN	1863	PB	BX58SYH	1878	WA	BX09OZE	1893	WA	BX09OZV
1849	WA	BX58SXO	1864	PB	BX58SYJ	1879	WA	BX09OZF	1894	WA	BX09OZW
1850	WA	BX58SXP	1865	PB	BX58SYO	1880	WA	BX09OZG	1895	WA	BX09PAO
1851	WA	BX58SXR	1866	PB	BX58SYP	1881	WA	BX09OZH	1896	WA	BX09PBF
1852	WA	BX58SXS	1867	PB	BX58SYR	1882	WA	BX09OZJ	1897	WA	BX09PBO
1853	WA	BX58SXT	1868	PB	BX58SYS	1883	WA	BX09OZK	1898	WA	BX09PBU
1854	WA	BX58SXU	1869	PB	BX58SYT	1884	WA	BX09OZL	1899	WA	BX09PBZ
1855	WA	BX58SXV	1870	PB	BX58SYU	1885	WA	BX09OZM	1900	WA	BX09PCF
1856	WA	BX58SXW	1871	PB	BX58SYV	1886	WA	BX09OZN	1901	WA	BX09PCO
1857	WA	BX58SXY	1872	PB	BX58SYW	1887	WA	BX09OZO	1902	WA	BX09PCU
1858	WA	BX58SXZ	1873	PB	BX58SYY	1888	WA	BX09OZP	1903	WA	BX09PCV
1859	WA	BX58SYA	1874	PB	BX58SYZ	1889	WA	BX09OZR	1904	WA	BX09PCY
1860	WA	BX58SYC	1875	PB	BX58SZC	1890	WA	BX09OZS	1905	PB	BX09PCZ
1861	WA	BX58SYE	1876	PB	BX58SZD	1891	WA	BX09OZT	1906	PB	BX09PDO
1862	WA	BX58SYG	1877	PB	BX58SZE	1892	WA	BX09OZU	1907	PB	BX09PDU

Dundee was allocated twenty-nine Volvo B7RLEs, two of which were initially used by Volvo for promotional purposes. Shown is the route branding applied to 2036, SP61CUU, as it heads for Ninewells Hospital on the cross-city route. *Richard Godfrey*

1909-1953

Scania OmniLink CK230 UB   Scania   N43F   2009-10

1909	YW	BX59NSU	1921	YW	BX59NTL	1932	AG	BX10ACJ	1943	AG	BX10AEB
1910	YW	BX59NSV	1922	YW	BX59NTM	1933	AG	BX10ACO	1944	AG	BX10AEC
1911	YW	BX59NSY	1923	YW	BX59NTN	1934	AG	BX10ACU	1945	AG	BX10AED
1912	YW	BX59NSZ	1924	YW	BX10ABF	1935	AG	BX10ACV	1946	AG	BX10AEE
1913	YW	BX59NTA	1925	YW	BX10ABK	1936	AG	BX10ACY	1947	AG	BX10AEF
1914	YW	BX59NTC	1926	YW	BX10ABN	1937	AG	BX10ACZ	1948	AG	BX10AEG
1915	YW	BX59NTD	1927	YW	BX10ABO	1938	AG	BX10ADO	1949	AG	BX10AEJ
1916	YW	BX59NTE	1928	YW	BX10ABU	1939	AG	BX10ADU	1950	AG	BX10AEK
1917	YW	BX59NTF	1929	YW	BX10ABV	1940	AG	BX10ADV	1951	AG	BX10AEL
1918	YW	BX59NTG	1930	YW	BX10ABZ	1941	AG	BX10ADZ	1952	AG	BX10AEM
1919	YW	BX59NTJ	1931	AG	BX10ACF	1942	AG	BX10AEA	1953	AG	BX10AEN
1920	YW	BX59NTK									

2001-2052

Volvo B7RLE   Wrightbus Eclipse Urban   N42F   2011   2030/1 ex Volvo 2011

2001	WN	BX61LHY	2014	WN	BX61LJY	2027	WN	BX61LKO	2040	DD	SP61CTO
2002	WN	BX61LHZ	2015	WN	BX61LJZ	2028	WN	BX61LKP	2041	DD	SP61CTU
2003	WN	BX61LJA	2016	WN	BX61LKA	2029	WN	BX61LKU	2042	DD	SP61CTV
2004	WN	BX61LJC	2017	WN	BX61LKC	2030	DD	BG59FYF	2043	DD	SP61CTX
2005	WN	BX61LJE	2018	WN	BX61LKD	2031	DD	BK10MGE	2044	DD	SP61CTY
2006	WN	BX61LJF	2019	WN	BX61LKE	2032	DD	SP61CUH	2045	DD	SP61CTZ
2007	WN	BX61LJJ	2020	WN	BX61LKF	2033	DD	SP61CUJ	2046	DD	SP61CUA
2008	WN	BX61LJK	2021	WN	BX61LKG	2034	DD	SP61CUK	2047	DD	SP61CUC
2009	WN	BX61LJL	2022	WN	BX61LKH	2035	DD	SP61CUO	2048	DD	SP61CUG
2010	WN	BX61LJN	2023	WN	BX61LKJ	2036	DD	SP61CUU	2049	DD	SP61CSY
2011	WN	BX61LJO	2024	WN	BX61LKL	2037	DD	SP61CUV	2050	DD	SP61CSZ
2012	WN	BX61LJU	2025	WN	BX61LKM	2038	DD	SP61CUW	2051	DD	SP61CTE
2013	WN	BX12DJO	2026	WN	BX61LKN	2039	DD	SP61CTK	2052	DD	SP61CTF

2053-2098

Volvo B7RLE   Wrightbus Eclipse Urban   N42F   2012

2053	DD	SP12DAA	2065	WN	BX61XBL	2077	WN	BX61XBZ	2088	PE	BX12DCE
2054	DD	SP12DAO	2066	WN	BX61XBM	2078	PE	BX61XCA	2089	PE	BX12DCF
2055	DD	SP12DAU	2067	WN	BX61XBN	2079	PE	BX61XCB	2090	PE	BX12DCO
2056	DD	SP12DBO	2068	WN	BX61XBO	2080	PE	BX61XCC	2091	PE	BX12DCU
2057	DD	SP12DBU	2069	WN	BX61XBP	2081	PE	BX12DAO	2092	PE	BX12DCV
2058	DD	SP12DBV	2070	WN	BX61XBR	2082	PE	BX12DAU	2093	PE	BX12DCY
2059	WN	BX61XBE	2071	WN	BX61XBS	2083	PE	BX12DBO	2094	PE	BX12DCZ
2060	WN	BX61XBF	2072	WN	BX61XBT	2084	PE	BX12DBU	2095	PE	BX12DKF
2061	WN	BX61XBG	2073	WN	BX61XBU	2085	PE	BX12DBV	2096	PE	BX12DDE
2062	WN	BX61XBH	2074	WN	BX61XBV	2086	PE	BX12DBY	2097	PE	BX12DDF
2063	WN	BX61XBJ	2075	WN	BX61XBW	2087	PE	BX12DBZ	2098	PE	BX12DDU
2064	WN	BX61XBK	2076	WN	BX61XBY						

Further Volvo B7RLEs have arrived in the West Midlands during 2012 and 2013. Allocated to Birmingham Central depot in Digbeth is 2152, BX12DJK, the last vehicle from the 2012 intake. It is seen on route 98 from Rubery Park which combined with 99 provides a frequent service between Queen Elizabeth Hospital, Birmingham University and the city centre. *Richard Godfrey*

2099-2152

Volvo B7RLE — Wrightbus Eclipse Urban — N42F — 2012

2099	AG	BX12DDK	2113	AG	BX12DFG	2127	BC	BX12DGU	2140	BC	BX12DHM
2100	AG	BX12DDL	2114	AG	BX12DFJ	2128	BC	BX12DGV	2141	BC	BX12DHN
2101	AG	BX12DDN	2115	AG	BX12DFK	2129	BC	BX12DGY	2142	BC	BX12DHO
2102	AG	BX12DDO	2116	AG	BX12DFL	2130	BC	BX12DGZ	2143	BC	BX12DHP
2103	AG	BX12DDU	2117	AG	BX12DFN	2131	BC	BX12DHA	2144	BC	BX12DHU
2104	AG	BX12DDV	2118	AG	BX12DFO	2132	BC	BX12DHC	2145	BC	BX12DHV
2105	AG	BX12DDY	2119	AG	BX12DFP	2133	BC	BX12DHD	2146	BC	BX12DHY
2106	AG	BX12DDZ	2120	AG	BX12DFU	2134	BC	BX12DHE	2147	BC	BX12DHZ
2107	AG	BX12DEU	2121	AG	BX12DFV	2135	BC	BX12DHF	2148	BC	BX12DJD
2108	AG	BX12DFA	2122	AG	BX12DFY	2136	BC	BX12DHG	2149	BC	BX12DJE
2109	AG	BX12DFC	2123	AG	BX12DFZ	2137	BC	BX12DHU	2150	BC	BX12DJF
2110	AG	BX12DFD	2124	BC	BX12DGE	2138	BC	BX12DHK	2151	BC	BX12DJJ
2111	AG	BX12DFE	2125	BC	BX12DGF	2139	BC	BX12DHL	2152	BC	BX12DJK
2112	AG	BX12DFF	2126	BC	BX12DGO						

2153-2177

Volvo B7RLE — Wrightbus Eclipse Urban — N42F — 2013

2153	CV	BD12TFZ	2160	CV	BX13JSZ	2166	CV	BX13JUA	2172	CV	BX13JUK
2154	PE	BX13JUJ	2161	CV	BX13JTO	2167	CV	BX13JUC	2173	CV	BX13JUO
2155	CV	BX13JRV	2162	CV	BX13JTU	2168	CV	BX13JUE	2174	CV	BX13JUT
2156	CV	BX13JRZ	2163	CV	BX13JTV	2169	CV	BX13JUF	2175	CV	BX13JUU
2157	CV	BX13JSU	2164	CV	BX13JTY	2170	CV	BX13JUH	2176	CV	BX13JUV
2158	CV	BX13JSV	2165	CV	BX13JTZ	2171	CV	BX13JUU	2177	CV	BX13JUW
2159	CV	BX13JSY									

3225	YW	MOF225	Daimler CVG6	Metro-Cammell	B37/28R	1955
3237	DD	S237EWU	Optare Solo M850	Optare	N26F	1998

3601-3614

Dennis Dart SLF 8.9m — Alexander ALX200 — N28F — 2000 — Connex, 2002

3601	WB	W601MWJ	3605	WB	W605MWJ	3609	u	W609MWJ	3612	WB	W612MWJ
3602	WB	W602MWJ	3606	u	W606MWJ	3610	WB	C8NEX	3613	u	W613MWJ
3603	WB	W603MWJ	3607	u	W607MWJ	3611	u	W611MWJ	3614	WB	W614MWJ
3604	u	W604MWJ	3608	WB	W608MWJ						

Allocated to Wolverhampton are all the fleet's Optare Spectra-bodied DAF DB250s. Representing the type is 4003, S403NVP, seen in the town centre. *Dave Heath*

4001-4022   DAF DB250   Optare Spectra   N43/29F   1998-99

4001	WN	R1NEG	4007	WN	S407NVP	4012	WN	S412NVP	4018	WN	T418UON
4002	WN	R2NEG	4008	WN	S408NVP	4013	WN	T413UON	4019	WN	T419UON
4003	WN	S403NVP	4009	WN	S409NVP	4015	WN	T415UON	4020	WN	T420UON
4004	WN	S404NVP	4010	WN	S410NVP	4016	WN	T416UON	4021	WN	T421UON
4005	WN	S405NVP	4011	WN	S411NVP	4017	WN	T417UON	4022	WN	T422UON
4006	WN	S406NVP									

4023-4124   Volvo B7TL   Plaxton President   N45/29F*   1999-2000 *4120-4 are BC45/25F

4023	AG	V423MOA	4049	WB	V49MOA	4074	AG	V74MOA	4100	AG	V410MOA
4024	AG	V424MOA	4050	AG	V450MOA	4075	AG	V75MOA	4101	AG	V101MOA
4025	AG	V425MOA	4051	AG	V51MOA	4076	AG	V76MOA	4102	AG	V102MOA
4026	AG	V426MOA	4052	AG	V52MOA	4077	AG	V477MOA	4103	AG	V103MOA
4027	AG	V427MOA	4053	AG	V53MOA	4078	AG	V78MOA	4104	YW	V104MOA
4028	AG	V428MOA	4054	WB	V54MOA	4079	AG	V79MOA	4105	YW	V105MOA
4029	AG	V429MOA	4055	WB	V455MOA	4080	AG	V480MOA	4106	YW	V106MOA
4031	AG	V431MOA	4056	YW	V56MOA	4081	AG	V81MOA	4107	YW	V107MOA
4032	AG	V32MOA	4057	AG	V57MOA	4082	AG	V82MOA	4108	YW	V108MOA
4033	AG	V433MOA	4058	AG	V58MOA	4083	WB	V83MOA	4109	YW	V109MOA
4034	AG	V34MOA	4059	AG	V59MOA	4084	WB	V84MOA	4110	YW	W411DOE
4035	AG	V35MOA	4060	AG	V460MOA	4085	WB	V85MOA	4111	AG	W411DOP
4036	AG	V36MOA	4061	AG	V61MOA	4086	WB	V86MOA	4112	AG	W112DOP
4037	AG	V37MOA	4062	AG	V62MOA	4087	WB	V87MOA	4113	WB	W113DOP
4038	AG	V38MOA	4063	AG	V63MOA	4089	YW	V89MOA	4114	WB	W114DOP
4039	AG	V39MOA	4064	AG	V64MOA	4090	YW	V490MOA	4115	WB	W415BOV
4040	AG	V440MOA	4065	AG	V65MOA	4091	YW	V91MOA	4116	DD	W116DOP
4041	AG	V41MOA	4066	AG	V466MOA	4092	YW	V92MOA	4117	DD	W117DOP
4042	AG	V42MOA	4067	AG	V67MOA	4093	YW	V93MOA	4118	DD	W118DOP
4043	AG	V43MOA	4068	AG	V68MOA	4094	YW	V94MOA	4119	DD	W119DOP
4044	WB	V544MOA	4069	AG	V69MOA	4095	YW	V95MOA	4120	DD	W412DOE
4045	AG	V45MOA	4070	AG	V470MOA	4096	YW	V96MOA	4121	DD	W421DOP
4046	AG	V46MOA	4071	AG	V71MOA	4097	YW	V97MOA	4122	DD	W122DOP
4047	WB	V47MOA	4072	AG	V72MOA	4098	YW	V98MOA	4123	DD	W523DOP
4048	WB	V48MOA	4073	AG	V73MOA	4099	AG	V499MOA	4124	DD	W124DOP

4125-4224 — Dennis Trident — Alexander ALX400 — N47/28F — 2001

4125	WA	Y716TOH	4150	BC	Y745TOH	4175	BC	Y776TOH	4200	PE	Y806TOH
4126	WA	Y717TOH	4151	BC	Y746TOH	4176	BC	Y778TOH	4201	PE	Y807TOH
4127	WA	Y718TOH	4152	BC	Y747TOH	4177	BC	Y779TOH	4202	PE	Y808TOH
4128	WA	Y719TOH	4153	BC	Y748TOH	4178	BC	Y781TOH	4203	CV	Y809TOH
4129	WA	Y721TOH	4154	BC	Y749TOH	4179	BC	Y782TOH	4204	CV	Y811TOH
4130	WA	Y722TOH	4155	BC	Y751TOH	4180	BC	Y783TOH	4205	CV	Y812TOH
4131	WA	Y723TOH	4156	BC	Y752TOH	4181	BC	Y784TOH	4206	CV	Y813TOH
4132	WA	Y724TOH	4157	BC	Y753TOH	4182	BC	Y786TOH	4207	CV	Y814TOH
4133	WA	Y726TOH	4158	BC	Y754TOH	4183	BC	Y787TOH	4208	CV	Y815TOH
4134	WA	Y727TOH	4159	BC	Y756TOH	4184	BC	Y788TOH	4209	CV	Y816TOH
4135	PE	Y728TOH	4160	BC	Y757TOH	4185	BC	Y789TOH	4210	CV	Y817TOH
4136	WA	Y729TOH	4161	BC	Y758TOH	4186	BC	Y791TOH	4211	CV	Y818TOH
4137	WA	Y731TOH	4162	BC	Y759TOH	4187	BC	Y792TOH	4212	CV	Y819TOH
4138	WA	Y732TOH	4163	BC	Y761TOH	4188	BC	Y793TOH	4213	CV	Y821TOH
4139	BC	Y733TOH	4164	BC	Y762TOH	4189	BC	Y794TOH	4214	CV	Y822TOH
4140	BC	Y734TOH	4165	BC	Y763TOH	4190	BC	Y795TOH	4215	CV	Y823TOH
4141	BC	Y735TOH	4166	BC	Y764TOH	4191	BC	Y796TOH	4216	CV	Y824TOH
4142	BC	Y736TOH	4167	BC	Y766TOH	4192	BC	Y797TOH	4217	CV	Y825TOH
4143	BC	Y737TOH	4168	BC	Y767TOH	4193	PE	Y798TOH	4218	BC	Y826TOH
4144	BC	Y738TOH	4169	BC	Y768TOH	4194	PE	Y799TOH	4219	CV	Y827TOH
4145	BC	Y739TOH	4170	BC	Y769TOH	4195	PE	Y801TOH	4220	CV	Y828TOH
4146	BC	Y741TOH	4171	BC	Y771TOH	4196	PE	Y802TOH	4221	CV	Y829TOH
4147	BC	Y742TOH	4172	BC	Y772TOH	4197	PE	Y803TOH	4222	CV	Y831TOH
4148	BC	Y743TOH	4173	BC	Y773TOH	4198	PE	Y804TOH	4223	CV	Y833TOH
4149	BC	Y744TOH	4174	BC	Y774TOH	4199	PE	Y805TOH	4224	CV	Y834TOH

4225-4304 — Volvo B7TL — Alexander ALX400 — N47/27F — 2001

4225	PB	BU51RRO	4245	PB	BU51RUV	4265	WB	BU51RWE	4285	PB	BU51RXN
4226	PB	BU51RRV	4246	PB	BU51RUW	4266	WB	BU51RWF	4286	PB	BU51RXO
4227	WB	BU51RRX	4247	PB	BU51RVA	4267	WB	BU51RWJ	4287	PB	BU51RXP
4228	WB	BU51RRY	4248	WB	BU51RVC	4268	WB	BU51RWK	4288	PB	BU51RXR
4229	WB	BU51RRZ	4249	PB	BU51RVE	4269	WB	BU51RWL	4289	PB	BU51RXS
4230	WB	BU51RSO	4250	PB	BU51RVF	4270	WB	BU51RWN	4290	WB	BU51RXT
4231	WB	BU51RSV	4251	PB	BU51RVJ	4271	WB	BU51RWO	4291	WB	BU51RXV
4232	WB	BU51RSX	4252	PB	BU51RVK	4272	WB	BU51RWV	4292	WB	BU51RXW
4233	WB	BU51RSZ	4253	PB	BU51RVL	4273	WB	BU51RWW	4293	WB	BU51RXX
4234	PB	BU51RSY	4254	PB	BU51RVM	4274	WB	BU51RWX	4294	WB	BU51RXZ
4235	PB	BU51RTO	4255	PB	BU51RVN	4275	WB	BU51RWY	4295	WB	BU51RYA
4236	PB	BU51RTV	4256	PB	BU51RVO	4276	PB	BU51RWZ	4296	WB	BU51RYB
4237	PB	BU51TRX	4257	PB	BU51RVP	4277	PB	BU51RXB	4297	WB	BU51RYD
4238	PB	BU51TRZ	4258	PB	BU51RVR	4278	PB	BU51RXC	4298	WB	BU51RYF
4239	PB	BU51RYA	4259	PB	BU51RVT	4279	PB	BU51RXD	4299	WB	BU51RYG
4240	PB	BU51RUC	4260	PB	BU51RVV	4280	PB	BU51RXG	4300	PB	ST02MZV
4241	PB	BU51RUH	4261	PB	BU51RVW	4281	PB	BU51RXH	4301	PB	ST02MZO
4242	PB	BU51RUJ	4262	PB	BU51RVX	4282	PB	BU51RXJ	4302	PB	ST02MZP
4243	PB	BU51RUO	4263	PB	BU51RVY	4283	PB	BU51RXK	4303	PB	ST02MZN
4244	PB	BU51RUR	4264	WB	BU51RVZ	4284	PB	BU51RXM	4304	PB	ST02MZU

Pictured in Blackpool while on a National Express extra, 4128, Y719TOH, is one of the 2001 intake of Dennis Tridents. All the Tridents for West Midlands carry Alexander ALX400 bodies.
John Young

Plaxton President bodywork features in just one order for vehicles with National Express West Midlands. This comprises one hundred Volvo B7TLs. Illustrating the type is 4096, V96MOA, pictured in Kingstanding while heading for West Bromwich. *Richard Godfrey*

4305-4414

			Dennis Trident			Alexander ALX400			N47/28F	2002-03		
4305	WA	BP51HDD	4333	YW	BX02AUF	4361	YW	BX02AVU	4388	YW	BV52OBF
4306	WA	BP51HDE	4334	YW	BX02AUH	4362	YW	BX02AVV	4389	YW	BV52OBG
4307	WA	BP51HDF	4335	YW	BX02AUJ	4363	YW	BX02AVY	4390	YW	BV52OBH
4308	WA	BP51HDG				4364	BC	BV52OAA	4391	YW	BV52OBJ
4309	WA	BP51HDH	4337	YW	BX02AUL	4365	BC	BV52OAB	4392	YW	BV52OBK
4310	WA	BP51HDJ	4338	YW	BX02AUM	4366	BC	BV52OAC	4393	YW	BV52OBT
4311	YW	BP51HDK	4339	YW	BX02AUN	4367	BC	BV52OAD	4394	YW	BV52OBX
4312	YW	BP51HDL	4340	YW	BX02AUO	4368	BC	BV52OAE	4395	YW	BV52OBY
4313	YW	BX02APY	4341	YW	BX02AUP	4369	YW	BV52OAG	4396	CV	BV52OBL
4314	YW	BP51HDO	4342	YW	BX02AUR	4370	YW	BV52OAU	4397	CV	BV52OBM
4315	YW	BX02APZ	4343	YW	BX02AUT	4371	YW	BV52OAH	4398	CV	BV52OBN
4316	BC	BX02ARF	4344	YW	BX02AUU	4372	YW	BV52OAJ	4399	CV	BV52OBO
4317	BC	BX02ARU	4345	YW	BX02AUV	4373	YW	BV52OAL	4400	CV	BV52OBP
4318	BC	BX02ARZ	4346	YW	BX02AUW	4374	YW	BV52OAM	4401	CV	BV52OBR
4319	CV	BX02ASO	4347	YW	BX02AUY	4375	YW	BV52OAN	4402	CV	BV52OBS
4320	BC	BX02ASU	4348	YW	BX02AVB	4376	YW	BV52OAO	4403	CV	BV52OBU
4321	BC	BX02ASV	4349	YW	BX02AVD	4377	YW	BV52OAP	4404	CV	BV52OBW
4322	CV	BX02ASZ	4350	YW	BX02AVE	4378	YW	BV52OAS	4405	CV	BV52OBZ
4323	BC	BX02ATK	4351	YW	BX02AVF	4379	YW	BV52OAW	4406	CV	BV52OCA
4324	BC	BX02ATN	4352	YW	BX02AVG	4380	YW	BV52OAX	4407	CV	BV52OCB
4325	BC	BX02ATO	4353	YW	BX02AVJ	4381	YW	BV52OAY	4408	CV	BV52OCC
4326	BC	BX02ATU	4354	YW	BX02AVK	4382	YW	BV52OAZ	4409	CV	BV52OCD
4327	BC	BX02ATV	4355	YW	BX02AVL	4383	YW	BV52OBA	4410	CV	BV52OCE
4328	BC	BX02ATY	4356	YW	BX02AVN	4384	WN	BV52OBB	4411	CV	BV52OCF
4329	WA	BX02ATZ	4357	YW	BX02AVO	4385	WN	BV52OBC	4412	CV	BV52OCG
4330	WA	BX02AUA	4358	YW	BX02AVP	4386	YW	BV52OBD	4413	CV	BV52OCH
4331	WA	BX02AUC	4359	YW	BX02AVR	4387	YW	BV52OBE	4414	CV	BV52OCJ
4332	WA	BX02AUE	4360	YW	BX02AVT						

4415-4424

			Volvo B7TL			Alexander ALX400			N47/27F	2003		
4415	CV	BV52OCK	4418	CV	BV52OCN	4421	CV	BV52OCR	4423	CV	BV52OCU
4416	CV	BV52OCL	4419	CV	BV52OCO	4422	CV	BV52OCS	4424	CV	BV52OCW
4417	CV	BV52OCM	4420	CV	BV52OCP						

More recent Volvo chassis carry Wrightbus bodywork. Seen outside 'The West Brom' in West Bromwich is 4506, BU53UMC. All the double-decks allocated to this town comprise Volvo B7TLs numbering just short of a hundred. *Dave Heath*

4425-4474 — TransBus Trident / TransBus ALX400 — N45/28F — 2003

No.	Op	Reg	No.	Op	Reg	No.	Op	Reg	No.	Op	Reg
4425	BC	BJ03ETR	4438	BC	BJ03EUH	4451	CV	BJ03EUZ	4463	BC	BJ03EVR
4426	BC	BJ03ETT	4439	BC	BJ03EUK	4452	CV	BJ03EVB	4464	BC	BJ03EVT
4427	BC	BJ03ETU	4440	BC	BJ03EUL	4453	CV	BJ03EVC	4465	BC	BJ03EVU
4428	BC	BJ03ETV	4441	BC	BJ03EUM	4454	CV	BJ03EVD	4466	BC	BJ03EVV
4429	BC	BJ03ETX	4442	BC	BJ03EUN	4455	BC	BJ03EVF	4467	BC	BJ03EVW
4430	BC	BJ03ETY	4443	BC	BJ03EUP	4456	BC	BJ03EVG	4468	BC	BJ03EVX
4431	BC	BJ03ETZ	4444	BC	BJ03EUR	4457	BC	BJ03EVH	4469	BC	BJ03EVY
4432	BC	BJ03EUA	4445	BC	BJ03EUT	4458	BC	BJ03EVK	4470	BC	BJ03EWA
4433	BC	BJ03EUB	4446	BC	BJ03EUU	4459	BC	BJ03EVL	4471	BC	BJ03EWB
4434	BC	BJ03EUC	4447	BC	BJ03EUV	4460	BC	BJ03EVM	4472	BC	BJ03EWC
4435	BC	BJ03EUD	4448	BC	BJ03EUW	4461	BC	BJ03EVN	4473	BC	BJ03EWD
4436	BC	BJ03EUE	4449	BC	BJ03EUX	4462	BC	BJ03EVP	4474	BC	BJ03EWE
4437	BC	BJ03EUF	4450	CV	BJ03EUY						

4475-4534 — Volvo B7TL / Wrightbus Eclipse Gemini — N43/29F — 2003-04

No.	Op	Reg	No.	Op	Reg	No.	Op	Reg	No.	Op	Reg
4475	PB	BJ03EWF	4490	PB	BJ03EWY	4505	WB	BJ03EXR	4520	WB	BU53UMX
4476	PB	BJ03EWG	4491	PB	BJ03EWZ	4506	WB	BU53UMC	4521	WB	BU53UMY
4477	PB	BJ03EWH	4492	PB	BJ03EXA	4507	WB	BU53UMD	4522	WB	BU53UNA
4478	PB	BJ03EWK	4493	PB	BJ03EXB	4508	WB	BU53UME	4523	WB	BU53UNB
4479	PB	BJ03EWL	4494	PB	BJ03EXC	4509	WB	BU53UMF	4524	WB	BU53UNE
4480	PB	BJ03EWM	4495	PB	BJ03EXD	4510	WB	BU53UMG	4525	WB	BU53UNF
4481	PB	BJ03EWN	4496	PB	BJ03EXE	4511	WB	BU53UPE	4526	WB	BU53UNG
4482	PB	BJ03EWP	4497	PB	BJ03EXF	4512	AG	BU53UMJ	4527	WB	BU53UNH
4483	PB	BJ03EWR	4498	PB	BJ03EXG	4513	AG	BU53UMK	4528	WB	BU53UNJ
4484	PB	BJ03EWS	4499	PB	BJ03EXH	4514	AG	BU53UML	4529	WB	BU53UNK
4485	PB	BJ03EWT	4500	PB	BJ03EXK	4515	PB	BU53UMM	4530	WB	BU53UNL
4486	PB	BJ03EWU	4501	PB	BJ03EXL	4516	PB	BU53UMR	4531	WB	BU53UNM
4487	PB	BJ03EWV	4502	PB	BJ03EXM	4517	WB	BU53UMT	4532	WB	BU53UNN
4488	PB	BJ03EWW	4503	WB	BJ03EXN	4518	WB	BU53UMV	4533	WB	BU53UNP
4489	PB	BJ03EWX	4504	WB	BJ03EXP	4519	WB	BU53UMW	4534	WB	BU53UNR

4535-4564

TransBus Trident   TransBus ALX400   N43/28F   2004

4535	WN	BL53EDF	4543	WN	BL53EDX	4551	WN	BL53EEN	4558	WN	BL53EEW
4536	WN	BL53EDJ	4544	WN	BL53EEA	4552	WN	BL53EEO	4559	WN	BL53EEX
4537	WN	BL53EDK	4545	WN	BL53EEB	4553	WN	BL53EEP	4560	WN	BL53EEY
4538	WN	BL53EDO	4546	WN	BL53EEF	4554	WN	BL53EER	4561	WN	BL53EEZ
4539	WN	BL53EDP	4547	WN	BL53EEG	4555	WN	BL53EET	4562	WN	BL53EFA
4540	WN	BL53EDR	4548	WN	BL53EEH	4556	WN	BL53EEU	4563	WN	BL53EFB
4541	WN	BL53EDU	4549	WN	BL53EEJ	4557	WN	BL53EEV	4564	WN	BL53EFC
4542	WN	BL53EDV	4550	WN	BL53EEM						

4565-4609

TransBus Trident   TransBus ALX400   N43/28F   2004

4565	WN	BU04BHX	4577	WN	BU04BKE	4588	WN	BU04BLJ	4599	WN	BX54DDE
4566	WN	BU04BHY	4578	WN	BU04BKF	4589	WN	BU04BLK	4600	WN	BX54DDF
4567	WN	BU04BHZ	4579	WN	BU04BKG	4590	WN	BU04BLN	4601	WN	BX54DDJ
4568	WN	BU04BJE	4580	WN	BU04BKJ	4591	WN	BU04BLV	4602	WN	BX54DDK
4569	WN	BU04BJF	4581	WN	BU04BKK	4592	WN	BU04BLX	4603	WN	BX54DDL
4570	WN	BU04BJJ	4582	WN	BU04BKL	4593	WN	BU04BLZ	4604	WN	BX54DDN
4571	WN	BU04BJK	4583	WN	BU04BKN	4594	WN	BX54DCU	4605	WN	BX54DDO
4572	WN	BU04BJV	4584	WN	BU04BKV	4595	WN	BU04BMZ	4606	WN	BX54DDU
4573	WN	BU04BJX	4585	WN	BU04BKX	4596	WN	BX54DCV	4607	WN	BX54DDV
4574	WN	BU04BJZ	4586	WN	BU04BKZ	4597	WN	BX54DCY	4608	WN	BX54DDY
4575	WN	BU04BKA	4587	WN	BU04BLF	4598	WN	BX54DDA	4609	WN	BX54DDZ
4576	WN	BU04BKB									

4610-4634

ADL Trident 10.5m   ADL ALX400   N43/28F   2004-05

4610	BC	BX54DEU	4617	BC	BX54XSE	4623	BC	BX54XSL	4629	BC	BX54XRV
4611	BC	BX54DFA	4618	BC	BX54XSF	4624	BC	BX54XSM	4630	BC	BX54XRW
4612	BC	BX54DFC	4619	BC	BX54XSG	4625	BC	BX54XRO	4631	BC	BX54XRY
4613	BC	BX54DFD	4620	BC	BX54XSH	4626	BC	BX54XRR	4632	BC	BX54XRZ
4614	BC	BX54DFE	4621	BC	BX54XSJ	4627	BC	BX54XRT	4633	BC	BX54XSA
4615	BC	BX54XSC	4622	BC	BX54XSK	4628	BC	BX54XRU	4634	BC	BX54XSB
4616	BC	BX54XSD									

4635-4696

Volvo B7TL   Wrightbus Eclipse Gemini   N43/29F   2004-05   *4680-6 are NC42/29F

4635	WB	BX54DFF	4651	AG	BX54XRM	4667	AG	BX54DHE	4682	WA	BX54XPP
4636	WB	BX54DFG	4652	AG	BX54XRN	4668	AG	BX54DHF	4683	WA	BX54XTA
4637	WB	BX54DFJ	4653	AG	BX54XRR	4669	AG	BX54DHG	4684	WA	BX54XTB
4638	WB	BX54DFK	4654	AG	BX54XPT	4670	AG	BX54XRH	4685	WA	BX54XTC
4639	WB	BX54DFV	4655	AG	BX54XPZ	4671	AG	BX54XRJ	4686	WA	BX54XTD
4640	WB	BX54DFY	4656	AG	BX54XRA	4672	AG	BX54XRK	4687	CV	BU05HEV
4641	WB	BX54DFZ	4657	AG	BX54XRE	4673	AG	BX54XRL	4688	CV	BU05HFE
4642	WB	BX54DGE	4658	AG	BX54DFN	4674	AG	BX54XPU	4689	CV	BU05HFF
4643	AG	BX54DGY	4659	AG	BX54DFO	4675	AG	BX54XPV	4690	CV	BU05HFH
4644	AG	BX54DGZ	4660	AG	BX54DFP	4676	AG	BX54XPW	4691	CV	BU05HFJ
4645	AG	BX54DHA	4661	AG	BX54DFU	4677	AG	BX54XPY	4692	CV	BU05HFL
4646	AG	BX54DHC	4662	AG	BX54DGF	4678	AG	BX54XRC	4693	CV	BU05HFO
4647	AG	BX54XRD	4663	AG	BX54DGO	4679	AG	BX54XPM	4694	CV	BU05HFP
4648	AG	BX54XRE	4664	AG	BX54DGU	4680	WA	BX54XPN	4695	CV	BU05HFR
4649	AG	BX54XRF	4665	AG	BX54DGV	4681	WA	BX54XPO	4696	CV	BU05HFS
4650	AG	BX54XRG	4666	AG	BX54DHD						

4697	PB	YN55PXB	Scania OmniCity N94UD	Scania	N45/27F	2005
4698	PB	BX55XOA	ADL Trident 2	ADL Enviro 400	N45/33F	2005

4700-4717

Volvo B7TL   Wrightbus Eclipse Gemini   N43/29F   2006

4700	WB	BU06CWR	4705	WB	BU06CWY	4710	WB	BU06CXD	4714	WB	BU06CXJ
4701	WB	BU06CWT	4706	WB	BU06CWZ	4711	WB	BU06CXE	4715	WB	BU06CXK
4702	WB	BU06CWV	4707	WB	BU06CXA	4712	WB	BU06CXG	4716	WB	BU06CXL
4703	WB	BU06CWW	4708	WB	BU06CXB	4713	WB	BU06CXH	4717	WB	BU06CXM
4704	WB	BU06CWX	4709	WB	BU06CXC						

The first thirteen of the 2011 intake of Enviro 400s were sent to Coventry. Illustrating the type as it passes along Corporation Street is 4831, BX61LKY. Further examples from the 2013 delivery have also been allocated to the city. *Richard Godfrey*

4718-4776

			ADL Trident 2 10.5m			ADL Enviro 400			N45/32F	2007-08			
4718	PB	BU07LGO	4733	WA	BV57XHX	4748	YW	BV57XJN	4763	WA	BV57XKG		
4719	PB	BU07LGV	4734	WA	BV57XHY	4749	YW	BV57XJO	4764	WA	BV57XKH		
4720	PB	BU07LGW	4735	WA	BV57XHZ	4750	YW	BV57XJP	4765	WA	BV57XKJ		
4721	PB	BU07LGX	4736	WA	BV57XJA	4751	YW	BV57XJT	4766	WA	BV57XKK		
4722	PB	BU07LGY	4737	WA	BV57XJB	4752	YW	BV57XJU	4767	WA	BV57XKL		
4723	PB	BU07LGZ	4738	YW	BV57XJC	4753	YW	BV57XJW	4768	WA	BV57XKM		
4724	PB	BU07LHA	4739	YW	BV57XJD	4754	YW	BV57XJX	4769	WA	BV57XKN		
4725	PB	BU07LHB	4740	YW	BV57XJE	4755	YW	BV57XJY	4770	WA	BV57XKO		
4726	PB	BU07LHC	4741	YW	BV57XJF	4756	YW	BV57XJZ	4771	WA	BV57XKP		
4727	PB	BU07LHD	4742	YW	BV57XJG	4757	YW	BV57XKA	4772	WA	BV57XKS		
4728	PB	BV57XHR	4743	YW	BV57XJH	4758	YW	BV57XKB	4773	WA	BV57XKT		
4729	PB	BV57XHS	4744	YW	BV57XJJ	4759	YW	BV57XKC	4774	WA	BV57XKU		
4730	PB	BV57XHT	4745	YW	BV57XJK	4760	YW	BV57XKD	4775	WA	BV57XKW		
4731	PB	BV57XHU	4746	YW	BV57XJL	4761	YW	BV57XKE	4776	WA	BV57XKX		
4732	PB	BV57XHW	4747	YW	BV57XJM	4762	YW	BV57XKF					

4777-4781

			Scania OmniCity N230 UD			Scania			N45/31F	2008			
4777	PB	BV57XKY	4779	PB	BV57XLA	4780	PB	BU08EHZ	4781	PB	BV57XLC		
4778	PB	BV57XKZ											

4800-4829

			ADL Trident 2 10.5m			ADL Enviro 400			N45/32F	2009			
4800	PE	BX09PDV	4808	PE	BX09PFG	4816	PE	BX09PFZ	4823	PE	BX09PGY		
4801	PE	BX09PDY	4809	PE	BX09PFJ	4817	PE	BX09PGE	4824	PE	BX09PGZ		
4802	PE	BX09PDZ	4810	PE	BX09PFK	4818	PE	BX09PGF	4825	PE	BX09PHA		
4803	PE	BX09PEO	4811	PE	BX09PFN	4819	PE	BX09PGK	4826	PE	BX09PHF		
4804	PE	BX09PFA	4812	PE	BX09PFO	4820	PE	BX09PGG	4827	PE	BX09PHJ		
4805	PE	BX09PFD	4813	PE	BX09PFU	4821	PE	BX09PGU	4828	PE	BX09PHK		
4806	PE	BX09PFE	4814	PE	BX09PFV	4822	PE	BX09PGV	4829	PE	BX09PHN		
4807	PE	BX09PFF	4815	PE	BX09PFY								

The Trident 2 was introduced to replace the Trident (1) at the same time as the Enviro 400 body was unveiled. Following an initial batch of sixty, thirty more were delivered to West Midlands in 2009 with further orders placed up to the present. Seen near Moor Street rail station and with lettering for route 33 is 4846, **BX61LLT**. *Richard Godfrey*

4830-4879

ADL Trident 2 10.5m   ADL Enviro 400   N45/32F   2011

No	Depot	Reg	No	Depot	Reg	No	Depot	Reg	No	Depot	Reg
4830	CV	BX61LKV	4843	PB	BX61LLO	4856	PB	BX61LMM	4868	WA	BX61LLN
4831	CV	BX61LKY	4844	PB	BX61LLP	4857	WA	BX61LMO	4869	WA	BX61LNM
4832	CV	BX61LKZ	4845	PB	BX61LLR	4858	WA	BX61LMU	4870	WA	BX61LNN
4833	CV	BX61LLA	4846	PB	BX61LLT	4859	WA	BX61LMV	4871	WA	BX61LNO
4834	CV	BX61LLC	4847	PB	BX61LLU	4860	WA	BX61LMY	4872	WA	BX61LNP
4835	CV	BX61LNA	4848	PB	BX61LLV	4861	WA	BX61LLD	4873	WA	BX61LNR
4836	CV	BX61LND	4849	PB	BX61LLW	4862	WA	BX61LLE	4874	WA	BX61LNT
4837	CV	BX61LNE	4850	PB	BX61LLZ	4863	WA	BX61LLF	4875	WA	BX61LNU
4838	CV	BX61LNF	4851	PB	BX61LME	4864	WA	BX61LLG	4876	WA	BX61LNV
4839	CV	BX61LNG	4852	PB	BX61LMF	4865	WA	BX61LLJ	4877	WA	BX61LNW
4840	CV	BX61LNH	4853	PB	BX61LMJ	4866	WA	BX61LLK	4878	WA	BX61LNY
4841	CV	BX61LNJ	4854	PB	BX61LMK	4867	WA	BX61LLM	4879	WA	BX61LNZ
4842	CV	BX61LNK	4855	PB	BX61LML						

4880-4913

ADL E40D   ADL Enviro 400   N45/32F   2013

No	Depot	Reg	No	Depot	Reg	No	Depot	Reg	No	Depot	Reg
4880	WA	BX13JVL	4889	CV	BX13JVE	4898	BC	BX13JVV	4906	BC	BX13JWF
4881	WA	BX13JVM	4890	CV	BX13JVF	4899	BC	BX13JVW	4907	BC	BX13JWG
4882	WA	BX13JVN	4891	CV	BX13JVG	4900	BC	BX13JVY	4908	BC	BX13JWJ
4883	WA	BX13JVO	4892	CV	BX13JVH	4901	BC	BX13JVZ	4909	BC	BX13JWK
4884	WA	BX13JVP	4893	CV	BX13JVJ	4902	BC	BX13JWA	4910	BC	BX13JWL
4885	CV	BX13JUY	4894	CV	BX13JVK	4903	BC	BX13JWC	4911	BC	BX13JWM
4886	CV	BX13JVA	4895	BC	BX13JVR	4904	BC	BX13JWD	4912	BC	BX13JWN
4887	CV	BX13JVC	4896	BC	BX13JVT	4905	BC	BX13JWE	4913	BC	BX13JWO
4888	CV	BX13JVD	4897	BC	BX13JVU						

4914-4939

ADL E40D   ADL Enviro 400   N45/32F   2013

No			No			No			No		
4914	-	-	4921	-	-	4928	-	-	4934	-	-
4915	-	-	4922	-	-	4929	-	-	4935	-	-
4916	-	-	4923	-	-	4930	-	-	4936	-	-
4917	-	-	4924	-	-	4931	-	-	4937	-	-
4918	-	-	4925	-	-	4932	-	-	4938	-	-
4919	-	-	4926	-	-	4933	-	-	4939	-	-
4920	-	-	4927	-	-						

Gaining in popularity is the hybrid version of the Enviro 400, and the latest sales make it the UK's best selling hybrid-electric bus. Its breakthrough technology derives from a partnership between ADL and BAe Systems and introduces a new era of quieter, greener and more fuel efficient public transport. Its green credentials are reflected in the livery as shown by 5407, BX61LHJ pictured at Harborne. *Richard Godfrey*

5401-5409

ADL E40H · ADL Enviro 400 · N45/32F · 2011

5401	BC	BX61LHC	5404	BC	BX61LHF	5406	BC	BX61LHH	5408	BC	BX61LHK
5402	BC	BX61LHD	5405	BC	BX61LHG	5407	BC	BX61LHJ	5409	BC	BX61LHL
5403	BC	BX61LHE								

5410-5421

ADL E40H · ADL Enviro 400 · N45/32F · 2013

5410	WN	BX13JOA	5413	WN	BX13JOU	5416	WN	BX13JPJ	5419	WN	BX13JPV
5411	WN	BX13JOH	5414	WN	BX13JOV	5417	WN	BX13JPO	5420	WN	BX13JPY
5412	WN	BX13JOJ	5415	WN	BX13JPF	5418	WN	BX13JPU	5421	WN	BX13JRO

5422-5430

ADL E40H · ADL Enviro 400 · N45/32F · 2013

5422	DD	SP13BRX	5425	DD	SP13BSU	5427	DD	SP13BSX	5429	DD	SP13BSZ
5423	DD	SP13BRZ	5426	DD	SP13BSV	5428	DD	SP13BSY	5430	DD	SP13BTE
5424	DD	SP13BSO								

5501-5509

Volvo B5LH · Wrightbus Gemeni 2 · N41/27F · 2011

5501	BC	BX61LHM	5504	BC	BX61LHP	5506	BC	BX61LHT	5508	BC	BX61LHV
5502	BC	BX61LHN	5505	BC	BX61LHR	5507	BC	BX61LHU	5509	BC	BX61LHW
5503	BC	BX61LHO								

5510-5518

Volvo B5LH · Wrightbus Gemeni 2 · N41/27F · 2013

5510	WN	BX13JNF	5513	WN	BX13JNL	5515	WN	BX13JNO	5517	WN	BX13JNV
5511	WN	BX13JNJ	5514	WN	BX13JNN	5516	WN	BX13JNU	5518	WN	BX13JNZ
5512	WN	BX13JNK								

6012-6021

Mercedes-Benz Citaro O530G · Mercedes-Benz · AN56D · 2003

6012	CV	BJ03ESN	6015	CV	BJ03ESY	6018	CV	BJ03ETE	6020	CV	BJ03ETK
6013	CV	BJ03ESU	6016	CV	BJ03ETA	6019	CV	BJ03ETF	6021	CV	BJ03ETL
6014	CV	BJ03ESV	6017	CV	BJ03ETD					

6022-6032

Scania OmniCity N94UA · Scania · AN58D · 2004

6022	PB	S1TWM	6025	PB	BX54DNF	6028	PB	BX54DNO	6031	PB	BX54DOA
6023	PB	BX54DND	6026	PB	BX54DNJ	6029	PB	BX54DNV	6032	PB	BX54DOH
6024	PB	BX54DNE	6027	PB	BX54DNN	6030	PB	BX54DNY			

7001-7018 — Volvo B7TL — Wrightbus Eclipse Gemini — N45/29F — 2005

7001	DD	SP54CHF	7006	DD	SP54CHL	7011	DD	SP54CGO	7015	DD	SP54CGY
7002	DD	SP54CHG	7007	DD	SP54CHN	7012	DD	SP54CGU	7016	DD	SP54CGZ
7003	DD	SP54CHH	7008	DD	SP54CHO	7013	DD	SP54CGV	7017	DD	SP54CHC
7004	DD	SP54CHJ	7009	DD	SP54CGG	7014	DD	SP54CGX	7018	DD	SP54CHD
7005	DD	SP54CHK	7010	DD	SP54CGK						

7019-7033 — Scania OmniLink CK230 UB — Scania — N43F — 2010

7019	PB	SP10CXA	7023	PB	SP10CXE	7027	PB	SP10CXJ	7031	PB	SP10CWX
7020	PB	SP10CXB	7024	PB	SP10CXF	7028	PB	SP10CXK	7032	PB	SP10CWY
7021	PB	SP10CXC	7025	PB	SP10CXG	7029	PB	SP10CWV	7033	PB	SP10CWZ
7022	PB	SP10CXD	7026	PB	SP10CXH	7030	PB	SP10CWW			

7067	DD	Y722CJW	Volvo B7L	Wright Eclipse	N37F	1996
7084	u	R84GNW	Dennis Dart SLF 10.1m	Wright Crusader	N36F	1997
7086	u	R86GNW	Dennis Dart SLF 10.1m	Wright Crusader	N36F	1997
7115	u	R466XDA	Volvo B10L	Wright Liberator	N43F	1997

7122-7151 — Volvo B10L — Wright Liberator — N43F — 1997

7122	u	P122KSL	7128	DD	P128KSL	7140	u	P140KSL	7146	DD	P146RSN
7123	u	P123KSL	7129	DD	P129KSL	7141	u	P141KSL	7147	DD	P147RSN
7124	DD	P124KSL	7132	u	P132KSL	7142	u	P142RSN	7148	DD	P148RSN
7125	u	P125KSL	7136	w	P136KSL	7143	w	P143RSN	7149	u	P149RSN
7126	u	P126KSL	7138	DD	P138KSL	7144	DD	P144RSN	7150	u	P150RSN
7127	DD	P127KSL	7139	u	P139KSL	7145	DD	P145RSN	7151	DD	P151RSN

7152-7161 — Volvo B10BLE — Wright Renown — N45F — 1998

7152	DD	R152RSN	7155	DD	R155RSN	7158	DD	R158RSN	7160	DD	R160RSN
7153	DD	R153RSN	7156	DD	R156RSN	7159	DD	R159RSN	7161	DD	R161RSN
7154	DD	R154RSN	7157	DD	R157RSN						

7165-7179 — Volvo B10BLE — Wright Renown — N45F — 1999

7165	DD	V165ESL	7169	DD	V169ESL	7173	DD	V173ESL	7177	DD	V177ESL
7166	DD	V166ESL	7170	DD	V170ESL	7174	DD	V174ESL	7178	u	V178ESL
7167	DD	V167ESL	7171	DD	V171ESL	7175	DD	V175ESL	7179	DD	V179ESL
7168	DD	V168ESL	7172	DD	V172ESL	7176	DD	V176ESL			

7241	DD	S233EWU	Optare Solo M850	Optare	N26F	1998	
7242	DD	S231EWU	Optare Solo M850	Optare	N26F	1998	
7243	DD	S235EWU	Optare Solo M850	Optare	N26F	1998	
7308	DD	T577ASN	Optare Solo M920	Optare	N31F	1999	
7309	DD	T307UOX	Optare Solo M850	Optare	N31F	1999	
7323	DD	YJ54UBR	Optare Solo M850	Optare	N28F	2004	Wilfreda, Adwick-le-Street
7344	DD	YP02LCA	Optare Solo M850	Optare	N28F	2002	Connex, 2002
7345	DD	YP02LCE	Optare Solo M850	Optare	N28F	2002	Connex, 2002
7419	t	N23FWU	DAF SB220	Ikarus CitiBus	B51F	1996	
9951	t	D951NDA	MCW Metrobus DR102/59	MCW	B43/26F	1986	
9955	t	D955NDA	MCW Metrobus DR102/59	MCW	B43/26F	1986	
9959	t	D959NDA	MCW Metrobus DR102/59	MCW	B43/26F	1986	

Articulated buses have been slow to take hold in the British market where the double-deck has been more popular. But thirty-two are in service in the West Midlands, a mix of three types. Allocated to Perry Barr, the Scania product is a low-floor OmniCity N94UA represented by 6023, BX54DND. It was heading along Chester Road in Tyburn on route 67 when pictured. *Richard Godfrey*

8321-8352 · ADL Dart 4 9.5m · ADL Enviro 200 · N22F · 2008

8321	HO	SN08AAU	8329	HO	SN08ABU	8337	HO	SN08ACV	8345	HO	SN08ADZ
8322	HO	SN08AAV	8330	HO	SN08ABV	8338	HO	SN08ACX	8346	HO	SN08AEA
8323	HO	SN08AAX	8331	HO	SN08ABX	8339	HO	SN08ACY	8347	HO	SN08AEB
8324	HO	SN08AAY	8332	HO	SN08ABZ	8340	HO	SN08ACZ	8348	HO	SN08AEC
8325	HO	SN08AAZ	8333	HO	SN08ACF	8341	HO	SN08ADO	8349	HO	SN08AED
8326	HO	SN08ABF	8334	HO	SN08ACJ	8342	HO	SN08ADU	8350	HO	SN08AEE
8327	HO	SN08ABK	8335	HO	SN08ACO	8343	HO	SN08ADV	8351	HO	SN08AEF
8328	HO	SN08ABO	8336	HO	SN08ACU	8344	HO	SN08ADX	8352	HO	SN08AEG

8353	SH	T503TOL	Volvo B6BLE	Wright Crusader	N37F	1999

8354-8358 · ADL E20D 8.8m · ADL Enviro 200 · N29F · 2012

8354	HO	MX61BBE	8356	HO	MX61BBJ	8357	HO	MX61BBK	8358	HO	MX61BBN
8355	HO	MX61BBF									

8541-8547 · Mercedes-Benz Citaro O530 GLE · AN29D · 2008

8541	SC	KX58GUA	8543	SC	KX58GUD	8545	SC	KX58GUF	8547	SC	KX58GUH
8542	SC	KX58GUC	8544	SC	KX58GUE	8546	SC	KX58GUG			

8548-8553 · Mercedes-Benz Citaro O530 GLE · AN28D · 2003 · Quality Line, 2008

8548	RE	BU53AWN	8550	RE	BU53AWP	8552	RE	BU53AWT	8553	RE	BU53AWV
8549	RE	BU53AWO	8551	RE	BU53AWR						

8554-8560 · Mercedes-Benz Citaro O530 LE · N21D · 2008

8554	SC	KX58GVJ	8556	SC	KX58GVL	8558	SC	KX58GTU	8560	SC	KX58GTZ
8555	SC	KX58GVK	8557	SC	KX58GVM	8559	SC	KX58GTY			

8561	SC	KX58GUJ	ADL Dart 4	ADL Enviro 200	N25F	2008
8562	SC	KX58GUK	ADL Dart 4	ADL Enviro 200	N25F	2008
8563	SC	KX58GUO	ADL Dart 4	ADL Enviro 200	N25F	2008

8564-8573

Mercedes-Benz Sprinter 515cdi KVC — M9 — 2009

8564	SC	KX58BJK	8567	SC	KX58BJO	8570	SC	KX58BFA	8572	SC	KX09CJO
8565	SC	KX58BJV	8568	SC	KX58BKA	8571	SC	KX58BJY	8573	SC	KX09CJU
8566	SC	KX58BJU	8569	SC	KX58BJZ						

8574-8579

Mercedes-Benz Citaro O530 GLE — AN28D — 2003 — Stagecoach

8574	SC	LX03HCE	8576	SC	LX03HCL	8578	SC	LX03HDE	8579	SC	LX03DD
8575	SC	LX03HCG	8577	SC	LX03HCU						

8600-8605

NAW Cobus 2700s — Cobus — N15T

8600	AL	8600	8602	AL	8602	8604	AL	8604	8605	AL	8605
8601	AL	8601	8603	AL	8603						

8606-8622

DAF SB220 — East Lancs Myllennium — N29D — 2000 — Aviation Defence, 2009

8606	AL	X831NWX	8611	AL	X836NWX	8616	AL	X841NWX	8620	RE	X845NWX
8607	AL	X832NWX	8612	AL	X837NWX	8617	AL	X842NWX	8621	RE	X846NWX
8608	AL	X833NWX	8614	AL	X839NWX	8618	RE	X843NWX	8622	RE	X847NWX
8610	AL	X835NWX	8615	AL	X840NWX	8619	AL	X844NWX			

8637-8640

MAN 14.220 — MCV Evolution — N28D — 2006

8637	AL	AE55MVF	8638	AL	AE55MVG	8639	AL	AE55MVH	8640	AL	AE55MVJ

8641-8645

NAW Cobus 2700s — Cobus — N15T — 2010

8641	SC	8641	8643	SC	8643	8644	SC	8644	8645	SC	8645
8642	SC	8642									

8646-8657

Mercedes-Benz Citaro O530 — AN30D — 2010

8646	AL	BK10EHT	8649	AL	BK10EHW	8652	AL	BK10EHZ	8655	AL	BK10EJX
8647	AL	BK10EHU	8650	AL	BK10EHX	8653	AL	BK10EJU	8656	AL	BK10EJY
8648	AL	BK10EHV	8651	AL	BK10EHY	8654	AL	BK10EJV	8657	AL	BK10EJZ

8658-8663

NAW Cobus 2700s — Cobus — N15T — 2010

8658	SC	8658	8660	SC	8660	8662	SC	8662	8663	SC	8663
8659	SC	8659	8661	SC	8661						

8664	AL	N470VPJ	Mercedes-Benz 811D	Wright Nimbus	B21F	1996	British Airways, 2012
8665	AL	N472VPJ	Mercedes-Benz 811D	Wright Nimbus	B21F	1996	British Airways, 2012
8666	AL	P849BPB	Mercedes-Benz 811D	Wright Nimbus	B21F	1996	British Airways, 2012

8667-8677

Ford Transit — Ford — M16 — 2012

8667	AL	HN62DYV	8670	AL	HN62FMM	8673	AL	HN62FMU	8676	AL	HN62DYX
8668	AL	HN62EAA	8671	AL	HN62FMN	8674	AL	HN62FMV	8677	AL	HN62DYY
8669	AL	HN62FML	8672	AL	HN62FMO	8675	AL	HN62DYW			

8678	AL	VO12PBU	Volkswagen Caravelle	Volkswagen	M16	2012
8679	AL	CN60AKJ	Mercedes-Benz 811D	Mercedes-Benz	M16	2012

Special event vehicle:

184	DD	ETS964	Daimler CVG6	Metro-Cammell	B37/28R	1955

Previous registrations:

2133PL	M36TRR		
5414PH	R884TSR		
A8TPT	T434GSP		
H3KFC	W869VGY		
JSU542	P973KTS		
K5KFC	W452AKN		
LVG263	T435GSP		
M8KFC	W453AKN		
		NSV621	V74DSN
		NSV622	V73DSN
		PYJ136	P10TAY
		USR591	-
		USU661	R91GTM
		USU662	R92GTM
		YX06AWM	MCH98

Depots and allocations:

Birmingham (Summer Road, Acocks Green) - AG

Scania Omnilink	1931	1932	1933	1934	1935	1936	1937	1938
	1939	1940	1941	1942	1943	1944	1945	1946
	1947	1948	1949	1950	1951	1952	1953	
Volvo B7RLE	2099	2100	2101	2102	2103	2104	2105	2106
	2107	2108	2109	2110	2111	2112	2113	2114
	2115	2116	2117	2118	2119	2120	2121	2122
	2123							
Volvo B7TL	4023	4024	4025	4026	4027	4028	4029	4031
	4032	4033	4034	4035	4036	4037	4038	4039
	4040	4041	4042	4043	4045	4046	4050	4051
	4052	4058	4059	4060	4061	4062	4063	4064
	4065	4066	4067	4068	4069	4070	4071	4072
	4073	4074	4075	4076	4077	4078	4079	4080
	4081	4082	4099	4100	4101	4102	4103	4111
	4112	4643	4644	4645	4646	4647	4648	4649
	4650	4651	4652	4653	4654	4655	4656	4657
	4658	4659	4660	4661	4662	4663	4664	4665
	4666	4667	4668	4669	4670	4671	4672	4673
	4674	4675	4676	4677	4678	4679		

Birmingham (Liverpool Street, Digbeth) - BC

Enviro 200	801	802	803	804	805	806	807	808
	809							
Volvo B7RLE	2124	2125	2126	2127	2128	2129	2130	2131
	2132	2133	2134	2135	2136	2137	2138	2139
	2140	2141	2142	2143	2144	2145	2146	2147
	2148	2149	2150	2151	2152			
Trident	4139	4140	4141	4142	4143	4144	4145	4146
	4147	4148	4149	4150	4151	4152	4153	4154
	4155	4156	4157	4158	4159	4160	4161	4162
	4163	4164	4165	4166	4167	4168	4169	4170
	4171	4172	4173	4174	4175	4176	4177	4178
	4179	4180	4181	4182	4183	4184	4185	4186
	4187	4188	4189	4190	4191	4192	4218	4316
	4317	4318	4320	4321	4323	4324	4325	4326
	4327	4328	4364	4365	4366	4367	4368	4425
	4426	4427	4428	4429	4430	4431	4432	4433
	4434	4435	4436	4437	4438	4439	4440	4441
	4442	4443	4444	4445	4446	4447	4448	4449
	4455	4456	4457	4458	4459	4460	4461	4462
	4463	4464	4465	4466	4467	4468	4469	4470
	4471	4472	4473	4474	4610	4611	4612	4613
	4614	4615	4616	4617	4618	4619	4620	4621
	4622	4623	4624	4625	4626	4627	4628	4629
	4630	4631	4632	4633	4634			
Enviro 400	4895	4896	4897	4898	4899	4900	4901	4902
	4903	4904	4905	4906	4907	4908	4909	4910
	4911	4912	4913					
Enviro 400 Hybris	5401	5402	5403	5404	5405	5406	5407	5408
	5409							
Volvo B5LH	5501	5502	5503	5504	5505	5506	5507	5508
	5509							

Birmingham (Bordesley Green) - BY

Scania Omnilink	1788	1789	1790	1791	1792	1793	1794	1795
	1796	1797	1798	1799	1800	1801	1802	1803
	1804	1805	1806	1807	1808	1809	1810	1811
	1812	1813	1814	1815	1816	1817	1818	1819
	1820	1821	1822	1823	1824	1825	1826	1827
	1828	1829	1830	1831	1832	1833	1834	1835
	1836							

Bishops Stortford (Start Hill, Great Hollingbury) - SH

Scania K340	1	2	3	4	6	7	8	9
	10	11	12	13	14	15	16	17
	18	19	20	23	24	25	26	32
	33	35	36	37	38	39	95	
Volvo B12B	60	61	62	64	66	72		
Volvo B9R	136	137	138	139	140	141	142	143

Coventry (Ford Street) - CV

Solo	3240							
Mercedes-Benz O405	1547	1548	1550	1558	1563	1564	1566	1568
	1569	1570	1571	1572	1579	1591	1594	1608
	1610	1612	1625	1634	1635	1636	1655	1656
	1659	1678	1680	1703				
Volvo B7RLE	2153	2155	2156	2157	2158	2159	2160	2161
	2162	2163	2164	2165	2166	2167	2168	2169
	2170	2171	2172	2173	2174	2175	2176	2177
Trident	4203	4204	4205	4206	4207	4208	4209	4210
	4211	4212	4213	4214	4215	4216	4217	4219
	4220	4221	4222	4223	4224	4319	4322	4396
	4397	4398	4399	4400	4401	4402	4403	4404
	4405	4406	4407	4408	4409	4410	4411	4412
	4413	4414	4450	4451	4452	4453	4454	
Volvo B7TL	4415	4416	4417	4418	4419	4420	4421	4422
	4423	4424	4687	4688	4689	4690	4691	4692
	4693	4694	4695	4696				
Enviro 400	4830	4831	4832	4833	4834	4835	4836	4837
	4838	4839	4840	4841	4842	4885	4886	4887
	4888	4889	4890	4891	4892	4893	4894	
MB O405GN	6012	6013	6014	6015	6016	6017	6018	6019
	6020	6021						

Crawley (Whetstone Close, Tinsley Green) - CY

Volvo B12B	44	47	61	62	63	64	66	67
	68	69	70	71	72	73	77	78
	79	80	81	82	83	84	85	86
Volvo B9R	110	111	112	113	114	115	123	124
	125	126	127	128	129	130	131	132
	133	134	135					
Mercedes-Benz	99							
DAF SB3000	950							

Dundee (East Dock Street) - DD

Optare Solo	295	298	300	321	322	3237	7241	7242
	7308	7323	7344	7345				
Volvo B10L	7127	7128	7129	7138	7144	7145	7146	7147
	7148	7151						
Volvo B10BLE	7152	7153	7154	7155	7156	7157	7158	7159
	7160	7161	7165	7166	7167	7168	7169	7170
	7171	7172	7173	7174	7175	7176	7177	7179
Volvo B7RLE	2030	2031	2032	2033	2034	2035	2036	2037
	2038	2039	2040	2041	2042	2043	2044	2045
	2046	2047	2048	2049	2050	2051	2052	2053
	2054	2055	2056	2057	2058			
Olympian	7269	7270						
Volvo B7TL	4116	4117	4118	4119	4120	4121	4122	4123
	4124	7001	7002	7003	7004	7005	7006	7007
	7008	7009	7010	7011	7012	7013	7014	7015
	7016	7017	7018					
Enviro 400	5422	5423	5424	5425	5426	5427	5428	5429
	5430							

Kingswinford (Pensnett Industrial Estate) - PE

Volvo B6	582							
Enviro 200	824	825	826	827	828	829	830	
Mercedes-Benz O405	1515	1516	1518	1520	1521	1525	1536	1540
	1541	1543	1545	1546	1549	1553	1554	1573
	1593	1614	1616	1620	1621	1627	1628	1629
	1630	1631	1632	1633	1637	1638	1639	1640
	1641	1642	1643	1645	1646	1647	1648	1649
	1657	1658	1665	1704	1705	1706	1707	1743
Volvo B7RLE	2078	2079	2080	2081	2082	2083	2084	2085
	2086	2087	2088	2089	2090	2091	2092	2093
	2094	2095	2096	2097	2098	2154		
Trident 2	4135	4193	4194	4195	4196	4197	4198	4199
	4200	4201	4202	4800	4801	4802	4803	4804
	4805	4806	4807	4808	4809	4810	4811	4812
	4813	4814	4815	4817	4818	4819	4820	4821
	4822	4823	4824	4825	4826	4827	4828	4829

Luton

Volvo B9R	C140	C141	C142	C143	C145	C146	C147	C148
	C149	C150	C151	C152	C153	C154	C155	C156
	C157	C158	C159	C160	C161			

Birmingham (Wellhead Lane, Perry Barr) - PB

Solo	286	287	303	319	320			
Volvo B10L	1430							
Scania OmniLink	1837	1838	1839	1840	1841	1842	1843	1844
	1845	1846	1847	1863	1864	1865	1866	1867
	1868	1869	1870	1871	1872	1873	1874	1875
	1876	1877	1905	1906	1907	7019	7020	7021
	7022	7023	7024	7025	7026	7027	7028	7029
	7030	7031	7032	7033				
Scania Artic	6022	6023	6024	6025	6026	6027	6028	6029
	6030	6031	6032					
Volvo B7TL	4225	4226	4234	4235	4236	4237	4238	4239
	4240	4241	4242	4243	4244	4245	4246	4247
	4249	4250	4251	4252	4253	4254	4255	4256
	4257	4258	4259	4260	4261	4262	4263	4276
	4277	4278	4279	4280	4281	4282	4283	4284
	4285	4286	4287	4288	4289	4300	4301	4302
	4303	4304	4475	4476	4477	4478	4479	4480
	4481	4482	4483	4484	4485	4486	4487	4488
	4489	4490	4491	4492	4493	4494	4495	4496
	4497	4498	4499	4500	4501	4502	4515	4516
OmniCity	4697	4777	4778	4779	4780	4781		
Enviro 400	4698	4718	4719	4720	4721	4722	4723	4724
	4725	4726	4727	4728	4729	4730	4731	4732
	4843	4844	4845	4846	4847	4848	4849	4850
	4851	4852	4853	4854	4855	4856		

Walsall (Carl Street) - WA

Volvo B6	244	547	669	673	677			
Volvo B10L	1419	1421	1431	1433	1434	1436	1438	1439
	1440	1444	1453	1454	1459	1474	1475	1477
	1479							
Volvo B7RLE	1750	1751	1752	1753	1754	1755	1756	1757
	1758	1759	1760	1761	1762	1763	1764	1765
	1766	1767	1768	1769	1770	1771	1772	1773
	1774	1775	1776	1777	1778	1779	1780	1781
	1782	1783	1784	1785	1786	1787		
Scania OmniLink	1848	1849	1850	1851	1852	1853	1854	1855
	1856	1857	1858	1859	1860	1861	1862	1878
	1879	1880	1881	1882	1883	1884	1885	1886
	1887	1888	1889	1890	1891	1892	1893	1894
	1895	1896	1897	1898	1899	1900	1901	1902
	1903	1904						
Trident	4125	4126	4127	4128	4129	4130	4131	4132
	4133	4134	4136	4137	4138	4305	4306	4307
	4308	4309	4329	4330	4331	4332		
Volvo B7TL	4680	4681	4682	4683	4684	4685	4686	
Enviro 400	4733	4734	4735	4736	4737	4763	4764	4765
	4766	4767	4768	4769	4770	4771	4772	4773
	4774	4775	4776	4857	4858	4859	4860	4861
	4862	4863	4864	4865	4866	4867	4868	4869
	4870	4871	4872	4873	4874	4875	4876	4877
	4878	4879	4880	4881	4882	4883	4884	

West Bromwich (Oak Lane) - WB

Volvo B6	519	524	533	534	564	566	568	569
	584	591	680					
Enviro 200	810	811	812	813	814	815	816	817
	818	819	820	821	822	823		
Dart	3601	3602	3603	3605	3608	3610	3612	3614
Mercedes-Benz O405	1523	1556	1560	1561	1577	1582	1585	1586
	1589	1592	1599	1607	1613	1618	1651	1652
	1653	1666	1667	1668	1694	1695	1696	1697
	1698	1699	1700	1701	1702			
Volvo B7TL	4044	4047	4048	4049	4053	4054	4055	4057
	4083	4084	4085	4086	4087	4113	4114	4115
	4227	4228	4229	4230	4231	4232	4233	4248
	4264	4265	4266	4267	4268	4269	4270	4271
	4272	4273	4274	4275	4290	4291	4292	4293
	4294	4295	4296	4297	4298	4299	4503	4504
	4505	4506	4507	4508	4509	4510	4511	4512
	4513	4514	4517	4518	4519	4520	4521	4522
	4523	4524	4525	4526	4527	4528	4529	4530
	4531	4532	4533	4534	4535	4536	4537	4538
	4539	4540	4541	4542	4700	4701	4702	4703
	4704	4705	4706	4707	4708	4709	4710	4711
	4712	4713	4714	4715	4716	4717		

West Drayton (Sipson Road) - Hotel Hopper, Airlinks - SC/SR

Scania K340	22	51	52	53	58			
Volvo B12B	96	102						
Volvo B9R	110	111	112	113	114	115	116	117
	118	119	120	121	122	123	124	125
	126	127	128	128	130	131	132	133
	134	135	136	137	138	139	144	
Volvo B6BLE	8353	8625	8626	8627	8628	8629		
Dart	8623	8624						
Enviro 200	8321	8322	8323	8324	8325	8326	8327	8328
	8329	8330	8331	8332	8333	8334	8335	8336
	8337	8338	8339	8340	8341	8342	8343	8344
	8345	8346	8347	8348	8349	8350	8351	8352
	8561	8562	8563					
DAF SB220	8606	8607	8608	8610	8611	8612	8614	8615
	8616	8617	8618	8620				
Cobus 2700	8600	8601	8602	8603	8604	8605		
MB Sprinter	8570							
MB Citaro	8554	8555	8556	8557	8558	8559	8560	8646
	8647	8648	8649	8650	8651	8652	8653	8654
	8655	8656	8657					
MB Citaro artic	8541	8542	8543	8544	8545	8546	8547	8548
	8549	8550	8551	8552	8553			

Wolverhampton (Park Lane) - WN

Type							
Volvo B6LE							
508	554	555	581	586	598	600	601
620	626	632	633	634	638	639	640
662							
Mercedes-Benz O405							
1650	1654	1660	1661	1662	1669	1670	1671
1672	1673	1674	1675	1676	1677	1679	1681
1682	1683	1684	1685	1686			
Volvo B7RLE							
2001	2002	2003	2004	2005	2006	2007	2008
2009	2010	2011	2012	2013	2014	2015	2016
2017	2018	2019	2020	2021	2022	2023	2024
2025	2026	2027	2028	2029	2059	2060	2061
2062	2063	2064	2065	2066	2067	2068	2069
2070	2071	2072	2073	2074	2075	2076	2077
VDL DB250							
4001	4002	4003	4004	4005	4006	4007	4008
4009	4010	4011	4012	4013	4015	4016	4017
4018	4019	4020	4021	4022			
Trident							
4535	4536	4537	4538	4539	4540	4541	4542
4543	4544	4545	4546	4547	4548	4549	4550
4551	4552	4553	4554	4555	4556	4557	4558
4559	4560	4561	4562	4563	4564	4565	4566
4567	4568	4569	4570	4571	4572	4573	4574
4575	4576	4577	4578	4579	4580	4581	4582
4583	4584	4585	4586	4587	4588	4589	4590
4591	4592	4593	4594	4595	4596	4597	4598
4599	4600	4601	4602	4603	4604	4605	4606
4607	4608	4609					
Enviro 400 Hybrid							
5410	5411	5412	5413	5414	5415	5416	5417
5418	5419	5420	5421				
Volvo B5LH							
5510	5511	5512	5513	5514	5515	5516	5517
5518							

Birmingham (Yardley Wood Road, Yardley Wood) - YW

Type							
Volvo B10L							
1406	1407	1408	1411	1413	1432	1447	1450
1457							
Scania OmniLink							
1909	1910	1911	1912	1913	1914	1915	1916
1917	1918	1919	1920	1921	1922	1923	1924
1925	1926	1927	1928	1929	1930		
Daimler CVG6							
3225							
Volvo B7TL							
4056	4089	4090	4091	4092	4093	4094	4095
4096	4097	4098	4104	4105	4106	4107	4108
4109	4110						
Trident							
4310	4311	4312	4313	4314	4315	4333	4334
4335	4337	4338	4339	4340	4341	4342	4343
4344	4345	4346	4347	4348	4349	4350	4351
4352	4353	4354	4355	4356	4357	4358	4359
4360	4361	4362	4363	4369	4370	4371	4372
4373	4374	4375	4376	4377	4378	4379	4380
4381	4382	4383	4384	4385	4386	4387	4388
4389	4390	4391	4392	4393	4394	4395	
Enviro 400							
4738	4739	4740	4741	4742	4743	4744	4745
4746	4747	4748	4749	4750	4751	4752	4753
4754	4755	4756	4757	4758	4759	4760	4761
4762	4799						

Driving School, Reserve and stored:

Remainder

The King's Ferry - Travelink - V.I.P. - Land Yachts

The Kings Ferry Ltd, The Travel Centre, 199 Eastcourt Lane, Gillingham, ME8 6HW

101	Y1CHT	Mercedes-Benz Vario O815	Medio	C19F	2005	Blueprint, Watford, 2006
102	Y20CHT	Mercedes-Benz Vario O815	Medio	C19F	2003	Blueprint, Watford, 2006
108	YP52CUU	Scania OmniTown N94 UB	Castrosua Corsa	N34F	2003	Scania demonstrator, 2005
201	FN02VBD	Irisbus EuroMidi CC80.E.18	Indcar Maxim 2	C29F	2002	
202	FN02VBE	Irisbus EuroMidi CC80.E.18	Indcar Maxim 2	C29F	2002	
203	BF61HBJ	Mercedes-Benz Tourino O510	Mercedes-Benz	C28FT	2011	
204	BF61HBK	Mercedes-Benz Tourino O510	Mercedes-Benz	C28FT	2011	
401	YJ04HVS	VDL Bus SB4000	Van Hool T9 Alizée	C49FT	2004	Westbus, 2009
402	YJ04HVU	VDL Bus SB4000	Van Hool T9 Alizée	C49FT	2004	Westbus, 2009
403	FJ61EXA	Volvo B9R	Caetano Levanté	C49FT	2011	
404	FJ61EXC	Volvo B9R	Caetano Levanté	C49FT	2011	
405	FJ61EXD	Volvo B9R	Caetano Levanté	C49FT	2011	
406	FJ61EXE	Volvo B9R	Caetano Levanté	C49FT	2011	
407	FJ61EXB	Volvo B9R	Caetano Levanté	C49FT	2011	
408	GN51WCA	Scania K124 IB4	Van Hool T9 Alizée	C49FT	2001	
409	FJ12GAX	Volvo B9R	Caetano Levanté	C49FT	2012	
410	FJ12GBE	Volvo B9R	Caetano Levanté	C49FT	2012	
411	FJ12GBO	Volvo B9R	Caetano Levanté	C49FT	2012	
412	FJ12GBU	Volvo B9R	Caetano Levanté	C49FT	2012	
413	FJ12GBV	Volvo B9R	Caetano Levanté	C49FT	2012	
420	H6KFC	Scania L94 IB	Van Hool T9 Alizée	C49FT	2000	
423	K8KFC	Scania L94 IB	Irizar Century 12.35	C49FT	2000	
426	J6TKF	Scania L94 IB	Irizar Century 12.35	C49FT	2000	

Representing The Kings Ferry fleet is 616, FJ10EZO, one of only eleven Mercedes-Benz OC500s that carry Caetano Levanté bodywork. It is seen on one of the commuter routes linking London with the Medway Towns. *Colin Lloyd*

501	FJ11RAU	Volvo B9R	Caetano Levanté	C53FT	2011
502	FJ11RAX	Volvo B9R	Caetano Levanté	C53FT	2011
503	FJ11RBF	Volvo B9R	Caetano Levanté	C53FT	2011
517	FD54DHL	Volvo B7R	Sunsundegui Sideral 330	C53F	2005
518	FD54DHM	Volvo B7R	Sunsundegui Sideral 330	C53F	2005
519	FJ05ANV	Volvo B7R	Sunsundegui Sideral 330	C53F	2005
520	FJ05AOD	Volvo B7R	Sunsundegui Sideral 330	C53F	2005
610	FJ10EZG	Mercedes-Benz OC500	Caetano Levanté	C53FT	2010
611	FJ10EZH	Mercedes-Benz OC500	Caetano Levanté	C51FT	2010
612	FJ10EZK	Mercedes-Benz OC500	Caetano Levanté	C51FT	2010
613	FJ10EZL	Mercedes-Benz OC500	Caetano Levanté	C49FT	2010
614	FJ10EZM	Mercedes-Benz OC500	Caetano Levanté	C53FT	2010
615	FJ10EZM	Mercedes-Benz OC500	Caetano Levanté	C53FT	2010
616	FJ10EZO	Mercedes-Benz OC500	Caetano Levanté	C53FT	2010
617	FJ10EZP	Mercedes-Benz OC500	Caetano Levanté	C51FT	2010
618	FJ10EZR	Mercedes-Benz OC500	Caetano Levanté	C51FT	2010
619	FJ60KUN	Mercedes-Benz OC500	Caetano Levanté	C57FT	2010
620	FJ60KUO	Mercedes-Benz OC500	Caetano Levanté	C57FT	2010
621	FJ61EXF	Volvo B13R 13.5m	Caetano Levanté	C59FT	2011
622	FJ61EXG	Volvo B13R 13.5m	Caetano Levanté	C59FT	2011
623	FJ61EXH	Volvo B13R 13.5m	Caetano Levanté	C59FT	2011
624	FJ12GBF	Volvo B13R 13.5m	Caetano Levanté	C59FT	2011
701	GJ52OMZ	Scania K114 EB6	Berkhof Axial 100	C55/19DT	2003
702	YR52VFE	Scania K114 EB6	Berkhof Axial 100	C55/19DT	2003
703	GN03TYB	Scania K114 EB6	Berkhof Axial 100	C55/19DT	2003
704	GJ52MUV	Scania K114 EB6	Berkhof Axial 100	C55/19DT	2003
705	GJ02JJL	Scania K114 EB6	Berkhof Axial 100	C55/19DT	2002
706	GJ02LUZ	Scania K114 EB6	Berkhof Axial 100	C55/19DT	2002
707	YT61GRU	Scania K400 EB6	VDL Axial 100	C55/19DT	2011
708	YT61GRX	Scania K400 EB6	VDL Axial 100	C55/19DT	2011
901	V1PKF	Scania K380 EB6	Irizar PB	C38FT	2008
902	YT12RLV	Scania K400 EB6	Irizar PB	C38FT	2009
903	YT59NZZ	Scania K400 EB6	Irizar PB	C38FT	2009
904	Y4PKF	Scania K114 EB6	Irizar PB	C34FT	2006
905	V5PKF	Scania K124 EB6	Irizar PB	C34FT	2004
906	YT60OSO	Scania K400 EB6	Irizar PB	C38FT	2009
907	V11PKF	Scania K400 EB6	Irizar PB	C38FT	2005
908	YT11LPX	Scania K400 EB6	Irizar PB	C38FT	2011
909	V9PKF	Scania K380 EB6	Irizar PB	C38FT	2008
910	YT61GRF	Scania K400 EB6	Irizar PB	C38FT	2011

Ancillary vehicle:

TC2	E75DRM	DAF SB3000	Van Hool Alizée	TV	1988	Camm's, Nottingham, 2007

Previous registrations:

A16TKF	V998JKK	V4PKF	YN56AAE
E75DRM	4671TR, SIB2632	V5PKF	YN54AKF
H6KFC	W903XKR	V11PKF	YN05HFX
J6TKF	Y875TKU	Y1CHT	BX55FYC
K8KFC	W533YKN	Y10CHT	YN04YBA
L6KFC	Y447TKN	Y20CHT	BU53AXY, L7MOA
L7KFC	Y451TKN	Y30CHT	BU53AXZ, L7MOC
M2KFC	Y449TKN	Y50CHT	YN04YBB

Depots: Eastcourt Lane, Gillingham (outstation: Cullet Drive, Queensborough, Isle of Sheppey); Oakington Barracks, Longstanton,

Web: www.thekingsferry.co.uk

RATP GROUP

London United, Busways House, Wellington Road, Twickenham, TW2 5NX

ADE1-45

				ADL E400D 10.1m			ADL Enviro 400			N41/24D	2012			
1	AV	YX12FNG	13	AV	YX12FNU	24	AV	YX62AEW	35	AV	YX62ARZ
2	AV	YX12FNH	14	AV	YX12FNV	25	AV	YX62AGU	36	AV	YX62BXF
3	AV	YX12FNJ	15	AV	YX12FNW	26	AV	YX12FON	37	AV	YX62BXR
4	AV	YX12FNK	16	AV	YX12FNY	27	AV	YX12FOP	38	AV	YX62BXU
5	AV	YX12FNL	17	AV	YX12FNZ	28	AV	YX12GHU	39	AV	YX62BXY
6	AV	YX12FNM	18	AV	YX12FOA	29	AV	YX12GHK	40	AV	YX62BXZ
7	AV	YX12FNN	19	AV	YX12FOC	30	AV	YX12GHN	41	AV	YX62BYG
8	AV	YX12FNO	20	AV	YX12FOD	31	AV	YX12GHO	42	AV	YX62BYJ
9	AV	YX12FNP	21	AV	YX12FOF	32	AV	YX12GHU	43	AV	YX62BYK
10	AV	YX12FNR	22	AV	YX12FOH	33	AV	YX62AHE	44	AV	YX62BZE
11	AV	YX12FNS	23	AV	YX12FOJ	34	AV	YX62AOE	45	AV	YX62BZS
12	AV	YX12FNT									

ADE46-73

				ADL E400D 10.1m			ADL Enviro 400			N41/24D	2012			
46	PK	YX62BBO	53	PK	YX62BGF	60	PK	YX62BKO	67	PK	YX62BPO
47	PK	YX62BBZ	54	PK	YX62BHD	61	PK	YX62BLZ	68	PK	YX62BPU
48	PK	YX62BCK	55	PK	YX62BHW	62	PK	YX62BMV	69	PK	YX62BPZ
49	PK	YX62BCV	56	PK	YX62BJF	63	PK	YX62BMY	70	PK	YX62BUA
50	PK	YX62BFL	57	PK	YX62BJU	64	PK	YX62BNO	71	PK	YX62BUE
51	PK	YX62BFU	58	PK	YX62BJZ	65	PK	YX62BNV	72	PK	YX62BVN
52	PK	YX62BGE	59	PK	YX62BKF	66	PK	YX62BPF	73	PK	YX62BWO

London United is one of many operators of London Buses and is owned by the RATP Group, an international public transport operator owned by the government of France. In 2009, the Caisse des dépôts et consignations, the majority owner of the Transdev group, started negotiations with Veolia Environnement to merge Transdev with Veolia Transport. As part of the resulting agreement, made in May 2010, it was agreed that the RATP Group, which had a minority shareholding in Transdev, would take over ownership of some of Transdev's operations in lieu of cash payment. This had a considerable impact on Transdev's London bus operations, as it was agreed that London United would transfer to the RATP Group, whilst London Sovereign would remain with Transdev and become part of the merged Veolia Transdev group. Enviro 400 ADH16, SN60BYM, is shown working route 94 at Holland Park. *Richard Godfrey*

The length of the ADL Enviro 200 most frequently found in London is the 10.2 metre version which seats 29 in dual-door format, where as the 29-seat single-doored 8.9metre model is popular in provincial fleets. Illustrating the former type is DE94, SN10CAX, shown passing through Barnes while operating route 72 to Roehampton. *Richard Godfrey*

ADH1-22

ADL E400H 10.1m   ADL Enviro 400   N37/26D   2009-10

1	V	SN58EOR	7	S	SN60BYB	13	S	SN60BYJ	18	S	SN60BYP
2	V	SN58EOS	8	S	SN60BYC	14	S	SN60BYK	19	S	SN60BYR
3	S	SN60BXX	9	S	SN60BYD	15	S	SN60BYL	20	S	SN60BYS
4	S	SN60BXY	10	S	SN60BYF	16	S	SN60BYM	21	S	SN60BYT
5	S	SN60BXZ	11	S	SN60BYG	17	S	SN60BYO	22	S	SN60BYU
6	S	SN60BYA	12	S	SN60BYH						

ADH23-51

ADL E400H 10.1m   ADL Enviro 400   N37/26D   2013

23	V	YX62FAU	31	V	YX62FJD	38	V	YX62FMV	45	V	YX62FSS
24	V.	YX62FCM	32	V	YX62FJV	39	V	YX62FNZ	46	V	YX62FTD
25	V	YX62FCO	33	V	YX62FKE	40	V	YX62FOA	47	V	YX62FTF
26	V	YX62FDY	34	V	YX62FKK	41	V	YX62FPC	48	V	YX62FTP
27	V	YX62FFB	35	V	YX62FLH	42	V	YX62FPF	49	V	YX62FTZ
28	V	YX62FFG	36	V	YX62FME	43	V	YX62FPK	50	V	YX62FUT
29	V	YX62FHA	37	V	YX62FMG	44	V	YX62FSE	51	V	YX62FUU
30	V	YX62FHO									

DE1-49

ADL Dart 4 10.2m   ADL Enviro 200   N29D   2008-09

1	HH	YX58DVA	14	HH	YX58DVR	26	FW	YX09HJU	38	S	YX09HKT
2	HH	YX58DVB	15	HH	YX58DVT	27	FW	YX09HJV	39	S	YX09HKH
3	HH	YX58DVC	16	HH	YX58DVU	28	FW	YX09HJY	40	S	YX09HKJ
4	HH	YX58DVF	17	HH	YX58DVV	29	FW	YX09HJZ	41	S	YX09HKK
5	HH	YX58DVG	18	HH	YX58DVW	30	FW	YX09HKZ	42	S	YX09HKL
6	HH	YX58DVH	19	HH	YX58DUV	31	FW	YX09HLA	43	S	YX09HKM
7	HH	YX58DVJ	20	HH	YX58DUY	32	S	YX09HKA	44	S	YX09HKN
8	HH	YX58DVK	21	HH	YX58DWK	33	S	YX09HKB	45	S	YX09HKO
9	HH	YX58DVL	22	HH	YX09HJJ	34	S	YX09HKC	46	S	YX09HKP
10	HH	YX58DVM	23	FW	YX09HJK	35	S	YX09HKD	47	S	YX09HKT
11	HH	YX58DVN	24	FW	YX09HJN	36	S	YX09HKE	48	S	YX09HKU
12	HH	YX58DVO	25	FW	YX09HJO	37	S	YX09HKR	49	S	YX09HKV
13	HH	YX58DVP									

DE57-92

ADL Dart 4 10.2m   ADL Enviro 200   N29D   2008   NCP, London, 2010

57	TV	SK07DXE	66	TV	SK07DXR	75	S	SK07DYC	84	S	SK07DYP
58	TV	SK07DXF	67	TV	SK07DXS	76	S	SK07DYD	85	S	SK07DYS
59	TV	SK07DXG	68	TV	SK07DXT	77	S	SK07DYF	86	S	SK07DYT
60	TV	SK07DXH	69	TV	SK07DXU	78	S	SK07DYG	87	S	SK07DYU
61	TV	SK07DXJ	70	TV	SK07DXV	79	S	SK07DYH	88	S	SK07DYV
62	TV	SK07DXL	71	TV	SK07DXW	80	S	SK07DYJ	89	S	SK07DYW
63	TV	SK07DXM	72	TV	SK07DXX	81	S	SK07DYM	90	S	SK07DYX
64	TV	SK07DXO	73	TV	SK07DXY	82	S	SK07DYN	91	S	SK07DYY
65	TV	SK07DXP	74	TV	SK07DXZ	83	S	SK07DYO	92	S	VX58DXA

Pictured in Longford while operating route H98 from Hayes End is DLE11, SN60EBM, and one of seventeen based at Hounslow. *Richard Godfrey*

DE93-128 · ADL Dart 4 10.2m · ADL Enviro 200 · N29D · 2010

93	S	SN10CAV	102	S	SN10CCD	111	FW	YX60CAO	120	FW	YX60CCD
94	S	SN10CAX	103	S	SN10CCE	112	FW	YX60CAU	121	FW	YX60CCE
95	S	SN10CBF	104	S	SN10CCF	113	FW	YX60CAV	122	FW	YX60CCF
96	S	SN10CBO	105	S	SN10CCJ	114	FW	YX60CBF	123	FW	YX60CCJ
97	S	SN10CBU	106	S	SN10CCK	115	FW	YX60CBO	124	FW	YX60CCK
98	S	SN10CBV	107	S	SN10CCO	116	FW	YX60CBU	125	FW	YX60CCN
99	S	SN10CBX	108	S	SN10CCU	117	FW	YX60CBV	126	FW	YX60CCO
100	S	SN10CBY	109	FW	YX60CAA	118	FW	YX60CBY	127	FW	YX60BZH
101	S	SN10CCA	110	FW	YX60CAE	119	FW	YX60CCA	128	FW	YX60BZJ

DLE1-25 · ADL Dart 4 10.8m · ADL Enviro 200 · N32D · 2011

1	AV	SN60EAX	8	AV	SN60EBJ	14	HH	SN60EBU	20	AV	SN60ECD
2	AV	SN60EAY	9	AV	SN60EBK	15	HH	SN60EBV	21	AV	SN60ECE
3	AV	SN60EBA	10	HH	SN60EBL	16	HH	SN60EBX	22	AV	SN60ECF
4	AV	SN60EBC	11	AV	SN60EBM	17	HH	SN60EBZ	23	AV	SN60ECJ
5	AV	SN60EBD	12	HH	SN60EBO	18	HH	SN60ECA	24	AV	SN60ECT
6	AV	SN60EBF	13	HH	SN60EBP	19	AV	SN60ECC	25	AV	SN60ECV
7	AV	SN60EBG									

DP1-11 · Dennis Dart SLF 10.7m · Plaxton Pointer 2 · N36F · 1998

1	FWt	S301MKH	7	Vt	S307MKH	10	Vt	S310MKH	11	Vt	S311MKH
6	Vt	S306MKH									

DPS549-552 · Dennis Dart SLF 10.1m · Plaxton Pointer 2 · N27D* · 2001 · *seating varies

549	u	Y549XAG	551	u	Y551XAG	552	u	Y552XAG	

DPS579-592 · Dennis Dart SLF 10.1m · Alexander ALX200 · N30D · 2001

579	TV	SN51TAU	583	V	SN51TAV	587	V	SN51TBO	590	TV	SN51TDZ
580	TV	SN51TBY	584	FW	SN51TBZ	588	TV	SN51TCJ	591	TV	SN51TBU
581	TV	SN51TCV	585	FW	SN51TCX	589	TV	SN51TCY	592	TR	SN51TCK
582	HH	SN51TDV	586	V	SN51TDX						

DPK613	TV	SN51SXG	Dennis Dart SLF 8.8m	Plaxton Pointer MPD	N29F	2001
DPK614	TV	SN51SXH	Dennis Dart SLF 8.8m	Plaxton Pointer MPD	N29F	2001

DPK615 TV	SN51SXJ	Dennis Dart SLF 8.8m	Plaxton Pointer MPD	N29F	2001	
DPK624 TV	SN06JPV	ADL Dart 8.8m	ADL Mini Pointer	N23F	2006	
DPK625 TV	SN06JPX	ADL Dart 8.8m	ADL Mini Pointer	N23F	2006	

DPS624-680
TransBus Dart 10.1m — TransBus Pointer — N27F* — 2002 — *seating varies

624	u	SK02XGT	649	TV	LG02FFT	660	AV	LG02FGF	671	u	LG02FHA
625	u	SK02XGU	650	TV	LG02FFU	661	FW	LG02FGJ	672	u	LG02FHB
626	u	SK02XGV	651	TV	LG02FFV	662	TV	LG02FGK	673	HH	LG02FHC
641	u	LG02FFK	652	TV	LG02FFW	663	FW	LG02FGM	674	HH	LG02FHD
642	u	LG02FFL	653	TV	LG02FFX	664	V	LG02FGN	675	HH	LG02FHE
643	u	LG02FFM	654	TV	LG02FFY	665	FW	LG02FGO	676	HH	LG02FHF
644	u	LG02FFN	655	FW	LG02FFZ	666	TV	LG02FGP	677	HH	LG02FHH
645	u	LG02FFO	656	TV	LG02FGA	667	FW	LG02FGU	678	HH	LG02FHJ
646	u	LG02FFP	657	TV	LG02FGC	668	u	LG02FGV	679	HH	LG02FHK
647	u	LG02FFR	658	TV	LG02FGD	669	u	LG02FGX	680	HH	LG02FHL
648	TV	LG02FFS	659	FW	LG02FGE	670	FW	LG02FGZ			

DPS681-694
TransBus Dart SLF 10.1m — TransBus Pointer — N27D* — 2003 — *seating varies

681	FW	SN03LDY	685	FW	SN03LEV	689	FW	SN03LFE	692	TV	SN03LFH
682	FW	SN03LDZ	686	FW	SN03LFA	690	FW	SN03LFF	693	TV	SN03LFJ
683	u	SN03LEF	687	FW	SN03LFB	691	TV	SN03LFG	694	V	SN03LFK
684	FW	SN03LEJ	688	S	SN03LFD						

DPS701-727
ADL Dart SLF 10.1m — ADL Pointer — N28D — 2005 — NCP, London, 2010

701	V	SN55HKD	708	HH	SN55HKL	715	HH	SN55HKW	722	TV	SN55HLC
702	V	SN55HKE	709	HH	SN55HKM	716	HH	SN55HKX	723	u	SN55DVR
703	V	SN55HKF	710	HH	SN55HKO	717	HH	SN55HKY	724	u	SN55DVT
704	V	SN55HKG	711	HH	SN55HKP	718	V	SN55HSD	725	u	SN55DVU
705	V	SN55HKH	712	HH	SN55HKT	719	V	SN55HSE	726	u	SN55DVV
706	V	SN55HKJ	713	HH	SN55HKU	720	V	SN55HKZ	727	S	SN55DVW
707	HH	SN55HKK	714	HH	SN55HKV	721	TV	SN55HLA			

RML880 FW	WLT880	AEC Routemaster RH2H1	Park Royal	B40/32R	1961	

HDE1-5
ADL Hybrid Dart 10.2m — ADL Enviro 200 — N29F — 2009

1	TV	SN09CHC	3	TV	SN09CHF	4	TV	SN09CHG	5	TV	SN09CHH
2	TV	SN09CHD									

MCL1-7
Mercedes-Benz Citaro O530 LE — Mercedes-Benz — N35D — 2011

1	AV	BD11LWN	3	AV	BD11LWP	5	AV	BD11LWS	7	AV	BD11LWU
2	AV	BD11LWO	4	AV	BD11LWR	6	AV	BD11LWT			

MV3-8
MAN 11.190 — Optare Vecta — N42F — 1995

3	Vt	N283DWY	6	Vt	N286DWY	7	Vt	N287DWY	8	Vt	N288DWY

OT1-16
Optare Tempo X1200 — Optare — N34D — 2011

1	AV	YJ11EHG	5	AV	YJ11EHM	9	AV	YJ11EHR	13	AV	YJ11EHV
2	AV	YJ11EHH	6	AV	YJ11EHN	10	AV	YJ11EHS	14	AV	YJ11EHW
3	AV	YJ11EHK	7	AV	YJ11EHO	11	AV	YJ11EHT	15	AV	YJ11EHX
4	AV	YJ11EHL	8	AV	YJ11EHP	12	AV	YJ11EHU	16	AV	YJ11EHZ

OV1-19
Optare Versa V1040 — Optare — N27D — 2008-09

1	V	YJ58VBA	6	V	YJ58VBF	11	V	YJ58VBN	16	V	YJ58VBV
2	V	YJ58VBB	7	V	YJ58VBG	12	V	YJ58VBO	17	V	YJ58VBX
3	V	YJ58VBC	8	V	YJ58VBK	13	V	YJ58VBP	18	V	YJ58VBY
4	V	YJ58VBD	9	V	YJ58VBL	14	V	YJ58VBT	19	V	YJ58VBZ
5	V	YJ58VBE	10	V	YJ58VBM	15	V	YJ58VBU			

OV50-66
Optare Versa V1040 — Optare — N27D — 2009

50	PK	YJ58PHY	55	PK	YJ09EZF	59	PK	YJ09EYW	63	PK	YJ09EZA
51	PK	YJ58PHZ	56	PK	YJ09EYT	60	PK	YJ09EYX	64	PK	YJ09EZB
52	PK	YJ58PJO	57	PK	YJ09EYU	61	PK	YJ09EYY	65	PK	YJ09EZC
53	PK	YJ58PJU	58	PK	YJ09EYV	62	PK	YJ09EYZ	66	PK	YJ09EZD
54	PK	YJ09EZE									

SDE1-10
ADL Dart 4 8.9m — ADL Enviro 200 — N26F — 2008

1	TV	YX08MFO	4	TV	YX08MDZ	7	TV	YX08MEV	9	TV	YX08MHM
2	TV	YX08MDV	5	TV	YX08MFN	8	TV	YX08MFA	10	TV	YX08MFK
3	TV	YX08MDY	6	TV	YX08MEU						

Joining the fleet in 2011 and used on route 203 are seven Mercedes-Benz Citaro integral vehicles. Introduced in 1997 and manufactured in Mannheim (Germany), Ligny-en-Barrois (France) and Sámano (Spain), the Citaro was revised in 2005 to coincide with the introduction of Euro IV-, Euro V- and EEV-compliant engines. Minor technical alterations, mainly to accommodate the new generation of engines, were made while the external design received a less angular face-lift. 15m and some 18m articulated versions are also now built at the Setra facility in Neu Ulm. MCL6, BD11LWT, is shown. *Richard Godfrey*

SDE11-17

ADL Dart 4 8.9m   ADL Enviro 200   N26F   2007   NCP, London, 2010

11	PK	SK07HLM	13	PK	SK07HLO	15	PK	SK07HLR	17	PK	SK07HLV
12	PK	SK07HLN	14	PK	SK07HLP	16	PK	SK07HLU			

SLE43-64

Scania N94UD 10.8m   East Lancs OmniDekka   N45/26D   2005

43	FW	YN55NKM	49	FW	YN55NKU	55	FW	YN55NLD	60	FW	YN55NLL
44	FW	YN55NKO	50	FW	YN55NKW	56	u	YN55NLE	61	FW	YN55NLM
45	FW	YN55NKP	51	FW	YN55NKX	57	u	YN55NLG	62	FW	YN55NLO
46	FW	YN55NKR	52	FW	YN55NKZ	58	FW	YN55NLJ	63	FW	YN55NLP
47	FW	YN55NKS	53	FW	YN55NLA	59	FW	YN55NLK	64	FW	YN55NLR
48	FW	YN55NKT	54	FW	YN55NLC						

SP1-15

Scania OmniCity CN94 UD 10.7m Scania   N41/23D   2006-07

1	HH	YN56FCA	5	AV	YN56FCF	9	AV	YN56FBB	13	AV	YN56FBX
2	HH	YN56FCC	6	AV	YN56FCG	10	AV	YN56FBO	14	AV	YN56FBY
3	HH	YN56FCD	7	AV	YN56FCJ	11	AV	YN56FBU	15	AV	YN56FBZ
4	HH	YN56FCE	8	AV	YN56FBA	12	AV	YN56FBV			

SP16-37

Scania OmniCity CN230 UD 10.8m Scania   N41/22D   2008

16	HH	YN08DEU	22	HH	YN08DHG	28	FW	YN08DHP	33	S	YN08DHZ
17	HH	YN08DHA	23	HH	YN08DHJ	29	S	YN08DHU	34	S	YN08MRU
18	HH	YN08DHC	24	FW	YN08DHK	30	S	YN08DHV	35	S	YN08MRV
19	HH	YN08DHD	25	AV	YN08DHL	31	S	YN08DHX	36	S	YN08MRX
20	HH	YN08DHE	26	FW	YN08DHM	32	S	YN08DHY	37	S	YN08MRY
21	HH	YN08DHF	27	FW	YN08DHO						

SP38-67

Scania OmniCity CN230 UD   Scania   N41/22D   2009

38	S	YP58ACF	46	AV	YT09BNA	54	FW	YT09BNN	61	FW	YT09ZCL
39	AV	YP58ACJ	47	AV	YT09BNB	55	FW	YT09BJU	62	FW	YT09ZCN
40	S	YP58ACO	48	AV	YT09BND	56	FW	YT09ZCA	63	FW	YT09ZCO
41	AV	YT09BKA	49	AV	YT09BNE	57	FW	YT09ZCE	64	FW	YT09ZCU
42	AV	YT09BMO	50	AV	YT09BNF	58	FW	YT09ZCF	65	FW	YT09BJV
43	AV	YT09BMU	51	AV	YT09BNJ	59	FW	YT09ZCJ	66	FW	YT09BJX
44	AV	YT09BMY	52	FW	YT09BNK	60	FW	YT09ZCK	67	FW	YT09BJY
45	AV	YT09BMZ	53	FW	YT09BNL						

Following on from the OmniDekka, over two hundred integral OmniCity double-deck buses were placed in London service by Transdev. London's Park Lane is the location for this view of SP140, YP59ODW, as it works route 10 from Stamford Brook depot. *Richard Godfrey*

SP88-108   Scania OmniCity CN230 UD   Scania   N41/22D   2009

88	FW	YT59SFK	94	FW	YT59SFY	99	FW	YT59SGX	104	FW	YT59SFF
89	FW	YT59SFN	95	FW	YT59SFZ	100	FW	YT59SGY	105	FW	YT59DXY
90	FW	YT59SFO	96	FW	YT59SGO	101	FW	YT59SGZ	106	FW	YT59DXZ
91	FW	YT59SFU	97	FW	YT59SGU	102	FW	YT59SHJ	107	FW	YT59DYX
92	FW	YT59SFV	98	FW	YT59SGV	103	FW	YT59SHV	108	FW	YT59DYY
93	FW	YT59SFX									

SP109-125   Scania OmniCity CN230 UD   Scania   N41/22D   2009

109	S	YR59FYO	114	S	YR59FYV	118	S	YR59FYZ	122	S	YR59FZD
110	S	YR59FYP	115	S	YR59FYW	119	S	YR59FZA	123	S	YR59FZE
111	S	YR59FYS	116	S	YR59FYX	120	S	YR59FZB	124	S	YR59FZF
112	S	YR59FYT	117	S	YR59FYY	121	S	YR59FZC	125	S	YR59FZG
113	S	YR59FYU									

SP126-164   Scania OmniCity CN230 UD   Scania   N41/22D   2009-10

126	S	YT59PBF	136	AV	YP59ODS	146	V	YP59OEE	156	V	YP59OER
127	S	YT59PBO	137	V	YP59ODT	147	V	YP59OEF	157	V	YP59OES
128	S	YT59PBV	138	V	YP59ODU	148	V	YP59OEG	158	V	YP59OET
129	S	YT59PBX	139	V	YP59ODV	149	V	YP59OEH	159	V	YP59OEU
130	S	YT59PBY	140	V	YP59ODW	150	V	YP59OEJ	160	V	YP59OEV
131	S	YT59PBZ	141	V	YP59ODX	151	V	YP59OEK	161	V	YP59OEW
132	S	YT59PCF	142	V	YP59OEA	152	V	YP59OEL	162	V	YP59OEX
133	S	YT59PCO	143	V	YP59OEB	153	V	YP59OEM	163	V	YP59OEY
134	S	YT59PCU	144	V	YP59OEC	154	V	YP59OEN	164	V	YP59OEZ
135	S	YT59PBU	145	V	YP59OED	155	V	YP59OEO			

SP165-206   Scania OmniCity CN230 UD   Scania   N41/22D   2010

165	HH	YT10UWA	176	HH	YT10XBZ	187	HH	YT10XCL	197	HH	YR10FGD
166	HH	YT10UWB	177	HH	YT10XCA	188	HH	YT10XCM	198	HH	YR10FGE
167	HH	YT10UWD	178	HH	YT10XCB	189	HH	YT10XCN	199	HH	YR10FGF
168	HH	YT10UWF	179	HH	YT10XCC	190	HH	YT10XCO	200	HH	YR10FGG
169	HH	YT10UWG	180	HH	YT10XCD	191	HH	YR10FFW	201	HH	YR10FGJ
170	HH	YT10UWH	181	HH	YT10XCE	192	HH	YR10FFX	202	HH	YR10FGK
171	HH	YT10XBU	182	HH	YT10XCF	193	HH	YR10FFY	203	HH	YR10FGM
172	HH	YT10XBV	183	HH	YT10XCG	194	HH	YR10FFZ	204	HH	YR10FGN
173	HH	YT10XBW	184	HH	YT10XCH	195	HH	YR10FGA	205	HH	YR10FGO
174	HH	YT10XBX	185	HH	YT10XCJ	196	HH	YR10FGC	206	HH	YR10FGP
175	HH	YT10XBY	186	HH	YT10XCK						

A body style now confined to history is the East Lancs Myllennium Vyking, a model designed for the Volvo B7TL. The East Lancs facility in Blackburn was acquired by Optare and subsequently closed. Illustrating the type while working route 9 at Hyde Park Corner is VLE7, PG04WHK. *Richard Godfrey*

TA204-225
Dennis Trident 9.9m — Alexander ALX400 4.4m — N43/20D — 2000-01

204	FW	SN51SYA	210	FW	SN51SYJ	216	HH	SN51SYV	221	FW	SN51SZC
205	FW	SN51SYC	211	FW	SN51SYO	217	HH	SN51SYW	222	FW	SN51SZD
206	FW	SN51SYE	212	FW	SN51SYR	218	HH	SN51SYX	223	FW	SN51SZE
207	FW	SN51SYF	213	FW	SN51SYS	219	FW	SN51SYY	224	FW	SN51SZT
208	FW	SN51SYG	214	FW	SN51SYT	220	FW	SN51SYZ	225	FW	SN51SZU
209	FW	SN51SYH	215	HH	SN51SYU						

TA229-250
TransBus Trident 9.9m — TransBus ALX400 4.4m — N43/19D — 2002

229	TV	LG02FAA	235	TV	LG02FAU	241	TV	LG02FBF	246	TV	LG02FBO
230	TV	LG02FAF	236	TV	LG02FBA	242	TV	LG02FBJ	247	TV	LG02FBU
231	TV	LG02FAJ	237	TV	LG02FBB	243	TV	LG02FBK	248	TV	LG02FBV
232	TV	LG02FAK	238	TV	LG02FBC	244	TV	LG02FBL	249	TV	LG02FBX
233	TV	LG02FAM	239	TV	LG02FBD	245	TV	LG02FBN	250	TV	LG02FBY
234	TV	LG02FAO	240	TV	LG02FBE						

TA281-286
TransBus Trident 9.9m — TransBus ALX400 4.4m — N43/19D — 2002

281	TV	LG02FDY	283	TV	LG02FEF	285	TV	LG02FEJ	286	TV	LG02FEK
282	TV	LG02FDZ	284	TV	LG02FEH						

TA312-346
TransBus Trident 9.9m — TransBus ALX400 4.4m — N43/19D — 2003

312	TV	SN03DZJ	321	FW	SN03DZX	330	FW	SN03EAW	339	FW	SN03EBL
313	FW	SN03DZK	322	FW	SN03EAA	331	FW	SN03EAX	340	FW	SN03EBM
314	FW	SN03DZM	323	FW	SN03EAC	332	FW	SN03EBA	341	FW	SN03LFL
315	FW	SN03DZP	324	FW	SN03EAE	333	FW	SN03EBC	342	FW	SN03LFM
316	FW	SN03DZR	325	FW	SN03EAF	334	FW	SN03EBD	343	FW	SN03LFP
317	FW	SN03DZS	326	FW	SN03EAG	335	FW	SN03EBF	344	FW	SN03LFR
318	FW	SN03DZT	327	FW	SN03EAJ	336	FW	SN03EBG	345	FW	SN03LFS
319	FW	SN03DZV	328	FW	SN03EAM	337	FW	SN03EBJ	346	FW	SN03LFT
320	TV	SN03DZW	329	FW	SN03EAP	338	FW	SN03EBK			

TLA1-32
TransBus Trident 10.5m — TransBus ALX400 — N45/22D — 2003-04

1	S	SN53EUF	9	S	SN53EUR	17	S	SN53KHR	25	S	SN53KJA
2	S	SN53EUH	10	S	SN53EUT	18	FW	SN53KHT	26	S	SN53KJE
3	FW	SN53EUJ	11	S	SN53EUU	19	FW	SN53KHU	27	S	SN53KJF
4	FW	SN53EUK	12	S	SN53EUV	20	FW	SN53KHV	28	S	SN53KJJ
5	TV	SN53EUL	13	S	SN53EUW	21	FW	SN53KHW	29	S	SN53KJK
6	HH	SN53EUM	14	S	SN53EUX	22	S	SN53KHX	30	S	SN53KJO
7	S	SN53EUO	15	S	SN53EUY	23	FW	SN53KHY	31	S	SN53KJU
8	S	SN53EUP	16	S	SN53EUZ	24	S	SN53KHZ	32	S	SN53KJV

VA6-10
Volvo Olympian   Alexander RH   B45/29F   1996

6	FW	N136YRW	8	FW	N138YRW	9	FW	N139YRW	10	FW	N140YRW
7	FW	N137YRW								

VA45-54
Volvo Olympian   Alexander RH   B47/25D   1998

45	FW	R945YOV	48	FW	R948YOV	49	FW	R949YOV	54	FW	R954YOV
46	FW	R946YOV								

VA62-104
Volvo B7TL 10.1m   Alexander ALX400 4.4m   N43/17D   2000   *Seating varies

62	S	V178OOE	74	AV	V190OOE	85	FW	V208OOE	92	FW	W126EON
63	FW	V179OOE	80	AV	V203OOE	86	FW	W116EON	101	u	W137EON
64	S	V180OOE	82	TV	V205OOE	87	TV	W117EON	102	u	W138EON
71	FW	V187OOE	83	TV	V206OOE	90	u	W122EON	103	u	W139EON
72	u	V188OOE	84	TV	V207OOE	91	u	W124EON	104	u	W141EON

VB1	FW	HF53OBG	Volvo B12M	Plaxton Paragon	C49FT	2993	Yellow Buses, 2011
VB2	FW	HF53OBH	Volvo B12M	Plaxton Paragon	C49FT	2993	Yellow Buses, 2011

VP105-112
Volvo B7TL 10.1m   Plaxton President 4.4m   N41/19D*   2000   *seating varies

105	AV	W448BCW	107	AV	W451BCW	109	TW	W453BCW	111	AV	W457BCW
106	AV	W449BCW	108	AV	W452BCW	110	AV	W454BCW	112	AV	W458BCW

VA293-311
Volvo B7TL 10.1m   TransBus ALX400 4.4m   N45/20D   2002-03

293	AV	SK52MKV	298	S	SK52MPY	303	AV	SK52URZ	308	AV	SK52USG
294	AV	SK52MSO	299	S	SK52URV	304	AV	SK52USB	309	AV	SK52USH
295	AV	SK52MPU	300	S	SK52URW	305	AV	SK52USC	310	S	SK52USJ
296	S	SK52MPV	301	S	SK52URX	306	AV	SK52USD	311	S	SK52USL
297	S	SK52MPX	302	S	SK52URY	307	AV	SK52USF			

VE1-10
Volvo B7TL 10.4m   East Lancs Myllennium Vyking N45/19D   2004

1	S	PG04WGN	4	S	PG04WGV	7	S	PG04WGY	9	S	PG04WHA
2	S	PG04WGP	5	S	PG04WGW	8	S	PG04WGZ	10	S	PG04WHB
3	S	PG04WGU	6	S	PG04WGX					

VLE1-26
Volvo B7TL 11m   East Lancs Myllennium Vyking N47/22D   2004

1	V	PG04WHC	7	V	PG04WHK	13	V	PG04WHS	19	V	PG04WHY
2	V	PG04WHD	8	V	PG04WHL	14	V	PG04WHT	20	V	PG04WJA
3	V	PG04WHE	9	V	PG04WHM	15	V	PG04WHU	21	V	PA04CYC
4	V	PG04WHF	10	V	PG04WHN	16	V	PG04WHV	22	V	PA04CYE
5	V	PG04WHH	11	V	PG04WHP	17	V	PG04WHW	23	V	PA04CYF
6	V	PG04WHJ	12	V	PG04WHR	18	V	PG04WHX	26	V	PA04CYJ

Depots and allocations:

Fulwell (Wellington Road) - FW

Dart	DP1	DP11	DPS584	DPS585	DPS655	DPS659	DPS661	DPS663
	DPS665	DPS667	DPS670	DPS681	DPS682	DPS684	DPS685	DPS686
	DPS687	DPS689	DPS690					
Enviro 200	DE23	DE24	DE25	DE26	DE27	DE28	DE29	DE30
	DE31	DE109	DE110	DE111	DE112	DE113	DE114	DE115
	DE116	DE117	DE118	DE119	DE120	DE121	DE122	DE123
	DE124	DE125	DE126	DE127	DE128			
Enviro 200 Hybrid	HDE1	HDE2	HDE3	HDE4	HDE5			
Volvo B12M	BB1	BB2						
Olympian	VA7	VA8	VA9	VA10	VA46	VA48	VA49	VA54
	VA63	VA71	VA81	VA85	VA689	VA92		
Trident	TA204	TA205	TA206	TA207	TA208	TA209	TA210	TA211
	TA212	TA213	TA214	TA219	TA220	TA221	TA222	TA223
	TA224	TA225	TA313	TA314	TA315	TA316	TA317	TA318
	TA319	TA320	TA321	TA322	TA323	TA324	TA325	TA326
	TA327	TA328	TA329	TA330	TA331	TA332	TA333	TA334
	TA335	TA336	TA337	TA338	TA339	TA340	TA341	TA342
	TA343	TA344	TA345	TA346	TLA3	TLA4		
Scania DD	SLE43	SLE44	SLE45	SLE46	SLE47	SLE48	SLE49	SLE50
	SLE51	SLE53	SLE54	SLE55	SLE58	SLE59	SLE60	SLE61
	SLE62	SLE63	SLE64	SP24	SP26	SP27	SP28	SP52
	SP53	SP54	SP55	SP56	SP57	SP58	SP59	SP60
	SP61	SP62	SP63	SP64	SP65	SP66	SP67	SP88
	SP89	SP90	SP91	SP92	SP93	SP94	SP95	SP96

SP97	SP98	SP99	SP100	SP101	SP102	SP103	SP104
SP105	SP106	SP107	SP108				

Hounslow (Kingsley Road) - AV

Enviro 200	DLE1	DLE2	DLE3	DLE4	DLE5	DLE6	DLE7	DLE8
	DLE9	DLE10	DLE11	DLE12	DLE13	DLE14	DLE15	DLE16
	DLE17	DLE18	DLE19	DLE20	DLE21	DLE22	DLE23	DLE24
	DLE25							
Optare Tempo	OT1	OT2	OT3	OT4	OT5	OT6	OT7	OT8
	OT9	OT10	OT11	OT12	OT13	OT14	OT15	OT16
Volvo B7TL	VA74	VA80	VM1	VP105	VP106	VP107	VP108	VP110
	VP111							
Mercedes-Benz Citaro	MCL1	MCL2	MCL3	MCL4	MCL5	MCL6	MCL7	
Scania	SP5	SP6	SP7	SP8	SP9	SP10	SP11	SP12
	SP13	SP14	SP15	SP25	SP39	SP41	SP42	SP43
	SP44	SP45	SP46	SP47	SP48	SP49	SP50	SP51
	SP136							
Enviro 400	ADE1	ADE2	ADE3	ADE4	ADE5	ADE6	ADE7	ADE8
	ADE9	ADE10	ADE11	ADE12	ADE13	ADE14	ADE15	ADE16
	ADE17	ADE18	ADE19	ADE20	ADE21	ADE22	ADE23	ADE24
	ADE25	ADE26	ADE27	ADE28	ADE29	ADE30	ADE31	ADE32
	ADE33	ADE34	ADE35	ADE36	ADE37	ADE38	ADE39	ADE40
	ADE41	ADE42	ADE43	ADE44	ADE45			

Hounslow Heath (Pulborough Way) - HH

Dart	DPS582	DPS673	DPS674	DPS675	DPS677	DPS678	DPS679	DPS680
	DPS707	DPS708	DPS709	DPS710	DPS711	DPS712	DPS713	DPS714
	DPS715	DPS716	DPS717					
Enviro 200	DE1	DE2	DE3	DE4	DE5	DE6	DE7	DE8
	DE9	DE10	DE11	DE12	DE13	DE14	DE15	DE16
Trident	TA215	TA216	TA217	TA218	TLA6			
Scania OmniCity DD	SP1	SP2	SP3	SP4	SP16	SP17	SP18	SP19
	SP20	SP21	SP22	SP23	SP165	SP166	SP167	SP168
	SP169	SP170	SP171	SP172	SP173	SP174	SP175	SP176
	SP177	SP178	SP179	SP180	SP181	SP182	SP183	SP184
	SP185	SP186	SP187	SP188	SP189	SP190	SP191	SP192
	SP193	SP194	SP195	SP196	SP197	SP198	SP199	SP200
	SP201	SP202	SP203	SP204	SP205	SP206		

Park Royal (Atlas Road) - PK

Enviro 200	DE76	DE77	DE78	DE79	DE80	DE81	DE82	DE83
	DE84	SDE11	SDE12	SDE13	SDE14	SDE15	SDE16	SDE17
Optare Versa	OV50	OV51	OV52	OV53	OV54	OV55	OV56	OV57
	OV58	OV59	OV60	OV61	OV62	OV63	OV64	OV65
	OV66							
Enviro 400	ADE46	ADE47	ADE48	ADE49	ADE50	ADE51	ADE52	ADE53
	ADE54	ADE55	ADE56	ADE57	ADE58	ADE59	ADE60	ADE61
	ADE62	ADE63	ADE64	ADE65	ADE66	ADE67	ADE68	ADE69
	ADE70	ADE71	ADE72	ADE73				

Shepherd's Bush (Wells Road) - S

Dart	DPS688							
Enviro 200	DE32	DE33	DE34	DE35	DE36	DE37	DE38	DE39
	DE40	DE41	DE42	DE43	DE44	DE45	DE46	DE47
	DE48	DE49	DE75	DE85	DE86	DE87	DE88	DE89
	DE90	DE91	DE92	DE93	DE94	DE95	DE96	DE97
	DE98	DE99	DE100	DE101	DE102	DE103	DE104	DE105
	DE106	DE107	DE108					
Trident	TLA1	TLA2	TLA3	TLA4	TLA5	TLA6	TLA7	TLA8
	TLA17	TLA18	TLA19	TLA20	TLA21	TLA22	TLA23	TLA24
	TLA25	TLA26	TLA27	TLA29	TLA30			
Volvo B7TL	VE1	VE2	VE3	VE4	VE5	VE6	VE7	VE8
	VE10	VA62	VA64					
Scania	SP29	SP30	SP31	SP32	SP33	SP34	SP35	SP36
	SP37	SP38	SP40	SP109	SP110	SP111	SP112	SP113
	SP114	SP115	SP116	SP117	SP118	SP119	SP120	SP121

	SP122	SP123	SP124	SP125	SP126	SP127	SP128	SP129
	SP130	SP131	SP132	SP133	SP134	SP135		
Enviro 400	ADH3	ADH4	ADH5	ADH6	ADH7	ADH8	ADH9	ADH10
	ADH11	ADH12	ADH13	ADH14	ADH15	ADH16	ADH17	ADH18
	ADH19	ADH20	ADH21	ADH22				

Stamford Brook (Chiswick High Road, Chiswick) - V

Dart	DPS581	DPS583	DPS586	DPS587	DPS664	DPS694	DPS701	DPS702
Versa	OV1	OV2	OV3	OV4	OV5	OV6	OV7	OV8
	OV9	OV10	OV11	OV12	OV13	OV14	OV15	OV16
	OV17	OV18	OV19					
Volvo B7TL	VE9	VLE1	VLE2	VLE3	VLE4	VLE5	VLE6	VLE7
	VLE8	VLE9	VLE10	VLE11	VLE12	VLE13	VLE14	VLE15
	VLE16	VLE17	VLE18	VLE19	VLE20	VLE21	VLE22	VLE23
	VLE26							
Scania	SP137	SP138	SP139	SP140	SP141	SP142	SP143	SP144
	SP145	SP146	SP147	SP148	SP149	SP150	SP151	SP152
	SP153	SP154	SP155	SP156	SP157	SP158	SP159	SP160
	SP161	SP162	SP163	SP164				
Enviro 400 Hybrid	ADH1	ADH2	ADH23	ADH24	ADH25	ADH26	ADH27	ADH28
	ADH29	ADH30	ADH31	ADH32	ADH33	ADH34	ADH35	ADH36
	ADH37	ADH38	ADH39	ADH40	ADH41	ADH42	ADH43	ADH44
	ADH45	ADH46	ADH47	ADH48	ADH49	ADH50	ADH51	

Tolworth (Day's Yard, Kingston Road) - TV

Dart	DPS579	DPS580	DPS588	DPS589	DPS590	DPS591	DPS592	DPK613
	DPK614	DPK615	DPK624	DPK625	DPS648	DPS649	DPS650	DPS651
	DPS652	DPS653	DPS654	DPS656	DPS657	DPS658	DPS660	DPS662
	DPS666	DPS691	DPS692	DPS693	DPS721	DPS722		
Enviro 200	DE57	DE58	DE59	DE60	DE61	DE62	DE63	DE64
	DE65	DE66	DE67	DE68	DE69	DE70	DE71	DE72
	DE73	DE74	SDE1	SDE2	SDE3	SDE4	SDE5	SDE6
	SDE7	SDE8	SDE9	SDE10				
Volvo B7TL	VP109							
Trident	TA229	TA230	TA231	TA232	TA233	TA234	TA235	TA236
	TA237	TA238	TA239	TA240	TA241	TA242	TA243	TA244
	TA245	TA246	TA247	TA248	TA249	TA250	TA281	TA282
	TA283	TA284	TA285	TA286	TA312	TLA5		

Twickenham (Rugby Road) - TV

Dart	DP1	DP11						
Volvo B12M	VB1	VB2						
Olympian	VA7	VA8	VA9	VA10	VA26	VA48	VA49	VA50
	VA53							

Epsom Coaches was founded by the Richmond family in 1920 and in April 2012 the company joined the French group RATP. Although historically known for its coach business, Epsom has expanded into bus operation under the Quality Line name. Delivered in 2004, OP18, YN53SVP, operates route S4 through Wrythe Lane, St Helier. *Mark Lyons*

QUALITY LINE

HR Richmond Ltd, Blenheim Road, Epsom, KT19 9AF

DD1-10

			ADL Trident 2			ADL Enviro 400			N41/26D	2007		
1	EB	SK07DZA	4	EB	SK07DZD	7	EB	SK07DZG	9	EB	SK07DZJ
2	EB	SK07DZB	5	EB	SK07DZE	8	EB	SK07DZH	10	EB	SK07DZL
3	EB	SK07DZC	6	EB	SK07DZF						

DD11	EB	SN11BVG	ADL Trident 2	ADL Enviro 400	N41/26D	2011
DD12	EB	SN11BVH	ADL Trident 2	ADL Enviro 400	N41/26D	2011
DD13	EB	YX61FYR	ADL E40D	ADL Enviro 400	N41/26D	2012

EP1	EC	FJ11GLF	Volvo B9R	Caetano Levanté	C48FT	2011
EP2	EC	FJ11GMV	Volvo B9R	Caetano Levanté	C48FT	2011
EP3	EC	FJ61EYK	Volvo B9R	Caetano Levanté	C48FT	2012
EP4	EC	FJ61EYL	Volvo B9R	Caetano Levanté	C48FT	2012
ET1	EBt	HV52WSZ	TransBus Dart 10.1m	Caetano Nimbus	N31D	2002
MCL1	EB	BW03ZMZ	Mercedes-Benz Citaro O530		N38D	2003

MCL8-17

			Mercedes-Benz Citaro O530						N38D	2003		
8	EB	BN12EOP	11	EB	BN12EOT	14	EB	BN12EOW	16	EB	BN12EOY
9	EB	BN12EOR	12	EB	BN12EOU	15	EB	BN12EOX	17	EB	BN12EOZ
10	EB	BN12EOS	13	EB	BN12EOV						

OP04-13

			Optare Solo M850			Optare			N25F	2002-03		
04	EB	YE52FHL	07	EB	YE52FHO	10	EB	YE52FHS	12	EB	YN03ZXF
05	EB	YE52FHM	08	EB	YE52FHP	11	EB	YE52FGU	13	EB	YN53SWF
06	EB	YE52FHN	09	EB	YE52FHR						

OP14-21

			Optare Solo M850			Optare			N25F	2004		
14	EB	YN53SUF	16	EB	YN53SVL	18	EB	YN53SVP	20	EB	YN53ZXA
15	EB	YN53SVK	17	EB	YN53SVO	19	EB	YN53SVR	21	EB	YN53ZXB

Outside the TfL area Quality Line uses its traditional maroon and cream scheme as illustrated by Optare Solo OP14, YN53SUF, seen in Epsom itself. *Mark Lyons*

OP23-30 — Optare Solo M850 — Optare — N24F — 2009

No		Reg	No		Reg	No		Reg	No		Reg
23	EB	YJ09MHK	25	EB	YJ09MHM	27	EB	YJ09MHO	29	EB	YJ09MHV
24	EB	YJ09MHL	26	EB	YJ09MHN	28	EB	YJ09MHU	30	EB	YJ09MHX

No		Reg	Model	Body	Seating	Year
OP31	EB	YJ11EJA	Optare Solo M850	Optare	N23F	2011
OP32	EB	YJ11EJC	Optare Solo M850	Optare	N23F	2011
OP33	EB	YJ11EJD	Optare Solo M850	Optare	N23F	2011
OP34	EB	YJ13HJN	Optare Solo M890 SR	Optare	N23F	2013

OPL01-08 — Optare Solo M970 SR — Optare — N25D — 2012

No		Reg	No		Reg	No		Reg	No		Reg
01	EB	YJ62FUD	03	EB	YJ62FVN	05	EB	YJ62FWB	07	EB	YJ62FXG
02	EB	YJ62FUG	04	EB	YJ62FVT	06	EB	YJ62FXA	08	EB	YJ62FXK

OV01-13 — Optare Versa V1110 — Optare — N29D — 2010-12

No		Reg	No		Reg	No		Reg	No		Reg
01	EB	YJ60KGA	05	EB	YJ60KGK	08	EB	YJ60KGP	11	EB	YJ12PKY
02	EB	YJ60KGE	06	EB	YJ60KGN	09	EB	YJ12PKV	12	EB	YJ12PKZ
03	EB	YJ60KGF	07	EB	YJ60KGO	10	EB	YJ12PKX	13	EB	YJ12PLF
04	EB	YJ60KGG									

SD38-42 — ADL Dart SLF 9m — East Lancs Myllennium — N26F — 2005

No		Reg	No		Reg	No		Reg	No		Reg
38	EB	PL05PLN	40	EB	PL05PLU	41	EB	PL05PLV	42	EB	PL05PLX
39	EB	PL05PLO									

SD43-51 — ADL Dart 4 9.5m — East Lancs Esteem — N25D — 2007

No		Reg	No		Reg	No		Reg	No		Reg
43	EB	PE56UFH	46	EB	PE56UFL	48	EB	PE56UFN	50	EB	PE56UFR
44	EB	PE56UFJ	47	EB	PE56UFM	49	EB	PE56UFP	51	EB	PE56UFS
45	EB	PE56UFK									

No		Reg	Model	Body	Seating	Year
SD52	EB	PN07KRZ	ADL Dart 4 9m	East Lancs Esteem	N23F	2007
SD53	EB	PN07KSE	ADL Dart 4 9m	East Lancs Esteem	N23F	2007
SD54	EB	LJ08RJY	ADL Dart 4 8.9m	ADL Enviro 200	N26F	2008

503	EC	YN08DMV	Mercedes-Benz Vario O816	Plaxton Cheetah	C25F	2008
504	EC	YN08DMX	Mercedes-Benz Vario O816	Plaxton Cheetah	C25F	2008
716	EC	BU04EXV	Setra S315 GT-HD	Setra	C53F	2004
717	EC	BU04EXW	Setra S315 GT-HD	Setra	C53F	2004
718	EC	BU04EXX	Setra S315 GT-HD	Setra	C53F	2004
719	EC	BX54ECF	Setra S315 GT-HD	Setra	C53F	2005
720	EC	BX54ECJ	Setra S315 GT-HD	Setra	C53F	2005
813	EC	BU53ZWN	Setra S315 GT-HD	Setra	C48FT	2004
814	EC	BU53ZWP	Setra S315 GT-HD	Setra	C48FT	2004
815	EC	BU53ZWR	Setra S315 GT-HD	Setra	C48FT	2004
816	EC	BU04EXT	Setra S315 GT-HD	Setra	C48FT	2004
901	EC	BU06CSF	Setra S416 GT-HD	Setra	C49FT	2006
902	EC	BU06CSO	Setra S416 GT-HD	Setra	C49FT	2006
903	EC	BX56VTY	Setra S416 GT-HD	Setra	C44FT	2007
904	EC	BX56VTZ	Setra S416 GT-HD	Setra	C44FT	2007
905	EC	BX58URT	Setra S416 GT-HD	Setra	C44FT	2009
906	EC	BX60OPD	Setra S416 GT-HD	Setra	C44FT	2011
907	EC	BX60OPE	Setra S416 GT-HD	Setra	C44FT	2011

Previous registration:

W813AAY   W813AAY, A9HRR

Web: www.epsomcoaches.com

Depot with allocations:

Epsom (Blenheim Road) - EB

Solo	OP04	OP05	OP06	OP07	OP08	OP09	OP10	OP11
	OP12	OP13	OP14	OP15	OP16	OP17	OP18	OP19
	OP20	OP21	OP23	OP24	OP25	OP26	OP27	OP28
	OP29	OP30	OP31	OP32	OP33	OP34	OPL1	OPL2
	OPL3	OPL4	OPL5	OPL6	OPL7	OPL8		
Dart	SD38	SD39	SD40	SD41	SD42			
Enviro 200	SD43	SD44	SD45	SD46	SD47	SD48	SD49	SD50
	SD51	SD52	SD53	SD54				
Versa	OV1	OV2	OV3	OV4	OV5	OV6	OV7	OV8
	OV9	OV10	OV11	OV12	OV13			
Citaro	MCL1	MCL8	MCL9	MCL10	MCL11	MCL12	MCL13	MCL14
	MCL15	MCL16	MCL17					
Trident 2	DD01	DD02	DD03	DD04	DD05	DD06	DD07	DD08
	DD09	DD10	DD11	DD12	DD13			

Epsom coach unit (Blenheim Road) - EC

Mercedes-Benz	503	504						
Setra S315	716	717	718	719	720	813	814	815
	816							
Setra S416	901	902	903	904	905	906	907	
Volvo B9R	EP01	EP02	EP03	EP04				

Selwyns Travel Ltd, Cavendish Farm Road, Runcorn, WA7 4LU

No.		Reg	Chassis	Body	Layout	Year	Notes
37	RU	FJ06GGA	MAN 14.280	Caetano Enigma	C39F	2006	
38	BR	FJ06GGO	MAN 14.280	Caetano Enigma	C39F	2006	
48	RU	SEL23	DAF SB4000	Van Hool T9 Alizée	C51FT	2004	
49	RU	SEL133	DAF SB4000	Van Hool T9 Alizée	C51FT	2004	
69	BR	SEL702	DAF SB3000	Van Hool Alizée HE	C57F	1998	Armchair, Brentford, 2002
90	BR	SEL36	DAF SB3000	Van Hool T9 Alizée	C55F	2002	
100	BR	SEL73	DAF SB3000	Van Hool Alizée HE	C57F	1999	Armchair, Brentford, 2002
103	BR	TJI6925	DAF SB4000	Van Hool T9 Alizée	C49FT	2003	
104	BR	SEL392	DAF SB4000	Van Hool T9 Alizée	C53F	2003	
105	RU	SEL853	DAF SB4000	Van Hool T9 Alizée	C49FT	2004	
106	BR	352STG	DAF SB4000	Van Hool T9 Alizée	C53F	2004	
107	BR	YJ04BYH	VDL Bus SB4000	Van Hool T9 Alizée	C49FT	2004	
109	RU	YJ54CFD	VDL Bus SB4000	Van Hool T9 Alizée	C49FT	2004	
111	RU	YJ05PWE	VDL Bus SB4000	Van Hool T9 Alizée	C49FT	2005	
112	BR	YJ05PWF	VDL Bus SB4000	Van Hool T9 Alizée	C49FT	2005	
113	RU	FN06EBO	Volvo B12B	Caetano Levanté	C49FT	2006	
114	BR	FJ06PAO	Volvo B12B	Caetano Levanté	C49FT	2006	
115	RU	FJ06PBF	Volvo B12B	Caetano Levanté	C49FT	2006	
116	BR	FJ06PBO	Volvo B12B	Caetano Levanté	C49FT	2006	
119	BR	YN56OSG	Mercedes-Benz Vario O814	Plaxton Cheetah	C29F	2006	
120	BR	YN56OSJ	Mercedes-Benz Vario O814	Plaxton Cheetah	C29F	2006	
122	RU	YJ04BOV	VDL Bus SB4000	Van Hool T9 Alizée	C49FT	2004	Ashton, St Helens, 2007
123	RU	YJ04HHZ	VDL Bus SB4000	Van Hool T9 Alizée	C49FT	2004	Arriva Bus & Coach, 2007
124	RU	YJ04HHY	VDL Bus SB4000	Van Hool T9 Alizée	C49FT	2004	Arriva Bus & Coach, 2007
126	RU	YJ04BJF	VDL Bus SB4000	Van Hool T9 Alizée	C49FT	2004	Fishwick, Leyland, 2008
127	RU	YJ05PXF	VDL Bus SB4000	Van Hool T9 Alizée	C49FT	2005	Gain Travel, Wibsey, 2008
128	RU	YJ06LFV	VDL Bus SB4000	Van Hool T9 Alizée	C51FT	2006	Ciy Circle, Edinburgh, 2008
129	RU	YJ08DGY	VDL Bus SB4000	VDL Berkhof Axial 50	C57FT	2008	
130	RU	YJ08DHF	VDL Bus SB4000	VDL Berkhof Axial 50	C57FT	2008	
131	RU	FJ58AJU	Scania K340 EB4	Caetano Levanté	C49FT	2009	
132	RU	FJ58AJV	Scania K340 EB4	Caetano Levanté	C49FT	2009	
137	BR	YN09KHO	Mercedes-Benz Vario O816	Plaxton Cheetah	C29F	2009	
138	BR	YN09KHP	Mercedes-Benz Vario O816	Plaxton Cheetah	C29F	2009	
139	RU	FJ59APX	Scania K340 EB4	Caetano Levanté	C49FT	2009	
140	RU	FJ59APY	Scania K340 EB4	Caetano Levanté	C49FT	2009	
141	RU	YN10FKM	Volvo B9R	Plaxton Elite	C48FT	2010	
142	RU	YN10FKO	Volvo B9R	Plaxton Elite	C48FT	2010	
143	RU	YN10FKP	Volvo B9R	Plaxton Elite	C48FT	2010	
144	RU	YN10FKR	Volvo B9R	Plaxton Elite	C48FT	2010	
145	RU	YN10FKS	Volvo B9R	Plaxton Elite	C48FT	2010	
146	RU	YN10FKT	Volvo B9R	Plaxton Elite	C48FT	2010	
147	RU	YN10FKV	Volvo B9R	Plaxton Elite	C48FT	2010	
149	RU	MX60EGK	Mercedes-Benz Sprinter 413 cdi	KVC	C16F	2010	
150	BR	DK60AMX	Mercedes-Benz Sprinter 413 cdi	KVC	C16F	2010	
151	RU	MX60EKH	Mercedes-Benz Sprinter 413 cdi	KVC	C16F	2010	
152	RU	YN60FMO	Mercedes-Benz Vario O816	Plaxton Cheetah	C29F	2011	
153	RU	YN11AYA	Volvo B9R	Plaxton Elite	C48FT	2011	
154	RU	YN11AYB	Volvo B9R	Plaxton Elite	C48FT	2011	
155	RU	YN11AYC	Volvo B9R	Plaxton Elite	C48FT	2011	
156	RU	YN11AYD	Volvo B9R	Plaxton Elite	C48FT	2011	
159	RU	YN11FTU	Mercedes-Benz Vario O816	Plaxton Cheetah	C29F	2011	
160	BR	YN11FTV	Mercedes-Benz Vario O816	Plaxton Cheetah	C29F	2011	
161	BR	FJ11MLV	Volvo B9R	Caetano Levanté	C48FT	2011	
162	BR	YN06TFY	Scania K114 EB4	VDL Berkhof Axial 50	C57FT	2006	Haytons, Manchester, 2011
163	BR	MHZ9321	Volvo B12M	Jonckheere Mistral 50	C39FT	2002	Haytons, Manchester, 2011
165	RU	FJ61EWF	Volvo B9R	Caetano Levanté	C48FT	2011	
166	RU	FJ61EWG	Volvo B9R	Caetano Levanté	C48FT	2011	
167	RU	FJ61EWH	Volvo B9R	Caetano Levanté	C48FT	2011	
168	RU	FJ61EWK	Volvo B9R	Caetano Levanté	C48FT	2011	
169	RU	FJ61EWL	Volvo B9R	Caetano Levanté	C48FT	2011	
170	RU	FJ61EWM	Volvo B9R	Caetano Levanté	C48FT	2011	
171	BR	FJ61EWB	Volvo B9R	Caetano Levanté	C48FT	2011	
172	BR	FJ61EWZ	Volvo B9R	Caetano Levanté	C48FT	2011	
173	BR	FJ61EXK	Volvo B9R	Caetano Levanté	C48FT	2011	

In March 2013 RATP Dev UK acquired Selwyns, which has more than 200 staff across depots in Manchester, Runcorn and St Helens and also operates under the Haytons name. Selwyns Travel was established in 1968 and continues to operate as an independent division of RATP Dev UK and will be led by founder and managing director Selwyn Jones. Number 163, MHZ9321, a Jonckheere Mistral-bodied Volvo B12M is shown. *John Young*

174	BR	FJ61EXL	Volvo B9R	Caetano Levanté	C48FT	2011	
175	BR	W201EAG	Volvo B10M-62	Plaxton Panther	C53F	2000	Haytons, Manchester, 2011
177	BR	SH51MHU	Optare Solo M920	Optare	N30F	2002	Haytons, Manchester, 2011
179	BR	FY02OTF	Mercedes-Benz Atego 1223L	Ferqui Solara	C39F	2002	Haytons, Manchester, 2011
182	BR	YN55WSO	Volvo B12B	Plaxton Panther	C49FT	2005	Haytons, Manchester, 2011
183	BR	PO56PCF	MAN 18.310	Maropolo Viaggio 350	S70F	2007	Haytons, Manchester, 2011
184	BR	BD08DZX	Mercedes-Benz Tourismo	Mercedes-Benz	C36FT	2008	Haytons, Manchester, 2011
186	BR	FJ60EFU	Volvo B9R	Caetano Levanté	C48FT	2010	Haytons, Manchester, 2011
187	BR	FJ60EFV	Volvo B9R	Caetano Levanté	C48FT	2010	Haytons, Manchester, 2011
188	RU	FJ60EFW	Volvo B9R	Caetano Levanté	C48FT	2010	Haytons, Manchester, 2011
190	SH	DE52NWY	Tecnobus	Tecnobus Pantheon	N11C	2002	
191	SH	DE52NXU	Tecnobus	Tecnobus Pantheon	N11C	2002	
192	SH	DE52NXV	Tecnobus	Tecnobus Pantheon	N11C	2002	
193	SH	DE52NXW	Tecnobus	Tecnobus Pantheon	N11C	2002	
194	SH	DE52NYX	Tecnobus	Tecnobus Pantheon	N11C	2002	
195	SH	DE52NYY	Tecnobus	Tecnobus Pantheon	N11C	2002	
199	BR	T133AUA	DAF DB250	Plaxton President	N45/22F	1999	Network Colchester, 2012
200	BR	YJ57BBE	VDL DB250	East Lancs Lowlander	N51/29F	2007	Bryline, Boston, 2012
201	BR	YJ57BNB	VDL DB250	East Lancs Lowlander	N51/29F	2007	Bryline, Boston, 2012
202	BR	PJ02PZN	Dennis Trident 9.9m	Plaxton President	N41/27F	2002	RHT, Whitney, 2012
204	RU	FN62CCV	Volvo B9R	Caetano Levanté	C48FT	2013	
205	RU	FN62CCZ	Volvo B9R	Caetano Levanté	C48FT	2013	
206	RU	FN62CDE	Volvo B9R	Caetano Levanté	C48FT	2013	
208	RU	FJ13DZZ	Volvo B9R	Caetano Levanté	C48FT	2013	
209	RU	FJ13EBC	Volvo B9R	Caetano Levanté	C48FT	2013	
210	RU	FJ13EBD	Volvo B9R	Caetano Levanté	C48FT	2013	
211	RU	FJ13EBF	Volvo B9R	Caetano Levanté	C48FT	2013	

Previous registrations:

352STG	YJ53VDO	SEL133	YJ04HHC-
MHZ9321	GT02WAG	SEL392	YJ03PPZ
MHZ9322	GT02WAM	SEL702	R39GNW, 98D70419
SEL23	YJ04HHB	SEL853	YJ53VDN
SEL36	YJ51EKX	TJI6925	YJ03PPY
SEL73	T185AUA		

Depots: Melbourne Avenue, Manchester Airport; Cavendish Farm Road, Runcorn and Sherdley Road Industrial Estate, St. Helens. **Web:** www.selwyns.co.uk

Bournemouth Transport Ltd, Yeomans Way, Bournemouth, BH8 0BQ

SA7-17 — Optare Tempo X1200 — Optare — N41F — 2009

7	R7TYB	10	R10TYB	13	R13TYB	16	T16TYB
8	R8TYB	11	R11TYB	14	R14TYB	17	T17TYB
9	R9TYB	12	R12TYB	15	R15TYB		

SB18-28 — Optare Versa V1100 — Optare — N38F — 2008

18	T18TYB	21	T21TYB	24	T24TYB	27	T27TYB
19	T19TYB	22	T22TYB	25	T25TYB	28	T28TYB
20	T20TYB	23	T23TYB	26	T26TYB		

SB31	YX61EMV	ADL E20D 10.8m	ADL Enviro 200	N38F	2012

SA101-107 — Optare Tempo X1200 — Optare — N41F — 2010

101	YJ10MDE	103	YJ10MDK	105	YJ10MDO	107	YJ10MDV
102	YJ10MDF	104	YJ10MDN	106	YJ10MDU		

DA110-115 — Volvo B7TL — East Lancs Vyking — N43/31F — 2004-05

110	HF04JWJ	112	HF04JWL	114	HF05HNB	115	HF05HNC
111	HF04JWK	113	HF05HNA				

DA120-124 — Volvo B9TL — Wrightbus Eclipse Gemini — N45/29F — 2011

120	HF11HCO	122	HF11HCU	123	HF11HCV	124	HF11HCX
121	HF11HCP						

DH180	HF03ODU	Volvo B7TL	Wrightbus Eclipse	N47/31F	2003	
DH181	HF03ODV	Volvo B7TL	Wrightbus Eclipse	N47/31F	2003	
DH182	HF03ODW	Volvo B7TL	Wrightbus Eclipse	N47/31F	2003	
DH183	HF04JWD	Volvo B7TL	Wrightbus Eclipse	N45/31F	2004	
DH184	HF04JWE	Volvo B7TL	Wrightbus Eclipse	N45/31F	2004	
DH185	HF04JWG	Volvo B7TL	Wrightbus Eclipse	N45/31F	2004	
DB186	SK07DYB	ADL Trident 2	ADL Enviro 400	N45/33F	2007	ADL demonstrator, 2007

DH208-214 — Volvo Citybus B10M-50 — Alexander RH — B47/33F — 1988-89

208	E208GCG	212	F212WRU	213	F213WRU	214	F214WRU
211	F211WRU						

DC270-278 — Dennis Trident 10.5m — East Lancs Lolyne — N51/33F — 1999

270	T270BPR	273	T273BPR	275	T275BPR	277	T277BPR
271	T271BPR	274	T274BPR	276	T276BPR	278	T278BPR
272	T272BPR						

DD281	X201UMS	Dennis Trident 9.8m	Alexander ALX400	N43/25F	2000	RATP London, 2011
DD282	X202UMS	Dennis Trident 9.8m	Alexander ALX400	N43/25F	2000	RATP London, 2011
DD283	X203UMS	Dennis Trident 9.8m	Alexander ALX400	N43/25F	2000	RATP London, 2011
DD284	V189OOE	Volvo B7TL	Alexander ALX400	N43/25F	2000	RATP London, 2011
DD285	V428DRA	Dennis Trident 12m	East lancs Lolyne	N49/34F	2000	RATP London, 2012

321	FJ07DVY	Volvo B12B	Caetano Levanté	C49FT	2007	
322	FJ07DVZ	Volvo B12B	Caetano Levanté	C49FT	2007	
323	FJ07DWA	Volvo B12B	Caetano Levanté	C49FT	2007	
324	FJ07DWC	Volvo B12B	Caetano Levanté	C49FT	2007	
328	FJ59AOV	Scania K340 EB4	Caetano Levanté	C49FT	2009	
329	FJ59ARO	Scania K340 EB4	Caetano Levanté	C49FT	2009	

330-341 — Volvo B9R — Caetano Levanté — C48FT — 2011-13

330	FJ60HYN	333	FJ61EWD	336	FJ61GZM	339	FJ12FXT
331	FJ60HYO	334	FJ61EWE	337	FJ61GZN	340	FJ13DZX
332	FJ61EWC	335	FJ61GZL	338	FJ12FXE	341	FJ13DZY

DB411-418 — Volvo B7TL — East Lancs Vyking — N45/31F — 2001

411	Y411CFX	413	Y413CFX	415	Y415CFX	417	Y417CFX
412	Y412CFX	414	Y414CFX	416	Y416CFX	418	Y418CFX

DB420-428 — Volvo B7TL — East Lancs Vyking — N45/31F — 2002-03

420	HJ02HFD	422	HJ02HFF	424	HJ02HFH	427	HF03ODS
421	HJ02HFE	423	HJ02HFG	426	HF03ODR	428	HF03ODT

The company was formerly owned by the local council and became known as Yellow Buses Bournemouth. The name was changed to Transdev Yellow Buses when Transdev bought the company in December 2005. Yellow Buses became part of RATP in May 2010 along with London United following an agreement to transfer part of the French Government's holding. Latterly operating in Shropshire with Minsterley Motors, Plaxton-bodied Volvo B7RLE 802, DX57REU, is seen in its coastal setting. *Richard Godfrey*

DB430	HJ02HFA	Volvo B7TL		East Lancs Vyking		CO45/31F	2002	
DB431	HJ02HFB	Volvo B7TL		East Lancs Vyking		CO45/31F	2002	
DB432	HJ02HFC	Volvo B7TL		East Lancs Vyking		CO45/31F	2002	

SE475-482

				Dennis Dart SLF		East Lancs Spryte	N37F	1998
475	R475NPR	477	R477NPR	479	R479NPR	481	R481NPR	
476	R476NPR	478	R478NPR	480	R480NPR	482	R482NPR	

SE484	P990AFV	Dennis Dart SLF 10.2m	East Lancs Spryte	N32F	1997	Go-Ahead Meteor, 2006
SE485	P991AFV	Dennis Dart SLF 10.2m	East Lancs Spryte	N32F	1997	Go-Ahead Meteor, 2006
SE487	P135LNF	Dennis Dart SLF 10.2m	East Lancs Spryte	N32F	1997	Go-Ahead Meteor, 2006
SE488	R524YRP	Dennis Dart SLF 10.2m	East Lancs Spryte	N32F	1997	Choice, Wednesfield, 2006
SE489	S399HVV	Dennis Dart SLF 10.2m	East Lancs Spryte	N32F	1997	People's Express, 2006
SE490	S401HVV	Dennis Dart SLF 10.2m	East Lancs Spryte	N32F	1997	People's Express, 2006
SE491	T464HNH	Dennis Dart SLF 10.7m	Plaxton Pointer 2	N36F	1999	NCP, Heathrow, 2006
SE492	W681TNV	Dennis Dart SLF 10.7m	Plaxton Pointer 2	N39F	1999	Cross Gates Coaches, 2006
SE493	W689TNV	Dennis Dart SLF 10.7m	Plaxton Pointer 2	N39F	1999	Flights-Hallmark, 2006
SE494	Y431PBD	Dennis Dart SLF 10.2m	East Lancs Flyte	N27F	2001	Manchester Airport, 2006
SE495	Y432PBD	Dennis Dart SLF 10.2m	East Lancs Flyte	N27F	2001	Manchester Airport, 2006

SD500-503

				VDL Bus SB120		Wrightbus Cadet 2	N39F	2005
500	HF05LYT	501	HF05LYU	502	HF05LYV	503	HF05LYW	

SD504-513

		ADL Dart 4		ADL Enviro 200		N39F	2005	Manchester Airport, 2007
504	SN55DVH	507	SN55DVL	510	SN55HSG	512	SN55HTD	
505	SN55DVJ	508	SN55DVM	511	SN55HSX	513	SN55HTF	
506	SN55DVK	509	SN55DVO					

SD514	YJ51ELX	DAF SB120	Wrightbus Cadet	N39F	2001	Transdev, 2009
SD515	HF57BKN	ADL Dart 4	ADL Enviro 200	N37F	2008	
SD516	GN07FDE	ADL Dart 4	ADL Enviro 200	N38F	2007	NX Kings Ferry, 2012
SD517	AY07CUA	ADL Dart 4	ADL Enviro 200	N38F	2007	Carters, Ipswich, 2012
SD518	KX07OOY	ADL Dart 4	ADL Enviro 200	N38F	2007	Webberbus, 2012
SC591	SJ56GBY	TransBus E300	TransBus Enviro 300	N44F	2007	Veolia, 2011
SC592	SJ56GCF	TransBus E300	TransBus Enviro 300	N44F	2007	Veolia, 2011

Seen in its winter guise is convertible open-top 430, HJ02HFA. Visible in this view are the hooks to enable the roof to be removed and the seal required when the roof is in place. Yellow Buses are in the process of adding class letters to their fleet numbers and these are shown in the accompanying list. *Richard Godfrey*

SD701	VU02TSY	Optare Solo M920	Optare	N29F	2002	*Operated for Dorset CC*
SD702	FY52RZC	Optare Solo M920	Optare	N29F	2002	*Operated for Dorset CC*
SD751	CE52UWR	Optare Solo M850	Optare	N27F	2002	*Operated for Dorset CC*
SD752	CE52UWS	Optare Solo M850	Optare	N27F	2002	*Operated for Dorset CC*
SD753	CE52UWU	Optare Solo M920	Optare	N27F	2002	*Operated for Dorset CC*
SD781	MX07OWU	ADL Dart 4 8.9m	ADL Enviro 200	N29F	2007	Meridian Line, 2012
SD782	YX09NZF	ADL Dart 4 8.9m	ADL Enviro 200	N29F	2009	Veolia, 2012
SD783	OU08AYF	ADL Dart 4 8.9m	ADL Enviro 200	N29F	2008	Heyfordian, Bicester, 2012
SD784	OU08AYG	ADL Dart 4 8.9m	ADL Enviro 200	N29F	2008	Heyfordian, Bicester, 2012
SD785	EU08FHD	ADL Dart 4 8.9m	ADL Enviro 200	N29F	2008	SMC, Harlow, 2012

SC801-807

		Volvo B7RLE	Plaxton Centro	N44F	2007-08	Minsterley Motors, 2012

801	DX57JXS	803	DX57TVW	805	YN08NLG	807	DX09GYS
802	DX57REU	804	YN08NKH	806	YN08NLJ		

SA851-858

		Wrightbus Streetlite DF 11.5m	Wrightbus	N44F	2013

851	HF13FZL	853	HF13FZN	855	HF13FZP	857	HF13FZS
852	HF13FZM	854	HF13FZO	856	HF13FZR	858	HF13FZT

Special event vehicles:

112	DLJ112L	Daimler Fleetline CRL6	Alexander AL	B43/31F	1973	
143	AJT143T	Leyland Fleetline FE30ALR	Alexander AL	B43/31F	1978	
245	ADV299A	Leyland Atlantean PDR1/1	Metro-Cammell	CO44/31F	1961	Leisurelink, 1996
248	928GTA	Leyland Atlantean PDR1/1	Metro-Cammell	CO44/31F	1961	Leisurelink, 1996

Ancilliary vehicles:

T473	P473BLJ	Dennis Dart SLF 10m	East Lancs Spryte	N37F	1997
T474	P474BLJ	Dennis Dart SLF 10m	East Lancs Spryte	N37F	1997

Previous registration:

ADV299A	925GTA

BATH CITYSTGHTSEEING

Bath Bus Company, 6 North Parade, Bath, BA1 1LF

RM1978	CF	ALD978B	AEC Routemaster R2RH	Park Royal	B36/28R	1964	Aintree Coachlines, 2010
307	WI	WLT307	Volvo Olympian	Northen Counties Palatine	PO48/27D	1995	London Central, 2004
248	CF	N548LHG	Volvo Olympian	Northen Counties Palatine	PO48/27D	1995	London Central, 2004
267	WI	P767SWC	Volvo Olympian	Alexander RH	PO47/31F	1997	Dublin Bus, 2010
357	BA	P757SWC	Volvo Olympian	Alexander RH	O47/31F	1997	Dublin Bus, 2010
274	EB	P774SWC	Volvo Olympian	Alexander RH	PO47/27D	1997	Dublin Bus, 2011
318	CF	P718SWC	Volvo Olympian	Alexander RH	O47/31F	1997	Dublin Bus, 2008
373	EB	P773SWC	Volvo Olympian	Alexander RH	O47/27D	1997	Dublin Bus, 2011
372	CF	P772SWC	Volvo Olympian	Alexander RH	O47/27D	1997	Dublin Bus, 2011
376	EB	P776SWC	Volvo Olympian	Alexander RH	O47/27D	1997	Dublin Bus, 2011
364	EB	S464ATV	Volvo Olympian	East Lancs Pyoneer	O49/35F	1999	Imperial, Southall, 2010
391	WI	V901FEC	Dennis Trident 9.9m	East Lancs Lolyne	O45/21D	1999	Ensignbus, 2011
393	CF	V903FEC	Dennis Trident 9.9m	East Lancs Lolyne	O45/21D	1999	Ensignbus, 2011
A501	BA	SK52URX	Volvo B7TL	Alexander ALX400	N45/20D	2002	RATP London, 2013
A502	BA	SK52URY	Volvo B7TL	Alexander ALX400	N45/20D	2002	RATP London, 2013
A503	BA	SK52USG	Volvo B7TL	Alexander ALX400	N45/20D	2003	RATP London, 2013
A504	BA	SK52USH	Volvo B7TL	Alexander ALX400	N45/20D	2003	RATP London, 2013
A505	BA	SK52USJ	Volvo B7TL	Alexander ALX400	N45/20D	2003	RATP London, 2013
381	BA	EU04CPV	Volvo B7L	Ayats Bravo City	O59/26F	2004	
272	BA	EU05VBG	Volvo B7L	Ayats Bravo	PO55/24F	2005	
273	BA	EU05VBJ	Volvo B7L	Ayats Bravo	PO55/24F	2005	
274	BA	EU05VBK	Volvo B7L	Ayats Bravo	PO55/24F	2005	
275	BA	EU05VBP	Volvo B7L	Ayats Bravo	PO55/24F	2005	
276	CF	EU05VBT	Volvo B7L	Ayats Bravo	PO55/24F	2005	
372	BA	EU05BZM	Volvo B7L	Ayats Bravo City	O55/24F	2005	
373	BA	EU05VBL	Volvo B7L	Ayats Bravo City	O55/24F	2005	
374	BA	EU05VBM	Volvo B7L	Ayats Bravo City	O55/24F	2005	
375	BA	EU05VBN	Volvo B7L	Ayats Bravo City	O55/24F	2005	
376	CF	EU05VBO	Volvo B7L	Ayats Bravo City	O55/24F	2005	
355	WI	YN55NKZ	Scania N94UD	East Lancs OmniDekka	N45/26F	2005	RATP London, 2012
301	BA	PN10FNR	Volvo B9TL	Optare Visionaire	O51/31F	2010	
302	BA	PN10FNS	Volvo B9TL	Optare Visionaire	O51/31F	2010	
360	WI	AE60GRU	Volvo B9TL	MCV	O(70)F	2010	Rotala, 2012

Depots: Bath (BA); Cardiff (CF); Eastbourne (EB) and Windsor (WI).

Latterly operated by Rotala's Wessex Connect operation Volvo B9TL AE60GRU was converted to open-top following a low-bridge incident. The bodywork was the first double-deck from MCV for the British market, a product which has attracted comparatively few buyers. It is seen passing the Guildhall while operating the tour of Windsor. *Richard Godfrey*

The Manchester Metrolink network continues to grow with the extension to East Didsbury being opened on 23rd May 2013. Work continues in the direction of Ashton and Tameside. Fleet changes have seen the withdrawal of some of the early Firema trams with the number of Bombardier Flexity Swifts now expected to reach ninety-four. 3013 is seen in High Street. *Mark Lyons*

MANCHESTER METROLINK

Manchester Metrolink, Metrolink House, Queens Road, Manchester, M8 0RY

1001-1026   GEC Alsthom   Firema   AB86T   1991-92

1001u	1005u	1009	1012	1015u	1018u	1021	1024
1002	1006u	1010u	1013	1016	1019u	1022	1025
1003	1007	1011u	1014	1017	1020u	1023	1026
1004u	1008u						

2001-2006   GEC Alsthom   Firema   AB86T   1999

2001	2002	2003	2004	2005	2006

3001-3094   Bombardier Flexity Swift HF   Bombardier Wien   AB80T   2009 and on order

3001	3013	3025	3037	3049	3061	3073	3084
3002	3014	3026	3038	3050	3062	3074	3085
3003	3015	3027	3039	3051	3063	3075	3086
3004	3016	3028	3040	3052	3064	3076	3087
3005	3017	3029	3041	3053	3065	3077	3088
3006	3018	3030	3042	3054	3066	3078	3089
3007	3019	3031	3043	3055	3067	3079	3090
3008	3020	3032	3044	3056	3068	3080	3091
3009	3021	3033	3045	3057	3069	3081	3092
3010	3022	3034	3046	3058	3070	3082	3093
3011	3023	3035	3047	3059	3071	3083	3094
3012	3024	3036	3048	3060	3072		

ROTALA

Central Connect - Diamond - Flights Hallmark - Ludlows - Wessex Connect - Preston Bus

Diamond Bus Co Ltd; Flights Hallmark Ltd; Central Connect Ltd; Wessex Connect Ltd; Ludlows of Halesowen Ltd, Beacon House, Long Acre, Birmingham, B7 5JJ

Preston Bus Ltd, 229 Deepdale Road, Preston, PR1 6NY

10014	BH	FOR35T	VDL Futura FHD12-340			VDL Bova		C49FT	2008		
10021	HR	A8FTG	Volvo B12B			Plaxton Panther		C49FT	2007		
10521	BH	491NFC	Volvo B12B			Plaxton Panther		C49FT	2005	Veolia, 2012	
10522	BH	Y40HMC	Volvo B12B			Plaxton Panther		C49FT	2004	Burton. Haverhill, 2012	
10523	BH	CN05DZH	Volvo B12B			Plaxton Panther		C49FT	2005	Veolia, 2012	

11516-11520
			Volvo B12B		Plaxton Panther	C49FT	2004	Veolia, 2011

11516	BH	FA04LJK	11518	BH	Y60HMC	11519	HR	Y50HMC	11520	BH	Y20HMC
11517	BH	Y30HMC									

13101-13114
			Volvo B9R		Caetano Levanté	C49FT	2011

13101	BH	FJ11GLK	13105	BH	FJ11GKV	13109	BH	FJ11MLE	13112	BH	FJ11MLL
13102	BH	FJ11GLZ	13106	BH	FJ11GKX	13110	BH	FJ11MLF	13113	BH	FJ11MLN
13103	BH	FJ11GKP	13107	BH	FJ11GJO	13111	BH	FJ11MLK	13114	BH	FJ11MLO
13104	BH	FJ11GKU	13108	BH	FJ11GJU						

13115	BH	FN06FLC	Volvo B12B		Caetano Levanté	C49FT	2006	First, 2012
13116	HR	FN06FLD	Volvo B12B		Caetano Levanté	C49FT	2006	First, 2012
14001	HR	BX09SOU	Mercedes-Benz Vario O816		Plaxton Cheetah	C29F	2009	
14002	HR	BX09SVJ	Mercedes-Benz Vario O816		Plaxton Cheetah	C29F	2009	
14013	BH	SF10EBN	Mercedes-Benz Vario O816		Plaxton Cheetah	C29F	2010	

14023-14027
			Mercedes-Benz Vario O816		Plaxton Cheetah	C29F	2010

14023	HR	KX60DWE	14025	HR	KX60DWG	14026	HR	KX60DWJ	14027	HR	KX60DWK
14024	HR	KX60DWF									

Rotala is an Alternative Investment Market listed company, which owns a number of English bus operations principally in the West Midlands, the South West (Bristol and Bath), and more recently in Preston. Seen in Central Connect livery is Plaxton Primo 20807, BX56BVE, pictured in Sutton Coldfield. *Mark Lyons*

14502	HR	YJ57EYL	Mercedes-Benz Vario 0814	Sitcar Beluga 2	C27F	2007	
14517	HR	WA57CYX	Mercedes-Benz Vario 0814	Sitcar Beluga 2	C27F	2007	
14518	BH	VX08HZS	Mercedes-Benz Vario 0814	Mellor	B29F	2008	Gemini Travel, 2012
15000	KR	MX08MYT	Optare Solo M950	Optare	N30F	2008	Maytree, Bolton, 2013
15102	HR	YN08FEO	Mercedes-Benz Sprinter 515	KVC	C16F	2008	
15516	u	BD57WCX	Mercedes-Benz Sprinter	Unvi Riada 45	C16F	2007	
20000	HR	YK11EKW	Optare Solo M960	Optare	N30F	2010	
20001	KE	SN05HDE	ADL Dart SLF 8.8m	ADL Mini Pointer	N29F	2005	Davidson, Bathgate, 2010
20002	TI	KP02PUY	Dennis Dart SLF 8.8m	Plaxton Pointer MPD	N28F	2002	Waverley Travel, 2005
20003	TI	KP02PUX	Dennis Dart SLF 8.8m	Plaxton Pointer MPD	N29F	2002	Waverley Travel, 2005
20004	KR	MX06BPE	Optare Solo M850	Optare	N25F	2006	
20007	HR	BU08ADZ	Enterprise EB01	Plaxton Primo	N28F	2008	
20008	KE	CW03XDM	Optare Solo M850	Optare	N29F	2003	
20010	BH	YJ56AUA	Optare Solo M850	Optare	N28F	2006	
20011	HR	BU08ACX	Enterprise EB01	Plaxton Primo	N28F	2008	
20013	KR	MX06BPK	Optare Solo M850	Optare	N25F	2006	
20014	BH	YJ10MFY	Optare Solo M960 SR	Optare	N33F	2010	
20015	BH	YJ10MFX	Optare Solo M960 SR	Optare	N33F	2010	
20016	BH	YJ10MFV	Optare Solo M960 SR	Optare	N33F	2010	
20023	KE	SN05HDD	ADL Dart SLF 8.8m	ADL Mini Pointer	N29F	2005	Davidson, Bathgate, 2010
20024	AV	BX04MZV	Mercedes-Benz Sprinter 411cdi	Mercedes-Benz	M16	2004	Rossendale, 2012
20026	KR	MX08MZG	Optare Solo M950	Optare	N33F	2008	Maytree, Bolton, 2010
20027	BH	YJ10MFZ	Optare Solo M960 SR	Optare	N33F	2010	
20032	TI	MV54EEO	ADL Dart SLF 8.8m	ADL Mini Pointer	N29F	2005	Bluebird, Middleton, 2010
20058	HR	KX58LJA	Enterprise EB01	Plaxton Primo	N28F	2008	
20100	TI	KP02PVA	Dennis Dart SLF 8.8m	Plaxton Pointer MPD	N29F	2002	Norbus, Kirkby, 2007
20101	HR	KX08OML	Enterprise EB01	Plaxton Primo	N28F	2008	
20104	BR	KP02PUY	Dennis Dart SLF 8.8m	Plaxton Pointer MPD	N29F	2002	Travel Wright, Newark, '06
20113	u	Y3JPT	Dennis Dart SLF 8.8m	Plaxton Pointer MPD	N29F	2001	JP Travel, Middleton, 2006
20114	u	Y2JPT	Dennis Dart SLF 8.8m	Plaxton Pointer MPD	N29F	2001	JP Travel, Middleton, 2006
20132	BR	Y32YVV	Dennis Dart SLF 8.8m	Plaxton Pointer MPD	N28F	2001	Zaks, Birmingham, 2008
20136	BR	Y36YVV	Dennis Dart SLF 8.8m	Plaxton Pointer MPD	N28F	2001	Zaks, Birmingham, 2008
20182	u	W181DNO	Dennis Dart SLF 9.4m	Plaxton Pointer 2	N35F	2000	East London, 2009
20183	AV	X183BNH	Dennis Dart SLF 8.8m	Plaxton Pointer MPD	N29F	2000	Zaks, Birmingham, 2007
20184	AV	X184BNH	Dennis Dart SLF 8.8m	Plaxton Pointer MPD	N29F	2000	Birmingham MT, 2007
20201	RH	KX03JBU	TransBus Dart 8.8m	TransBus Mini Pointer	N29F	2003	
20202	TI	KU52YJX	Dennis Dart SLF 8.8m	Plaxton Pointer MPD	N29F	2002	Jay, Greengairs, 2007
20203	BH	KX03HZK	TransBus Dart 8.8m	TransBus Mini Pointer	N29F	2003	Waverley Travel, 2010
20204	u	W204DNO	Dennis Dart SLF 9.4m	Plaxton Pointer 2	N31F	2000	East London, 2009
20205	TI	KU52YJT	Dennis Dart SLF 8.8m	Plaxton Pointer MPD	N29F	2002	Doyle, Ripley, 2007
20206	TI	KU52YJS	Dennis Dart SLF 8.8m	Plaxton Pointer MPD	N29F	2002	Doyle, Ripley, 2007

20207-20233

			Dennis Dart SLF 9.3m*	Plaxton Pointer 2	N31F	2000	East London, 2009
20207	u	W207DNO	20209	u	W209DNO	20223	TI	W223DNO	20232	u	W232DNO
20208	u	W208DNO	20211	u	W211DNO	20229	u	W229DNO	20233	u	W233DNO

20251-20254

			Dennis Dart SLF 8.8m	Alexander ALX200	N29F	2001	Bluebird, Middleton, 2010
20251	AV	Y251KNB	20252	BH	Y252KNB	20253	AV	Y253KNB	20254	AV	Y254KNB

20263	u	Y263KNB	Dennis Dart SLF 8.9m	Alexander ALX200	N29F	2001	South Gloucestershire, '06
20274	BH	Y274FJN	Dennis Dart SLF 10.1m	Alexander ALX200	N35F	2001	East London, 2009
20300	AV	BU53AWR	Mercedes-Benz Sprinter 413	Koch	N16F	2003	Arriva Midlands, 2008
20301	u	BU53AWP	Mercedes-Benz Sprinter 413	Koch	N16F	2003	Arriva Midlands, 2008
20302	TI	KX03JBE	TransBus Dart 8.8m	TransBus Mini Pointer	N29F	2003	
20304	RH	KX03HZJ	TransBus Dart 8.8m	TransBus Mini Pointer	N29F	2003	Pulham, Bourton, 2006
20305	u	BW03ZVA	Mercedes-Benz Sprinter 413	Koch	N16F	2003	Hatts, Foxham, 2008
20306	u	BW03ZVB	Mercedes-Benz Sprinter 413	Koch	N16F	2003	Hatts, Foxham, 2008
20307	KE	BW03ZVC	Mercedes-Benz Sprinter 413	Koch	N16F	2003	Hatts, Foxham, 2008
20312	u	BU52AXB	Mercedes-Benz Sprinter 413	Koch	N16F	2003	Hatts, Foxham, 2008
20361	KE	W361ABD	Dennis Dart SLF 8.8m	Plaxton Pointer MPD	N29F	2000	Thames Travel, 2003
20366	KE	W366ABD	Dennis Dart SLF 8.8m	Plaxton Pointer MPD	N29F	2000	Thames Travel, 2003
20401	KE	YJ61CHD	Optare Solo M950 SR	Optare	N30F	2011	
20402	KE	YJ61CHF	Optare Solo M950 SR	Optare	N30F	2011	
20403	KE	YJ61CHG	Optare Solo M950 SR	Optare	N30F	2011	
20469	u	T469HNH	Dennis Dart SLF 8.8m	Plaxton Pointer MPD	N29F	1999	Norbus, Kirby, 2008
20490	u	P516RYM	Dennis Dart SLF 10.1m	Plaxton Pointer 2	N32F	1996	
20500	AV	KP54BYV	ADL Dart SLF 8.8m	ADL Mini Pointer	N29F	2005	

Wessex Connect is the fleetname used for the Bristol services. Bus operation began in Bristol in April 2007 and by June of that year the bus business of South Gloucestershire Bus and Coach Company had been acquired. Allocated to the Avon depot is 20516, YX09HYZ, an Alexander Dennis Dart with Enviro 200 bodywork. *Richard Godfrey*

20501-20507

			Dennis Dart SLF 8.8m	Plaxton Pointer MPD	N28F	1999	Go-West Midlands, 2008

20501	TI	S758RNE	20503	RH	T71JBA	20505	TI	V267BNV	20507	TI	V942DNB
20502	TI	S759RNE	20504	RH	V266BNV	20506	u	V941DNB			

20508	TI	KP02PUE	Dennis Dart SLF 8.8m	Plaxton Pointer MPD	N28F	2002	Go-West Midlands, 2008
20511	TI	KX54NKZ	Dennis Dart SLF 8.8m	ADL Pointer MPD	N29F	2005	Jack, Edinburgh, 2012
20512	AV	KX57OWM	ADL Dart 4 8.9m	ADL Enviro 200	N29F	2008	OFJ, Heathrow, 2012
20515	AV	YX09HZE	ADL Dart 4 8.9m	ADL Enviro 200	N29F	2009	Veolia, 2012
20516	AV	YX09HYZ	ADL Dart 4 8.9m	ADL Enviro 200	N29F	2009	Veolia, 2012
20517	AV	YX09HYY	ADL Dart 4 8.9m	ADL Enviro 200	N29F	2009	Veolia, 2012
20518	TI	KU02YUA	Dennis Dart SLF 8.8m	Plaxton Pointer MPD	N29F	2002	Jones, Llanfaethlu, 2008
20519	TI	KP51UFC	Dennis Dart SLF 8.8m	Plaxton Pointer MPD	N29F	2002	Thames Travel, 2008
20520	AV	YX09HZC	ADL Dart 4 8.9m	ADL Enviro 200	N29F	2009	Veolia, 2012
20522	TI	MX57UPW	Optare Solo M880	Optare	N28F	2008	
20523	u	W448DOP	Dennis Dart SLF 10.7m	Plaxton Pointer 2	N39F	2000	
20524	AV	YX09HZB	ADL Dart 4 8.9m	ADL Enviro 200	N29F	2009	Veolia, 2012
20525	AV	YX09HYW	ADL Dart 4 8.9m	ADL Enviro 200	N29F	2009	Veolia, 2012
20526	AV	BA02EAA	ADL Dart 4 8.9m	ADL Enviro 200	N29F	2007	Reay, Wigton, 2012
20527	AV	BA05EAA	ADL Dart 4 8.9m	ADL Enviro 200	N29F	2007	Reay, Wigton, 2012
20528	AV	KX57OVU	ADL Dart 4 8.9m	ADL Enviro 200	N29F	2008	JPT, Middleton, 2012
20529	AV	KX57OVT	ADL Dart 4 8.9m	ADL Enviro 200	N29F	2008	JPT, Middleton, 2012
20533	RH	X372CUY	Dennis Dart SLF 8.8m	Plaxton Pointer MPD	N29F	2000	Pullman, Crofty, 2009
20535	TI	KW02CVV	Dennis Dart SLF 8.8m	Plaxton Pointer MPD	N29F	2002	National Express, 2010
20536	TI	KW02CXG	Dennis Dart SLF 8.8m	Plaxton Pointer MPD	N29F	2002	National Express, 2010
20537	RH	Y37YVV	Dennis Dart SLF 8.8m	Plaxton Pointer MPD	N28F	2001	Travel London, 2010

20538-20542

			Optare Solo M920	Optare	N26F	2003	Airparks, Birmingham, '10

20538	TI	KS03EXG	20540	TI	KS03EXL	20541	TI	KS03EXM	20542	TI	KS03EXP
20539	TI	KS03EXN									

20543	TI	YT51EAO	Dennis Dart SLF 8.8m	Plaxton Pointer MPD	N29F	2002	Connex, 2008
20544	TI	KP51UFB	Dennis Dart SLF 8.8m	Plaxton Pointer MPD	N29F	2002	Thames Travel, 2008
20545	TI	W573JVV	Dennis Dart SLF 8.8m	Plaxton Pointer MPD	N29F	2000	Pete's Travel, 2008
20546	u	T468HNH	Dennis Dart SLF 8.8m	Plaxton Pointer MPD	N29F	1999	Norbus, Kirby, 2008
20571	u	W571JVV	Dennis Dart SLF 8.8m	Plaxton Pointer MPD	N29F	2000	People's Express, 2003

20572	KE	W572JVV	Dennis Dart SLF 8.8m	Plaxton Pointer MPD	N29F	2000	People's Express, 2003
20573	RH	W573JVV	Dennis Dart SLF 8.8m	Plaxton Pointer MPD	N29F	2000	People's Express, 2003
20574	TI	KP51SXW	Dennis Dart SLF 8.8m	Plaxton Pointer MPD	N29F	2001	National Express, 2010
20601	TI	KP51UFH	Dennis Dart SLF 8.8m	Plaxton Pointer MPD	N29F	2002	Thames Travel, 2007
20602	TI	KU52YJZ	Dennis Dart SLF 8.8m	Plaxton Pointer MPD	N29F	2002	Jay, Greengairs, 2007
20603	AV	KP54BYX	ADL Dart SLF 8.8m	ADL Mini Pointer	N29F	2005	
20604	BH	KP51UFG	Dennis Dart SLF 8.8m	Plaxton Pointer MPD	N29F	2002	Thames Travel, 2007
20605	TI	KP51SXX	Dennis Dart SLF 8.8m	Plaxton Pointer MPD	N29F	2001	A1A, Birkenhead, 2002
20606	TI	KU51KZH	Dennis Dart SLF 8.8m	Plaxton Pointer MPD	N29F	2002	Norbus, Kirkby, 2007
20607	BH	KP51UFJ	Dennis Dart SLF 8.8m	Plaxton Pointer MPD	N29F	2002	Thames Travel, 2007
20608	RH	KU52YJY	Dennis Dart SLF 8.8m	Plaxton Pointer MPD	N29F	2002	Jay, Greengairs, 2007
20610	KE	KP54BYW	ADL Dart SLF 8.8m	ADL Mini Pointer	N29F	2005	
20646	u	T546HNH	Dennis Dart SLF 10.7m	Plaxton Pointer 2	N39F	1999	Armchair, Brenford, 2007

20652-20660

			Dennis Dart SLF	Plaxton Pointer MPD	N29F	1999-2002	
20652	KE	V652HEC	20654	KE	V654HEC	20657	KE	V657HEC	20660	KE	V660HEC
20653	KE	V653HEC	20656	u	V656HEC	20658	KE	V658HEC

20701-20708

			Optare Solo M920 SR	Optare	N32F	2008	Stagecoach, 2010
20701	PR	PN08SVK	20703	PR	PN08SVO	20705	PR	PN08SVR	20707	PR	PN08SVT
20702	PR	PN08SVL	20704	PR	PN08SVP	20706	PR	PN08SVS	20708	PR	PN08SVU

20762	PR	PN52ZVL	Optare Solo M850	Optare	N29F	2002	Stagecoach, 2010
20767	PR	PN52ZVS	Optare Solo M850	Optare	N29F	2002	Stagecoach, 2010

20769-20776

			Optare Solo M850	Optare	N29F	2006	Stagecoach, 2010
20769	PR	PO56RNZ	20771	PR	PO56ROU	20773	PR	PO56RPV	20776	PR	PO56RPZ
20770	PR	PO56ROH	20772	PR	PO56RPU

20777-20780

			Optare Solo M880	Optare	N28F	2007	Stagecoach, 2010
20777	PR	PN07NTK	20778	PR	PN07NTL	20779	PR	PN57NFF	20780	PR	PN57NFG

20781-20791

			Optare Solo M920	Optare	N32F	2005-06	Stagecoach, 2010
20781	PR	PE55WMD	20784	PR	PO56RRU	20787	PR	PO56RRY	20790	PR	PO56RSV
20782	PR	PE55WMF	20785	PR	PO56RRV	20788	PR	PO56RRZ	20791	PR	PO56RSX
20783	PR	PE55WMG	20786	PR	PO56RRX	20789	PR	PO56RSU

20792-20797

			Optare Solo M950	Optare	N32F	2007	Stagecoach, 2010
20792	PR	PN07NTJ	20794	PR	PN07NTO	20796	PR	PN07NTU	20797	PR	PN07NTV
20793	PR	PN07NTM	20795	PR	PN07NTT

20804	AV	KP54BYT	ADL Dart SLF 8.8m	ADL Mini Pointer	N29F	2005	
20805	TI	KP54BYR	ADL Dart SLF 8.8m	ADL Mini Pointer	N29F	2005	
20806	AV	YX09HZD	ADL Dart 4 8.9m	ADL Enviro 200	N29F	2009	Veolia, 2012
20807	u	BX56BVE	Enterprise EB01	Plaxton Primo	N28F	2007	
20808	u	YX56JUE	Enterprise EB01	Plaxton Primo	N28F	2007	
20809	u	YX56JUC	Enterprise EB01	Plaxton Primo	N28F	2007	
20810	KR	BX56BKA	Optare Solo M850	Optare	N25F	2007	
20811	KR	BX56BJZ	Optare Solo M850	Optare	N25F	2007	
20812	BH	BX56BPY	Enterprise EB01	Plaxton Primo	N28F	2007	
20813	u	BX56BPU	Enterprise EB01	Plaxton Primo	N28F	2007	
20814	HR	YJ08PKN	Optare Solo M880	Optare	N25F	2008	Newport Transport, 2012
20815	BH	YJ08PKK	Optare Solo M850	Optare	N25F	2008	Newport Transport, 2012
20816	BH	YJ57YCG	Optare Solo M850	Optare	N25F	2008	Newport Transport, 2012
20817	BH	YJ57YCK	Optare Solo M850	Optare	N25F	2008	Newport Transport, 2012
20818	HR	YJ08PKO	Optare Solo M850	Optare	N25F	2008	Newport Transport, 2012
20819	BH	YJ57YCH	Optare Solo M850	Optare	N25F	2008	Newport Transport, 2012
20820	AV	SF57FZK	ADL Dart 4 8.9m	ADL Enviro 200	N29F	2007	Central Taxi, Felling, 2012
20821	AV	SF07VOB	ADL Dart 4 8.9m	ADL Enviro 200	N29F	2007	Reay, Wigton, 2012
20823	HR	P11FTG	Optare Solo M1020	Optare	N20D	2007	Airparks, Edinburgh, 2012
20824	AV	YX09HZG	ADL Dart 4 8.9m	ADL Enviro 200	N29F	2009	Veolia, 2012
20825	BH	SF54ORK	Optare Solo M850	Optare	N27F	2004	
20826	BH	SF54HWG	Optare Solo M850	Optare	N27F	2004	
20827	BH	L5PPN	Optare Solo M850	Optare	N27F	2004	
20828	BH	YN04LXS	Optare Solo M850	Optare	N27F	2004	
20829	BH	YJ56AUC	Optare Solo M880	Optare	N27F	2004	
20830	BH	YJ56AUH	Optare Solo M880	Optare	N27F	2006	
20831	BH	YJ06YPP	Optare Solo M880	Optare	N27F	2006	Coachcare, Leicester, 2012
20832	BH	YJ06YPR	Optare Solo M880	Optare	N27F	2006	Coachcare, Leicester, 2012
20833	BH	SF54ORL	Optare Solo M850	Optare	N27F	2006	Ayrways, Patna, 2012

In January 2011, Preston Bus Limited became the next acquisition for Rotala. This purchase established a new hub for Rotala in the north west of England. In 2012, three Wrightbus Streetlite buses that had been used for development work at Wrightbus were added to that allocation with 20907, DRZ4018, showing the livery applied to the Preston unit. *Richard Godfrey*

20834	BH	SF54ORC	Optare Solo M850	Optare	N27F	2004	Ayrways, Patna, 2012
20836	BH	YJ54BUE	Optare Solo M850	Optare	N27F	2004	Rossendale Transport, '12
20837	BH	YJ54BUF	Optare Solo M850	Optare	N27F	2004	Rossendale Transport, '12
20838	BH	YJ54BUO	Optare Solo M850	Optare	N27F	2004	Rossendale Transport, '12
20839	BH	YJ54BUA	Optare Solo M850	Optare	N27F	2004	Rossendale Transport, '12
20840	BH	YJ54BUH	Optare Solo M850	Optare	N27F	2004	Rossendale Transport, '12
20841	KR	MX09HJG	Optare Solo M950	Optare	N27F	2004	Airparks, Edinburgh, 2012
20842	HR	MX58KZM	Optare Solo M880 SL	Optare	N27F	2009	Sheffield CT, 2012
20843	HR	MX58ACJ	Optare Solo M880 SL	Optare	N27F	2008	Sheffield CT, 2012
20844	KR	MX58KZG	Optare Solo M950	Optare	N27F	2009	Andrew, Lerwick, 2012
20845	BH	MX08DHO	Optare Solo M1020	Optare	N27F	2008	Airparks, Edinburgh, 2012
20846	u	BX56BVF	Enterprise EB01	Plaxton Primo	N28F	2007	
20847	KR	YG02DJZ	Optare Solo M850	Optare	N28F	2002	Coachcare, Leicester, 2012
20848	RH	KU52RXW	TransBus Dart SLF 10.7m	Plaxton Pointer 2	N37F	2002	Yourbus, Nottingham, 2012
20849	TI	KU52RYH	TransBus Dart SLF 10.7m	Plaxton Pointer 2	N37F	2002	Yourbus, Nottingham, 2012
20850	RH	KU52RYK	TransBusDart SLF 10.7m	Plaxton Pointer 2	N37F	2002	Yourbus, Nottingham, 2012
20851	KR	KU52RYN	TransBus Dart SLF 10.7m	Plaxton Pointer 2	N37F	2002	Yourbus, Nottingham, 2012
20852	TI	LG02FFC	Dennis Dart SLF 8.8m	Plaxton Pointer MPD	N29F	2002	Yourbus, Nottingham, 2012
20853	KR	LG02FFD	Dennis Dart SLF 8.8m	Plaxton Pointer MPD	N29F	2002	Yourbus, Nottingham, 2012
20854	KR	LG02FFE	Dennis Dart SLF 8.8m	Plaxton Pointer MPD	N29F	2002	Yourbus, Nottingham, 2012
20855	TI	LG02FFH	Dennis Dart SLF 8.8m	Plaxton Pointer MPD	N29F	2002	Yourbus, Nottingham, 2012
20856	TI	LG02FFJ	Dennis Dart SLF 8.8m	Plaxton Pointer MPD	N29F	2002	Yourbus, Nottingham, 2012
20867	TI	W767URP	Dennis Dart SLF 8.8m	Plaxton Pointer MPD	N29F	2000	
20899	KE	V899DNB	Dennis Dart SLF 8.8m	Plaxton Pointer MPD	N29F	1999	Selwyns, Runcorn, 2002
20904	AV	X704UKS	Dennis Dart SLF 8.8m	Plaxton Pointer MPD	N29F	2000	Shuttle Buses, 2006
20905	u	Y705TGH	Dennis Dart SLF 10.1m	Plaxton Pointer 2	N29F	2001	Go-Ahead London, 2010
20906	TI	KP54BYO	ADL Dart SLF 8.8m	ADL Mini Pointer	N29F	2005	
20907	PR	DRZ4018	Wrightbus Streetlite WF 9.5m	Wrightbus	N37	2011	Wrightbus, 2012
20908	PR	CRZ7495	Wrightbus Streetlite WF 8.8m	Wrightbus	N37	2011	Wrightbus, 2012
20909	PR	BRZ9662	Wrightbus Streetlite WF 9.5m	Wrightbus	N37	2010	Wrightbus, 2012
20910	AV	EU08FHC	ADL Enviro 4 8.9m	ADL Enviro 200	N29F	2008	SM Travel, Harlow, 2012
20911	AV	SN56AWZ	ADL Dart 4 8.9m	ADL Enviro 200	N29F	2006	Irvine, Law, 2012
20912	TI	MX57UPT	Optare Solo M880 SL	Optare	N27F	2008	RH Transport, Whitney, '12
20913	TI	MX57UPS	Optare Solo M880 SL	Optare	N27F	2008	RH Transport, Whitney, '12
20914	u	BU05HDV	ADL Dart SLF 8.8m	ADL Mini Pointer	N29F	2005	SM Travel, Harlow, 2012
20915	u	BU05HDO	ADL Dart SLF 8.8m	ADL Mini Pointer	N29F	2005	SM Travel, Harlow, 2012

20916-20921			Optare Solo M970 SR	Optare	N32F	2013

20916	AV	YJ62FHZ	20918	AV	YJ62FGF	20920	AV	YJ62FHR	20921	AV	YJ62FHV
20917	AV	YJ62FFZ	20919	AV	YJ62FGP					

During 2013 Rotala acquired the Redditch and Kidderminster operations of First and brought them into the Diamond brand. The Red Diamond operation is based at the depot in Redditch and the services run from both depots are mostly local contracted ones. Pictured leaving Worcester bus station, and displaying its former fleet number, is Dennis Dart 20646, T546HNH, which has recently been placed into reserve. *Richard Godfrey*

20972	KE	Y972GPN	Dennis Dart SLF 8.8m	Plaxton Pointer MPD	N29F	2001	Thames Travel, 2007
20973	AV	Y973GPN	Dennis Dart SLF 8.8m	Plaxton Pointer MPD	N29F	2001	Thames Travel, 2007
21009	BH	SN05FLR	ADL Dart SLF 8.8m	ADL Pointer	N29F	2005	Bryans, Derry, 2007
21500	u	BV58MKX	Mercedes-Benz Sprinter 515	Mercedes-Benz	C16F	2008	
21501	AV	KP54BYU	ADL Dart SLF 8.8m	ADL Mini Pointer	N29F	2005	
22003	HR	T5EEV	Optare Solo M880 Electrilc	Optare	N29F	2009	

30000-30006
Volvo B7RLE — Plaxton Centro — N45F — 2007

| 30000 | BH | BX07BRV | 30002 | BH | BX07KPP | 30004 | KE | BX07AXO | 30006 | AV | BX07AYU |
| 30001 | AV | WX07UOB | 30003 | AV | BX07KPO | 30005 | AV | BX07KPN | | | |

30007-30011
VDL Bus SB120 — Plaxton Centro — N42F — 2007

| 30007 | AV | YJ07JRV | 30009 | AV | X30COV | 30010 | AV | YJ07JJU | 30011 | AV | YJ07JJO |
| 30008 | AV | X300COV | | | | | | | | | |

30013	RH	Y3NBB	Dennis Dart SLF 10.7m	Alexander ALX200	N38F	2001
30018	BH	AE10CTO	ADL Dart 4 11.3m	MCV Evolution	N39F	2010
30019	BH	BV10ZJU	Mercedes-Benz Citaro O530LE	Mercedes-Benz	N42F	2010
30021	TI	AE10CTO	ADL Dart 4 11.3m	MCV Evolution	N39F	2010
30030	BH	BF60OFA	Mercedes-Benz Citaro O530LE	Mercedes-Benz	N42F	2010
30103	PR	BF60OEV	Mercedes-Benz Citaro O530LE	Mercedes-Benz	N42F	2010

30104-30112
ADL Dart 4 11.3m — MCV Evolution — N40F — 2010

30104	HR	AE10CUH	30107	HR	AE10CTV	30109	HR	AE10CTZ	30111	RH	AE10CSF
30105	HR	AE10CUJ	30108	HR	AE10CTY	30110	HR	AE10CTU	30112	HR	AE10CTX
30106	HR	AE10CUK									

30113-30118
Scania OmniLink K230 UB — Scania — N45F — 2011

| 30113 | AV | YS10XBO | 30115 | AV | YT61FEU | 30117 | AV | YT61FEO | 30118 | AV | YT61FEM |
| 30114 | AV | YT61FEV | 30116 | AV | YT61FEP | | | | | | |

| 30120 | HR | B14WTS | MAN 14.220 | MCV Evolution | N38F | 2008 |
| 30121 | HR | B15WTS | MAN 14.220 | Plaxton Centro | N38F | 2008 |

Supplied to the Black Diamond operation in 2012 were fifteen Optare Versa buses including one of which is a hybrid example, 30129, YJ12GTY, seen shortly after delivery in Kingstanding Road, Birmingham. The Diamond Bus Company became part of Rotala group following the acquisition of Go West Midlands in March 2008 from the Go-Ahead Group. *Richard Godfrey*

30122-30136
Optare Versa V1100   Optare   N37F   2012

30122	PR	YJ61JJU	30126	PR	YJ61JJL	30130	BH	YJ12GTZ	30134	BH	YJ12GUF
30123	PR	YJ61JJE	30127	PR	YJ61JJO	30131	PR	YJ12GUA	30135	BH	YJ12GUG
30124	PR	YJ61JJF	30128	BH	YJ12GUE	30132	BH	YJ12GUC	30136	BH	YJ12GUH
30125	PR	YJ61JJK	30129	BH	YJ12GTY	30133	BH	YJ12GUD			

30153-30159
Dennis Dart SLF 10.7m   Plaxton Pointer 2   N34F   1999   Centra, Staines, 2007

30153	w	T153OGC	30156	w	T156OGC	30157	w	T157OGC	30159	w	T159OGC

30201-30214
DAF SB120   Wrightbus Cadet   N39F   2001-02   Go-West Midlands, 2008

30201	TI	YJ51EKA	30205	TI	YJ51EKE	30209	TI	YD02PZJ	30212	TI	YD02PZM
30202	TI	YJ51EKB	30206	TI	YJ51EKF	30210	TI	YD02PZK	30213	TI	YD02PZN
30204	TI	YJ51EKD	30207	TI	YJ51EKG	30211	TI	YD02PZL	30214	TI	YD02PZO

30216	TI	YJ51EKM	DAF SB120	Wrightbus Cadet	N39F	2002	
30217	u	Y283HUA	DAF SB120	Wrightbus Cadet	N39F	2001	Ludlows, Halesowen, 2009
30218	TI	X808NWX	DAF SB120	Wrightbus Cadet	N39F	2000	Ludlows, Halesowen, 2009
30301	HR	BX57CCN	MAN 14.220	MCV Evolution	N38F	2008	
30378	u	S378TMB	Dennis Dart SLF 11.3m	Plaxton Pointer SPD	N39D	1999	Weavaway, Newbury, 2007

30382-30388
Dennis Dart SLF 10.7m   Alexader ALX200   N37F   1999   Dawson Rentals, 2009

30382	u	V382SVV	30384	u	V384SVV	30387	u	V387SVV	30388	u	V388SVV
30383	u	V383SVV									

30401	BH	BN09FWS	Mercedes-Benz Citaro O530LE	Mercedes-Benz	N42F	2009	Mercedes-Benz, 2010
30402	KE	A9UOB	Volvo B7L 11.8m	Wrightbus Eclipse Metro	N31D	2002	Volvo demonstrator, 2007
30404	BH	YJ61CHH	Optare Versa V1100	Optare	N37F	2011	
30405	BH	YJ61CHK	Optare Versa V1100	Optare	N37F	2011	
30426	TI	S397HVV	Dennis Dart SLF 10.7m	Plaxton Pointer 2	N39F	1999	Go-West Midlands, 2008
30427	TI	S404JUA	Dennis Dart SLF 10.7m	Plaxton Pointer 2	N39F	1998	Go-West Midlands, 2008
30428	RH	S405JUA	Dennis Dart SLF 10.7m	Plaxton Pointer 2	N39F	1998	Go-West Midlands, 2008

30431-30434
Dennis Dart SLF   Wright Crusader   N40F   1999   Go-West Midlands, 2008

30431	u	T442EBD	30432	u	T443EBD	30433	u	T445EBD	30434	TI	T447EBD

Wessex operates U10, U18 and X18 services using the Uniconnect brand. These services link the University of Bath with its surrounding areas. Whilst being specifically intended to meet students' requirements, they are open to all passengers. Illustrating the livery applied to this branding is 30925, BX62FAK, one of six Volvo B7RLEs added to the fleet in 2012. *Richard Godfrey*

30436	u	V386JWK	Dennis Dart SLF			Plaxton Pointer 2	N41F	1999	Go-West Midlands, 2008
30437	TI	V377SVV	Dennis Dart SLF 10.7m			Plaxton Pointer 2	N39F	1999	Go-West Midlands, 2008
30438	TI	V391SVV	Dennis Dart SLF 10.7m			Plaxton Pointer 2	N39F	1999	Go-West Midlands, 2008
30439	TI	W567JVV	Dennis Dart SLF 10.1m			Plaxton Pointer 2	N39F	1999	Go-West Midlands, 2008
30444	u	S393HVV	Dennis Dart SLF 10.7m			Plaxton Pointer 2	N37F	1999	Go-West Midlands, 2008
30454	TI	Y211HEJ	Dennis Dart SLF			Plaxton Pointer 2	N39F	2000	Go-West Midlands, 2008
30455	TI	Y212HEJ	Dennis Dart SLF			Plaxton Pointer 2	N39F	2000	Go-West Midlands, 2008

30486-30489			Dennis Dart SLF 10.7m			Plaxton Pointer 2	N31D	2000	Go-West Midlands, 2008
30486	TI	W337VGX	30488	TI	W335VGX	30489	TI	W336VGX	

30500	KR	MW52PZR	TransBus Dart 9.5m			TransBus Pointer	N31F	2003	

30501-30507			Volvo B7RLE			Plaxton Centro	N45F	2008	
30501	AV	BX58APK	30503	AV	BX58AOY	30505	AV	BX58AOV	30507	AV	BX58AON
30502	AV	BX58APF	30504	AV	BX58AOW	30506	AV	BX58AOU			

30508	AV	FJ57CYV	Volvo B7RLE			Wrightbus Eclipse Urban	N45D	2007	
30509	AV	FJ57CYT	Volvo B7RLE			Wrightbus Eclipse Urban	N45D	2007	
30512	TI	S377TMB	Dennis Dart SLF 11.3m			Plaxton Pointer SPD	N41F	1998	Arriva NW & Wales, 2007
30513	TI	S396HVV	Dennis Dart SLF 10.7m			Plaxton Pointer 2	N39F	1996	Dawson Rentals, 2008
30516	RH	W906JNF	Dennis Dart SLF 10.8m			Alexander ALX200	N38F	2000	Go-West Midlands, 2008
30520	u	W142WGT	Dennis Dart SLF 9.2m			Plaxton Pointer 2	N37F	2000	Mitcham Belle, 2008
30525	AV	BX62FEU	Volvo B7RLE			Wrightbus Eclipse Urban 2	N44D	2012	
30526	AV	BX62FDC	Volvo B7RLE			Wrightbus Eclipse Urban 2	N44D	2012	
30527	AV	BX62FEM	Volvo B7RLE			Wrightbus Eclipse Urban 2	N44D	2012	
30636	BR	X637AKW	Dennis Dart SLF 10.7m			Plaxton Pointer 2	N39F	2000	
30637	BR	X637AKW	Dennis Dart SLF 10.7m			Plaxton Pointer 2	N39F	2000	
30701	KE	MW52PZP	TransBus Dart 9.5m			TransBus Pointer	N31F	2003	
30704	BH	KX57OVS	MAN 14.220 10.8			Plaxton Centro	N38F	2007	Grant Palmer, Dunstable

30801-30806			MAN 14.240			Plaxton Centro	N38F	2008	30802/5 Kent CC, 2008
30801	TI	WX58FRU	30803	TI	BU08DBO	30805	TI	KX08HMY	30806	TI	WX58FRV
30802	TI	KX08HMZ	30804	TI	KX57OVV						

30807-30812			Volvo B7RLE			Plaxton Centro	N45F	2008	
30807	TI	BU08DCO	30809	TI	BU08DCX	30811	TI	WX58FSA	30812	KE	BX58AOZ
30808	TI	BU08DCE	30810	TI	BU08DCF						

In January 2013 it was announced that Rotala had acquired two freehold depots (Kidderminster and Redditch) along with thirty-six buses from First Group. Initially the vehicles gained Diamond names on the First livery as shown by 30935, VX54MTE, one of three ADL Enviro 300s allocated to Kidderminster that were included in the sale. *Mark Doggett*

30813	AV	FJ57CYW	Volvo B7RLE					Wrightbus Eclipse Urban	N45D	2007	
30814	AV	FJ57CYU	Volvo B7RLE					Wrightbus Eclipse Urban	N45D	2007	
30815	AV	FJ57CYS	Volvo B7RLE					Wrightbus Eclipse Urban	N45D	2007	
30816	KE	BX58AOO	Volvo B7RLE					Plaxton Centro	N45F	2008	

30821-30828
Volvo B7RLE — Plaxton Centro — N45F — 2009

| 30821 | TI | BX09SHZ | 30823 | TI | BX09SJU | 30825 | TI | BX09SRO | 30827 | TI | BX09SNY |
| 30822 | TI | BX09SJO | 30824 | TI | BX09SJV | 30826 | TI | BX09SNV | 30828 | TI | BX09SNZ |

30831	RH	MX08PZH	MAN 14.220 10.8					Plaxton Centro	N38F	2008	JPT, Middleton, 2012
30832	TI	MX08NNU	Volvo B7RLE					Wrightbus Eclipse Urban	N45D	2008	Midland Classic, 2012
30833	TI	AE57FXW	Volvo B7RLE					Wrightbus Eclipse Urban	N45D	2007	Midland Classic, 2012
30834	TI	BU08DAO	Volvo B7RLE					Wrightbus Eclipse Urban	N45D	2007	Midland Classic, 2012

30850-30862
Volvo B7RLE — Wrightbus Eclipse Urban — N45F — 2007-08

30850	RH	BU08DAO	30854	RH	WX58FSE	30857	RH	BU08DHO	30860	RH	WX58FRR
30851	RH	BU08DBX	30855	RH	WX58FRZ	30858	RH	BU08DHP	30861	RH	MX07OYT
30852	RH	BU08DBV	30856	RH	WX58FSD	30859	RH	WX58FSC	30862	RH	BU08MTE

30875	u	T875HGT	Dennis Dart SLF 10.7m					Plaxton Pointer 2	N33D	1999	Centra, Staines, 2007
38876	KE	T876HGT	Dennis Dart SLF 10.7m					Plaxton Pointer 2	N33D	1999	Centra, Staines, 2007
30877	u	T877HGT	Dennis Dart SLF 10.7m					Plaxton Pointer 2	N33D	1999	Centra, Staines, 2007

30901-30905
Dennis Dart SLF — Alexander ALX200 — N38F — 2000 — Go-West Midlands, 2008

| 30901 | AV | W901JNF | 30903 | BR | W903JNF | 30904 | AV | W904JNF | 30905 | BR | W905JNF |
| 30902 | BR | W902JNF | | | | | | | | | |

| 30910 | PR | PRN909 | Scania N230 UB | | | | | East Lancs Esteem | N40F | 2007 | Stagecoach, 2010 |

30911-30917
Scania N94 UB — East Lancs Esteem — N40F — 2006 — Stagecoach, 2010

| 30911 | PR | PL06RYO | 30915 | PR | PO56JDK | 30916 | PR | PO56JDU | 30917 | PR | PL56JDX |
| 30912 | PR | PL06RYP | | | | | | | | | |

30918-30921
Scania N230 UB — East Lancs Esteem — N40F — 2007-08 — Stagecoach, 2010

| 30918 | PR | PN57NFA | 30919 | PR | PN57NFC | 30920 | PR | PN57NFD | 30921 | PR | PN57NFE |

| 30922 | HR | B20WTS | MAN 14.220 10.7 | | | | | Plaxton Centro | N38F | 2010 | Supertravel, Liverpool, '12 |

30923-30928
Volvo B7RLE — Wrightbus Eclipse Urban 2 — N44F — 2012

| 30923 | BH | BX62FGD | 30925 | KE | BX62FAK | 30927 | KE | BX62FZP | 30928 | KE | BX62FYY |
| 30924 | KE | BX62FZL | 30926 | KE | BX62FBF | | | | | | |

30929	TI	KX07OOW	ADL Dart 4 10.8m		ADL Enviro 200	N37F	2007	Webberbus, Bridgewater
30930	KR	VX54MUC	ADL Dart 10.8m		ADL Pointer	N37F	2004	First 2013
30931	KR	VX54MUO	ADL Dart 10.8m		ADL Pointer	N37F	2004	First 2013
30932	KR	VX54MUP	ADL Dart 10.8m		ADL Pointer	N37F	2004	First 2013
30933	KR	VX54MSU	ADL E300 12m		ADL Enviro 300	N44F	2005	First 2013
30934	KR	VX54MSY	ADL E300 12m		ADL Enviro 300	N44F	2005	First 2013
30935	KR	VX54MTE	ADL E300 12m		ADL Enviro 300	N44F	2005	First 2013

30936-30943 — Volvo B7RLE — Wrightbus Eclipse Urban 2 — N44F — 2013

30936	AV	BK13NZM	30938	AV	BK13NZO	30940	TI	BK13NZR	30942	TI	BK13NZT
30937	AV	BK13NZN	30939	AV	BK13NZP	30941	TI	BK13NZS	30943	TI	BK13NZU

31082	t	K128UFV	DAF SB220		Optare Delta	TV	1993	Stagecoach, 2010
31110	u	P10FTG	Dennis Dart SLF 10.6m		Plaxton Pointer 2	N40F	1996	Dunn-Line, 2004
31181	u	S81DOX	Dennis Dart SLF 10.8m		Marshall Capital	N43F	1998	A-Line, Bedworth, 2002
31215	PR	G215KRN	Leyland Lynx LX2R11C15Z4R		Leyland Lynx	B45F	1989	Stagecoach, 2010
31305	u	S305MKH	Dennis Dart SLF 10.7m		Plaxton Pointer 2	N36F	1998	London United, 2009
31309	u	V509NOF	Dennis Dart SLF 11.3m		Plaxton Pointer SPD	N41F	1996	Zaks, Birmingham, 2008
31395	u	S395HVV	Dennis Dart SLF 11.3m		Plaxton Pointer 2	N39F	1996	Dawson Rentals, 2008
31401	u	R401XFL	Dennis Dart SLF 11.3m		Marshall Capital	N42F	1997	Halton Transport, 2007
31457	u	R457LGH	Dennis Dart SLF 10.1m		Plaxton Pointer	N36F	1997	Go-Ahead London, 2009
31458	u	R478LGH	Dennis Dart SLF 10.1m		Plaxton Pointer	N36F	1997	Go-Ahead London, 2009
31483	u	R407FFC	Dennis Dart SLF		Wright Crusader	N30D	1998	Go-West Midlands, 2008
31490	u	S490MCC	Dennis Dart SLF 10.7m		Plaxton Pointer 2	N39F	1998	Caelloi, Pwllheli, 2001
31495	u	S405TMB	Dennis Dart SLF 10.7m		Plaxton Pointer 2	N41F	1999	Bus Eireann, 2007
31496	u	S496MCC	Dennis Dart SLF 10.7m		Plaxton Pointer 2	N40F	1998	Express Motors, 2005
31500	KR	R610YCR	Dennis Dart SLF 10.7m		Plaxton Pointer 2	N37F	1998	First, 2013
31501	KR	R220MSA	Dennis Dart SLF 10.7m		Plaxton Pointer 2	N37F	1998	First, 2013
31502	u	P402MLA	Dennis Dart SLF 10.1m		Plaxton Pointer	N34F	1996	First, 2013
31503	u	P403MLA	Dennis Dart SLF 10.1m		Plaxton Pointer	N34F	1996	First, 2013
31504	u	P404MLA	Dennis Dart SLF 10.1m		Plaxton Pointer	N34F	1996	First, 2013
31505	u	P405MLA	Dennis Dart SLF 10.1m		Plaxton Pointer	N34F	1996	First, 2013
31506	u	P406MLA	Dennis Dart SLF 10.1m		Plaxton Pointer	N34F	1996	First, 2013
31507	u	P455CCV	Dennis Dart SLF 10.7m		Plaxton Pointer 2	N35F	1997	First, 2013
31508	u	P401MLA	Dennis Dart SLF 10.1m		Plaxton Pointer	N34F	1996	First, 2013
31510	u	P457CAH	Dennis Dart SLF 10.7m		Plaxton Pointer 2	N35F	1997	First, 2013
31516	u	M255MRW	Dennis Lance 11m		Plaxton Verde	B49F	1994	First, 2013
31793	u	S793RRL	Dennis Dart SLF 10.7m		Plaxton Pointer 2	N41F	1998	Dawson Rentals, 2010

40005-40008 — Dennis Trident 9.9m — Alerxander ALX400 — N43/20D — 2002 — London United, 2010

40005	AV	LG02FDP	40006	AV	LG02FDO	40007	AV	LG02FDV	40008	AV	LG02FDX

40030	AV	YT61FEX	Scania OmniCity CN230 OUD		Scania	N45/24F	2011	
40112	FI	Y2NBB	Dennis Trident		Plaxton President	N47/29F	2001	
40406	PR	PO56RSY	Scania OmniDekka N94 UD		East Lancs	N47/33F	2007	Stagecoach, 2010
40407	PR	PO56RSZ	Scania OmniDekka N94 UD		East Lancs	N47/33F	2007	Stagecoach, 2010
40409	FI	PO51UMX	Dennis Trident 9.9m		East Lancs Lolyne	N46/20D	2001	Go-Ahead London, 2009
40410	FI	PO51UMY	Dennis Trident 9.9m		East Lancs Lolyne	N46/20D	2001	Go-Ahead London, 2009
40503	AV	FJ57CZG	Volvo B9TL		Wrightbus Eclipse Gemini	N44/24D	2007	
40510	AV	FJ57CZC	Volvo B9TL		Wrightbus Eclipse Gemini	N44/24D	2007	
40515	AV	YN08MOF	Scania OmniCity CN230 UB		Scania	N45/24F	2008	Scania demonstrator, 2009

40540-40544 — Dennis Trident 10.5m — Plaxton President — N45/29F — 1996 — Lothian Buses, 2010

40540	PR	V540ESC	40542	PR	V542ESC	40543	PR	V543ESC	40544	PR	V544ESC
40541	PR	V541ESC								

40582-40599 — Dennis Trident — East Lancs Pyoneer — N45/30F — 1999-2001 Stagecoach, 2010

40582	PR	X182RRN	40587	PR	X187RRN	40592	PR	V192EBV	40596	PR	V196EBV
40583	PR	X183RRN	40588	PR	X188RRN	40593	PR	V193EBV	40597	PR	X197RRN
40584	PR	X184RRN	40589	PR	X189RRN	40594	PR	V194EBV	40598	PR	X198RRN
40585	PR	X185RRN	40590	PR	V190EBV	40595	PR	V195EBV	40599	PR	X199RRN
40586	PR	X186RRN	40591	PR	V191EBV					

40600	PR	X388NNO	Dennis Trident		Alexander ALX400	N45/30F	2001	Stagecoach, 2012
40601	PR	X385NNO	Dennis Trident		Alexander ALX400	N45/30F	2001	Stagecoach, 2012

40602-40605 — Volvo B9TL — Wrightbus Gemini Eclipse 2 — N45/30F — 2012

40602	AV	BX62FUO	40603	AV	BX62FNV	40604	AV	BX62FOJ	40605	AV	BX62FUU

For many years Midland Red West operated almost no double-decks but recent times have seen First introduce Dennis Tridents into Redditch for the Birmingham service. Nine of these were included in the sale from First with 40617, T885KLF, which latterly operated in London, showing here its new names but former fleet number. *Mark Doggett*

40606-40609
Volvo B5LH — Wrightbus Gemini Eclipse 2 — N43/28F — 2013

40606	PR	PR62TON	40607	PR	PO62LNU	40608	PR	PO62LNF	40609	PR	PO62LNN

40610-40618
Dennis Trident — Plaxton President — N39/21F — 1999 — First, 2013

40610	RH	V857HBY	40613	RH	V877HBY	40615	RH	V882HBY	40617	RH	T885KLF
40611	RH	V860HBY	40614	RH	T881KLF	40616	RH	T884KLF	40618	RH	V886HBY
40612	RH	V862HBY									

40619-40622
Volvo B5LH — Wrightbus Gemini Eclipse 2 — N43/28F — 2013

40619	PR	PE13JYY	40620	PR	PE13JYZ	40621	PR	PE13JZA	40622	PR	PE13JZB

40623	RH	V894HLH	Dennis Trident	Plaxton President	N43/23F	2000	First, 2013

40624-40629
Dennis Trident — Plaxton President — N45/30F — 2000 — Yourbus, Nottingham, 2012

40624	u	X603EGK	40626	u	X607EGK	40628	u	X609EGK	40629	u	X701EGK
40625	u	X606EGK	40627	u	X608EGK						

42551-42554
Leyland Olympian ON2R50C13Z4 — Northern Counties Palatine — B47/30F — 1991 — Stagecoach, 2010

42551	PR	H101BFR	42552	PR	H102BFR	42553	PR	H103BFR	42554	PR	H104BFR

42556	PR	J976PRW	Leyland Olympian ON2R50C13Z4	Leyland	B47/31F	1991	Stagecoach, 2010

42557-42562
Leyland Olympian ON2R50C13Z4 — Leyland — B47/31F — 1992 — Stagecoach, 2010

42557	PR	J107KCW	42559	PR	J109KCW	42560	PR	J110KCW	42562	PR	J112KCW
42558	PR	J108KCW							

42564	RH	K123URP	Volvo Citybus B10M-50	Alexander RV	BC47/35F	1992	First, 2013
42565	RH	K126URP	Volvo Citybus B10M-50	Alexander RV	BC47/35F	1992	First, 2013

In January 2011 Rotala took over the Preston Bus operation that Stagecoach Group was required to sell by the competition authorities. Illustrating the new livery applied by Rotala is one of two Tridents new to East London, 40600, X388NNO. It is seen in the Sherwood district of the city while operating an Asda special. *Dave Heath*

Previous registrations:

491NFC	CN05DZF	FOR35T	YJ08VPC
A8FTG	FB07AAF	KV51KZH	KV51KZH, T5BUS
A9UOB	LF51CYC	P10FTG	P10FTG, L6BOB
B12WTS	BX57CCN	P11FTG	MX57BBV
B14WTS	BX57CDN	T5EEV	JY09EZR
B15WTS	BU08ANV	Y20HMC	FJ54ZPG
B20WTS	MX59KUF	Y30HMC	FR04LJL
BA02EAA	SF07URJ	Y40HMC	YU04XFB
BA05EAA	SF07URL	Y50HMC	FD54DHO
BU08HTE	BU08DBY	Y60HMC	FD54DHN
BU51ZAK	FE51RDX	YN04AHA	YN04AHA, N1EOS

Depots and allocations

Avonmouth (Port Edward Centre, BS11 9HS) - AV (Wessex Connect)

Mercedes-Benz	20024	20300						
Optare Solo	20916	20917	20918	20919	20920	20921		
Dart	20183	20184	20251	20253	20254	20500	20603	20604
	20904	20973	21501	30901				
Enviro 200	20512	20515	20516	20517	20520	20524	20525	20526
	20527	20528	20529	20806	20820	20821	20824	20910
	20911							
Volvo B7RLE	30000	30001	30003	30005	30006	30501	30502	30503
	30504	30505	30506	30507	30508	30509	30525	30526
	30527	30813	30814	30815	30936	30937	30938	30939
VDL SB200	30007	30008	30009	30010	30011			
Trident	40005	40006	40007	40008	40112			
Volvo B9TL	40503	40510	40602	40603	40604	40605		
Scania OmniCity	40030	40515						

In March 2013 Preston Bus received four Volvo B5LH hybrid buses. These feature Wrightbus bodywork and are used principally on routes 22 and 23. Receiving the vehicles on behalf of Preston Bus was Managing Director, Bob Dunn, who said at the time, "These new Volvo buses have been purchased for our busy city centre routes and will be used daily by the Preston public". Representing the new arrivals is **40608, PO62LNF.** *Richard Godfrey*

Birmingham (Flights Coach Station, Long Acre, B7 5JJ) - BH (Flights)

Mercedes-Benz	14013	14518						
Volvo B9R	13101	13102	13103	13104	13105	13106	13107	13108
	13109	13110	13111	13112	13113	13114		
Volvo B12B	11021	11516	11517	11518	11520	11521	11522	11523
	13115							
VDL Bova	10014							
Volvo B7RLE	30923							

Birmingham (BRM Bus Division, Long Acre, B7 5JJ) - BR (Central Connect)

Plaxton Primo	20812							
Optare Solo	20010	20014	20015	20016	20027	20815	20816	20817
	20819	20825	20826	20827	20828	20829	20830	20831
	20832	20833	20834	20836	20837	20838	20839	20840
	20845							
Optare Versa	30128	30129	30130	30132	30133	30134	30135	30136
	30404	30405						
Dart	20104	20132	20136	20203	20252	20274	20604	20607
	21009	30637	30905					
MAN 14.220	30704	30801						
Citaro	30019	30030	30401					

Heathrow (Green Lane, Hounslow, TW4 6HB) - HR

Sprinter	15102							
Plaxton Primo	20007	20011	20058	20101	20102			
Optare Solo	20000	20814	20818	20823	20842	20843	22003	
Dart	30384							
Enviro 200	30104	30105	30106	30107	30108	30109	30110	30112
MAN 14.220	30120	30121	30922					
Volvo B12B	11519	13116						

Keynsham (Gypsy Lane, Burnett, BS31 2ED) - KE - Wessex Connect

Mercedes-Benz	20307							
Optare Solo	20008	20401	20402	20403				
Dart	20001	20023	20361	20366	20572	20610	20652	20653
	20654	20657	20658	20660	20972	30876	30904	
Volvo B7RLE	30002	30004	30402	30812	30816	30924	30925	30926
	30927	30928						

Kidderminster (Island Drive) - KR

Optare Solo	15000	20004	20013	20026	20810	20811	20841	20844
	20847							
Dart	20851	20853	20854	30500	30930	30931	30932	31500
	31501	31510	31516					

Preston (Deepdale Road, PR1 6NY) - PR

Optare Solo	20701	20702	20703	20704	20705	20706	20707	20708
	20762	20767	20769	20770	20771	20772	20773	20776
	20777	20778	20779	20780	20781	20782	20783	20784
	20785	20786	20787	20788	20789	20790	20791	20792
	20793	20794	20795	20796	20797			
Streetlite WF	20907	20908	20909					
Citaro	30103							
Optare Versa	30122	30123	30124	30125	30126	30127	30131	
Scania N94	30911	30912	30915	30916	30917			
Scania N230	30910	30918	30919	30920	30921			
Leyland Lynx	31215							
Olympian	42551	42552	42553	42554	42556	42557	42558	42559
	42560	42562						
Trident	40582	40583	40584	40585	40586	40587	40588	40589
	40590	40591	40592	40593	40594	40595	40596	40597
	40598	40599	40600	40601				
Scania OmniDekka	40406	40607						
Volvo B5LH	40606	40607	40608	40609	40619	40620	40621	

Redditch (Church Road, B97 4AB) - RH (Diamond)

Dart	20201	20304	20503	20504	20533	20537	20573	20608
	20848	20850	30013	30428	30516	30636	30701	31502
	31503	31506	31507	31508				
Enviro 200	30111							
MAN 14.240	30802	30803	30804	30805	30831			
Volvo B7RLE	30850	30851	30852	30854	30855	30856	30857	30858
	30859	30860	30861	30862				
Enviro 300	30933	30934	30935					
Dennis Trident	40540	40541	40542	40543	40544	40610	40611	40612
	40613	40614	40615	40616	40617	40618	40623	
Volvo Citybus	42564	42565						

Tividale (Hallbridge Way, Oldbury, B69 3HW) - TI (Diamond)

Optare Solo	20522	20538	20539	20540	20541	20542	20912	20913
DAF SB120	30201	30202	30204	30205	30206	30207	30209	30210
	30211	30212	30213	30214	30216	30218		
Dart	20002	20003	20032	20100	20202	20205	20206	20223
	20302	20501	20502	20505	20507	20508	20511	20518
	20519	20535	20536	20543	20544	20574	20601	20602
	20605	20606	20805	20849	20852	20855	20856	20867
	20906							
Enviro 200	30929							
MAN 14.220	30806							
Volvo B7RLE	30807	30808	30809	30810	30811	30821	30822	30823
	30824	30825	30826	30827	30828	30832	30833	30834
	20940	20941	20942	20943				

Stored, Unallocated - u/w - Remainder

TRANSDEV

Transdev Burnley & Pendle - Transdev Harrogate & District - Transdev Keighley & District - Transdev Lancashire United - Yorkshire Coastliner - Transdev York

Burnley & Pendle Travel Ltd; Lancashire United Ltd;

Harrogate & District Travel Ltd; Yorkshire Coastliner Ltd, Prospect Park, Broughton Way, Starbeck, Harrogate, HG2 7NY

Transdev York Ltd, 5 Dean Mill, Plumbe Street, Burnley, BB11 3AG

Travelspeed Ltd, 5 Dean Mill, Plumbe Street, Burnley, BB11 3AG

Keighley & District Travel Ltd; Blazefield House, Russell Street, Keighley, BD21 2JX

11	BP	G281UMJ	Leyland Olympian ONCL10/1RZ	Leyland	B47/31F	1989	Arriva The Shires, 2004
12	HD	G289UMJ	Leyland Olympian ONCL10/1RZ	Leyland	B47/31F	1989	Arriva The Shires, 2004
13	BB	H546GKX	Leyland Olympian ON2R50C13Z4	Leyland	B47/31F	1991	Blue Bus, Bolton, 2004
14	BB	H549GKX	Leyland Olympian ON2R50C13Z4	Leyland	B47/31F	1991	Blue Bus, Bolton, 2004
15	BB	H550GKX	Leyland Olympian ON2R50C13Z4	Leyland	B47/31F	1991	Blue Bus, Bolton, 2004
16	BB	N416JBV	Volvo Olympian	Northern Counties Palatine	B47/30F	1995	London Central, 2004
17	BB	N424JBV	Volvo Olympian	Northern Counties Palatine	B47/30F	1995	London Central, 2004
18	BB	N425JBV	Volvo Olympian	Northern Counties Palatine	B47/30F	1995	London Central, 2004
39	u	B738GSC	Leyland Olympian ONTL11/2R	Eastern Coach Works	B51/32D	1984	Lothian Buses, 2001

50-58										
			Leyland Olympian ONTL11/2R	Eastern Coach Works			B51/32D	1984-86	Lothian Buses, 2001-04	
50	u	B750GSC	**51**	u	B751GSC	**54**	w	B754GSC	**58**	u	C792SFS

101-106										
			BMC Condor 220	BMC			S57F	2005-06	*Operated on behalf of Metro*	
101	KD	YK55ZZY	**103**	KD	YK55AAE	**105**	KD	YK55AVB	**106**	KD	YK55AVC
102	KD	YK55AAF	**104**	KD	YK55AUC					

Transdev is a subsidiary of Caisse des dépôts et consignations and was created in 1990. To celebrate the centenary of Accrington Corporation buses Olympian 163, F263YTJ was repainted in traditional colours. It is seen in Reedly while heading for Burnley.
Richard Godfrey

Carrying Lancashire United colours, Optare Versa 271, YJ57XWK, heads for Chorley on a service 124, a route once associated with Ribble's operation. *Richard Godfrey*

108-115

			BMC Condor 220			BMC			S57F	2006	*Operated on behalf of Metro*
108	KD	YK55AVE	**110**	KD	YK06DNO	**112**	KD	YK06EHM	**114**	KD	YK56LKA
109	KD	YK55AVL	**111**	KD	YK06EHL	**113**	KD	YJ06WTY	**115**	KD	YK55LJZ

116	BP	N116UHP	Volvo Olympian	Alexander Royale	BC43/29F	1995	National Express, 2005
117	KD	YK56WGC	BMC Condor 220	BMC	S57F	2007	*Operated on behalf of Metro*
118	KD	YK55AVD	BMC Condor 220	BMC	S57F	2005	*Operated on behalf of Metro*
125	BP	B251NVN	Leyland Olympian ONLXB/1RV	Eastern Coach Works	B45/32F	1989	Arriva NW & Wales, 2006
127	KD	YK55AUA	BMC Condor 220	BMC	S57F	2005	*Operated on behalf of Metro*
128	KD	YK55AUN	BMC Condor 220	BMC	S57F	2005	*Operated on behalf of Metro*
129	KD	YK55AUO	BMC Condor 220	BMC	S57F	2005	*Operated on behalf of Metro*
140	HD	L140BFV	Dennis Javelin 11m	Plaxton Première Interurban	BC60F	1994	Stagecoach NW, 2001
150	HD	L150BFV	Dennis Javelin 11m	Plaxton Première Interurban	BC60F	1994	Stagecoach NW, 2001
151	u	G51FKG	Scania N113DRB	Alexander RH	B47/33F	1989	Newport Bus, 2005
152	u	G52FKG	Scania N113DRB	Alexander RH	B47/33F	1989	Newport Bus, 2005
155	HD	L155BFV	Dennis Javelin 11m	Plaxton Première Interurban	BC60F	1994	Stagecoach NW, 2001
157	HD	L157BFV	Dennis Javelin 11m	Plaxton Première Interurban	BC60F	1994	Stagecoach NW, 2001
162	BB	F262YTJ	Leyland Olympian ONCL10/1RZ	Northern Counties	B47/30F	1989	Arriva NW & Wales, 2006
163	u	F263YTJ	Leyland Olympian ONCL10/1RZ	Northern Counties	B47/30F	1989	Arriva NW & Wales, 2006
165	HD	L106SDY	Dennis Javelin 11m	Plaxton Première Interurban	BC60F	1993	Stagecoach NW, 2001
196	u	F96PRE	Leyland Olympian ONCL10/1RZ	Alexander RL	B47/32F	1988	Arriva NW & Wales, 2006

201-205

			Volvo B10BLE			Wright Renown			N44F*	1999	Ambassador, 2005
										201/4 are S57F	
201	KD	T126OAH	**203**	u	T128OAH	**204**	HD	T129OAH	**205**	u	T125OAH
202	u	T127OAH									

206-210

			Volvo B10BLE			Wright Renown			N44F	1999	
206	BB	V206EBV	**208**	KD	V208EBV	**209**	KD	V209EBV	**210**	HD	V210EBV
207	BB	V207EBV									

211	BB	T124OAH	Volvo B10BLE	Wright Renown	N44F	1999	Ambassador, 2005
212	BB	T122OAH	Volvo B10BLE	Wright Renown	N44F	1999	Ambassador, 2005

Transdev has increased the number and frequency of services into Manchester from the north in recent years. Linking Blackburn and Haslingden with the city is route X41 which now requires double-decks. Seen passing traditional Lancashire stone cottages is 404, YJ04LYP, a Volvo B7TL fitted with Wrightbus bodywork. *Richard Godfrey*

251-276

			Optare Versa V1100			Optare			N37F		2008		
251	YK	YJ57XVN	258	u	YJ57XVV	264	BP	YJ57XWB	271	BB	YJ57XWK		
252	u	YJ57XVO	259	BP	YJ57XVW	265	u	YJ57XWC	272	BB	YJ57XWV		
253	u	YJ57XVP	260	BP	YJ57XVX	266	BP	YJ57XWD	273	YK	YJ57XWW		
254	BP	YJ57XVR	261	BP	YJ57XVY	267	BP	YJ57XWE	274	BB	YJ08PKX		
255	BP	YJ57XVS	262	BP	YJ57XVZ	268	BP	YJ57XWF	275	YK	YJ08PKY		
256	BP	YJ57XVT	263	u	YJ57XWA	269	BP	YJ57XWG	276	YK	YJ08PKZ		
257	BP	YJ57XVU											

277-286

			Optare Versa V1100			Optare			N37F		2012		
277	HG	YJ12MZN	280	HG	YJ12MZT	283	HG	YJ12MZW	285	BP	YJ12MZY		
278	HG	YJ12MZO	281	HG	YJ12MZU	284	HG	YJ12MZX	286	BP	YJ12MZZ		
279	HG	YJ12MZP	282	HG	YJ12MZV								

301	u	KE51WUO	Volvo B10M-62	Plaxton Paragon	C53F	2001	
302	HD	KE51WUP	Volvo B10M-62	Plaxton Paragon	C53F	2001	

305-309

			Volvo B10BLE		Wrightbus Renown		NC44F	2002	
305	HD	YC51LXX	307	HD	YC51LXZ	308	HD	YC51LYA	309	HD	YC51LYD
306	HD	YC51LXY							

347	u	A604NYG	Leyland Olympian ONLXB/1R	Eastern Coach Works	B41/29F	1984	

401-404

			Volvo B7TL		Wrightbus Eclipse Gemini		NC41/28F	2004		
401	BB	YJ04LYG	402	BB	YJ04LYH	403	BB	YJ04LYK	404	BB	YJ04LYP

405-410

			Volvo B7TL		Wrightbus Eclipse Gemini		NC41/28F	2006		
405	BB	YK55ATN	407	BB	YK55ATU	409	YK	YK55ATX	410	YK	YK55ATY
406	BB	YK55ATO	408	BB	YK55ATV						

411-420

			Volvo B9TL		Wrightbus Eclipse Gemini		NC41/29F	2008		
411	MA	FJ08BYH	414	MA	FJ08BYM	417	MA	FJ08BYV	419	MA	FJ08BYX
412	MA	FJ08BYK	415	MA	FJ08BYN	418	MA	FJ08BYW	420	MA	FJ08BYZ
413	MA	FJ08BYL	416	MA	FJ08BYU						

Nestled in the heart of Nidderdale, which is an Area of Outstanding Natural Beauty, Pateley Bridge is the perfect place to start exploring the Yorkshire Dales. Seen in the village on its return journey into Harrogate is Volvo B10BLE 307, YC51LXZ. As an additional feature for this rural service, high-back seating is fitted in its Wrightbus Renown body. *John Young*

421-424 · Volvo B9TL · Wrightbus Eclipse Gemini · NC41/29F · 2011

421	MA	BD11CEA	422	MA	BD11CEF	423	MA	BD11CEJ	424	MA	BD11CEK

425-428 · Volvo B9TL · Wrightbus Eclipse Gemini · NC41/29F · 2013

425	MA	BF62UXV	426	MA	BF62UXW	427	MA	BF62UXX	428	MA	BF62UXY

438	KD	YD02UMY	Volvo B7TL	Plaxton President	NC43/27F	2002
439	BB	YD02UMZ	Volvo B7TL	Plaxton President	NC43/27F	2002
440	BB	YD02UNB	Volvo B7TL	Plaxton President	NC43/27F	2002

450-455 · Volvo B7RLE · Wrightbus Eclipse Urban · BN44F · 2005

450	KD	YJ05FNH	452	KD	YJ05FNL	454	KD	YJ05FNN	455	KD	YJ05FNO
451	KD	YJ05FNK	453	KD	YJ05FNM						

504	HD	N504HWY	Volvo B10B-58	Alexander Strider	S59F	1996
509	HD	N509HWY	Volvo B10B-58	Alexander Strider	S59F	1996
530	KD	R530TWR	Volvo B10BLE	Wright Renown	S57F	1999
531	KD	R531TWR	Volvo B10BLE	Wright Renown	S57F	1999

540-544 · Volvo B10BLE · Wright Renown · S57F · 1999

540	KD	T540AUA	542	KD	T542AUA	543	KD	T543AUA	544	KD	T544AUA
541	KD	T541AUA									

557-577 · Volvo B10BLE · Wright Renown · NC47F* · 2000 · *557/61/2 are S57F

557	KD	X557YUG	564	u	X564YUG	569	u	X569YUG	575	w	X575YUG
561	KD	W561CWX	566	u	X566YUG	573	u	X573YUG	576	w	X576YUG
562	KD	X562YUG	567	u	X567YUG	574	BB	X574YUG	577	u	X577YUG
563	u	X563YUG									

601-615 · Volvo B6BLE · Wright Crusader 2 · NC36F · 2000

601	w	W601CWX	608	w	W608CWX	611	w	W611CWX	613	w	W613CWX
607	w	W607CWX	609	w	W609CWX	612	w	W612CWX	615	w	W615CWX

The Yorkshire Coastliner network uses modern dual-purpose vehicles that later transfer to local services. The six Optare Versa buses which were illustrated in the last edition of this handbook have moved on and the service is now provided entirely by double-deck Volvo B9TLs. Providing a map of the route network is 423, BD11CEJ, one of four supplied for the route in 2011. It is seen in York while returning from the coast. *Tony Wilson*

641	w	P641UUG	Volvo B6LE			Wright Crusader		NC38F	1997	
642	w	P642UUG	Volvo B6LE			Wright Crusader		NC38F	1997	
643	w	P643UUG	Volvo B6LE			Wright Crusader		NC38F	1997	
665	w	PK51LJX	Dennis Dart SLF			Plaxton Pointer MPD		N29F	2002	
667	w	PK51LJY	Dennis Dart SLF			Plaxton Pointer MPD		N29F	2002	
703	BB	YG52GDJ	Dennis Dart SLF 8.8m			Plaxton Pointer MPD		NC29F	2002	
704	BB	YG52GDK	Dennis Dart SLF 8.8m			Plaxton Pointer MPD		NC29F	2002	
705	BB	YG52GDO	Dennis Dart SLF 8.8m			Plaxton Pointer MPD		NC29F	2002	

706-720

TransBus Dart 8.8m — TransBus Mini Pointer — N29F — 2004

706	BB	YJ04LXN	710	KD	YJ04LXT	714	KD	YJ04LXX	718	KD	YJ04LYC
707	BB	YJ04LXP	711	KD	YJ04LXU	715	BP	YJ04LXY	719	YK	YJ04LYD
708	BP	YJ04LXR	712	KD	YJ04LXV	716	KD	YJ04LXZ	720	BP	YJ04LYF
709	u	YJ04LXS	713	KD	YJ04LXW	717	KD	YJ04LYA			

| 848 | w | V548JBH | Dennis Dart SLF 10.1m | | | Plaxton Pointer 2 | | N36F | 1999 | Mitchell Belle, 2001 |

940-962

Dennis Javelin 11m — Plaxton Première Interurban — S60F — 1993-94 — Stagecoach NW, 2001

| 940 | HD | M940JBO | 947 | HD | M947JBO | 949 | HD | M949JBO | 962 | HD | M102CCD |
| 942 | HD | M942JBO | 948 | HD | M948JBO | | | | | | |

| 963 | KD | S63VNM | Volvo Olympian | | | Northern Counties Palatine | | B32/29F | 1998 | |
| 964 | BP | S64VNM | Volvo Olympian | | | Northern Counties Palatine | | B32/29F | 1998 | |

971-978

Volvo Olympian — Northern Counties Palatine — B47/30F — 1991

| 971 | KD | H141GGS | 973 | KD | H143GGS | 975 | KD | H145GGS | 977 | KD | H147GGS |
| 972 | KD | H142GGS | 974 | KD | H144GGS | 976 | KD | H146GGS | 978 | KD | H148GGS |

983-989

Volvo Olympian — Northern Counties Palatine — B32/29F — 1998

| 983 | BB | S53VNM | 986 | BP | S56VNM | 988 | KD | S58VNM | 989 | KD | S59VNM |
| 984 | BB | S54VNM | 987 | KD | S57VNM | | | | | | |

Connecting York University with the city is a UniBus service provided by Transdev. Shown at the university end of the route is Volvo B10BLE 1012, YD02UMU. Many Transbus vehicles feature high-back seating. *Richard Godfrey*

1001-1004
Volvo B10BLE · Wrightbus Renown · NC47F · 2000

1001	KD	W616CWX	1002	KD	W617CWX	1003	KD	W618CWX	1004	KD	W619CWX

1012-1016
Volvo B10BLE · Wrightbus Renown · NC44F · 2002

1012	YK	YD02UMU	1014	BB	YD02UMW	1015	YK	YD02UMX	1016	YK	PN02HVZ
1013	YK	YD02UMV								

1039	KD	W139XRO	Volvo B10BLE	Wrightbus Renown	N47F	2000
1041	KD	X441YUB	Volvo B10BLE	Wrightbus Renown	NC47F	2000

1042-1078
Volvo B10BLE · Wrightbus Renown · NC44F · 2001

1042	BP	Y142HRN	1052	KD	Y152HRN	1063	KD	Y163HRN	1071	BP	Y171HRN
1043	BP	Y143HRN	1053	BP	Y153HRN	1064	YK	Y164HRN	1072	KD	Y172HRN
1044	KD	Y144HRN	1054	YK	Y154HRN	1065	KD	Y165HRN	1073	BP	Y173HRN
1046	BP	Y146HRN	1057	YK	Y157HRN	1066	BP	Y166HRN	1074	BP	Y174HRN
1047	BB	Y147HRN	1058	BP	Y158HRN	1067	BP	Y167HRN	1076	KD	Y176HRN
1048	KD	Y148HRN	1059	YK	Y159HRN	1068	BB	Y168HRN	1077	KD	Y177HRN
1049	KD	Y149HRN	1061	KD	Y161HRN	1069	BP	Y169HRN	1078	KD	Y178HRN
1051	BB	Y151HRN	1062	BP	Y162HRN					

1079-1103
Volvo B10BLE · Wrightbus Renown · NC44F · 2001-02

1079	KD	PO51MTE	1086	HD	PO51MTZ	1092	HD	PO51MUU	1098	BB	PN02HVY
1080	KD	PO51MTF	1087	HD	PO51MUA	1093	HD	PO51MUV	1099	BB	PN02HVX
1081	KD	PO51MTK	1088	BB	PO51MUB	1094	KD	PO51MUW	1100	BB	PN02HVW
1082	KD	PO51MTU	1089	BB	PO51MUC	1095	KD	PO51MUY	1101	BB	PN02HWA
1083	KD	PO51MTV	1090	HD	PO51MUE	1096	BB	PO51MVA	1102	BB	PN02HVJ
1084	HD	PO51MTX	1091	HD	PO51MUP	1097	BB	PN02HVV	1103	BB	PN02HVK
1085	HD	PO51MTY								

1104	BB	BU02BKV	Volvo B7L	Wrightbus Eclipse	NC41F	2002	Volvo demonstrator, 2002
1105	BB	Y814BOJ	Volvo B7L	Wrightbus Eclipse	N40F	2002	Volvo demonstrator, 2002
1107	YK	YJ60ADU	MAN 14.240	ADL Enviro 200	N37F	2010	York Pullman, 2012
1108	YK	YJ60ADV	MAN 14.240	ADL Enviro 200	N37F	2010	York Pullman, 2012
1129	KD	R529TWR	Volvo B10BLE	Wright Renown	NC47F	1998	

Passing through the village of Branham, Wrightbus Renown 1084, PO51MTX, illustrates the livery applied to the Harrogate-based services. The vehicle is operating the hourly 770 service from Harrogate to Leeds via Follifoot and Wetherby, which interworks with route 771. *Richard Godfrey*

1254	HG	V844FSG	Optare Solo M850	Optare	N28F	2000	EVE Coaches, Dunbar, 2004
1255	u	MX54KYF	Optare Solo M850	Optare	N27F	2004	Dearden, Darwen, 2006
1256	u	MX54KYE	Optare Solo M850	Optare	N27F	2004	Dearden, Darwen, 2006
1262	w	MX05EMK	Optare Solo M920	Optare	N29F	2005	Top-Line, York, 2008
1263	w	YJ56WUT	Optare Solo M880 SL	Optare	N27F	2007	Top-Line, York, 2008
1264	w	YJ56WUU	Optare Solo M880 SL	Optare	N27F	2007	Top-Line, York, 2008
1265	w	YJ56WUV	Optare Solo M880 SL	Optare	N27F	2007	Top-Line, York, 2008
1266	w	YJ56WUW	Optare Solo M880 SL	Optare	N27F	2007	Top-Line, York, 2008

1301-1308

Optare Tempo X1200 — Optare — N43F — 2010

1301	BB	YJ60KAA	1303	BB	YJ60KAK	1305	BB	YJ60KAU	1307	BB	YJ60KBE
1302	BB	YJ60KAE	1304	BB	YJ60KAO	1306	BB	YJ60KAX	1308	BB	YJ60KBF

1700-1705

Volvo B7RLE — Wrightbus Eclipse Urban — NC43F — 2003-04 — 1700, Volvo demonstrator

1700	HD	BU03SXK	1702	HD	YK04JYH	1704	HD	YK04JYL	1705	HD	YK04JYN
1701	HD	YK04JYG	1703	HD	YK04JYJ						

1800-1814

Volvo B7RLE — Wrightbus Eclipse Urban — NC44F — 2004-05

1800	HD	YK04JYP	1804	KD	YJ05FNT	1808	KD	YJ05KHF	1812	KD	YJ05KHL
1801	KD	YJ05FNP	1805	KD	YJ05KHC	1809	KD	YJ05KHG	1813	KD	YJ05KHM
1802	KD	YJ05FNR	1806	KD	YJ05KHD	1810	KD	YJ05KHH	1814	KD	YJ05KHO
1803	KD	YJ05FNS	1807	KD	YJ05KHE	1811	KD	YJ05KHK			

1815-1839

Volvo B7RLE — Wrightbus Eclipse Urban — NC44F — 2006-07

1815	BB	YJ56YDO	1822	BB	YJ07PBO	1828	BB	YJ07PCF	1834	BP	YJ07PCZ
1816	BB	YJ07OZU	1823	BB	YJ07PBU	1829	BB	YJ07PCO	1835	BB	YJ07PDK
1817	BP	YJ07OZV	1824	BB	YJ07PBV	1830	BB	YJ07PCU	1836	YK	YJ07PDO
1818	BB	YJ07OZW	1825	BB	YJ07PBX	1831	BB	YJ07PCV	1837	YK	YJ07PDU
1819	BB	YJ07OZX	1826	BB	YJ07PBY	1832	BB	YJ07PCX	1838	BP	YJ07PDV
1820	BB	YJ07PAO	1827	BB	YJ07PBZ	1833	BP	YJ07PCY	1839	YK	YJ07PDX
1821	BB	YJ07PBF									

1840	BB	BX07AZJ	Volvo B7RLE	Wrightbus Eclipse Urban	N45F	2007	Volvo demonstrator, 2007

Recent changes to the routes south of Blackburn have seen the Bolton service increase from hourly to every twenty minutes and renumbered 1, providing a frequent link between Egerton and Dunscar with Bolton centre. Seen on a short working to Darwen is 1878, BD12TEY, the last of seven Volvo B7RLEs added to the fleet in 2012. *Richard Godfrey*

1841-1850   Volvo B7RLE   Wrightbus Eclipse Urban   NC44F   2007-08

1841	BB	FJ57CZN	1844	KD	FJ08BZR	1847	KD	FJ08BZU
1842	BB	FJ57CZM	1845	KD	FJ08BZS	1848	KD	FJ08BZV
1843	KD	FJ08BZP	1846	KD	FJ08BZT			

1849	KD	FJ08BZW
1850	KD	FJ08BZX

1853-1871   Volvo B7RLE   Wrightbus Eclipse Urban 2   NC44F   2009

1853	BP	FJ58LSL	1858	BP	FJ58LSY	1863	BP	FJ58LSZ	1868	BP	FJ58LTN
1854	BP	FJ58LSN	1859	BP	FJ58LTK	1864	BP	FJ58LTE	1869	BP	FJ58LUA
1855	BP	FJ58LSO	1860	BP	FJ58LTA	1865	BP	FJ58LTT	1870	BP	FJ58LTX
1856	BP	FJ58LSU	1861	BP	FJ58LTF	1866	BP	FJ58LTU	1871	BP	FJ58LYV
1857	BP	FJ58LSV	1862	BP	FJ58LSX	1867	BP	FJ09KNV			

1872-1878   Volvo B7RLE   Wrightbus Eclipse Urban 2   NC44F   2012

1872	BB	BD12TDX	1874	BB	BD12TEJ	1876	BB	BD12TEU	1878	BB	BD12TEY
1873	BB	BD12TDZ	1875	BB	BD12TEO	1877	BB	BD12TEV			

2002	BP	L778SNO	Leyland Olympian ON2R50C13Z4	Alexander RH	B47/31F	1993	Top-Line, York, 2008
2003	BB	L779SNO	Leyland Olympian ON2R50C13Z4	Alexander RH	B47/31F	1993	Top-Line, York, 2008
2004	BP	R95LHK	Volvo Olympian	Alexander RH	B47/27F	1997	York Pullman, 2012
2005	HD	J113KCW	Leyland Olympian ON2R50C13Z4	Leyland	B47/31F	1992	York Pullman, 2012
2006	BB	M208VSX	Volvo Olympian	Alexander RH	B51/34F	1995	Thamesdown, 2012
2007	BB	M209VSX	Volvo Olympian	Alexander RH	B51/34F	1995	Thamesdown, 2012
2173	BB	C173ECK	Leyland Olympian ONLXB/1R	Eastern Coach Works	B42/28F	1985	Stagecoach NW, 2001

2701-2716   Volvo B7TL   Plaxton President   BC43/28F   2001

2701	KD	Y701HRN	2705	BB	Y705HRN	2709	HD	Y709HRN	2714	KD	Y714HRN
2702	BB	Y702HRN	2706	HD	B7BDV	2711	KD	Y711HRN	2715	KD	Y715HRN
2703	KD	Y703HRN	2707	YK	Y707HRN	2712	KD	Y712HRN	2716	YK	Y716HRN
2704	KD	Y704HRN	2708	HD	Y708HRN	2713	KD	Y713HRN			

2750-2764   Volvo B7TL   Wrightbus Eclipse Gemini   BC39/28F   2005

2750	BP	PJ05ZVW	2754	BP	PJ05ZWA	2758	BP	PJ05ZWE	2762	BP	PJ05ZWK
2751	BP	PJ05ZVX	2755	BP	PJ05ZWB	2759	BP	PJ05ZWF	2763	BP	PJ05ZWL
2752	BP	PJ05ZVY	2756	BP	PJ05ZWC	2760	BP	PJ05ZWG	2764	BP	PO55PYL
2753	BP	PJ05ZVZ	2757	BP	PJ05ZWD	2761	BP	PJ05ZWH			

Carrying 'The Witch Way' livery is 2761, PJ05ZWH, one of fifteen Volvo B7TLs that feature leather seating in their Wrightbus bodywork. It is seen in Reedley while heading for Manchester. *Richard Godfrey*

3601-3612

		Volvo B7TL			Wrightbus Eclipse Gemini		NC33/28F	2003-04	
3601	HD	X1VTD	3604	HD	X4VTD	3607	HD	X7VTD	3610	HD	X10VTD
3602	HD	X2VTD	3605	HD	X5VTD	3608	HD	X8VTD	3611	HD	X11VTD
3603	HD	X3VTD	3606	HD	X6VTD	3609	HD	X9VTD	3612	HD	X12VTD

3613	HD	BF62UXZ	Volvo B9TL	Wrightbus Eclipse Gemini 2	N33/28F	2013	
3614	HD	X14VTD	Volvo B7TL	Wrightbus Eclipse Gemini	BC39/28F	2005	
4008	YK	E308MSG	Leyland Olympian ONCL10/2RZ	Alexander RH	PO47/28F	1988	Top-Line, York, 2008
4009	YK	T407SMV	Dennis Trident	East Lancs	PO45/28F	1999	Top-Line, York, 2008
4010	YK	T408SMV	Dennis Trident	East Lancs	PO45/28F	1999	Top-Line, York, 2008
4011	YK	T409SMV	Dennis Trident	East Lancs	PO45/25F	1999	Top-Line, York, 2008

4012-4018

		Leyland Olympian ON2R50C13Z4	Alexander RH		O47/28F*	1988-92	York Pullman, 2012	
4012	YK	E307MSG	4014	YK	E314MSG	4016	YK	G336CSG	4018	YK	K875CSF
4013	YK	E313MSG	4015	w	F356WSC	4017	YK	G337CSG	*seating varies

4019	w	MTU118Y	Leyland Olympian ONLXB/1R	Eastern Coach Works	PO45/32F	1983	York Pullman, 2012

Ancillary vehicles:

T042	KD	V542JBH	Dennis Dart SLF 10.1m	Plaxton Pointer 2	N14D	1999	Mitcham Belle, 2001
T543	MA	V543JBH	Dennis Dart SLF 10.1m	Plaxton Pointer 2	N13D	1999	Mitcham Belle, 2001
T550	BB	V550JBH	Dennis Dart SLF 10.1m	Plaxton Pointer 2	N13D	1999	Mitcham Belle, 2001
T845	HD	V545JBH	Dennis Dart SLF 10.1m	Plaxton Pointer 2	N27F	1999	Mitcham Belle, 2001

Previous registrations:

B7BDV	Y706HRN		
H142GGS	H142GGS, H12SDW	X6VTD	YC53MXO
L778SNO	93D10171	X7VTD	YC53MXT
L779SNO	93D10172	X8VTD	YC53MXU
R95LHK	97D373	X9VTD	YC53MXV
X1VTD	YJ53CZY		
X2VTD	YC53MXN	X10VTD	YC53MXY
X3VTD	YC53MXM	X11VTD	YC53MXX
X4VTD	YC53MXP	X12VTD	YC53MXW
X5VTD	YC53MXR	X14VTD	PO55PYP
		V844FSG	V5EVE

London Sovereign

London Sovereign Ltd, Approach Road, Edgware, HA8 7AN

DE50-56 — ADL Dart 4 10.2m — ADL Enviro 200 — N29D — 2008-09

50	SO	YX59BYA	52	SO	YX59BYC	54	SO	YX59BYF	56	SO	YX59BYH
51	SO	YX59BYB	53	SO	YX59BYD	55	SO	YX59BYG			

DE57-99 — ADL Dart 4 10.2m — ADL Enviro 200 — N29D — 2011

57	BT	YX11GBE	68	SO	YX11GCV	79	SO	YX11FZF	90	SO	YX11FZS
58	BT	YX11GBF	69	SO	YX11GCY	80	SO	YX11FZG	91	SO	YX11FZT
59	BT	YX11GBO	70	SO	YX11GCZ	81	SO	YX11FZH	92	SO	YX11FZU
60	BT	YX11GBU	71	SO	YX11GDA	82	SO	YX11FZJ	93	SO	YX11FZV
61	BT	YX11GBV	72	SO	YX11GDE	83	SO	YX11FZK	94	SO	YX11FZW
62	BT	YX11GBY	73	SO	YX11GDF	84	SO	YX11FZL	95	SO	YX11FZY
63	BT	YX11GBZ	74	SO	YX11FZA	85	SO	YX11FZM	96	SO	YX11FZZ
64	BT	YX11GCF	75	SO	YX11FXB	86	SO	YX11FZN	97	SO	YX11COH
65	BT	YX11GCK	76	SO	YX11FZD	87	SO	YX11FZO	98	SO	YX11COJ
66	BT	YX11GCO	77	SO	YX11FZD	88	SO	YX11FZP	99	SO	YX11CNJ
67	BT	YX11GCU	78	SO	YX11FZE	89	SO	YX11FZR			

DPS599 SO SN51TBX — Dennis Dart SLF 10.1m — Alexander ALX200 — N30D — 2001

DPS627-640 — TransBus Dart 10.1m — TransBus Pointer — N27F* — 2002 — *seating varies

627	SO	SK02XGW	632	SO	SK02XHG	635	SO	SK02XHL	638	SO	SK02XHO
628	SO	SK02XGX	633	SO	SK02XHH	636	SO	SK02XHM	639	SO	SK02XHP
629	SO	SK02XHD	634	SO	SK02XHJ	637	SO	SK02XHN	640	SO	SK02XHR
630	SO	SK02XHE									

SDE18-24 — ADL Dart 4 8.9m — ADL Enviro 200 — N26F — 2010

18	BT	YX60BZA	20	BT	YX60BZC	22	BT	YX60BZE	24	BT	YX60BZG
19	BT	YX60BZB	21	BT	YX60BZD	23	BT	YX60BZF			

SLE1-6 — Scania N94UD 10.8m — East Lancs OmniDekka — N49/27D — 2004

1	BT	YN54OAA	3	BT	YN54OAC	5	BT	YN54OAG	6	BT	YN54OAH
2	BT	YN54OAB	4	BT	YN54OAE						

SLE21-42 — Scania N94UD 10.8m — East Lancs OmniDekka — N45/27D — 2005

21	BT	YN55NHT	27	BT	YN55NJE	33	BT	YN55NKA	38	BT	YN55NKG
22	BT	YN55NHU	28	BT	YN55NJF	34	BT	YN55NKC	39	BT	YN55NKH
23	BT	YN55NHV	29	BT	YN55NJJ	35	BT	YN55NKD	40	BT	YN55NKJ
24	BT	YN55NHX	30	BT	YN55NJK	36	BT	YN55NKE	41	BT	YN55NKK
25	BT	YN55NHY	31	BT	YN55NJU	37	BT	YN55NKF	42	BT	YN55NKL
26	BT	YN55NHZ	32	BT	YN55NJV						

SP68-87 — Scania OmniCity CN230 UD — Scania — N41/22D — 2009

68	BT	YT59RXR	73	BT	YT59RXX	78	BT	YT59RYC	83	BT	YT59RYJ
69	BT	YT59RXS	74	BT	YT59RXY	79	BT	YT59RYD	84	BT	YT59RYK
70	BT	YT59RXU	75	BT	YT59RXZ	80	BT	YT59RYF	85	BT	YT59RYM
71	BT	YT59RXV	76	BT	YT59RYA	81	BT	YT59RYG	86	BT	YT59RYN
72	BT	YT59RXW	77	BT	YT59RYB	82	BT	YT59RYH	87	BT	YT59RYO

VA7 BT N137YRW — Volvo Olympian — Alexander RH — B47/25D — 1997

VH1-23 — Volvo B5LH — Wrightbus Gemini 2 — N--/--D — On order

1	BT	BD13OHU	7	BT	BD13OJA	13	BT	BT13YWL	19	BT	BT13YWR
2	BT	BD13OHV	8	BT	BD13OJB	14	BT	BT13YWN	20	BT	BT13YWS
3	BT	BD13OHW	9	BT	BD13OJC	15	BT	BT13YWJ	21	BT	BT13YWW
4	BT	BD13OHX	10	BT	BD13OJE	16	BT	BT13YWM	22	BT	BT13YWU
5	BT	BD13OHY	11	BT	BD13OHJ	17	BT	BT13YWP	23	BT	BT13YWV
6	BT	BD13OHZ	12	BT	BT13YWK	18	BT	BT13YWO			

VPL220 BT N137YRW — Volvo B7TL — Plaxton President — N43/24D — 2001 — Metroline, Harrow, 2012

Transdev acquired both London Sovereign and London United in 2002 but in 2010 London United was transferred to the RATP Group leaving Transdev with just two depots in London. All of Sovereign's double-decks are allocated to Edgware depot. TransBus President-bodied Volvo B7TL VLP26, PJ53OVA, illustrates the type while loading at Elstree & Borehamwood station. *Richard Godfrey*

VLE27-39

						Volvo B7TL 11m			East Lancs Myllennium Vyking			N47/22D	2004	
27	BT	PA04CYK	31	BT	PA04CYT	34	BT	PO54ACJ	37	BT	PO54ACX			
28	BT	PA04CYL	32	BT	PO54ABZ	35	BT	PO54ACU	38	BT	PO54ACY			
29	BT	PA04CYP	33	BT	PO54ACF	36	BT	PO54ACV	39	BT	PO54ACZ			
30	BT	PA04CYS												

VLP18-27

						Volvo B7TL 10.6m			TransBus President 4.4m			N45/23D	2003	
18	BT	PJ53OUN	21	BT	PJ53OUU	24	BT	PJ53OUX	26	BT	PJ53OVA			
19	BT	PJ53OUO	22	BT	PJ53OUV	25	BT	PJ53OUY	27	BT	PJ53OVB			
20	BT	PJ53OUP	23	BT	PJ53OUW									

Depots and allocations:

Blackburn (Intack) - Transdev Lancashire United - BB

Dart	703	704	705	706	707			
Optare Versa	271	272	274					
Volvo B10BLE	206	207	211	212	574	1014	1047	1051
	1068	1088	1089	1096	1097	1098	1099	1100
	1101	1102	1103					
Volvo B7L	1104	1105						
Volvo B7RLE	1815	1816	1818	1819	1820	1821	1822	1823
	1824	1825	1826	1827	1828	1829	1830	1831
	1832	1835	1840	1841	1842	1872	1873	1874
	1875	1876	1877	1878				
Optare Tempo	1301	1302	1303	1304	1305	1306	1307	1308
Olympian	13	14	15	16	17	18	162	983
	984	2003	2007	2173				
Volvo B7TL	401	402	403	404	405	406	407	408
	439	440	2702	2705				

Burnley (Queensgate) - Transdev Burnley & Pendle - BP

Dart	708	715	720					
Optare Versa	254	255	256	257	259	260	261	262
	264	266	267	268	269	285	286	
Volvo B10BLE	1042	1043	1046	1053	1058	1062	1066	1067
	1069	1071	1072	1073	1074			
Volvo B7RLE	1817	1833	1834	1838	1853	1854	1855	1856
	1857	1858	1859	1860	1861	1862	1863	1864
	1865	1866	1867	1868	1869	1870	1871	
Olympian	11	116	964	986	2002	2004	2006	
Volvo B7TL	2750	2751	2752	2753	2754	2755	2756	2757
	2758	2759	2760	2761	2762	2763	2764	

Edgware (Station Road) - BT

Enviro 200	SDE18	SDE19	SDE20	SDE21	SDE22	SDE23	SDE24	DE57
	DE58	DE59	DE60	DE61	DE62	DE63	DE64	DE65
	DE66	DE67						
Olympian	VA7							
Scania N94 UD	SLE1	SLE2	SLE3	SLE4	SLE5	SLE6	SLE21	SLE22
	SLE23	SLE24	SLE25	SLE26	SLE27	SLE28	SLE29	SLE30
	SLE31	SLE32	SLE33	SLE34	SLE35	SLE36	SLE37	SLE38
	SLE39	SLE40	SLE41	SLE42				
Scania OmniCity dd	SP68	SP69	SP70	SP71				
	SP72	SP73	SP74	SP75	SP76	SP77	SP78	SP79
	SP80	SP81	SP82	SP83	SP84	SP85	SP86	SP87
Volvo B7TL	VLE27	VLE28	VLE29	VLE30	VLE31	VLE32	VLE33	VLE34
	VLE35	VLE36	VLE37	VLE38	VLE39	VPL18	VPL19	VPL20
	VPL21	VPL22	VPL23	VPL24	VPL25	VPL26	VPL27	VPL220
Volvo B5LH	VH1	VH2	VH3	VH4	VH5	VH6	VH7	VH8
	VH9	VH10	VH11	VH12	VH13	VH14	VH15	VH16
	VH17	VH18	VH19	VH20	VH21	VH22	VH23	

Harrogate (Broughton Way, Starbeck) - Transdev Harrogate & District - HD

Optare Solo	1254							
Optare Versa	277	278	279	280	281	282	283	284
Javelin	140	150	155	157	165	940	942	947
	948	949	962					
Volvo B10M	302							
Volvo B10B	504	509						
Volvo B10BLE	204	210	305	306	307	308	309	1084
	1085	1086	1087	1090	1091	1092	1093	
Volvo B7RLE	1700	1701	1702	1703	1704	1705	1800	
Olympian	12	125	2005					
Volvo B7TL	2706	2707	2708	2709	3601	3602	3603	3604	3605
	3606	3607	3608	3609	3610	3611	3612	3614
Volvo B9TL	3613							

Harrow (Pinner Road) - London Sovereign - SO

Dart	DPS599	DPS627	DPS628	DPS629	DPS630	DPS631	DPS632	DPS633
	DPS634	DPS635	DPS636	DPS637	DPS638	DPS639	DPS640	
Enviro 200	DE50	DE51	DE52	DE53	DE54	DE55	DE56	DE68
	DE69	DE70	DE71	DE72	DE73	DE74	DE75	DE76
	DE77	DE78	DE79	DE80	DE81	DE82	DE83	DE84
	DE85	DE86	DE87	DE88	DE89	DE90	DE91	DE92
	DE93	DE95	DE96	DE97	DE98	DE99		

Keighley (Suresnes Road) - Transdev Keighley & District - KD

Outstaion: Woodhouse Road, Keighley

Dart	710	711	712	713	714	716	717	718
Volvo B10BLE	201	208	209	530	531	540	541	542
	543	544	557	561	562	1001	1002	1003
	1004	1039	1041	1044	1048	1049	1052	1061
	1063	1065	1076	1077	1078	1079	1080	1081
	1082	1083	1094	1095	1129			
BMC Condor	101	102	103	104	105	106	108	109
	110	111	112	113	114	115	117	118
	127	128	129					
Volvo B7RLE	450	451	452	453	454	455	1801	1802
	1803	1804	1805	1806	1807	1808	1809	1810
	1811	1812	1813	1814	1843	1844	1845	1846
	1847	1848	1849	1850				
Olympian	963	971	972	973	974	975	976	977
	978	987	988	989				
Volvo B7TL	438	2701	2703	2704	2711	2712	2713	2714
	2715							

Malton (Railway Street) - Yorkshire Coastliner - MA

Volvo B9TL	411	412	413	414	415	416	417	418
	419	420	421	422	423	424	425	426
	427	428	429					

York (Fulford Industrial Estate) - Transdev York - YK

Dart	719							
Optare Versa	251	273	275	276				
MAN 14.220	1107	1108						
Volvo B10BLE	1012	1013	1015	1016	1054	1057	1059	1064
Volvo B7RLE	1836	1837	1839					
Olympian	4008	4012	4013	4016	4017	4018		
Trident	4009	4010	4011					
Volvo B7TL	409	410	2707	2716	2717	2718		

Stored, Unallocated - u/w -

Remainder

East Lancs-bodied Scania SLE32, YN55NHV, operates route13 in Park Street in May 2013. The Scania OmniDekka was introduced in 2003 and was initially based on Scania N94UD chassis. More recently sales have moved to Scania's own double-deck version of the OmniCity; class SP with London Sovereign.
Richard Godfrey

WELLGLADE

Trent Barton - Midland General - Kinchbus - Notts & Derby - TM Travel

Kinchbus Ltd; Notts & Derby Traction Co. Ltd; The Midland General Omnibus Co Ltd;
Barton Buses Ltd; Trent Motor Traction Co. Ltd, Mansfield Road, Heanor, DE75 7BG

1-7			Optare Solo M950 SL			Optare		N26F	2007		
1	LB	YJ07EFR	3	LB	YJ07EFT	5	LB	YJ07EFV	7	LB	YJ07EFX
2	LB	YJ07EFS	4	LB	YJ07EFU	6	LB	YJ07EFW			

10-14			Leyland Olympian ON2R56C13Z4			Alexander RH		B51/30D	1991-93		Lothian Buses, 2008-09
10	ND	J864TSC	12	ND	J871TSC	13	ND	K883CSF	14	ND	K894CSF
11	ND	J865TSC									

15	ND	M212VSX	Volvo Olympian			Alexander RH		B51/30D	1995		Lothian Buses, 2010
16	ND	M214VSX	Volvo Olympian			Alexander RH		B51/30D	1995		Lothian Buses, 2010
18	HW	C718LTO	Leyland Olympian ONLXB/1RV			Eastern Coach Works		B45/30F	1985		
20	ND	C720NNN	Leyland Olympian ONLXB/1RV			Eastern Coach Works		B45/30F	1985		

22-28			Volvo Olympian			Alexander Royale		B51/30D	1996-97		Lothian Buses, 2009
22	ND	N404GSX	25	ND	P410KSX	27	ND	P267PSX	28	ND	P256PSX
23	ND	N407GSX	26	ND	P260PSX						

29-32			Volvo B7TL			Plaxton President		N41/19D	2000		London United, 2011
29	ND	W467BCW	30	ND	W474BCW	31	ND	W475BCW	32	ND	W477BCW

33-39			Volvo B7TL			Plaxton President		N45/30F	2000		Lothian Buses, 2012
33	ND	W291PFS	35	ND	W293PFS	37	ND	W295PFS	39	ND	X683RDA
34	ND	W292PFS	36	ND	W294PFS	38	ND	W296PFS			

55	ND	R812NUD	Volvo B10M-62			Plaxton Expressliner 2		BC53F	1988		Oxford Citybus, 2012
56	ND	R813NUD	Volvo B10M-62			Plaxton Expressliner 2		BC53F	1988		Oxford Citybus, 2012

So far the only batch of Optare Tempo SRs in service are thirteen built for Wellglade and allocated to Nottingham. Illustrating the styling is 327, YJ12GWF, lettered for route i4. *Dave Heath*

Several of the once large batch of Volvo B10Bs have now left the fleet while others are in store. Pictured in London Road, Derby, is Notts & Derby liveried 132, M132PRA. The Paladin bodywork was principally built in Wigan. *Mark Lyons*

57-63

Volvo B10M-60 — Plaxton Première Interurban — C51F — 1997

No		Reg	No		Reg	No		Reg	No		Reg
57	N	YRC180	59	ND	R59RAU	61	w	R61RAU	63	ND	R63RAU
58	N	YRC181	60	w	R960RAU	62	D	YRC182			

64-71

Scania K94 IB4 — Irizar InterCentury 12.32 — C49F — 2004

No		Reg	No		Reg	No		Reg	No		Reg
64	D	FN04BRX	66	D	FN04BSU	68	D	FN04BSX	70	D	FN04BSZ
65	D	FN04BRZ	67	D	FN04BSV	69	D	FN04BSY	71	D	FN04BTE

72-76

Scania K320 IB4 — Irizar i4 — C47F — 2010

No		Reg	No		Reg	No		Reg	No		Reg
72	D	FJ10OXM	74	D	FJ10OXP	75	D	FJ10OXR	76	D	FJ10OXS
73	D	FJ10OXN									

105-127

Volvo B10B — Northern Counties Paladin — B49F — 1993-94

No		Reg	No		Reg	No		Reg	No		Reg
105	w	L105LRA	110	ND	L110LRA	116	A	L116LRA	123	ND	L123LRA
106	w	L106LRA	112	ND	L112LRA	117	w	L117LRA	126	ND	L126LRA
107	ND	L107LRA	113	DH	L113LRA	121	ND	L121LRA	127	ND	L127LRA
109	ND	L109LRA	114	ND	L114LRA	122	ND	L122LRA			

129-138

Volvo B10B — Northern Counties Paladin — B49F — 1994

No		Reg	No		Reg	No		Reg	No		Reg
129	ND	M129PRA	133	ND	M133PRA	136	ND	M136PRA	138	ND	M138PRA
132	ND	M132PRA	135	ND	M135PRA	137	ND	M137PRA			

201-222

Optare Excel L1150 — Optare — N45F — 2000

No		Reg	No		Reg	No		Reg	No		Reg
201	w	V201ENU	215	w	W215PRB	221	ND	W221PRB	222	ND	W302PRB

230-266

Optare Excel L1150 — Optare — N45F — 2000-01

No		Reg	No		Reg	No		Reg	No		Reg
230	ND	X998WRA	246	w	X236WRA	258	ND	Y258DRC	264	D	Y264DRC
234	LB	X234WRA	255	A	Y271DRC	259	ND	Y259DRC	265	D	Y265DRC
236	ND	X236WRA	256	w	Y256DRC	261	A	Y261DRC	266	D	Y266DRC
245	w	X236WRA	257	LM	Y257DRC	263	A	Y263DRC			

301-306

Optare Tempo X1200 — Optare — N42F — 2005

No		Reg	No		Reg	No		Reg	No		Reg
301	N	FD54JXZ	303	N	FD54JYB	305	N	FD54JYE	306	N	FD54JYF
302	N	FD54JYA	304	N	FD54JYC						

Black cats are associated with good luck and here our photographer was fortunate to picture Optare Temp 312, YJ07VSG, as it passes through Sutton in Ashfield while heading for Derby. Wellglade takes route lettering further than most operators by using a variety of liveries that are route specific.
Richard Godfrey

307-322			Optare Tempo X1200			Optare			N42F	2007	
307	D	YJ07VSA	311	LM	YJ07VSF	315	N	YJ07VSM	319	LB	YJ07VST
308	D	YJ07VSC	312	LM	YJ07VSG	316	N	YJ07VSN	320	LB	YJ07VSV
309	LM	YJ07VSD	313	N	YJ07VSK	317	LM	YJ07VSO	321	LB	YJ07VSX
310	LM	YJ07VSE	314	N	YJ07VSL	318	LM	YJ07VSP	322	LB	YJ07VSY

323-335			Optare Tempo X1200 SR			Optare			N41F	2012	
323	N	YJ07GWA	327	N	YJ07GWF	330	N	YJ07GWL	333	N	YJ07GWO
324	N	YJ07GWC	328	N	YJ07GWG	331	N	YJ07GWM	334	N	YJ07GWP
325	N	YJ07GWD	329	N	YJ07GWK	332	N	YJ07GWN	335	N	YJ07GWU
326	N	YJ07GWE									

401-431			Optare Solo M920			Optare			N34F	2000	
401	HW	V401JTO	412	LM	W412YAL	418	HW	W418YAL	425	HW	W425RTO
402	HW	V402JTO	413	D	W413YAL	420	LB	W471RTO	427	LM	X627ERB
403	ND	V403JTO	414	N	W414YAL	421	HW	W421RTO	428	A	X628ERB
404	u	V404JTO	415	HW	W415YAL	422	HW	W422RTO	429	A	X629ERB
405	A	V405JTO	416	D	W416YAL	423	HW	W423RTO	430	A	X612ERB
411	HW	W411YAL	417	A	W417YAL	424	HW	W424RTO	431	HW	X631ERB

432-466			Optare Solo M920			Optare			N33F	2002	
432	LM	FP51GXR	441	D	FP51GXV	450	LM	FE02KDX	459	LB	FE02KFG
433	LM	FP51GXS	442	N	FE02KCZ	451	LB	FE02KDZ	460	HW	FE02KFJ
434	LM	FP51GXT	443	HW	FE02KDF	452	LB	FE02KEJ	461	HW	FE02KFK
435	LM	FP51GXU	444	HW	FE02KDJ	453	ND	A20UOD	462	u	FE02KFL
436	LM	FP51GYE	445	HW	FE02KDK	454	ND	A12UOD	463	HW	FG02BGE
437	HW	FP51GXW	446	N	FE02KDN	455	HW	FE02KFA	464	HW	FG02BGF
438	N	FP51GXX	447	A	FE02KDO	456	ND	A18UOD	465	LB	FG02BGK
439	N	FP51GXY	448	D	FE02KDU	457	LM	FE02KFD	466	D	FG02BGO
440	u	FP51GXZ	449	A	FE02KDV	458	LB	FE02KFF			

467-490			Optare Solo M950			Optare			NC33F	2009-10	
467	A	FJ09MVR	473	A	FJ09MVX	479	A	FJ09MWE	485	N	FJ10EHG
468	A	FJ09MVS	474	A	FJ09MVY	480	D	FJ09MWF	486	N	FJ10EHH
469	A	FJ09MVT	475	A	FJ09MVZ	481	D	FJ09MWG	487	N	FJ10EHK
470	A	FJ09MVU	476	A	FJ09MWA	482	D	FJ09MWK	488	N	FJ10EHL
471	A	FJ09MVV	477	A	FJ09MWC	483	D	FJ09MWL	489	N	FJ10EHM
472	A	FJ09MVW	478	A	FJ09MWD	484	D	FJ10EHF	490	N	FJ10EHN

Wellglade was founded in 1989 to take over the services of Trent in the privatisation of the National Bus Company fleets. Since then the area of operation has expanded with the acquisition of TM Travel. Carrying *mango* livery at Matlock is Optare Solo 448, FE02KDU. *Tony Wilson*

491-500

						Optare Solo M950			Optare				NC33F	2011-12	
491	A	YJ11EKT	494	D	YJ12NBB	497	D	YJ12NBF	499	N	YJ12NAD
492	D	YJ11EKU	495	D	YJ12NBD	498	N	YJ12NAE	500	D	YJ12NAU
493	D	YJ12NBA	496	D	YJ12NBE						

598	D	YN03WRA	Scania L94 UB	Wrightbus Solar	N44F	2003	Felix, Stanley, 2013
599	D	YN04AGY	Scania L94 UB	Wrightbus Solar	N44F	2004	Felix, Stanley, 2013
600	D	YN05GZB	Scania L94 UB	Wrightbus Solar	N44F	2005	Felix, Stanley, 2013

601-635

Scania L94UB   WrightBus Solar   N44F   2003

601	LM	FJ03VVM	610	A	FJ03VVY	619	D	FJ03VWH	628	LB	FJ03VWU
602	LM	FJ03VVN	611	A	FJ03VVZ	620	N	FJ03VWK	629	LB	FJ03VWV
603	LM	FJ03VVP	612	A	FJ03VWA	621	N	FJ03VWL	630	LB	FJ03VWW
604	LM	FJ03VVR	613	D	FJ03VWB	622	N	FJ03VWR	631	D	FJ03VWY
605	N	FJ03VVS	614	D	FJ03VWC	623	LB	FJ03VWN	632	LM	FJ03VWX
606	N	FJ03VVT	615	D	FJ03VWD	624	D	FJ03VWP	633	LM	FJ03VXA
607	N	FJ03VVU	616	D	FJ03VWE	625	LB	FJ03VWM	634	N	FJ03VXB
608	N	FJ03VVW	617	D	FJ03VWF	626	LB	FJ03VWS	635	N	FJ03VXC
609	A	FJ03VVX	618	LB	FJ03VWG	627	LB	FJ03VWT			

636-667

Scania L94UB   WrightBus Solar   N44F   2004-05

636	N	FD53WWH	651	LM	FN04HSU	657	LM	FN04HSG	663	N	FN54AEB
637	N	FD53WWJ	652	LM	FN04HSD	658	LM	FN54AEV	664	LM	FN54AEC
638	LB	FD53WWK	653	LM	FN04HSZ	659	LM	FN54AEW	665	LM	FH54VRX
639	LB	FD53WWL	654	LM	FN04HTA	660	LM	FN54AEX	666	N	FH54VRY
649	LM	FN04HTV	655	LM	FN04HSE	661	LM	FN54AEY	667	LM	FH54VRZ
650	LM	FN04HSY	656	LM	FN04HSF	662	N	FN54AEZ			

668-692

Scania L94UB   WrightBus Solar   N44F   2006

668	N	FH05TKJ	675	D	FJ55AAU	681	A	FJ55ABK	687	D	FJ55BZO
668	N	FH05TKK	676	N	FJ55AAV	682	LM	FJ55ABN	688	D	FJ55BZP
670	D	FJ55AAE	677	A	FJ55AAX	683	D	FJ55ABO	689	D	FJ55BZR
671	A	FJ55AAF	678	N	FJ55AAY	684	D	FJ55ABV	690	D	FJ55BZS
672	A	FJ55AAK	679	LM	FJ55AAZ	685	D	FJ55BZM	691	D	FJ55BZT
673	LM	FJ55AAN	680	N	FJ55ABF	686	D	FJ55BZN	692	D	FJ55BZU
674	LM	FJ55AAO									

Recent orders from Optare saw thirty-nine Versa buses arrive during 2011-12. These are shared between Derby, Langley Mill and Sutton-in-Ashfield, where 821, YJ12PKD, is pictured carrying the colours of *the threes*, a route which links Mansfield with Nottingham. *Richard Godfrey*

693-698

Mercedes-Benz Citaro O530LE — Mercedes-Benz — N40F — 2009

693	A	BN09FXL	695	A	BN09FWW	697	A	BN09FWY	698	A	BN09FWZ
694	A	BN09FWV	696	A	BN09FWX						

No.	Op	Reg	No.	Op	Reg	No.	Op	Reg	No.	Op	Reg
693	A	BN09FXL	695	A	BN09FWW	697	A	BN09FWY	698	A	BN09FWZ
694	A	BN09FWV	696	A	BN09FWX						

701-727

Volvo B7RLE — Wightbus Eclipse Urban — N44F — 2008

No.	Op	Reg	No.	Op	Reg	No.	Op	Reg	No.	Op	Reg
701	N	FJ58KJK	708	N	FJ58KJZ	715	N	FJ58KKG	722	N	FJ58KKR
702	N	FJ58KJN	709	N	FJ58KKA	716	N	FJ58KKH	723	N	FJ58KKS
703	N	FJ58KJO	710	N	FJ58KKB	717	N	FJ58KKL	724	N	FJ58KKT
704	N	FJ58KJO	711	N	FJ58KKC	718	N	FJ58KKM	725	N	FJ58KKU
705	N	FJ58KJV	712	N	FJ58KKD	719	N	FJ58KKN	726	D	FJ08WHR
706	N	FJ58KJX	713	N	FJ58KKE	720	N	FJ58KKO	727	D	FJ08WHS
707	N	FJ58KJY	714	N	FJ58KKF	721	N	FJ58KKP			

728-751

Volvo B7RLE — Wightbus Eclipse Urban — N44F — 2009

No.	Op	Reg	No.	Op	Reg	No.	Op	Reg	No.	Op	Reg
728	D	FJ09BXG	734	D	FJ09BXO	740	LM	FJ09BXE	746	LM	FJ09XPE
729	D	FJ09BXH	735	D	FJ09BXP	741	D	FJ09BXF	747	LM	FJ09XPF
730	D	FJ09BXK	736	D	FJ09BXA	742	LM	FJ09XPA	748	LM	FJ09XPG
731	D	FJ09BXL	737	D	FJ09BXB	743	LM	FJ09XPB	749	LM	FJ09XPH
732	D	FJ09BXM	738	D	FJ09BXC	744	LM	FJ09XPC	750	LM	FJ09XPK
733	D	FJ09BXN	739	LM	FJ09BXD	745	LM	FJ09XPD	751	D	FJ09XPL

761-767

Volvo B7RLE — Plaxton Centro — N39F — 2008-10

No.	Op	Reg	No.	Op	Reg	No.	Op	Reg	No.	Op	Reg
761	LB	YN08CWT	763	LB	YN08CWV	765	LB	YN08CWX	767	LB	FL10NFV
762	LB	YN08CWU	764	LB	YN08CWW	766	LB	YN08CWY			

801-827

Optare Versa V1110 — Optare — N37F — 2011-12

No.	Op	Reg	No.	Op	Reg	No.	Op	Reg	No.	Op	Reg
801	LM	YJ11ENC	808	D	YJ11ENN	815	A	YJ12PJO	822	A	YJ12PKE
802	LM	YJ11ENE	809	D	YJ11ENO	816	A	YJ12PJU	823	A	YJ12PKF
803	LM	YJ11ENF	810	A	YJ12PHU	817	A	YJ12PJV	824	A	YJ12PKK
804	LM	YJ11ENH	811	A	YJ12PHV	818	A	YJ12PJX	825	A	YJ12PKN
805	LM	YJ11ENK	812	A	YJ12PHX	819	A	YJ12PJY	826	A	YJ12PKO
806	D	YJ11ENL	813	A	YJ12PHY	820	A	YJ12PKA	827	A	YJ12PKU
807	D	YJ11ENM	814	A	YJ12PHZ	821	A	YJ12PKD			

No.	Op	Reg	Chassis	Body	Seating	Year	
910	ND	P910CTO	Dennis Dart SLF	Plaxton Pointer	N39F	1996	
937	ND	S937UAL	Dennis Dart SLF	Plaxton Pointer 2	N41F*	1998	
950	ND	FP04CFE	TransBus Dart	TransBus Mini Pointer	N29F	2004	*Operated for Derby NHS Trust*

996-999

Optare Solo M950 Hybrid, Optare, N33F, 2012

996	N	YJ12GVD	997	N	YJ12GVE	998	N	YJ12GVF	999	N	YJ12GVG

1001-1008

Fiat Ducato, Rohill Harrier, N16F, 2001-04, *Derby Community Transport*

1001	ND	Y968LRC	1004	ND	Y961LRC	1006	ND	Y953LRC	1008	ND	BU04WFL
1002	ND	Y967LRC	1005	ND	Y954LRC	1007	ND	HF53BWC			

1010-1022

Mercedes-Benz Sprinter, Mercedes-Benz, N16F, 2001-10, *Derby Community Transport*

1010	ND	KX08HLV	1014	ND	KX59CYA	1017	ND	WX05WWT	1020	ND	WA51EDV
1011	ND	KX08HLW	1015	ND	KX59CYC	1018	ND	CE02HDY	1021	ND	CN51BKG
1012	ND	KX08HLY	1016	ND	GK51NGN	1019	ND	WJ02KNR	1022	ND	CA51FSD
1013	ND	KX08HLZ									

1102	HW	D188FYM	Leyland Olympian ONLXB/1RH	Eastern Coach Works	B42/26D	1986	Arriva London, 2010
1105	HW	G370YUR	Leyland Olympian ONCL10/1RZ	Alexander AL	B47/30F	1990	Thompson, Parkgate, 2004
1108	u	G532VBB	Leyland Olympian ON2R50C13Z4	Northern Counties	B47/27D	1990	Arriva London, 2005
1109	HW	G535VBB	Leyland Olympian ON2R50C13Z4	Northern Counties	B47/27D	1990	Arriva London, 2005
1111	HW	H784PVW	Leyland Olympian ON2R50C13Z4	Alexander AL	B47/31F	1991	Dublin Bus, 2008
1112	HW	J619CEV	Leyland Olympian ON2R50C13Z4	Alexander RH	B47/31F	1992	Dublin Bus, 2006
1113	HW	J628CEV	Leyland Olympian ON2R50C13Z4	Alexander RH	B47/31F	1992	Dublin Bus, 2006
1114	HW	J844TSC	Leyland Olympian ON2R56C13Z4	Alexander RH	B51/34F	1991	Lothian Buses, 2008
1115	HW	J850TSC	Leyland Olympian ON2R56C13Z4	Alexander RH	B51/34F	1991	Lothian Buses, 2008
1116	HW	J854TSC	Leyland Olympian ON2R56C13Z4	Alexander RH	B51/34F	1991	Lothian Buses, 2008
1117	HW	J353BSH	Leyland Olympian ON2R56C13Z4	Alexander RH	B51/34F	1991	Lothian Buses, 2010
1118	HW	K482GNN	Leyland Olympian ON2R56C14Z5	East Lancs	B49/35F	1992	City of Nottingham, 2005
1119	HW	L351MRR	Scania N113 DRB	East Lancs	B49/35F	1994	City of Nottingham, 2010
1120	HW	L352MRR	Scania N113 DRB	East Lancs	B49/35F	1994	City of Nottingham, 2010
1121	HW	L353MRR	Scania N113 DRB	East Lancs	B49/35F	1994	City of Nottingham, 2010
1122	HW	L720SNO	Leyland Olympian ON2R50C13Z4	Alexander RH	B47/31F	1993	Dublin Bus, 2006
1123	HW	L726SNO	Leyland Olympian ON2R50C13Z4	Alexander RH	B47/31F	1993	Dublin Bus, 2006
1124	HW	P337ROO	DAF DB250	Northern Counties Palatine 2	B43/29F	1997	Courtney, Bracknell, 2005
1125	HW	P487SWC	Volvo Olympian	Alexander RH	B47/31F	1996	Dublin Bus, 2008
1127	HW	R974KAR	Volvo Olympian	Alexander RH	B47/31F	1998	Dublin Bus, 2010
1128	HW	R977KAR	Volvo Olympian	Alexander RH	B47/31F	1998	Dublin Bus, 2010
1130	HW	R32LHK	Volvo Olympian	Alexander RH	B47/23D	1997	Dublin Bus, 2010
1131	HW	R93LHK	Volvo Olympian	Alexander RH	B47/23D	1997	Dublin Bus, 2010
1132	HW	R94LHK	Volvo Olympian	Alexander RH	B47/23D	1997	Dublin Bus, 2010
1137	w	S779RNE	Dennis Dart SLF 11.3m	Plaxton Pointer SPD	N41F	1998	Beaumont, Gloucester, '05
1139	HW	T112AUA	DAF SB3000	Ikarus Blue Danube 396	C49FT	1999	Alfa, Chorley, 2008
1141	HW	W261EWU	Optare Solo M850	Optare	N23F	2000	Arriva Scotland, 2007
1142	HW	W284EYG	Optare Solo M850	Optare	N21F	2000	HAD, Shotts, 2007
1143	HW	W285EYG	Optare Solo M850	Optare	N23F	2000	Norfolk Green, 2007
1144	HW	W286EYG	Optare Solo M850	Optare	N23F	2000	Arriva Scotland, 2007
1145	HW	W288EYG	Optare Solo M850	Optare	N28F	2000	HAD, Shotts, 2007
1146	HW	W289EYG	Optare Solo M850	Optare	N23F	2000	Courtney, Bracknell, 2007
1147	HW	W292EYG	Optare Solo M850	Optare	N23F	2000	Smith, Patna, 2007
1149	u	W923JNF	Dennis Dart SLF 10.8m	Alexander ALX200	N38F	2000	Connexions, Redhill, 2005
1150	HW	X732FPO	Optare Solo M920	Optare	N27F	2000	Hampshire CC, 2007
1151	HW	X941NUB	Optare Solo M850	Optare	N23F	2000	Raddoneur, Birkenhead, '07
1152	HW	X385VVY	Optare Solo M920	Optare	N30F	2001	APL, Crudwell, 2008
1154	HW	Y867PWT	Optare Solo M920	Optare	N29F	2001	Diamond Bus, 2007
1155	HW	Y198KNB	Optare Solo M920	Optare	N29F	2001	Beaumont, Gloucester, '02
1156	HW	LA02WMZ	Optare Solo M850	Optare	N29F	2002	Bristol Airport, 2008
1157	HW	YL02FKU	Optare Solo M850	Optare	N27F	2002	*Operated for South Yorkshire*
1158	HW	YL02FKV	Optare Solo M850	Optare	N27F	2002	*Operated for South Yorkshire*
1159	HW	FB02LFP	Optare Solo M920	Optare	N31F	2002	NCP, Paisley, 2007
1160	HW	MW52PZD	Optare Solo M920	Optare	N33F	2003	Selwyns, Runcorn, 2004
1161	HW	YG52DHC	Optare Solo M920	Optare	N33F	2003	
1162	HW	TM52BUS	Optare Solo M920	Optare	N33F	2002	
1163	HW	MX03YCN	Optare Solo M850	Optare	N29F	2003	K-Line, Honley, 2004
1164	HW	MX03YCP	Optare Solo M850	Optare	N29F	2003	Timeline, Melling, 2004
1165	HW	YN03ZXE	Optare Solo M920	Optare	N33F	2003	Birchill, Whitstable, 2008
1166	HW	MX03YDF	Optare Solo M920	Optare	N33F	2003	Hut, Finstock, 2006
1167	HW	1294RU	VDL Bus DB250	East Lancs Lowlander	N51/29F	2003	
1169	HW	MX04VLM	Optare Solo M920	Optare	N33F	2004	McNee, Ratho Station, '05
1171	HW	YN54SYG	VDL Bus DB250	East Lancs Lowlander	N45/24F	2004	
1174	HW	YT55TMT	ADL Dart	East Lancs Myllennium	N41F	2005	
1177	u	YN06CYO	VDL Bus SB120	Plaxton Centro	N40F	2006	
1179	u	YJ56KAO	VDL Bus SB120	Plaxton Centro	N40F	2006	

1180	HW	YN56AHY	Optare Solo M920	Optare	N33F	2006	
1181	HW	YN56OWP	Optare Solo M920	Optare	N33F	2006	
1182	u	YJ56JYA	VDL Bus SB120	Plaxton Centro	N40F	2007	
1185	HW	YJ07JNN	VDL Bus SB120	Plaxton Centro	N40F	2007	
1187	HW	YJ07JVE	VDL Bus SB120	Plaxton Centro	N40F	2007	
1189	HW	YJ07JWU	VDL Bus SB120	Plaxton Centro	N40F	2007	
1190	HW	YN07SYS	Optare Solo M780 SL	Optare	N27F	2007	
1191	HW	YJ57KFE	Optare Solo M880 SL	Optare	N28F	2007	
1193	HW	YJ57EHB	Optare Solo M950	Optare	N33F	2007	
1194	HW	YJ57EHC	Optare Solo M950	Optare	N33F	2007	
1195	HW	YJ57EHU	Optare Versa V1100	Optare	N38F	2007	Optare demonstrator, 2008
1196	HW	YN08DNU	Volvo B12M	Plaxton Paragon	C45FT	2008	
1197	HW	YJ08PFN	Optare Versa V1100	Optare	N40F	2008	
1199	u	YN08JWD	MAN 12.240	Plaxton Centro	N38F	2008	
1200	u	YN08JWE	MAN 12.240	Plaxton Centro	N38F	2008	
1201	HW	YN08NKW	Volvo B12M	Plaxton Paragon	C61F	2008	
1202	HW	YN58NDV	Optare Solo M880	Optare	N29F	2008	
1203	HW	YN09AOS	Volvo B7R	Plaxton Profile 70	S70F	2009	
1204	HW	P274PSX	Volvo Olympian	Alexander Royale	B51/30D	1997	Lothian Buses, 2010
1205	HW	YN04XZC	Optare Solo M920	Optare	N33F	2004	Docherty's Midland, 2010
1206	HW	YJ56WVN	Optare Solo M880 SL	Optare	N28F	2007	Peterborough CC, 2010

Special event vehicles:

		JRA635	Leyland Tiger PS1	Crossley	B35R	1947	Chesterfield
		Q723GHG	Leyland RETL11	Eastern Coach Works	B51F	1985	Leyland Bus
		FRN816W	Leyland Tiger TRCTL11/3R	Van Hool Alizée	C51F	1981	Leyland Bus
		VOY182X	Leyland Tiger TRCTL11/2R	Plaxton Viewmaster IV	C49FT	1981	British Airways
		CBV775Y	Leyland Royal Tiger B50	Leyland Doyen	C49FT	1983	Leyland Bus
191	D	YRC191	Leyland Tiger Cub PSUC1/1	Alexander	BC41F	1962	
A417	D	RC7927	BMMO SON	Willowbrook	B34F	1940	
1054	D	LRC454	Leyland Titan PD3/4	Willowbrook	H41/32R	1958	

Ancillary vehicles:

118-134

			Volvo B10B	Northern Counties Paladin	TV	1993-94	
118	LM	L118LRA	125	LM	L125LRA	131	LM	L131LRA	134	LM	L134LRA
124	LM	L124LRA	130	LM	L130LRA						

| 367 | LM | N367VRC | Dennis Lance 11m | Optare Sigma | B46F | 1995 | |
| 1103 | HW | D192FYM | Leyland Olympian ONLXB/1RH | Eastern Coach Works | B42/26D | 1986 | |

Representing the TM Travel allocation is 1171, YN54SYG, a VDL DB250 with East Lancs Lowlander bodywork. It was taking a break at Tideswell while working the Peak District route to Buxton from Sheffield.
Richard Godfrey

Previous registrations:

A12UOD	FE02KEU	R32LHK	98D20390
A18UOD	FE02KFC	R93LHK	97D368
A20UOD	FE02KEK	R94LHK	97D371
FB02LFP	YL02FKW	R812NUD	R3OXF
H784PVW	91D1089	R813NUD	R2OXF
J619CEV	92D127	R974KAR	98D20412
J628CEV	92D126	R977KAR	98D20396
L720SNU	93D10165	YRC180	P57CTO
L726SNU	93D10167	YRC181	P58CTO
P487SWC	96D304	YRC182	P62RAU

Web: www.trentbuses.co.uk

Allocations:-

Ashfield (Midland Road, Sutton Junction) - Trent Barton - A

Outstation: Hucknall

Optare Solo	405	417	428	429	430	447	449	467
	468	469	470	471	472	473	474	475
	476	477	478	479	491			
Excel	255	257	261	263				
Volvo B10B	116							
Scania L94	609	610	611	612	671	672	677	681
Mercedes-Benz Citaro	693	694	695	696	697	698		
Optare Versa	810	811	812	813	814	815	816	817
	818	819	820	821	822	823	824	825
	826	827						

Derby (Meadow Road) - Trent Barton - D

Outstations:- Ashbourne, Belper and Matlock.

Optare Solo	413	416	441	448	466	480	481	482
	483	484	492	493	494	495	496	497
	500							
Excel	265							
Optare Tempo	307	308						
Optare Versa	806	807	808	809				
Volvo B10M	60	62						
Scania coach	64	65	66	67	68	69	70	71
	72	73	74	75	76			
Scania L94	613	614	615	616	617	619	624	631
	670	675	683	684	685	686	687	688
	689	690	691	692				
Volvo B7RLE	726	727	728	729	730	731	732	733
	734	735	736	737	738	741	751	

Derby (Meadow Road) - Notts & Derby - Midland General - ND

Outstations:- Hucknall and Ashfield

Optare Solo	403	453	454	456				
Volvo B10M	55	56						
Excel	221	222	230	236	258	259		
Dart	910	937	950					
Volvo B10B	107	109	110	112	113	114	121	122
	123	126	127	129	132	133	135	136
	137	138						
Scania L94	598	599	600					
VDL SB200	791	792	793					
Olympian	10	11	12	13	14	15	16	18
	22	23	25	26	27	28		
Volvo B7TL	29	30	31	32	33	34	35	36
	37	38	39					

Langley Mill (Station Road) - Trent Barton - LM

Optare Solo	412	427	432	433	434	435	436	450
	457							
Optare Versa	801	802	803	804	805			
Tempo	309	310	311	312	317	318		
Scania L94	601	602	603	604	632	633	649	650
	651	652	653	654	655	656	657	658
	659	660	661	662	663	664	667	673
	674	679	682					
Volvo B7RLE	739	740	742	743	744	745	746	747
	748	749	750					

Loughborough (Sullivan Way, LE11 5QS) - Kinchbus - LB

Outstation: Leicester

Solo	1	2	3	4	5	6	7	420
	451	452	458	459	465			
Excel	234	264	266					
Scania L94	618	623	625	626	627	628	629	630
	638	639						
Volvo B7RLE	761	762	763	764	765	766	767	
Tempo	319	320	321	322				

Nottingham (Manvers Street) - Trent Barton - N

Outstations: Cropwell Bishop, Derby (Meadow Road) and Loughborough (Sullivan Way).

Optare Solo	414	438	439	442	446	485	486	487
	488	489	490	498	499	996	997	998
	999							
Optare Tempo	301	302	303	304	305	306	313	314
	315	316	323	324	325	326	327	328
	329	330	331	332	333	334	335	
Volvo B7RLE	701	702	703	704	705	706	707	708
	709	710	711	712	713	714	715	716
	717	718	719	720	721	722	723	724
	725							
Volvo B10M	57	58						
Scania L94	605	606	607	608	620	621	622	634
	635	636	637	662	663	665	666	668
	669	676	678	680				

Sheffield (Station Road, Halfway, S20 2GZ) - TM Travel

DAF coach	1139							
Volvo B9R	1203							
Volvo B12M	63	1196	1201					
Optare Solo	401	402	411	415	418	421	422	423
	424	425	431	437	443	444	445	455
	460	461	463	464	1141	1142	1143	1144
	1145	1146	1147	1150	1151	1152	1154	1155
	1156	1157	1158	1160	1161	1162	1163	1164
	1165	1166	1169	1180	1181	1190	1191	1193
	1194	1202	1205	1206				
Optare Versa	1195	1197						
Dart	1174							
VDL SB120	1185	1187	1189					
MAN 12.240	1198	1199	1200					
Olympian	20	1102	1105	1109	1111	1112	1113	1114
	1115	1116	1117	1122	1123	1125	1127	1128
	1130	1131	1132	1204				
Scania N113	1119	1120	1121					
DAF DB250	1124	1167	1171					

Unallocated/stored - u/w

Remainder

English Bus Handbook: Smaller Groups

YOURBUS

Yourbus - Dunn Line

Dunn Motor Traction Ltd, Heanor Gate Road, Heanor, DE75 7RJ

1201-1205			Wrightbus Streetlite WF 9.5m			Wrightbus		N37F	2012	
1201	HE	MX62GVL	**1203**	HE	MX62GVR	**1204**	HE	MX62GVV	**1205**	HE	MX62GVZ
1202	HE	MX62GVN								

1301-1307			Wrightbus Streetlite DF 10.8m			Wrightbus		N41F	2012	
1301	HE	MX62GOA	**1303**	HE	MX62GXK	**1305**	HE	MX62GXZ	**1307**	HE	MX62GWZ
1302	HE	MX62GXE	**1304**	HE	MX62GXY	**1306**	HE	MX62GWC		

1401	HE	SN10CDE	ADL Dart 4 10.8m		ADL Enviro 200	N37F	2010	Premiere, Nottingham, '13
1402	HE	SN10CDF	ADL E300 12m		ADL Enviro 300	N45F	2010	Premiere, Nottingham, '13
1403	HE	SN10CDK	ADL E300 12m		ADL Enviro 300	N45F	2010	Premiere, Nottingham, '13
1601	DH	YJ60KFK	Optare Solo M810SL EV		Optare	N26F	2010	
1602	DH	YJ60KFL	Optare Solo M810SL EV		Optare	N26F	2010	
1603	DH	YJ60KFN	Optare Solo M810SL EV		Optare	N26F	2010	
1604	DH	YJ60KFP	Optare Solo M810SL EV		Optare	N26F	2010	
2101	HE	BK10MFU	Volvo B9TL		Wrightbus Gemini 2	N45/30F	2012	Premiere, Nottingham, '13
2102	HE	BK10MFV	Volvo B9TL		Wrightbus Gemini 2	N45/30F	2012	Premiere, Nottingham, '13
2103	HE	FJ57CZB	Volvo B9TL		Wrightbus Gemini 2	N44/24D	2012	Premiere, Nottingham, '13

3001-3009			Mercedes-Benz Citaro O530 LE			Mercedes-Benz		N42F	2011	
3001	HE	BT11UWF	**3004**	HE	BT11UWJ	**3006**	HE	BT11UWL	**3008**	HE	BT11UWN
3002	HE	BT11UWG	**3005**	HE	BT11UWK	**3007**	HE	BT11UWM	**3009**	HE	BT11UWO
3003	HE	BT11UWH								

The low-entry model of the Mercedes-Benz Citaro now dominates Yourbus' service network. Pictured in Nottingham is 3002, BT11UWG, which carries lettering for the Chilwell routes. *Dave Heath*

Yourbus operates both type of Wrightbus Streetlite. Illustrating the door-forward model is 1305, MX62GXZ, which carries lettering for route 59. *Dave Heath*

3010-3023

		Mercedes-Benz Citaro O530 LE		Mercedes-Benz			N42F	2012		
3010	HE	BF62JZA	3014	HE	BF62JZG	3018	HE	BF62JZU	3021	HE	BF62JZX
3011	HE	BF62JZC	3015	HE	BF62JZR	3019	HE	BF62JZV	3022	HE	BF62JZY
3012	HE	BF62JZD	3016	HE	BF62JZS	3020	HE	BF62JZW	3023	HE	BF62JZZ
3013	HE	BF62JZE	3017	HE	BF62JZT						

3024-3033

		Mercedes-Benz Citaro O530 LE		Mercedes-Benz			N42F	2013		
3024	HE	-	3027	HE	-	3030	HE	-	3032	HE	-
3025	HE	-	3028	HE	-	3031	HE	-	3033	HE	-
3026	HE	-	3029	HE	-						

3501-3506

		Mercedes-Benz Citaro O530		Mercedes-Benz			N42F	2004	Epsom Coaches, 2012	
3501	HE	BU53AWX	3503	HE	BU53AWY	3505	HE	BU53AXA	3506	HE	BW03ZMY
3502	HE	BU53AWW	3504	HE	BU53AWZ						

3601	HE	BK10MFX	Volvo B7RLE	Plaxton Centro	N44F	2010	Premiere, Nottingham, '13
3602	HE	BK10MFY	Volvo B7RLE	Plaxton Centro	N44F	2010	Premiere, Nottingham, '13

3603-3606

		Volvo B7RLE			Wrightbus Eclipse Urban	N43F	2004	Rotala, 2013
3603	HE	SJ04DVH	3604	HE	SJ04DVK	3605	HE	SJ04DVL	3606	HE	SJ04DVM

4001-4028

		Volvo B9R		Caetano Levanté			C48FT	2011		
4001	HE	FJ60EHN	4008	HE	FJ60EFY	4015	HE	FJ60KVP	4022	DH	FJ11MME
4002	HE	FJ60HXW	4009	HE	FJ60EGY	4016	HE	FJ60KVR	4023	DH	FJ11MMF
4003	HE	FJ60HXZ	4010	HE	FJ60KVH	4017	DH	FJ11GLY	4024	DH	FJ11MMK
4004	HE	FJ60HYA	4011	HE	FJ60KVK	4018	DH	FJ11GKE	4025	DH	FJ11MMO
4005	HE	FJ60HYB	4012	HE	FJ60KVL	4019	DH	FJ11MLY	4026	DH	FJ11MMU
4006	HE	FJ60EGZ	4013	HE	FJ60KVM	4020	DH	FJ11MLZ	4027	DH	FJ11MMX
4007	HE	FJ60EFX	4014	HE	FJ60KVO	4021	DH	FJ11MMA	4028	DH	FJ11MOA

4029-4043

		Volvo B9R		Caetano Levanté			C48FT	2011-12		
4029	HE	FJ61EXM	4033	HE	FJ61EXR	4037	HE	FJ61EXV	4041	HE	FJ61EYA
4030	HE	FJ61EXN	4034	HE	FJ61EXS	4038	HE	FJ61EXW	4042	HE	FJ61EYC
4031	HE	FJ61EXO	4035	HE	FJ61EXT	4039	HE	FJ61EXX	4043	HE	FJ61EYD
4032	HE	FJ61EXP	4036	HE	FJ61EXU	4040	HE	FJ61EXZ			

Much of the work of Yourbus comprises National Express contracts with some fifty-five coaches now dedicated to that network. Representing them is 4107, FN06FLE, a Volvo B12B with Caetano Levanté bodywork. It was seen working a duty from Skipton to London route 5611. *Dave Heath*

4101-4110   Volvo B12B   Caetano Levanté   C49FT   2006   Veolia, 2011

4101	DH	FJ56PCF	4104	DH	FJ56PBY	4107	DH	FN06FLE	4109	DH	FN06FLG
4102	DH	FJ56PBU	4105	DH	FJ56PBZ	4108	DH	FN06FLF	4110	DH	FN06FKZ
4103	DH	FJ56PBX	4106	DH	FN06FLB						

4201	DH	FJ07DWL	Scania K340 EB4	Caetano Levanté	C49FT	2007	Veolia, 2011
4202	DH	FJ07DWK	Scania K340 EB4	Caetano Levanté	C49FT	2007	Veolia, 2011

Ancillary vehicle:

T1010	HE	PJ02RHA	Dennis Dart SLF	Plaxton Pointer 2	N37F	2002	Diamond, 2010

Allocations:-

Durham (Colliery Lane, Hetton-le-Hole, DH5 0BG) - DH

Optare Solo	1601	1602	1603	1604				
Volvo B9R	4017	4018	4019	4020	4021	4022	4023	4024
	4025	4026	4027	4028				
Volvo B12B	4101	4102	4103	4104	4105	4106	4107	4108
	4109	4110						
Scania K340	4201	4202						

Heanor (Heanor Gate Road, DE75 7RJ) - HE

Streetlite WF	1201	1202	1203	1204	1205			
Streetlite DF	1301	1303	1303	1304	1305	1306	1307	
Dart	1401	1402	1403					
Volvo B9TL	2101	2102	2103					
MB Citaro	3001	3002	3003	3004	3005	3006	3007	3008
	3009	3010	3011	3012	3013	3014	3015	3016
	3017	3018	3019	3020	3021	3022	3023	3501
	3502	3503	3504	3505	3506			
Volvo B7RLE	3601	3602	3603	3604	3605	3606		
Volvo B9R	4001	4002	4003	4004	4005	4006	4007	4008
	4009	4010	4011	4012	4013	4014	4015	4016
	4029	4030	4031	4032	4033	4034	4035	4036
	4037	4038	4039	4040	4041	4042	4043	

Vehicle index

340GUP	North East	B251NVN	Transdev	BJ03EUD	NX West Midlands
10RU	EYMS Group	B517UWW	Transdev	BJ03EUE	NX West Midlands
39EYD	EYMS Group	B521UWW	Transdev	BJ03EUF	NX West Midlands
80EYC	EYMS Group	B737GSC	Transdev	BJ03EUH	NX West Midlands
152FRH	EYMS Group	B738GSC	Transdev	BJ03EUK	NX West Midlands
165DKH	EYMS Group	B739GSC	Transdev	BJ03EUL	NX West Midlands
352STG	RATP Group	B747GSC	Transdev	BJ03EUM	NX West Midlands
491NFC	Rotala	B750GSC	Transdev	BJ03EUN	NX West Midlands
647JOE	EYMS Group	B751GSC	Transdev	BJ03EUP	NX West Midlands
787EYC	EYMS Group	B754GSC	Transdev	BJ03EUR	NX West Midlands
794EYD	EYMS Group	BA02EAA	Rotala	BJ03EUT	NX West Midlands
834EYD	EYMS Group	BA05EAA	Rotala	BJ03EUU	NX West Midlands
897EYX	EYMS Group	BC05JHO	Centrebus	BJ03EUV	NX West Midlands
1294RU	TrentBarton	BD08DZX	RATP Group	BJ03EUW	NX West Midlands
8225KH	EYMS Group	BD11CEA	Transdev	BJ03EUX	NX West Midlands
A1EYD	EYMS Group	BD11CEF	Transdev	BJ03EUY	NX West Midlands
A6EYC	EYMS Group	BD11CEJ	Transdev	BJ03EUZ	NX West Midlands
A7EYC	EYMS Group	BD11CEK	Transdev	BJ03EVB	NX West Midlands
A8EYC	EYMS Group	BD12TDX	Transdev	BJ03EVC	NX West Midlands
A8FTG	Rotala	BD12TDZ	Transdev	BJ03EVD	NX West Midlands
A9EYC	EYMS Group	BD12TEJ	Transdev	BJ03EVF	NX West Midlands
A9UOB	Rotala	BD12TEO	Transdev	BJ03EVG	NX West Midlands
A10EYC	EYMS Group	BD12TEU	Transdev	BJ03EVH	NX West Midlands
A10EYD	EYMS Group	BD12TEV	Transdev	BJ03EVK	NX West Midlands
A14EYC	EYMS Group	BD12TEY	Transdev	BJ03EVL	NX West Midlands
A15EYC	EYMS Group	BD12TFZ	NX West Midlands	BJ03EVM	NX West Midlands
A16EYC	EYMS Group	BD57WCX	Rotala	BJ03EVN	NX West Midlands
A17EYC	EYMS Group	BF60OEV	Rotala	BJ03EVP	NX West Midlands
A18EYC	EYMS Group	BF60OFA	Rotala	BJ03EVR	NX West Midlands
A18UOD	TrentBarton	BF60OFD	RATP Group	BJ03EVT	NX West Midlands
A19EYC	EYMS Group	BF60OFE	RATP Group	BJ03EVU	NX West Midlands
A20EYC	EYMS Group	BF61HBJ	NX Coaching	BJ03EVV	NX West Midlands
A20UOD	TrentBarton	BF61HBK	NX Coaching	BJ03EVW	NX West Midlands
A12UOD	TrentBarton	BF62JYR	Yourbus	BJ03EVX	NX West Midlands
A602NYG	Transdev	BF62JYS	Yourbus	BJ03EVY	NX West Midlands
A604NYG	Transdev	BF62JYT	Yourbus	BJ03EWA	NX West Midlands
AE06HBU	Centrebus	BF62JYU	Yourbus	BJ03EWB	NX West Midlands
AE06HBX	Centrebus	BF62JYV	Yourbus	BJ03EWC	NX West Midlands
AE10CSF	Rotala	BF62JYW	Yourbus	BJ03EWD	NX West Midlands
AE10CTO	Rotala	BF62JYX	Yourbus	BJ03EWE	NX West Midlands
AE10CTU	Rotala	BF62JYY	Yourbus	BJ03EWF	NX West Midlands
AE10CTV	Rotala	BF62JYZ	Yourbus	BJ03EWG	NX West Midlands
AE10CTX	Rotala	BF62JZA	Yourbus	BJ03EWH	NX West Midlands
AE10CTY	Rotala	BF62JZC	Yourbus	BJ03EWK	NX West Midlands
AE10CTZ	Rotala	BF62JZD	Yourbus	BJ03EWL	NX West Midlands
AE10CUH	Rotala	BF62JZE	Yourbus	BJ03EWM	NX West Midlands
AE10CUJ	Rotala	BF62JZG	Yourbus	BJ03EWN	NX West Midlands
AE10CUK	Rotala	BF62UXV	Transdev	BJ03EWP	NX West Midlands
AE10KHB	Rotala	BF62UXW	Transdev	BJ03EWR	NX West Midlands
AE55MVF	NX Coaching	BF62UXX	Transdev	BJ03EWS	NX West Midlands
AE55MVG	NX Coaching	BF62UXY	Transdev	BJ03EWT	NX West Midlands
AE55MVH	NX Coaching	BF62UXZ	Transdev	BJ03EWU	NX West Midlands
AE55MVJ	NX Coaching	BG59FYF	NX West Midlands	BJ03EWV	NX West Midlands
AE55MVL	Centrebus	BJ03ESN	NX West Midlands	BJ03EWW	NX West Midlands
AE55VGD	Centrebus	BJ03ESU	NX West Midlands	BJ03EWX	NX West Midlands
AE57FXW	Rotala	BJ03ESV	NX West Midlands	BJ03EWY	NX West Midlands
AE60GRU	RATP Group	BJ03ESY	NX West Midlands	BJ03EWZ	NX West Midlands
AE60GRU	RATP Group	BJ03ETA	NX West Midlands	BJ03EXA	NX West Midlands
ALD978B	RATP Group	BJ03ETD	NX West Midlands	BJ03EXB	NX West Midlands
ALD978B	RATP Group	BJ03ETE	NX West Midlands	BJ03EXC	NX West Midlands
AN09BUS	Centrebus	BJ03ETF	NX West Midlands	BJ03EXD	NX West Midlands
AV51AVA	Centrebus	BJ03ETK	NX West Midlands	BJ03EXE	NX West Midlands
AY07CUA	RATP Group	BJ03ETL	NX West Midlands	BJ03EXF	NX West Midlands
B5WER	Centrebus	BJ03ETR	NX West Midlands	BJ03EXG	NX West Midlands
B6WER	Centrebus	BJ03ETT	NX West Midlands	BJ03EXH	NX West Midlands
B7BVD	Transdev	BJ03ETU	NX West Midlands	BJ03EXK	NX West Midlands
B8WER	Centrebus	BJ03ETV	NX West Midlands	BJ03EXL	NX West Midlands
B12WTS	Rotala	BJ03ETX	NX West Midlands	BJ03EXM	NX West Midlands
B14WTS	Rotala	BJ03ETY	NX West Midlands	BJ03EXN	NX West Midlands
B15WTS	Rotala	BJ03ETZ	NX West Midlands	BJ03EXP	NX West Midlands
B20WTS	Rotala	BJ03EUA	NX West Midlands	BJ03EXR	NX West Midlands
B91SWX	Transdev	BJ03EUB	NX West Midlands	BK10EHT	NX Coaching
B92SWX	Transdev	BJ03EUC	NX West Midlands	BK10EHU	NX Coaching

Reg	Operator	Reg	Operator	Reg	Operator
BK10EHV	NX Coaching	BP51HDK	NX West Midlands	BU06CXH	NX West Midlands
BK10EHW	NX Coaching	BP51HDL	NX West Midlands	BU06CXJ	NX West Midlands
BK10EHX	NX Coaching	BP51HDO	NX West Midlands	BU06CXK	NX West Midlands
BK10EHY	NX Coaching	BRZ9662	Rotala	BU06CXL	NX West Midlands
BK10EHZ	NX Coaching	BT11UWF	Yourbus	BU06CXM	NX West Midlands
BK10EJU	NX Coaching	BT11UWG	Yourbus	BU07LGO	NX West Midlands
BK10EJV	NX Coaching	BT11UWH	Yourbus	BU07LGV	NX West Midlands
BK10EJX	NX Coaching	BT11UWJ	Yourbus	BU07LGW	NX West Midlands
BK10EJY	NX Coaching	BT11UWK	Yourbus	BU07LGX	NX West Midlands
BK10EJZ	NX Coaching	BT11UWL	Yourbus	BU07LGY	NX West Midlands
BK10MFU	Yourbus	BT11UWM	Yourbus	BU07LGZ	NX West Midlands
BK10MFV	Yourbus	BT11UWN	Yourbus	BU07LHA	NX West Midlands
BK10MFX	Yourbus	BT11UWO	Yourbus	BU07LHB	NX West Midlands
BK10MFY	Yourbus	BU02BKV	Transdev	BU07LHC	NX West Midlands
BK10MGE	NX West Midlands	BU03RTX	EYMS Group	BU07LHD	NX West Midlands
BK13NZM	Rotala	BU03SXK	Transdev	BU08ACX	Rotala
BK13NZN	Rotala	BU04BHX	NX West Midlands	BU08ADZ	Rotala
BK13NZO	Rotala	BU04BHY	NX West Midlands	BU08DAO	Rotala
BK13NZP	Rotala	BU04BHZ	NX West Midlands	BU08DBO	Rotala
BK13NZR	Rotala	BU04BJE	NX West Midlands	BU08DBV	Rotala
BK13NZS	Rotala	BU04BJF	NX West Midlands	BU08DBX	Rotala
BK13NZT	Rotala	BU04BJJ	NX West Midlands	BU08DCE	Rotala
BK13NZU	Rotala	BU04BJK	NX West Midlands	BU08DCF	Rotala
BK58URT	RATP Group	BU04BJV	NX West Midlands	BU08DCO	Rotala
BL53EDF	NX West Midlands	BU04BJX	NX West Midlands	BU08DCX	Rotala
BL53EDJ	NX West Midlands	BU04BJZ	NX West Midlands	BU08DHO	Rotala
BL53EDK	NX West Midlands	BU04BKA	NX West Midlands	BU08DHP	Rotala
BL53EDO	NX West Midlands	BU04BKD	NX West Midlands	BU08DYB	NX West Midlands
BL53EDP	NX West Midlands	BU04BKE	NX West Midlands	BU08EHZ	NX West Midlands
BL53EDR	NX West Midlands	BU04BKF	NX West Midlands	BU08MTE	Rotala
BL53EDU	NX West Midlands	BU04BKG	NX West Midlands	BU09JZT	NX West Midlands
BL53EDV	NX West Midlands	BU04BKJ	NX West Midlands	BU51RRO	NX West Midlands
BL53EDX	NX West Midlands	BU04BKK	NX West Midlands	BU51RRV	NX West Midlands
BL53EEA	NX West Midlands	BU04BKL	NX West Midlands	BU51RRX	NX West Midlands
BL53EEB	NX West Midlands	BU04BKN	NX West Midlands	BU51RRY	NX West Midlands
BL53EEF	NX West Midlands	BU04BKV	NX West Midlands	BU51RRZ	NX West Midlands
BL53EEG	NX West Midlands	BU04BKX	NX West Midlands	BU51RSO	NX West Midlands
BL53EEH	NX West Midlands	BU04BKZ	NX West Midlands	BU51RSV	NX West Midlands
BL53EEJ	NX West Midlands	BU04BLF	NX West Midlands	BU51RSX	NX West Midlands
BL53EEM	NX West Midlands	BU04BLJ	NX West Midlands	BU51RSY	NX West Midlands
BL53EEN	NX West Midlands	BU04BLK	NX West Midlands	BU51RSZ	NX West Midlands
BL53EEO	NX West Midlands	BU04BLN	NX West Midlands	BU51RTO	NX West Midlands
BL53EEP	NX West Midlands	BU04BLV	NX West Midlands	BU51RTV	NX West Midlands
BL53EER	NX West Midlands	BU04BLX	NX West Midlands	BU51RTX	NX West Midlands
BL53EET	NX West Midlands	BU04BLZ	NX West Midlands	BU51RTZ	NX West Midlands
BL53EEU	NX West Midlands	BU04BMZ	NX West Midlands	BU51RUA	NX West Midlands
BL53EEV	NX West Midlands	BU04EXT	RATP Group	BU51RUC	NX West Midlands
BL53EEW	NX West Midlands	BU04EXV	RATP Group	BU51RUH	NX West Midlands
BL53EEX	NX West Midlands	BU04EXW	RATP Group	BU51RUJ	NX West Midlands
BL53EEY	NX West Midlands	BU04EXX	RATP Group	BU51RUO	NX West Midlands
BL53EEZ	NX West Midlands	BU05HDO	Rotala	BU51RUR	NX West Midlands
BL53EFA	NX West Midlands	BU05HDV	Rotala	BU51RUV	NX West Midlands
BL53EFB	NX West Midlands	BU05HEV	NX West Midlands	BU51RUW	NX West Midlands
BL53EFC	NX West Midlands	BU05HFE	NX West Midlands	BU51RVA	NX West Midlands
BN09FWS	Rotala	BU05HFF	NX West Midlands	BU51RVC	NX West Midlands
BN09FWV	TrentBarton	BU05HFH	NX West Midlands	BU51RVE	NX West Midlands
BN09FWW	TrentBarton	BU05HFJ	NX West Midlands	BU51RVF	NX West Midlands
BN09FWX	TrentBarton	BU05HFL	NX West Midlands	BU51RVJ	NX West Midlands
BN09FWY	TrentBarton	BU05HFO	NX West Midlands	BU51RVK	NX West Midlands
BN09FWZ	TrentBarton	BU05HFP	NX West Midlands	BU51RVL	NX West Midlands
BN09FXL	TrentBarton	BU05HFR	NX West Midlands	BU51RVM	NX West Midlands
BN12EOP	RATP Group	BU05HFS	NX West Midlands	BU51RVN	NX West Midlands
BN12EOR	RATP Group	BU06CSF	RATP Group	BU51RVO	NX West Midlands
BN12EOS	RATP Group	BU06CSO	RATP Group	BU51RVP	NX West Midlands
BN12EOT	RATP Group	BU06CWR	NX West Midlands	BU51RVR	NX West Midlands
BN12EOU	RATP Group	BU06CWT	NX West Midlands	BU51RVT	NX West Midlands
BN12EOV	RATP Group	BU06CWV	NX West Midlands	BU51RVV	NX West Midlands
BN12EOW	RATP Group	BU06CWW	NX West Midlands	BU51RVW	NX West Midlands
BN12EOX	RATP Group	BU06CWX	NX West Midlands	BU51RVX	NX West Midlands
BN12EOY	RATP Group	BU06CWY	NX West Midlands	BU51RVY	NX West Midlands
BN12EOZ	RATP Group	BU06CWZ	NX West Midlands	BU51RVZ	NX West Midlands
BP51HDD	NX West Midlands	BU06CXA	NX West Midlands	BU51RWE	NX West Midlands
BP51HDE	NX West Midlands	BU06CXB	NX West Midlands	BU51RWF	NX West Midlands
BP51HDF	NX West Midlands	BU06CXC	NX West Midlands	BU51RWJ	NX West Midlands
BP51HDG	NX West Midlands	BU06CXD	NX West Midlands	BU51RWK	NX West Midlands
BP51HDH	NX West Midlands	BU06CXE	NX West Midlands	BU51RWL	NX West Midlands
BP51HDJ	NX West Midlands	BU06CXG	NX West Midlands	BU51RWN	NX West Midlands

BU51RWO	NX West Midlands	BV52OAB	NX West Midlands	BV57XFU	NX West Midlands
BU51RWV	NX West Midlands	BV52OAC	NX West Midlands	BV57XFW	NX West Midlands
BU51RWW	NX West Midlands	BV52OAD	NX West Midlands	BV57XFX	NX West Midlands
BU51RWX	NX West Midlands	BV52OAE	NX West Midlands	BV57XFY	NX West Midlands
BU51RWY	NX West Midlands	BV52OAG	NX West Midlands	BV57XFZ	NX West Midlands
BU51RWZ	NX West Midlands	BV52OAH	NX West Midlands	BV57XGA	NX West Midlands
BU51RXB	NX West Midlands	BV52OAJ	NX West Midlands	BV57XGB	NX West Midlands
BU51RXC	NX West Midlands	BV52OAL	NX West Midlands	BV57XGC	NX West Midlands
BU51RXD	NX West Midlands	BV52OAM	NX West Midlands	BV57XGD	NX West Midlands
BU51RXG	NX West Midlands	BV52OAN	NX West Midlands	BV57XGE	NX West Midlands
BU51RXH	NX West Midlands	BV52OAO	NX West Midlands	BV57XGF	NX West Midlands
BU51RXJ	NX West Midlands	BV52OAP	NX West Midlands	BV57XGG	NX West Midlands
BU51RXK	NX West Midlands	BV52OAS	NX West Midlands	BV57XGH	NX West Midlands
BU51RXM	NX West Midlands	BV52OAU	NX West Midlands	BV57XGJ	NX West Midlands
BU51RXN	NX West Midlands	BV52OAW	NX West Midlands	BV57XGK	NX West Midlands
BU51RXO	NX West Midlands	BV52OAX	NX West Midlands	BV57XGL	NX West Midlands
BU51RXP	NX West Midlands	BV52OAY	NX West Midlands	BV57XGM	NX West Midlands
BU51RXR	NX West Midlands	BV52OAZ	NX West Midlands	BV57XGN	NX West Midlands
BU51RXS	NX West Midlands	BV52OBA	NX West Midlands	BV57XGO	NX West Midlands
BU51RXT	NX West Midlands	BV52OBB	NX West Midlands	BV57XGP	NX West Midlands
BU51RXV	NX West Midlands	BV52OBC	NX West Midlands	BV57XGR	NX West Midlands
BU51RXW	NX West Midlands	BV52OBD	NX West Midlands	BV57XGS	NX West Midlands
BU51RXX	NX West Midlands	BV52OBE	NX West Midlands	BV57XGT	NX West Midlands
BU51RXZ	NX West Midlands	BV52OBF	NX West Midlands	BV57XGU	NX West Midlands
BU51RYA	NX West Midlands	BV52OBG	NX West Midlands	BV57XGW	NX West Midlands
BU51RYB	NX West Midlands	BV52OBH	NX West Midlands	BV57XGX	NX West Midlands
BU51RYD	NX West Midlands	BV52OBJ	NX West Midlands	BV57XGY	NX West Midlands
BU51RYF	NX West Midlands	BV52OBK	NX West Midlands	BV57XGZ	NX West Midlands
BU51RYG	NX West Midlands	BV52OBL	NX West Midlands	BV57XHA	NX West Midlands
BU53AWP	Rotala	BV52OBM	NX West Midlands	BV57XHB	NX West Midlands
BU53AWR	Rotala	BV52OBN	NX West Midlands	BV57XHC	NX West Midlands
BU53AWW	Yourbus	BV52OBO	NX West Midlands	BV57XHD	NX West Midlands
BU53AWX	Yourbus	BV52OBP	NX West Midlands	BV57XHE	NX West Midlands
BU53AWY	Yourbus	BV52OBR	NX West Midlands	BV57XHF	NX West Midlands
BU53AWZ	Yourbus	BV52OBS	NX West Midlands	BV57XHG	NX West Midlands
BU53AXA	Yourbus	BV52OBT	NX West Midlands	BV57XHH	NX West Midlands
BU53AXB	Rotala	BV52OBU	NX West Midlands	BV57XHJ	NX West Midlands
BU53AXN	NX Coaching	BV52OBW	NX West Midlands	BV57XHK	NX West Midlands
BU53AXO	NX Coaching	BV52OBX	NX West Midlands	BV57XHL	NX West Midlands
BU53AXP	NX Coaching	BV52OBY	NX West Midlands	BV57XHM	NX West Midlands
BU53AXR	NX Coaching	BV52OBZ	NX West Midlands	BV57XHN	NX West Midlands
BU53AXT	NX Coaching	BV52OCA	NX West Midlands	BV57XHO	NX West Midlands
BU53AXV	NX Coaching	BV52OCB	NX West Midlands	BV57XHP	NX West Midlands
BU53UMC	NX West Midlands	BV52OCC	NX West Midlands	BV57XHR	NX West Midlands
BU53UMD	NX West Midlands	BV52OCD	NX West Midlands	BV57XHS	NX West Midlands
BU53UME	NX West Midlands	BV52OCE	NX West Midlands	BV57XHT	NX West Midlands
BU53UMF	NX West Midlands	BV52OCF	NX West Midlands	BV57XHU	NX West Midlands
BU53UMG	NX West Midlands	BV52OCG	NX West Midlands	BV57XHW	NX West Midlands
BU53UMH	NX West Midlands	BV52OCH	NX West Midlands	BV57XHX	NX West Midlands
BU53UMJ	NX West Midlands	BV52OCJ	NX West Midlands	BV57XHY	NX West Midlands
BU53UMK	NX West Midlands	BV52OCK	NX West Midlands	BV57XHZ	NX West Midlands
BU53UML	NX West Midlands	BV52OCL	NX West Midlands	BV57XJA	NX West Midlands
BU53UMM	NX West Midlands	BV52OCM	NX West Midlands	BV57XJB	NX West Midlands
BU53UMR	NX West Midlands	BV52OCN	NX West Midlands	BV57XJC	NX West Midlands
BU53UMT	NX West Midlands	BV52OCO	NX West Midlands	BV57XJD	NX West Midlands
BU53UMV	NX West Midlands	BV52OCP	NX West Midlands	BV57XJE	NX West Midlands
BU53UMW	NX West Midlands	BV52OCR	NX West Midlands	BV57XJF	NX West Midlands
BU53UMX	NX West Midlands	BV52OCS	NX West Midlands	BV57XJG	NX West Midlands
BU53UMY	NX West Midlands	BV52OCU	NX West Midlands	BV57XJH	NX West Midlands
BU53UMZ	NX West Midlands	BV52OCW	NX West Midlands	BV57XJJ	NX West Midlands
BU53UNB	NX West Midlands	BV57XFB	NX West Midlands	BV57XJK	NX West Midlands
BU53UNE	NX West Midlands	BV57XFC	NX West Midlands	BV57XJL	NX West Midlands
BU53UNF	NX West Midlands	BV57XFD	NX West Midlands	BV57XJM	NX West Midlands
BU53UNG	NX West Midlands	BV57XFE	NX West Midlands	BV57XJN	NX West Midlands
BU53UNH	NX West Midlands	BV57XFF	NX West Midlands	BV57XJO	NX West Midlands
BU53UNJ	NX West Midlands	BV57XFG	NX West Midlands	BV57XJP	NX West Midlands
BU53UNK	NX West Midlands	BV57XFH	NX West Midlands	BV57XJT	NX West Midlands
BU53UNL	NX West Midlands	BV57XFJ	NX West Midlands	BV57XJU	NX West Midlands
BU53UNM	NX West Midlands	BV57XFK	NX West Midlands	BV57XJW	NX West Midlands
BU53UNN	NX West Midlands	BV57XFL	NX West Midlands	BV57XJX	NX West Midlands
BU53UNP	NX West Midlands	BV57XFM	NX West Midlands	BV57XJY	NX West Midlands
BU53UNR	NX West Midlands	BV57XFN	NX West Midlands	BV57XJZ	NX West Midlands
BU53ZWN	RATP Group	BV57XFO	NX West Midlands	BV57XKA	NX West Midlands
BU53ZWP	RATP Group	BV57XFP	NX West Midlands	BV57XKB	NX West Midlands
BU53ZWR	RATP Group	BV57XFR	NX West Midlands	BV57XKC	NX West Midlands
BV10ZJU	Rotala	BV57XFS	NX West Midlands	BV57XKD	NX West Midlands
BV52OAA	NX West Midlands	BV57XFT	NX West Midlands	BV57XKE	NX West Midlands

BV57XKF	NX West Midlands	BX07AXO	Rotala	BX10ABK	NX West Midlands
BV57XKG	NX West Midlands	BX07AYU	Rotala	BX10ABN	NX West Midlands
BV57XKH	NX West Midlands	BX07AZJ	Transdev	BX10ABO	NX West Midlands
BV57XKJ	NX West Midlands	BX07BRV	Rotala	BX10ABU	NX West Midlands
BV57XKK	NX West Midlands	BX07KPN	Rotala	BX10ABV	NX West Midlands
BV57XKL	NX West Midlands	BX07KPO	Rotala	BX10ABZ	NX West Midlands
BV57XKM	NX West Midlands	BX07KPP	Rotala	BX10ACF	NX West Midlands
BV57XKN	NX West Midlands	BX09OZE	NX West Midlands	BX10ACJ	NX West Midlands
BV57XKO	NX West Midlands	BX09OZF	NX West Midlands	BX10ACO	NX West Midlands
BV57XKP	NX West Midlands	BX09OZG	NX West Midlands	BX10ACU	NX West Midlands
BV57XKS	NX West Midlands	BX09OZH	NX West Midlands	BX10ACV	NX West Midlands
BV57XKT	NX West Midlands	BX09OZJ	NX West Midlands	BX10ACY	NX West Midlands
BV57XKU	NX West Midlands	BX09OZK	NX West Midlands	BX10ACZ	NX West Midlands
BV57XKW	NX West Midlands	BX09OZL	NX West Midlands	BX10ADO	NX West Midlands
BV57XKX	NX West Midlands	BX09OZM	NX West Midlands	BX10ADU	NX West Midlands
BV57XKY	NX West Midlands	BX09OZN	NX West Midlands	BX10ADV	NX West Midlands
BV57XKZ	NX West Midlands	BX09OZO	NX West Midlands	BX10ADZ	NX West Midlands
BV57XLA	NX West Midlands	BX09OZP	NX West Midlands	BX10AEA	NX West Midlands
BV58MKX	Rotala	BX09OZR	NX West Midlands	BX10AEB	NX West Midlands
BW03ZMY	Yourbus	BX09OZS	NX West Midlands	BX10AEC	NX West Midlands
BW03ZMZ	RATP Group	BX09OZT	NX West Midlands	BX10AED	NX West Midlands
BW03ZVA	Rotala	BX09OZU	NX West Midlands	BX10AEE	NX West Midlands
BW03ZVB	Rotala	BX09OZV	NX West Midlands	BX10AEF	NX West Midlands
BW03ZVC	Rotala	BX09OZW	NX West Midlands	BX10AEG	NX West Midlands
BX02APY	NX West Midlands	BX09PAO	NX West Midlands	BX10AEJ	NX West Midlands
BX02APZ	NX West Midlands	BX09PBF	NX West Midlands	BX10AEK	NX West Midlands
BX02ARF	NX West Midlands	BX09PBO	NX West Midlands	BX10AEL	NX West Midlands
BX02ARU	NX West Midlands	BX09PBU	NX West Midlands	BX10AEM	NX West Midlands
BX02ARZ	NX West Midlands	BX09PBZ	NX West Midlands	BX10AEN	NX West Midlands
BX02ASO	NX West Midlands	BX09PCF	NX West Midlands	BX12DAO	NX West Midlands
BX02ASU	NX West Midlands	BX09PCO	NX West Midlands	BX12DAU	NX West Midlands
BX02ASV	NX West Midlands	BX09PCU	NX West Midlands	BX12DBO	NX West Midlands
BX02ASZ	NX West Midlands	BX09PCV	NX West Midlands	BX12DBU	NX West Midlands
BX02ATK	NX West Midlands	BX09PCY	NX West Midlands	BX12DBV	NX West Midlands
BX02ATN	NX West Midlands	BX09PCZ	NX West Midlands	BX12DBY	NX West Midlands
BX02ATO	NX West Midlands	BX09PDO	NX West Midlands	BX12DBZ	NX West Midlands
BX02ATU	NX West Midlands	BX09PDU	NX West Midlands	BX12DCE	NX West Midlands
BX02ATV	NX West Midlands	BX09PDV	NX West Midlands	BX12DCF	NX West Midlands
BX02ATY	NX West Midlands	BX09PDY	NX West Midlands	BX12DCO	NX West Midlands
BX02ATZ	NX West Midlands	BX09PDZ	NX West Midlands	BX12DCU	NX West Midlands
BX02AUA	NX West Midlands	BX09PEO	NX West Midlands	BX12DCV	NX West Midlands
BX02AUC	NX West Midlands	BX09PFA	NX West Midlands	BX12DCY	NX West Midlands
BX02AUE	NX West Midlands	BX09PFD	NX West Midlands	BX12DCZ	NX West Midlands
BX02AUF	NX West Midlands	BX09PFE	NX West Midlands	BX12DDE	NX West Midlands
BX02AUH	NX West Midlands	BX09PFF	NX West Midlands	BX12DDF	NX West Midlands
BX02AUJ	NX West Midlands	BX09PFG	NX West Midlands	BX12DDJ	NX West Midlands
BX02AUL	NX West Midlands	BX09PFJ	NX West Midlands	BX12DDK	NX West Midlands
BX02AUM	NX West Midlands	BX09PFK	NX West Midlands	BX12DDL	NX West Midlands
BX02AUN	NX West Midlands	BX09PFN	NX West Midlands	BX12DDN	NX West Midlands
BX02AUO	NX West Midlands	BX09PFO	NX West Midlands	BX12DDO	NX West Midlands
BX02AUP	NX West Midlands	BX09PFU	NX West Midlands	BX12DDU	NX West Midlands
BX02AUR	NX West Midlands	BX09PFV	NX West Midlands	BX12DDV	NX West Midlands
BX02AUT	NX West Midlands	BX09PFY	NX West Midlands	BX12DDY	NX West Midlands
BX02AUU	NX West Midlands	BX09PGE	NX West Midlands	BX12DDZ	NX West Midlands
BX02AUV	NX West Midlands	BX09PGF	NX West Midlands	BX12DEU	NX West Midlands
BX02AUW	NX West Midlands	BX09PGK	NX West Midlands	BX12DFA	NX West Midlands
BX02AUY	NX West Midlands	BX09PGO	NX West Midlands	BX12DFC	NX West Midlands
BX02AVB	NX West Midlands	BX09PGU	NX West Midlands	BX12DFD	NX West Midlands
BX02AVD	NX West Midlands	BX09PGV	NX West Midlands	BX12DFE	NX West Midlands
BX02AVE	NX West Midlands	BX09PGY	NX West Midlands	BX12DFF	NX West Midlands
BX02AVF	NX West Midlands	BX09PGZ	NX West Midlands	BX12DFG	NX West Midlands
BX02AVG	NX West Midlands	BX09PHA	NX West Midlands	BX12DFJ	NX West Midlands
BX02AVJ	NX West Midlands	BX09PHF	NX West Midlands	BX12DFK	NX West Midlands
BX02AVK	NX West Midlands	BX09PHJ	NX West Midlands	BX12DFL	NX West Midlands
BX02AVL	NX West Midlands	BX09PHK	NX West Midlands	BX12DFN	NX West Midlands
BX02AVN	NX West Midlands	BX09PHN	NX West Midlands	BX12DFO	NX West Midlands
BX02AVO	NX West Midlands	BX09SHZ	Rotala	BX12DFP	NX West Midlands
BX02AVP	NX West Midlands	BX09SJO	Rotala	BX12DFU	NX West Midlands
BX02AVR	NX West Midlands	BX09SJU	Rotala	BX12DFV	NX West Midlands
BX02AVT	NX West Midlands	BX09SJV	Rotala	BX12DFY	NX West Midlands
BX02AVU	NX West Midlands	BX09SNV	Rotala	BX12DFZ	NX West Midlands
BX02AVV	NX West Midlands	BX09SNY	Rotala	BX12DGE	NX West Midlands
BX02AVY	NX West Midlands	BX09SNZ	Rotala	BX12DGF	NX West Midlands
BX02CMO	RATP Group	BX09SOU	Rotala	BX12DGO	NX West Midlands
BX02CMU	RATP Group	BX09SRO	Rotala	BX12DGU	NX West Midlands
BX04MXR	NX Coaching	BX09SVJ	Rotala	BX12DGV	NX West Midlands
BX04MZV	Rotala	BX10ABF	NX West Midlands	BX12DGY	NX West Midlands

Reg	Operator	Reg	Operator	Reg	Operator
BX12DGZ	NX West Midlands	BX13JVH	NX West Midlands	BX54DNV	NX West Midlands
BX12DHA	NX West Midlands	BX13JVJ	NX West Midlands	BX54DNY	NX West Midlands
BX12DHC	NX West Midlands	BX13JVK	NX West Midlands	BX54DOA	NX West Midlands
BX12DHD	NX West Midlands	BX13JVL	NX West Midlands	BX54DOH	NX West Midlands
BX12DHE	NX West Midlands	BX13JVM	NX West Midlands	BX54ECF	RATP Group
BX12DHF	NX West Midlands	BX13JVN	NX West Midlands	BX54ECJ	RATP Group
BX12DHG	NX West Midlands	BX13JVO	NX West Midlands	BX54XPM	NX West Midlands
BX12DHJ	NX West Midlands	BX13JVP	NX West Midlands	BX54XPN	NX West Midlands
BX12DHK	NX West Midlands	BX13JVR	NX West Midlands	BX54XPO	NX West Midlands
BX12DHL	NX West Midlands	BX13JVT	NX West Midlands	BX54XPP	NX West Midlands
BX12DHM	NX West Midlands	BX13JVU	NX West Midlands	BX54XPR	NX West Midlands
BX12DHN	NX West Midlands	BX13JVV	NX West Midlands	BX54XPT	NX West Midlands
BX12DHO	NX West Midlands	BX13JVW	NX West Midlands	BX54XPU	NX West Midlands
BX12DHP	NX West Midlands	BX13JVY	NX West Midlands	BX54XPV	NX West Midlands
BX12DHU	NX West Midlands	BX13JVZ	NX West Midlands	BX54XPW	NX West Midlands
BX12DHV	NX West Midlands	BX13JWA	NX West Midlands	BX54XPY	NX West Midlands
BX12DHY	NX West Midlands	BX13JWC	NX West Midlands	BX54XPZ	NX West Midlands
BX12DHZ	NX West Midlands	BX13JWD	NX West Midlands	BX54XRA	NX West Midlands
BX12DJD	NX West Midlands	BX13JWE	NX West Midlands	BX54XRB	NX West Midlands
BX12DJE	NX West Midlands	BX13JWF	NX West Midlands	BX54XRC	NX West Midlands
BX12DJF	NX West Midlands	BX13JWG	NX West Midlands	BX54XRD	NX West Midlands
BX12DJJ	NX West Midlands	BX13JWJ	NX West Midlands	BX54XRE	NX West Midlands
BX12DJK	NX West Midlands	BX13JWK	NX West Midlands	BX54XRF	NX West Midlands
BX12DJO	NX West Midlands	BX13JWL	NX West Midlands	BX54XRG	NX West Midlands
BX12DKF	NX West Midlands	BX13JWM	NX West Midlands	BX54XRH	NX West Midlands
BX13JNF	NX West Midlands	BX13JWN	NX West Midlands	BX54XRJ	NX West Midlands
BX13JNJ	NX West Midlands	BX13JWO	NX West Midlands	BX54XRK	NX West Midlands
BX13JNK	NX West Midlands	BX54DCU	NX West Midlands	BX54XRL	NX West Midlands
BX13JNL	NX West Midlands	BX54DCV	NX West Midlands	BX54XRM	NX West Midlands
BX13JNN	NX West Midlands	BX54DCY	NX West Midlands	BX54XRN	NX West Midlands
BX13JNO	NX West Midlands	BX54DDA	NX West Midlands	BX54XRO	NX West Midlands
BX13JNU	NX West Midlands	BX54DDE	NX West Midlands	BX54XRR	NX West Midlands
BX13JNV	NX West Midlands	BX54DDF	NX West Midlands	BX54XRT	NX West Midlands
BX13JNZ	NX West Midlands	BX54DDJ	NX West Midlands	BX54XRU	NX West Midlands
BX13JOA	NX West Midlands	BX54DDK	NX West Midlands	BX54XRV	NX West Midlands
BX13JOH	NX West Midlands	BX54DDL	NX West Midlands	BX54XRW	NX West Midlands
BX13JOJ	NX West Midlands	BX54DDN	NX West Midlands	BX54XRY	NX West Midlands
BX13JOU	NX West Midlands	BX54DDO	NX West Midlands	BX54XRZ	NX West Midlands
BX13JOV	NX West Midlands	BX54DDU	NX West Midlands	BX54XSA	NX West Midlands
BX13JPF	NX West Midlands	BX54DDV	NX West Midlands	BX54XSB	NX West Midlands
BX13JPJ	NX West Midlands	BX54DDY	NX West Midlands	BX54XSC	NX West Midlands
BX13JPO	NX West Midlands	BX54DDZ	NX West Midlands	BX54XSD	NX West Midlands
BX13JPU	NX West Midlands	BX54DEU	NX West Midlands	BX54XSE	NX West Midlands
BX13JPV	NX West Midlands	BX54DFA	NX West Midlands	BX54XSF	NX West Midlands
BX13JPY	NX West Midlands	BX54DFC	NX West Midlands	BX54XSG	NX West Midlands
BX13JRO	NX West Midlands	BX54DFD	NX West Midlands	BX54XSH	NX West Midlands
BX13JRU	NX West Midlands	BX54DFE	NX West Midlands	BX54XSJ	NX West Midlands
BX13JRV	NX West Midlands	BX54DFF	NX West Midlands	BX54XSK	NX West Midlands
BX13JRZ	NX West Midlands	BX54DFG	NX West Midlands	BX54XSL	NX West Midlands
BX13JSU	NX West Midlands	BX54DFJ	NX West Midlands	BX54XSM	NX West Midlands
BX13JSV	NX West Midlands	BX54DFK	NX West Midlands	BX54XTA	NX West Midlands
BX13JSY	NX West Midlands	BX54DFN	NX West Midlands	BX54XTB	NX West Midlands
BX13JSZ	NX West Midlands	BX54DFO	NX West Midlands	BX54XTC	NX West Midlands
BX13JTO	NX West Midlands	BX54DFP	NX West Midlands	BX54XTD	NX West Midlands
BX13JTU	NX West Midlands	BX54DFU	NX West Midlands	BX55XOA	NX West Midlands
BX13JTV	NX West Midlands	BX54DFV	NX West Midlands	BX56BJZ	Rotala
BX13JTY	NX West Midlands	BX54DFY	NX West Midlands	BX56BKA	Rotala
BX13JTZ	NX West Midlands	BX54DFZ	NX West Midlands	BX56BPU	Rotala
BX13JUA	NX West Midlands	BX54DGE	NX West Midlands	BX56BPY	Rotala
BX13JUC	NX West Midlands	BX54DGF	NX West Midlands	BX56BVE	Rotala
BX13JUE	NX West Midlands	BX54DGO	NX West Midlands	BX56BVF	Rotala
BX13JUF	NX West Midlands	BX54DGU	NX West Midlands	BX56VTY	RATP Group
BX13JUH	NX West Midlands	BX54DGV	NX West Midlands	BX56VTZ	RATP Group
BX13JUJ	NX West Midlands	BX54DGY	NX West Midlands	BX56XBS	NX West Midlands
BX13JUK	NX West Midlands	BX54DGZ	NX West Midlands	BX56XBT	NX West Midlands
BX13JUO	NX West Midlands	BX54DHA	NX West Midlands	BX56XBU	NX West Midlands
BX13JUT	NX West Midlands	BX54DHC	NX West Midlands	BX56XBV	NX West Midlands
BX13JUU	NX West Midlands	BX54DHD	NX West Midlands	BX56XBW	NX West Midlands
BX13JUV	NX West Midlands	BX54DHE	NX West Midlands	BX56XBY	NX West Midlands
BX13JUW	NX West Midlands	BX54DHF	NX West Midlands	BX56XBZ	NX West Midlands
BX13JUY	NX West Midlands	BX54DHG	NX West Midlands	BX56XCA	NX West Midlands
BX13JVA	NX West Midlands	BX54DND	NX West Midlands	BX56XCB	NX West Midlands
BX13JVC	NX West Midlands	BX54DNE	NX West Midlands	BX56XCC	NX West Midlands
BX13JVD	NX West Midlands	BX54DNF	NX West Midlands	BX56XCD	NX West Midlands
BX13JVE	NX West Midlands	BX54DNJ	NX West Midlands	BX56XCE	NX West Midlands
BX13JVF	NX West Midlands	BX54DNN	NX West Midlands	BX56XCF	NX West Midlands
BX13JVG	NX West Midlands	BX54DNO	NX West Midlands	BX56XCG	NX West Midlands

Reg	Operator	Reg	Operator	Reg	Operator
BX56XCH	NX West Midlands	BX59NTN	NX West Midlands	BX61LMY	NX West Midlands
BX56XCJ	NX West Midlands	BX61LHC	NX West Midlands	BX61LNA	NX West Midlands
BX56XCK	NX West Midlands	BX61LHD	NX West Midlands	BX61LND	NX West Midlands
BX56XCL	NX West Midlands	BX61LHE	NX West Midlands	BX61LNE	NX West Midlands
BX56XCM	NX West Midlands	BX61LHF	NX West Midlands	BX61LNF	NX West Midlands
BX56XCN	NX West Midlands	BX61LHG	NX West Midlands	BX61LNG	NX West Midlands
BX56XCO	NX West Midlands	BX61LHH	NX West Midlands	BX61LNH	NX West Midlands
BX56XCP	NX West Midlands	BX61LHJ	NX West Midlands	BX61LNJ	NX West Midlands
BX56XCR	NX West Midlands	BX61LHK	NX West Midlands	BX61LNK	NX West Midlands
BX56XCS	NX West Midlands	BX61LHL	NX West Midlands	BX61LNM	NX West Midlands
BX56XCT	NX West Midlands	BX61LHM	NX West Midlands	BX61LNN	NX West Midlands
BX56XCU	NX West Midlands	BX61LHN	NX West Midlands	BX61LNO	NX West Midlands
BX56XCV	NX West Midlands	BX61LHO	NX West Midlands	BX61LNP	NX West Midlands
BX56XCW	NX West Midlands	BX61LHP	NX West Midlands	BX61LNR	NX West Midlands
BX56XCY	NX West Midlands	BX61LHR	NX West Midlands	BX61LNT	NX West Midlands
BX56XCZ	NX West Midlands	BX61LHT	NX West Midlands	BX61LNU	NX West Midlands
BX56XDA	NX West Midlands	BX61LHU	NX West Midlands	BX61LNV	NX West Midlands
BX56XDB	NX West Midlands	BX61LHV	NX West Midlands	BX61LNW	NX West Midlands
BX56XDC	NX West Midlands	BX61LHW	NX West Midlands	BX61LNY	NX West Midlands
BX56XDD	NX West Midlands	BX61LHY	NX West Midlands	BX61LNZ	NX West Midlands
BX56XDE	NX West Midlands	BX61LHZ	NX West Midlands	BX61XBE	NX West Midlands
BX56XDG	NX West Midlands	BX61LJA	NX West Midlands	BX61XBF	NX West Midlands
BX56XDH	NX West Midlands	BX61LJC	NX West Midlands	BX61XBG	NX West Midlands
BX56XDJ	NX West Midlands	BX61LJE	NX West Midlands	BX61XBH	NX West Midlands
BX58AON	Rotala	BX61LJF	NX West Midlands	BX61XBJ	NX West Midlands
BX58AOO	Rotala	BX61LJJ	NX West Midlands	BX61XBK	NX West Midlands
BX58AOU	Rotala	BX61LJK	NX West Midlands	BX61XBL	NX West Midlands
BX58AOV	Rotala	BX61LJL	NX West Midlands	BX61XBM	NX West Midlands
BX58AOW	Rotala	BX61LJN	NX West Midlands	BX61XBN	NX West Midlands
BX58AOY	Rotala	BX61LJO	NX West Midlands	BX61XBO	NX West Midlands
BX58AOZ	Rotala	BX61LJU	NX West Midlands	BX61XBP	NX West Midlands
BX58APF	Rotala	BX61LJY	NX West Midlands	BX61XBR	NX West Midlands
BX58APK	Rotala	BX61LJZ	NX West Midlands	BX61XBS	NX West Midlands
BX58SXN	NX West Midlands	BX61LKA	NX West Midlands	BX61XBT	NX West Midlands
BX58SXO	NX West Midlands	BX61LKC	NX West Midlands	BX61XBU	NX West Midlands
BX58SXP	NX West Midlands	BX61LKD	NX West Midlands	BX61XBV	NX West Midlands
BX58SXR	NX West Midlands	BX61LKE	NX West Midlands	BX61XBW	NX West Midlands
BX58SXS	NX West Midlands	BX61LKF	NX West Midlands	BX61XBY	NX West Midlands
BX58SXT	NX West Midlands	BX61LKG	NX West Midlands	BX61XBZ	NX West Midlands
BX58SXU	NX West Midlands	BX61LKJ	NX West Midlands	BX61XCA	NX West Midlands
BX58SXV	NX West Midlands	BX61LKK	NX West Midlands	BX61XCB	NX West Midlands
BX58SXW	NX West Midlands	BX61LKL	NX West Midlands	BX61XCC	NX West Midlands
BX58SXY	NX West Midlands	BX61LKM	NX West Midlands	BX62FAK	Rotala
BX58SXZ	NX West Midlands	BX61LKN	NX West Midlands	BX62FBF	Rotala
BX58SYA	NX West Midlands	BX61LKO	NX West Midlands	BX62FDC	Rotala
BX58SYC	NX West Midlands	BX61LKP	NX West Midlands	BX62FEM	Rotala
BX58SYE	NX West Midlands	BX61LKU	NX West Midlands	BX62FEU	Rotala
BX58SYG	NX West Midlands	BX61LKV	NX West Midlands	BX62FGD	Rotala
BX58SYH	NX West Midlands	BX61LKY	NX West Midlands	BX62FNV	Rotala
BX58SYJ	NX West Midlands	BX61LKZ	NX West Midlands	BX62FOJ	Rotala
BX58SYO	NX West Midlands	BX61LLA	NX West Midlands	BX62FUO	Rotala
BX58SYP	NX West Midlands	BX61LLC	NX West Midlands	BX62FUU	Rotala
BX58SYR	NX West Midlands	BX61LLD	NX West Midlands	BX62FYY	Rotala
BX58SYS	NX West Midlands	BX61LLE	NX West Midlands	BX62FZL	Rotala
BX58SYT	NX West Midlands	BX61LLF	NX West Midlands	BX62FZP	Rotala
BX58SYU	NX West Midlands	BX61LLG	NX West Midlands	BX62SBY	NX West Midlands
BX58SYV	NX West Midlands	BX61LLJ	NX West Midlands	BX62SCV	NX West Midlands
BX58SYW	NX West Midlands	BX61LLK	NX West Midlands	BX62SEY	NX West Midlands
BX58SYY	NX West Midlands	BX61LLM	NX West Midlands	BX62SFJ	NX West Midlands
BX58SYZ	NX West Midlands	BX61LLN	NX West Midlands	BX62SFY	NX West Midlands
BX58SZC	NX West Midlands	BX61LLO	NX West Midlands	BX62SJU	NX West Midlands
BX58SZD	NX West Midlands	BX61LLP	NX West Midlands	BX62SKJ	NX West Midlands
BX58SZE	NX West Midlands	BX61LLR	NX West Midlands	BX62SKU	NX West Midlands
BX59NSU	NX West Midlands	BX61LLT	NX West Midlands	BX62SKV	NX West Midlands
BX59NSV	NX West Midlands	BX61LLU	NX West Midlands	BX62SLV	NX West Midlands
BX59NSY	NX West Midlands	BX61LLV	NX West Midlands	BX62SNF	NX West Midlands
BX59NSZ	NX West Midlands	BX61LLW	NX West Midlands	BX62SNK	NX West Midlands
BX59NTA	NX West Midlands	BX61LLZ	NX West Midlands	BX62SNU	NX West Midlands
BX59NTC	NX West Midlands	BX61LME	NX West Midlands	BX62SOH	NX West Midlands
BX59NTD	NX West Midlands	BX61LMF	NX West Midlands	BX62SUA	NX West Midlands
BX59NTE	NX West Midlands	BX61LMJ	NX West Midlands	BX62SVG	NX West Midlands
BX59NTF	NX West Midlands	BX61LMK	NX West Midlands	BX62SVP	NX West Midlands
BX59NTG	NX West Midlands	BX61LML	NX West Midlands	BX62SVU	NX West Midlands
BX59NTJ	NX West Midlands	BX61LMM	NX West Midlands	BX62SXD	NX West Midlands
BX59NTK	NX West Midlands	BX61LMO	NX West Midlands	BX62SXH	NX West Midlands
BX59NTL	NX West Midlands	BX61LMU	NX West Midlands	BX62SXR	NX West Midlands
BX59NTM	NX West Midlands	BX61LMV	NX West Midlands	BX62SYA	NX West Midlands

Reg	Operator	Reg	Operator	Reg	Operator
BX62SYC	NX West Midlands	FB02LFP	TrentBarton	FJ03VWL	TrentBarton
BX62SYW	NX West Midlands	FC07MCF	EYMS Group	FJ03VWM	TrentBarton
BX62SYZ	NX West Midlands	FD02SFE	Centrebus	FJ03VWN	TrentBarton
BX62SZC	NX West Midlands	FD05ANV	NX Coaching	FJ03VWP	TrentBarton
BX62SZD	NX West Midlands	FD05AOD	NX Coaching	FJ03VWR	TrentBarton
BX62SZE	NX West Midlands	FD51EYV	Centrebus	FJ03VWS	TrentBarton
BX62SZJ	NX West Midlands	FD51EYY	Centrebus	FJ03VWT	TrentBarton
C8NEX	NX West Midlands	FD53WWH	TrentBarton	FJ03VWU	TrentBarton
C173ECK	Transdev	FD53WWJ	TrentBarton	FJ03VWV	TrentBarton
C718LTO	TrentBarton	FD53WWK	TrentBarton	FJ03VWW	TrentBarton
C719LTO	TrentBarton	FD53WWL	TrentBarton	FJ03VWX	TrentBarton
C720NNN	TrentBarton	FD54DHL	NX Coaching	FJ03VWY	TrentBarton
C792SFS	Transdev	FD54DHM	NX Coaching	FJ03VXA	TrentBarton
CE52UWR	RATP Group	FD54JXZ	TrentBarton	FJ03VXB	TrentBarton
CE52UWS	RATP Group	FD54JYA	TrentBarton	FJ03VXC	TrentBarton
CE52UWU	RATP Group	FD54JYB	TrentBarton	FJ06FLH	NX Coaching
CE52UWX	Centrebus	FD54JYC	TrentBarton	FJ06GGA	RATP Group
CE52UWY	Centrebus	FD54JYE	TrentBarton	FJ06GGK	NX Coaching
CE52UWZ	Centrebus	FD54JYF	TrentBarton	FJ06GGO	RATP Group
CE52UXF	Centrebus	FE02BGE	TrentBarton	FJ06URG	NX Coaching
CN05DZH	Rotala	FE02BGF	TrentBarton	FJ06URH	NX Coaching
CRZ7495	Rotala	FE02BGK	TrentBarton	FJ06URO	NX Coaching
CW03XDM	Rotala	FE02BGO	TrentBarton	FJ07DVH	NX Coaching
D1WET	Centrebus	FE02KCZ	TrentBarton	FJ07DVK	NX Coaching
D188FYM	TrentBarton	FE02KDF	TrentBarton	FJ07DVL	NX Coaching
D192FYM	TrentBarton	FE02KDJ	TrentBarton	FJ07DVM	NX Coaching
D951NDA	NX West Midlands	FE02KDK	TrentBarton	FJ07DVN	NX Coaching
D955NDA	NX West Midlands	FE02KDN	TrentBarton	FJ07DVO	NX Coaching
D959NDA	NX West Midlands	FE02KDO	TrentBarton	FJ07DVP	NX Coaching
DAZ4302	Centrebus	FE02KDU	TrentBarton	FJ07DVR	NX Coaching
DE52NWY	RATP Group	FE02KDV	TrentBarton	FJ07DVY	RATP Group
DE52NXU	RATP Group	FE02KDX	TrentBarton	FJ07DVZ	RATP Group
DE52NXV	RATP Group	FE02KEJ	TrentBarton	FJ07DWA	RATP Group
DE52NYW	RATP Group	FE02KFA	TrentBarton	FJ07DWC	RATP Group
DE52NYX	RATP Group	FE02KFD	TrentBarton	FJ07DWK	Yourbus
DE52NYY	RATP Group	FE02KFF	TrentBarton	FJ07DWL	Yourbus
DK60AMX	RATP Group	FE02KFG	TrentBarton	FJ07DWN	NX Coaching
DRZ4018	Rotala	FE02KFJ	TrentBarton	FJ08BYH	Transdev
DX09GYS	RATP Group	FE02KFK	TrentBarton	FJ08BYK	Transdev
DX57JXS	RATP Group	FE02KFL	TrentBarton	FJ08BYL	Transdev
DX57REU	RATP Group	FE52KNS	Centrebus	FJ08BYM	Transdev
DX57TVW	RATP Group	FG56PAO	RATP Group	FJ08BYN	Transdev
E208GCG	RATP Group	FG56PBF	RATP Group	FJ08BYU	Transdev
E307MSG	Transdev	FG56PBO	RATP Group	FJ08BYV	Transdev
E308MSG	Transdev	FH05TKJ	TrentBarton	FJ08BYW	Transdev
E313MSG	Transdev	FH05TKK	TrentBarton	FJ08BYX	Transdev
E314MSG	Transdev	FH05URN	NX Coaching	FJ08BYZ	Transdev
EU03EUD	Centrebus	FH05URO	NX Coaching	FJ08BZP	Transdev
EU04BZY	Centrebus	FH05URP	NX Coaching	FJ08BZR	Transdev
EU04CPV	RATP Group	FH05URR	NX Coaching	FJ08BZS	Transdev
EU05BZM	RATP Group	FH06EAW	NX Coaching	FJ08BZT	Transdev
EU05VBG	RATP Group	FH06EAX	NX Coaching	FJ08BZU	Transdev
EU05VBJ	RATP Group	FH06EBO	RATP Group	FJ08BZV	Transdev
EU05VBK	RATP Group	FH06KGK	Centrebus	FJ08BZW	Transdev
EU05VBL	RATP Group	FH54VRX	TrentBarton	FJ08BZX	Transdev
EU05VBM	RATP Group	FH54VRY	TrentBarton	FJ08MBF	Centrebus
EU05VBN	RATP Group	FH54VRZ	TrentBarton	FJ08MBO	Centrebus
EU05VBO	RATP Group	FJ03VVM	TrentBarton	FJ08MBU	Centrebus
EU05VBP	RATP Group	FJ03VVN	TrentBarton	FJ08MBV	Centrebus
EU05VBT	RATP Group	FJ03VVP	TrentBarton	FJ08WHR	TrentBarton
EU08FHC	Rotala	FJ03VVR	TrentBarton	FJ08WHS	TrentBarton
EU08FHD	RATP Group	FJ03VVS	TrentBarton	FJ09BXA	TrentBarton
EYC73	EYMS Group	FJ03VVT	TrentBarton	FJ09BXB	TrentBarton
EYH876	EYMS Group	FJ03VVU	TrentBarton	FJ09BXC	TrentBarton
F43YHB	Transdev	FJ03VVW	TrentBarton	FJ09BXD	TrentBarton
F96PRE	Transdev	FJ03VVX	TrentBarton	FJ09BXE	TrentBarton
F211WRU	RATP Group	FJ03VVY	TrentBarton	FJ09BXF	TrentBarton
F212WRU	RATP Group	FJ03VVZ	TrentBarton	FJ09BXG	TrentBarton
F213WRU	RATP Group	FJ03VWA	TrentBarton	FJ09BXH	TrentBarton
F214WRU	RATP Group	FJ03VWB	TrentBarton	FJ09BXK	TrentBarton
F251YTJ	Transdev	FJ03VWC	TrentBarton	FJ09BXL	TrentBarton
F262YTJ	Transdev	FJ03VWD	TrentBarton	FJ09BXM	TrentBarton
F263YTJ	Transdev	FJ03VWE	TrentBarton	FJ09BXN	TrentBarton
F349WSC	Transdev	FJ03VWF	TrentBarton	FJ09BXO	TrentBarton
F356WSC	Transdev	FJ03VWG	TrentBarton	FJ09BXP	TrentBarton
FA04LJK	Rotala	FJ03VWH	TrentBarton	FJ09KNV	Transdev
		FJ03VWK	TrentBarton	FJ09MVR	TrentBarton

Reg	Operator	Reg	Operator	Reg	Operator
FJ09MVS	TrentBarton	FJ11MKL	NX Coaching	FJ55AAY	TrentBarton
FJ09MVT	TrentBarton	FJ11MKM	NX Coaching	FJ55AAZ	TrentBarton
FJ09MVU	TrentBarton	FJ11MKN	NX Coaching	FJ55ABF	TrentBarton
FJ09MVV	TrentBarton	FJ11MKU	NX Coaching	FJ55ABK	TrentBarton
FJ09MVW	TrentBarton	FJ11MKV	NX Coaching	FJ55ABN	TrentBarton
FJ09MVX	TrentBarton	FJ11MLE	Rotala	FJ55ABO	TrentBarton
FJ09MVY	TrentBarton	FJ11MLF	Rotala	FJ55ABV	TrentBarton
FJ09MVZ	TrentBarton	FJ11MLK	Rotala	FJ55BZM	TrentBarton
FJ09MWA	TrentBarton	FJ11MLL	Rotala	FJ55BZN	TrentBarton
FJ09MWC	TrentBarton	FJ11MLN	Rotala	FJ55BZO	TrentBarton
FJ09MWD	TrentBarton	FJ11MLO	Rotala	FJ55BZP	TrentBarton
FJ09MWE	TrentBarton	FJ11MLV	RATP Group	FJ55BZR	TrentBarton
FJ09MWF	TrentBarton	FJ11MLY	Yourbus	FJ55BZS	TrentBarton
FJ09MWG	TrentBarton	FJ11MLZ	Yourbus	FJ55BZT	TrentBarton
FJ09MWK	TrentBarton	FJ11MMA	Yourbus	FJ55BZU	TrentBarton
FJ09MWL	TrentBarton	FJ11MME	Yourbus	FJ56PBU	Yourbus
FJ09XPA	TrentBarton	FJ11MMF	Yourbus	FJ56PBX	Yourbus
FJ09XPB	TrentBarton	FJ11MMK	Yourbus	FJ56PBY	Yourbus
FJ09XPC	TrentBarton	FJ11MMO	Yourbus	FJ56PBZ	Yourbus
FJ09XPD	TrentBarton	FJ11MMU	Yourbus	FJ56PCF	Yourbus
FJ09XPE	TrentBarton	FJ11MMX	Yourbus	FJ56PFE	NX Coaching
FJ09XPF	TrentBarton	FJ11MOA	Yourbus	FJ56PFF	NX Coaching
FJ09XPG	TrentBarton	FJ11RAU	NX Coaching	FJ56YBV	Centrebus
FJ09XPH	TrentBarton	FJ11RAX	NX Coaching	FJ56YBW	Centrebus
FJ09XPK	TrentBarton	FJ11RBF	NX Coaching	FJ56ZWC	Centrebus
FJ09XPL	TrentBarton	FJ11RDO	NX Coaching	FJ57CYS	Rotala
FJ10EHF	TrentBarton	FJ11RDU	NX Coaching	FJ57CYT	Rotala
FJ10EHG	TrentBarton	FJ11RDV	NX Coaching	FJ57CYU	Rotala
FJ10EHH	TrentBarton	FJ12FXD	NX Coaching	FJ57CYV	Rotala
FJ10EHK	TrentBarton	FJ12FXE	RATP Group	FJ57CYW	Rotala
FJ10EHL	TrentBarton	FJ12FXT	RATP Group	FJ57CZB	Yourbus
FJ10EHM	TrentBarton	FJ12FYH	NX Coaching	FJ57CZC	Rotala
FJ10EHN	TrentBarton	FJ12FYL	NX Coaching	FJ57CZG	Rotala
FJ10EZG	NX Coaching	FJ12FYM	NX Coaching	FJ57CZM	Transdev
FJ10EZH	NX Coaching	FJ12FYN	NX Coaching	FJ57CZN	Transdev
FJ10EZK	NX Coaching	FJ12FYO	NX Coaching	FJ57KGZ	NX Coaching
FJ10EZL	NX Coaching	FJ12FYP	NX Coaching	FJ57KHA	NX Coaching
FJ10EZM	NX Coaching	FJ12FYR	NX Coaching	FJ57KHC	NX Coaching
FJ10EZN	NX Coaching	FJ12GAX	NX Coaching	FJ57KHD	NX Coaching
FJ10EZO	NX Coaching	FJ12GBE	NX Coaching	FJ57KHE	NX Coaching
FJ10EZP	NX Coaching	FJ12GBF	NX Coaching	FJ57KHF	NX Coaching
FJ10EZR	NX Coaching	FJ12GBO	NX Coaching	FJ57KHG	NX Coaching
FJ10EZV	NX Coaching	FJ12GBU	NX Coaching	FJ57KHK	NX Coaching
FJ10OXM	TrentBarton	FJ12GBV	NX Coaching	FJ57KHL	NX Coaching
FJ10OXN	TrentBarton	FJ13DZX	RATP Group	FJ57KHM	NX Coaching
FJ10OXP	TrentBarton	FJ13DZY	RATP Group	FJ57KHO	NX Coaching
FJ10OXR	TrentBarton	FJ13DZZ	RATP Group	FJ57KHP	NX Coaching
FJ10OXS	TrentBarton	FJ13EBC	RATP Group	FJ57KHR	NX Coaching
FJ11GJO	Rotala	FJ13EBD	RATP Group	FJ57KHT	NX Coaching
FJ11GJU	Rotala	FJ13EBF	RATP Group	FJ57KHX	NX Coaching
FJ11GJX	EYMS Group	FJ13EBG	NX Coaching	FJ57KHY	NX Coaching
FJ11GJY	EYMS Group	FJ13EBK	NX Coaching	FJ57KHZ	NX Coaching
FJ11GJZ	EYMS Group	FJ13EBL	NX Coaching	FJ57KJA	NX Coaching
FJ11GKA	EYMS Group	FJ13EBM	NX Coaching	FJ57KJE	NX Coaching
FJ11GKC	EYMS Group	FJ13EBN	NX Coaching	FJ57KJO	NX Coaching
FJ11GKE	Yourbus	FJ13EBO	NX Coaching	FJ57KJU	NX Coaching
FJ11GKP	Rotala	FJ13EBP	NX Coaching	FJ58AJU	RATP Group
FJ11GKU	Rotala	FJ13EBU	NX Coaching	FJ58AJV	RATP Group
FJ11GKV	Rotala	FJ13EBV	NX Coaching	FJ58KJK	TrentBarton
FJ11GKX	Rotala	FJ13EBX	NX Coaching	FJ58KJN	TrentBarton
FJ11GLF	RATP Group	FJ13EBZ	NX Coaching	FJ58KJO	TrentBarton
FJ11GLK	Rotala	FJ13ECA	NX Coaching	FJ58KJU	TrentBarton
FJ11GLV	EYMS Group	FJ13ECC	NX Coaching	FJ58KJV	TrentBarton
FJ11GLY	Yourbus	FJ13ECD	NX Coaching	FJ58KJX	TrentBarton
FJ11GLZ	Rotala	FJ13ECE	NX Coaching	FJ58KJY	TrentBarton
FJ11GMV	RATP Group	FJ13ECF	NX Coaching	FJ58KJZ	TrentBarton
FJ11MJK	NX Coaching	FJ13ECN	NX Coaching	FJ58KKA	TrentBarton
FJ11MJO	NX Coaching	FJ13ECT	NX Coaching	FJ58KKB	TrentBarton
FJ11MJU	NX Coaching	FJ53LZW	EYMS Group	FJ58KKC	TrentBarton
FJ11MJV	NX Coaching	FJ55AAE	TrentBarton	FJ58KKD	TrentBarton
FJ11MJX	NX Coaching	FJ55AAF	TrentBarton	FJ58KKE	TrentBarton
FJ11MJY	NX Coaching	FJ55AAK	TrentBarton	FJ58KKF	TrentBarton
FJ11MKD	NX Coaching	FJ55AAN	TrentBarton	FJ58KKG	TrentBarton
FJ11MKE	NX Coaching	FJ55AAO	TrentBarton	FJ58KKH	TrentBarton
FJ11MKF	NX Coaching	FJ55AAU	TrentBarton	FJ58KKL	TrentBarton
FJ11MKG	NX Coaching	FJ55AAV	TrentBarton	FJ58KKM	TrentBarton
FJ11MKK	NX Coaching	FJ55AAX	TrentBarton	FJ58KKN	TrentBarton

FJ58KKO	TrentBarton	FJ61EXG	NX Coaching	FN54AEV	TrentBarton
FJ58KKP	TrentBarton	FJ61EXH	NX Coaching	FN54AEW	TrentBarton
FJ58KKR	TrentBarton	FJ61EXK	RATP Group	FN54AEX	TrentBarton
FJ58KKS	TrentBarton	FJ61EXL	RATP Group	FN54AEY	TrentBarton
FJ58KKT	TrentBarton	FJ61EXM	Yourbus	FN54AEZ	TrentBarton
FJ58KKU	TrentBarton	FJ61EXN	Yourbus	FN56BWV	Centrebus
FJ58LSL	Transdev	FJ61EXO	Yourbus	FN56CZS	Centrebus
FJ58LSN	Transdev	FJ61EXP	Yourbus	FN62CCV	RATP Group
FJ58LSO	Transdev	FJ61EXR	Yourbus	FN62CCZ	RATP Group
FJ58LSU	Transdev	FJ61EXS	Yourbus	FN62CDE	RATP Group
FJ58LSV	Transdev	FJ61EXT	Yourbus	FN62CEA	EYMS Group
FJ58LSX	Transdev	FJ61EXU	Yourbus	FN62CEU	EYMS Group
FJ58LSY	Transdev	FJ61EXV	Yourbus	FN62CGX	EYMS Group
FJ58LSZ	Transdev	FJ61EXW	Yourbus	FOR35T	Rotala
FJ58LTA	Transdev	FJ61EXX	Yourbus	FP04CFE	TrentBarton
FJ58LTE	Transdev	FJ61EXZ	Yourbus	FP51GXR	TrentBarton
FJ58LTF	Transdev	FJ61EYA	Yourbus	FP51GXS	TrentBarton
FJ58LTK	Transdev	FJ61EYC	Yourbus	FP51GXT	TrentBarton
FJ58LTN	Transdev	FJ61EYD	Yourbus	FP51GXU	TrentBarton
FJ58LTT	Transdev	FJ61EYK	RATP Group	FP51GXV	TrentBarton
FJ58LTU	Transdev	FJ61EYL	RATP Group	FP51GXW	TrentBarton
FJ58LTV	Transdev	FJ61GZL	RATP Group	FP51GXX	TrentBarton
FJ58LTX	Transdev	FJ61GZM	RATP Group	FP51GXY	TrentBarton
FJ58LUA	Transdev	FJ61GZN	RATP Group	FP51GXZ	TrentBarton
FJ59AOV	RATP Group	FL10NFV	TrentBarton	FP51GYE	TrentBarton
FJ59APX	RATP Group	FM52GKV	Centrebus	FX04TJY	Centrebus
FJ59APY	RATP Group	FN02VBD	NX Coaching	FY02OTF	RATP Group
FJ59ARO	RATP Group	FN02VBE	NX Coaching	FY52RZC	RATP Group
FJ59FYS	Centrebus	FN04BRX	TrentBarton	G51FKG	Transdev
FJ59FYT	Centrebus	FN04BRZ	TrentBarton	G52FKG	Transdev
FJ60EFU	RATP Group	FN04BSU	TrentBarton	G127NGN	Centrebus
FJ60EFV	RATP Group	FN04BSV	TrentBarton	G215KRN	Rotala
FJ60EFW	RATP Group	FN04BSX	TrentBarton	G281UMJ	Transdev
FJ60EFX	Yourbus	FN04BSY	TrentBarton	G289UMJ	Transdev
FJ60EFY	Yourbus	FN04BSZ	TrentBarton	G336CSG	Transdev
FJ60EGY	Yourbus	FN04BTE	TrentBarton	G337CSG	Transdev
FJ60EGZ	Yourbus	FN04HSC	Centrebus	G370YUR	TrentBarton
FJ60EHN	Yourbus	FN04HSD	TrentBarton	G535VBB	TrentBarton
FJ60HXS	NX Coaching	FN04HSE	TrentBarton	G622OTV	Centrebus
FJ60HXT	NX Coaching	FN04HSF	TrentBarton	GJ52MUV	NX Coaching
FJ60HXU	NX Coaching	FN04HSG	TrentBarton	GJ52OMZ	NX Coaching
FJ60HXV	NX Coaching	FN04HSK	Centrebus	GK03NFT	EYMS Group
FJ60HXW	Yourbus	FN04HSL	Centrebus	GK04NZU	Centrebus
FJ60HXX	NX Coaching	FN04HSU	TrentBarton	GN03TYB	NX Coaching
FJ60HXY	NX Coaching	FN04HSV	Centrebus	GN07FDE	RATP Group
FJ60HXZ	Yourbus	FN04HSX	Centrebus	GN51WCA	NX Coaching
FJ60HYA	Yourbus	FN04HSY	TrentBarton	GX06AOE	Centrebus
FJ60HYB	Yourbus	FN04HSZ	TrentBarton	H6KFC	NX Coaching
FJ60HYN	RATP Group	FN04HTA	TrentBarton	H101BFR	Rotala
FJ60HYO	RATP Group	FN04HTC	Centrebus	H102BFR	Rotala
FJ60KUN	NX Coaching	FN04HTP	Centrebus	H103BFR	Rotala
FJ60KUO	NX Coaching	FN04HTT	Centrebus	H104BFR	Rotala
FJ60KVH	Yourbus	FN04HTU	Centrebus	H141GGS	Transdev
FJ60KVK	Yourbus	FN04HTV	TrentBarton	H142GGS	Transdev
FJ60KVL	Yourbus	FN06EBL	NX Coaching	H143GGS	Transdev
FJ60KVM	Yourbus	FN06EBM	NX Coaching	H144GGS	Transdev
FJ60KVO	Yourbus	FN06EBN	NX Coaching	H145GGS	Transdev
FJ60KVP	Yourbus	FN06FKZ	Yourbus	H146GGS	Transdev
FJ60KVR	Yourbus	FN06FLB	Yourbus	H147GGS	Transdev
FJ60KVS	NX Coaching	FN06FLC	Rotala	H148GGS	Transdev
FJ61EWB	RATP Group	FN06FLD	Rotala	H231LOM	Centrebus
FJ61EWC	RATP Group	FN06FLE	Yourbus	H242LOM	Centrebus
FJ61EWD	RATP Group	FN06FLF	Yourbus	H474CEG	Centrebus
FJ61EWE	RATP Group	FN06FLG	Yourbus	H546GKX	Transdev
FJ61EWF	RATP Group	FN06FMA	NX Coaching	H549GKX	Transdev
FJ61EWG	RATP Group	FN06FMC	NX Coaching	H550GKX	Transdev
FJ61EWH	RATP Group	FN07BYV	NX Coaching	H784PVW	TrentBarton
FJ61EWK	RATP Group	FN07BYW	NX Coaching	HF02HFH	RATP Group
FJ61EWL	RATP Group	FN07BYX	NX Coaching	HF03ODR	RATP Group
FJ61EWM	RATP Group	FN07BYZ	NX Coaching	HF03ODS	RATP Group
FJ61EWZ	RATP Group	FN07BZA	NX Coaching	HF03ODT	RATP Group
FJ61EXA	NX Coaching	FN07BZB	NX Coaching	HF03ODU	RATP Group
FJ61EXB	NX Coaching	FN07BZC	NX Coaching	HF03ODV	RATP Group
FJ61EXC	NX Coaching	FN08CHG	Centrebus	HF03ODW	RATP Group
FJ61EXD	NX Coaching	FN08CHH	Centrebus	HF04JWD	RATP Group
FJ61EXE	NX Coaching	FN54AEB	TrentBarton	HF04JWE	RATP Group
FJ61EXF	NX Coaching	FN54AEC	TrentBarton	HF04JWG	RATP Group

Reg	Operator	Reg	Operator	Reg	Operator	Reg	Operator
HF04JWJ	RATP Group	KP51UFG	Rotala	KX58GUO	NX Coaching
HF04JWK	RATP Group	KP51UFH	Rotala	KX58GVJ	NX Coaching
HF04JWL	RATP Group	KP51UFJ	Rotala	KX58GVK	NX Coaching
HF05HNA	RATP Group	KP54BYO	Rotala	KX58GVL	NX Coaching
HF05HNB	RATP Group	KP54BYR	Rotala	KX58GVM	NX Coaching
HF05HNC	RATP Group	KP54BYT	Rotala	KX58LJA	Rotala
HF05LUY	RATP Group	KP54BYU	Rotala	KX60DWE	Rotala
HF05LYT	RATP Group	KP54BYV	Rotala	KX60DWF	Rotala
HF05LYV	RATP Group	KP54BYW	Rotala	KX60DWG	Rotala
HF05LYW	RATP Group	KP54BYX	Rotala	KX60DWJ	Rotala
HF11HCO	RATP Group	KS03EXG	Rotala	KX60DWK	Rotala
HF11HCP	RATP Group	KS03EXL	Rotala	L5PPN	Rotala
HF11HCU	RATP Group	KS03EXM	Rotala	L71EKG	Centrebus
HF11HCV	RATP Group	KS03EXN	Rotala	L102LRA	Centrebus
HF11HCX	RATP Group	KS03EXP	Rotala	L103LRA	Centrebus
HF57BKN	RATP Group	KU02YUA	Rotala	L104LRA	Centrebus
HIL7745	EYMS Group	KU52RXW	Rotala	L106SDY	Transdev
HJ02HFA	RATP Group	KU52RYH	Rotala	L107LRA	TrentBarton
HJ02HFB	RATP Group	KU52RYK	Rotala	L108VDM	Centrebus
HJ02HFC	RATP Group	KU52RYN	Rotala	L109LRA	TrentBarton
HJ02HFD	RATP Group	KU52YJS	Rotala	L110LRA	TrentBarton
HJ02HFE	RATP Group	KU52YJT	Rotala	L112LRA	TrentBarton
HJ02HFF	RATP Group	KU52YJX	Rotala	L113LRA	TrentBarton
HJ02HFG	RATP Group	KU52YJY	Rotala	L114LRA	TrentBarton
HJZ9928	Centrebus	KU52YJZ	Rotala	L116LRA	TrentBarton
HJZ9929	Centrebus	KUI6564	Centrebus	L118LRA	TrentBarton
HV52WSZ	RATP Group	KUI9266	Centrebus	L121LRA	TrentBarton
J107KCW	Rotala	KUI9268	Centrebus	L122LRA	TrentBarton
J108KCW	Rotala	KV51KZH	Rotala	L123LRA	TrentBarton
J109KCW	Rotala	KW02CVV	Rotala	L124LRA	TrentBarton
J110KCW	Rotala	KW02CXG	Rotala	L125LRA	TrentBarton
J112KCW	Rotala	KX03HZJ	Rotala	L126LRA	TrentBarton
J113KCW	Transdev	KX03HZK	Rotala	L127LRA	TrentBarton
J353BSH	TrentBarton	KX03JBE	Rotala	L140BFV	Transdev
J619CEV	TrentBarton	KX03JBU	Rotala	L150BFV	Transdev
J628CEV	TrentBarton	KX03KYW	Centrebus	L155BFV	Transdev
J844TSC	TrentBarton	KX06APV	Centrebus	L157BFV	Transdev
J850TSC	TrentBarton	KX06APY	Centrebus	L170EKG	Centrebus
J854TSC	TrentBarton	KX06APZ	Centrebus	L172EKG	Centrebus
J864TSC	TrentBarton	KX07OOW	Rotala	L351MRR	TrentBarton
J865TSC	TrentBarton	KX07OOY	RATP Group	L352MRR	TrentBarton
J871TSC	TrentBarton	KX08HMY	Rotala	L353MRR	TrentBarton
J976PRW	Rotala	KX08HMZ	Rotala	L713JUD	Centrebus
K2YCL	Centrebus	KX08OML	Rotala	L720SNO	TrentBarton
K3YCL	Centrebus	KX09CJO	NX Coaching	L726SNO	TrentBarton
K4YCL	Centrebus	KX09CJU	NX Coaching	L778SNO	Transdev
K5YCL	Centrebus	KX54NKZ	Rotala	L779SNO	Transdev
K6YCL	Centrebus	KX55PFD	Centrebus	LA02WMZ	TrentBarton
K7YCL	Centrebus	KX55PFF	Centrebus	LG02FDO	Rotala
K8KFC	NX Coaching	KX55PFO	Centrebus	LG02FDP	Rotala
K104YTX	Centrebus	KX55PGE	Centrebus	LG02FDV	Rotala
K106YTX	Centrebus	KX57MTW	Rotala	LG02FDX	Rotala
K123URP	Rotala	KX57OVS	Rotala	LG02FFC	Rotala
K126URP	Rotala	KX57OVT	Rotala	LG02FFD	Rotala
K128UFV	Rotala	KX57OVU	Rotala	LG02FFE	Rotala
K242CHB	Centrebus	KX57OVV	Rotala	LG02FFH	Rotala
K728DAO	Centrebus	KX57OWM	Rotala	LG02FFJ	Rotala
K828NKH	Centrebus	KX58BFA	NX Coaching	LIL9666	Centrebus
K875CSF	Transdev	KX58BJK	NX Coaching	LJ08RJY	RATP Group
K883CSF	TrentBarton	KX58BJO	NX Coaching	LK07GTF	Centrebus
K894CSF	TrentBarton	KX58BJU	NX Coaching	LK51XGP	Transdev
KB10BUS	Centrebus	KX58BJV	NX Coaching	LK51XGP	Transdev
KE06NZW	Centrebus	KX58BJY	NX Coaching	LK53KVT	NX Coaching
KE06NZX	Centrebus	KX58BJZ	NX Coaching	LK53KVW	NX Coaching
KE06RXL	Centrebus	KX58BKA	NX Coaching	LK53KVX	NX Coaching
KE51WUO	Transdev	KX58GTU	NX Coaching	LK53KVY	NX Coaching
KE51WUP	Transdev	KX58GTY	NX Coaching	LK53KVZ	NX Coaching
KIW8606	Centrebus	KX58GTZ	NX Coaching	LK53KWB	NX Coaching
KP02PUE	Rotala	KX58GUA	NX Coaching	LK53KWD	NX Coaching
KP02PUV	Rotala	KX58GUC	NX Coaching	LK53KWE	NX Coaching
KP02PUX	Rotala	KX58GUD	NX Coaching	LN03AYL	Centrebus
KP02PVA	Rotala	KX58GUE	NX Coaching	LN03AYM	Centrebus
KP51SXW	Rotala	KX58GUF	NX Coaching	LX03HCE	NX Coaching
KP51SXX	Rotala	KX58GUG	NX Coaching	LX03HCG	NX Coaching
KP51UFB	Rotala	KX58GUH	NX Coaching	LX03HCL	NX Coaching
KP51UFC	Rotala	KX58GUJ	NX Coaching	LX03HCU	NX Coaching
		KX58GUK	NX Coaching	LX03HDE	NX Coaching

Reg	Operator	Reg	Operator	Reg	Operator
LX03HDE	NX Coaching	MX08DHO	Rotala	N746ANE	EYMS Group
LX51FGP	Centrebus	MX08DJJ	Centrebus	N748ANE	EYMS Group
LX51FGZ	Centrebus	MX08MYT	Rotala	NK53TJV	Centrebus
LX51FHC	Centrebus	MX08MYW	Centrebus	NY03PUV	Centrebus
LX51FHD	Centrebus	MX08MZG	Rotala	OU08AYF	RATP Group
LX51FHE	Centrebus	MX08NNU	Rotala	OU08AYG	RATP Group
LX51FPJ	Centrebus	MX08PZH	Rotala	P10FTG	Rotala
M102CCD	Transdev	MX09HJG	Rotala	P11FTG	Rotala
M113SLS	Centrebus	MX53FDG	Centrebus	P27MLE	Centrebus
M129PRA	TrentBarton	MX53FEG	Centrebus	P122KSL	NX West Midlands
M130PRA	TrentBarton	MX53FEH	Centrebus	P123KSL	NX West Midlands
M131PRA	TrentBarton	MX54KYE	Transdev	P125KSL	NX West Midlands
M132PRA	TrentBarton	MX54KYF	Transdev	P126KSL	NX West Midlands
M133PRA	TrentBarton	MX55BYK	Centrebus	P127KSL	NX West Midlands
M134PRA	TrentBarton	MX55WCW	Centrebus	P128KSL	NX West Midlands
M135PRA	TrentBarton	MX56NLP	Centrebus	P129KSL	NX West Midlands
M136PRA	TrentBarton	MX57UPS	Rotala	P130PPV	Centrebus
M137PRA	TrentBarton	MX57UPT	Rotala	P132KSL	NX West Midlands
M138PRA	TrentBarton	MX57UPW	Rotala	P132PPV	Centrebus
M205VSX	Transdev	MX58ACJ	Rotala	P135LNF	RATP Group
M209VSX	Transdev	MX58KZG	Rotala	P138KSL	NX West Midlands
M212VSX	TrentBarton	MX58KZM	Rotala	P139KSL	NX West Midlands
M214VSX	TrentBarton	MX60EGK	RATP Group	P140KSL	NX West Midlands
M255MRW	Rotala	MX60EKH	RATP Group	P141KSL	NX West Midlands
M389KVR	Centrebus	MX61BBE	NX Coaching	P158MLE	Centrebus
M521UTV	Centrebus	MX61BBF	NX Coaching	P160MLE	Centrebus
M723KPD	NX West Midlands	MX61BBJ	NX Coaching	P244AAP	NX West Midlands
M829RCP	Centrebus	MX61BBK	NX Coaching	P256PSX	TrentBarton
M844RCP	Centrebus	MX61BBN	NX Coaching	P260PSX	TrentBarton
M940JBO	Transdev	MX62GOA	Yourbus	P267PSX	TrentBarton
M942JBO	Transdev	MX62GVL	Yourbus	P274PSX	TrentBarton
M947JBO	Transdev	MX62GVN	Yourbus	P285WAT	EYMS Group
M948JBO	Transdev	MX62GVR	Yourbus	P286WAT	EYMS Group
M949JBO	Transdev	MX62GVV	Yourbus	P315DVE	NX West Midlands
MF51LZW	EYMS Group	MX62GVZ	Yourbus	P337ROO	TrentBarton
MF51LZX	EYMS Group	MX62GWC	Yourbus	P401EJW	NX West Midlands
MF51MBV	EYMS Group	MX62GWZ	Yourbus	P401MLA	Rotala
MF51MBX	EYMS Group	MX62GXE	Yourbus	P402EJW	NX West Midlands
MHZ9321	RATP Group	MX62GXK	Yourbus	P402MLA	Rotala
MK53BLU	EYMS Group	MX62GXY	Yourbus	P403EJW	NX West Midlands
MOF225	NX West Midlands	MX62GXZ	Yourbus	P403MLA	Rotala
MRY1W	Centrebus	N19FUG	Centrebus	P404EJW	NX West Midlands
MTU119Y	Transdev	N23FWU	NX West Midlands	P404MLA	Rotala
MV54EEO	Rotala	N116UHP	Transdev	P405EJW	NX West Midlands
MW52PZD	TrentBarton	N132XND	Centrebus	P405MLA	Rotala
MW52PZE	Centrebus	N137YRW	Transdev	P406EJW	NX West Midlands
MW52PZP	Rotala	N241WRW	NX Coaching	P406MLA	Rotala
MW52PZR	Rotala	N243WRW	NX Coaching	P407EJW	NX West Midlands
MX03YCM	Centrebus	N244WRW	NX Coaching	P408EJW	NX West Midlands
MX03YCN	TrentBarton	N245WRW	NX Coaching	P409EJW	NX West Midlands
MX03YCP	TrentBarton	N246WRW	NX Coaching	P409KSX	TrentBarton
MX03YCT	Centrebus	N344WOH	NX West Midlands	P410KSX	TrentBarton
MX03YCZ	Centrebus	N345WOH	NX West Midlands	P411EJW	NX West Midlands
MX03YDA	Centrebus	N349WOH	NX West Midlands	P412EJW	NX West Midlands
MX03YDF	TrentBarton	N350WOH	NX West Midlands	P413EJW	NX West Midlands
MX03YDG	Centrebus	N355WOH	NX West Midlands	P414EJW	NX West Midlands
MX04VLM	TrentBarton	N366WOH	NX West Midlands	P415EJW	NX West Midlands
MX04VLV	Centrebus	N367VRC	TrentBarton	P416EJW	NX West Midlands
MX04VMC	Centrebus	N368WOH	NX West Midlands	P418EJW	NX West Midlands
MX04VMG	Centrebus	N377WOH	NX West Midlands	P419EJW	NX West Midlands
MX05EKT	Centrebus	N384BOV	NX West Midlands	P420EJW	NX West Midlands
MX05EKV	Centrebus	N385BOV	NX West Midlands	P421EJW	NX West Midlands
MX05ELO	Centrebus	N386BOV	NX West Midlands	P422EJW	NX West Midlands
MX05ELU	Transdev	N404GSX	TrentBarton	P423EJW	NX West Midlands
MX05EMJ	Transdev	N407GSX	TrentBarton	P424EJW	NX West Midlands
MX05EMK	Transdev	N416JBV	Transdev	P426EJW	NX West Midlands
MX05ENF	Centrebus	N424JBV	Transdev	P427EJW	NX West Midlands
MX06BPE	Rotala	N425JBV	Transdev	P429EJW	NX West Midlands
MX06BPK	Rotala	N431CHL	Centrebus	P430EJW	NX West Midlands
MX06BPO	Centrebus	N432CHL	Centrebus	P431JJW	NX West Midlands
MX06BTE	Centrebus	N470VPJ	NX Coaching	P432JJW	NX West Midlands
MX07BCF	Centrebus	N472VPJ	NX Coaching	P433JJW	NX West Midlands
MX07BCO	Centrebus	N504HWY	Transdev	P434JJW	NX West Midlands
MX07JNL	Centrebus	N509HWY	Transdev	P435JJW	NX West Midlands
MX07JNN	Centrebus	N548LHG	RATP Group	P436JJW	NX West Midlands
MX07OWU	RATP Group	N548LHG	RATP Group	P437JJW	NX West Midlands
MX07OYT	Rotala	N632XBU	Centrebus	P438JJW	NX West Midlands

P439JJW	NX West Midlands	P772SWC	RATP Group	PJ53OUY	Transdev
P440JJW	NX West Midlands	P773SWC	RATP Group	PJ53OVA	Transdev
P441JOX	NX West Midlands	P773SWC	RATP Group	PJ53OVA	Transdev
P442JOX	NX West Midlands	P774SWC	RATP Group	PJ53OVB	Transdev
P443JOX	NX West Midlands	P774SWC	RATP Group	PJ53OVB	Transdev
P446JOX	NX West Midlands	P776SWC	RATP Group	PJI6431	Centrebus
P447JOX	NX West Midlands	P776SWC	RATP Group	PJZ9450	Centrebus
P448JOX	NX West Midlands	P849BPB	NX Coaching	PJZ9451	Centrebus
P449JOX	NX West Midlands	P910CTO	TrentBarton	PJZ9452	Centrebus
P450JOX	NX West Midlands	P955LDA	NX West Midlands	PK51LJX	Transdev
P451JOX	NX West Midlands	P960LOB	NX West Midlands	PK51LJY	Transdev
P452JOX	NX West Midlands	P990AFV	RATP Group	PL05PLN	RATP Group
P453JOX	NX West Midlands	P991AFV	RATP Group	PL05PLO	RATP Group
P454JOX	NX West Midlands	PA04CYK	Transdev	PL05PLU	RATP Group
P455JOX	NX West Midlands	PA04CYK	Transdev	PL05PLV	RATP Group
P456JOX	NX West Midlands	PA04CYL	Transdev	PL05PLX	RATP Group
P457JOX	NX West Midlands	PA04CYL	Transdev	PL05UBR	Transdev
P458JOX	NX West Midlands	PA04CYP	Transdev	PL05UBS	Transdev
P459JOX	NX West Midlands	PA04CYP	Transdev	PL06RYO	Rotala
P460JOX	NX West Midlands	PA04CYS	Transdev	PL06RYP	Rotala
P473BLJ	RATP Group	PA04CYS	Transdev	PL51LDJ	EYMS Group
P474BLJ	RATP Group	PA04CYT	Transdev	PL51LDU	EYMS Group
P487SWC	TrentBarton	PA04CYT	Transdev	PL51LDV	EYMS Group
P501KOX	NX West Midlands	PAZ3184	Centrebus	PL51LDX	Transdev
P501VRO	Centrebus	PAZ9346	Centrebus	PL51LDZ	EYMS Group
P502EJW	NX West Midlands	PE13JYY	Rotala	PL51LEF	EYMS Group
P503KOX	NX West Midlands	PE13JYZ	Rotala	PN02HVJ	Transdev
P504KOX	NX West Midlands	PE13JZA	Rotala	PN02HVK	Transdev
P505KOX	NX West Midlands	PE13JZB	Rotala	PN02HVV	Transdev
P507KOX	NX West Midlands	PE55WMD	Rotala	PN02HVW	Transdev
P508EJW	NX West Midlands	PE55WMF	Rotala	PN02HVX	Transdev
P508KOX	NX West Midlands	PE55WMG	Rotala	PN02HVY	Transdev
P509KOX	NX West Midlands	PE56UFH	RATP Group	PN02HVZ	Transdev
P510EJW	NX West Midlands	PE56UFJ	RATP Group	PN02HWA	Transdev
P510KOX	NX West Midlands	PE56UFK	RATP Group	PN02XBH	EYMS Group
P512KOX	NX West Midlands	PE56UFL	RATP Group	PN02XBP	EYMS Group
P514KOX	NX West Midlands	PE56UFM	RATP Group	PN02XBR	EYMS Group
P516EJW	NX West Midlands	PE56UFN	RATP Group	PN02XBS	EYMS Group
P516RYM	Rotala	PE56UFP	RATP Group	PN02XBT	Transdev
P517EJW	NX West Midlands	PE56UFR	RATP Group	PN02XBU	EYMS Group
P519EJW	NX West Midlands	PE56UFS	RATP Group	PN07KRZ	RATP Group
P524EJW	NX West Midlands	PJ02PZN	RATP Group	PN07KSE	RATP Group
P530EJW	NX West Midlands	PJ02RAU	EYMS Group	PN07NTJ	Rotala
P533EJW	NX West Midlands	PJ02RAX	EYMS Group	PN07NTK	Rotala
P534EJW	NX West Midlands	PJ02RBF	EYMS Group	PN07NTL	Rotala
P541EJW	NX West Midlands	PJ02RBV	EYMS Group	PN07NTM	Rotala
P544EJW	NX West Midlands	PJ02RBY	EYMS Group	PN07NTO	Rotala
P547EJW	NX West Midlands	PJ02RHA	Yourbus	PN07NTT	Rotala
P549EFL	EYMS Group	PJ05ZVW	Transdev	PN07NTU	Rotala
P554LDA	NX West Midlands	PJ05ZVX	Transdev	PN07NTV	Rotala
P557EFL	EYMS Group	PJ05ZVY	Transdev	PN08SVK	Rotala
P558EFL	EYMS Group	PJ05ZVZ	Transdev	PN08SVL	Rotala
P561MDA	NX West Midlands	PJ05ZWA	Transdev	PN08SVO	Rotala
P564MDA	NX West Midlands	PJ05ZWB	Transdev	PN08SVP	Rotala
P565EFL	EYMS Group	PJ05ZWC	Transdev	PN08SVR	Rotala
P566MDA	NX West Midlands	PJ05ZWD	Transdev	PN08SVS	Rotala
P574EFL	EYMS Group	PJ05ZWE	Transdev	PN08SVT	Rotala
P577EFL	EYMS Group	PJ05ZWF	Transdev	PN08SVU	Rotala
P604SAT	EYMS Group	PJ05ZWG	Transdev	PN10FNR	RATP Group
P605SAT	EYMS Group	PJ05ZWH	Transdev	PN10FNR	RATP Group
P606SAT	EYMS Group	PJ05ZWK	Transdev	PN10FNS	RATP Group
P607SAT	EYMS Group	PJ05ZWL	Transdev	PN10FNS	RATP Group
P608SAT	EYMS Group	PJ53OUN	Transdev	PN52ZVL	Rotala
P609SAT	EYMS Group	PJ53OUN	Transdev	PN52ZVS	Rotala
P610SAT	EYMS Group	PJ53OUO	Transdev	PN57NFA	Rotala
P611SAT	EYMS Group	PJ53OUO	Transdev	PN57NFC	Rotala
P641UUG	Transdev	PJ53OUP	Transdev	PN57NFD	Rotala
P642UUG	Transdev	PJ53OUP	Transdev	PN57NFE	Rotala
P643UUG	Transdev	PJ53OUU	Transdev	PN57NFF	Rotala
P718SWC	RATP Group	PJ53OUU	Transdev	PN57NFG	Rotala
P718SWC	RATP Group	PJ53OUV	Transdev	PO51MTE	Transdev
P749HND	Centrebus	PJ53OUV	TrentBarton	PO51MTF	Transdev
P757SWC	RATP Group	PJ53OUW	Transdev	PO51MTK	Transdev
P757SWC	RATP Group	PJ53OUW	Transdev	PO51MTU	Transdev
P767SWC	RATP Group	PJ53OUX	Transdev	PO51MTV	Transdev
P767SWC	RATP Group	PJ53OUX	Transdev	PO51MTX	Transdev
P772SWC	RATP Group	PJ53OUY	Transdev	PO51MTY	Transdev

Reg	Operator	Reg	Operator	Reg	Operator
PO51MTZ	Transdev	R130RLY	Centrebus	R477NPR	RATP Group
PO51MUA	Transdev	R132RLY	Centrebus	R477XDA	NX West Midlands
PO51MUB	Transdev	R140XOB	NX West Midlands	R478LGH	Rotala
PO51MUC	Transdev	R141RLY	Centrebus	R478NPR	RATP Group
PO51MUE	Transdev	R142RSN	NX West Midlands	R478XDA	NX West Midlands
PO51MUP	Transdev	R144RSN	NX West Midlands	R479NPR	RATP Group
PO51MUU	Transdev	R145RSN	NX West Midlands	R479XDA	NX West Midlands
PO51MUV	Transdev	R146RSN	NX West Midlands	R480NPR	RATP Group
PO51MUW	Transdev	R147RSN	NX West Midlands	R480XDA	NX West Midlands
PO51MUY	Transdev	R148RSN	NX West Midlands	R481NPR	RATP Group
PO51MVA	Transdev	R149RSN	NX West Midlands	R482NPR	RATP Group
PO51UMS	Centrebus	R149UAL	Centrebus	R484LGH	Centrebus
PO51UMW	Centrebus	R150RSN	NX West Midlands	R515XOB	NX West Midlands
PO51UMX	Rotala	R151RSN	NX West Midlands	R516XOB	NX West Midlands
PO51UMY	Rotala	R151UAL	Centrebus	R517XOB	NX West Midlands
PO51WNN	Centrebus	R152RSN	NX West Midlands	R518XOB	NX West Midlands
PO54ABZ	Transdev	R153RSN	NX West Midlands	R521XOB	NX West Midlands
PO54ACF	Transdev	R154RSN	NX West Midlands	R522XOB	NX West Midlands
PO54ACJ	Transdev	R155RSN	NX West Midlands	R524YRP	RATP Group
PO54ACU	Transdev	R155VLA	Centrebus	R526XOB	NX West Midlands
PO54ACV	Transdev	R155XOB	NX West Midlands	R529TWR	Transdev
PO54ACX	Transdev	R156RSN	NX West Midlands	R529XOB	NX West Midlands
PO54ACY	Transdev	R157RSN	NX West Midlands	R530TWR	Transdev
PO54ACZ	Transdev	R158RSN	NX West Midlands	R531TWR	Transdev
PO55PYL	Transdev	R159RSN	NX West Midlands	R533XOB	NX West Midlands
PO56JDK	Rotala	R160RSN	NX West Midlands	R534XOB	NX West Midlands
PO56JDU	Rotala	R160XOB	NX West Midlands	R536XOB	NX West Midlands
PO56JDX	Rotala	R160YON	NX West Midlands	R537XOB	NX West Midlands
PO56PCF	RATP Group	R161RSN	NX West Midlands	R538XOB	NX West Midlands
PO56RNZ	Rotala	R161UAL	Centrebus	R539XOB	NX West Midlands
PO56ROH	Rotala	R162UAL	Centrebus	R541XOB	NX West Midlands
PO56ROU	Rotala	R164UAL	Centrebus	R542XOB	NX West Midlands
PO56RPU	Rotala	R165XOB	NX West Midlands	R543XOB	NX West Midlands
PO56RPV	Rotala	R166UAL	Centrebus	R545XOB	NX West Midlands
PO56RPZ	Rotala	R220HCD	Centrebus	R546XOB	NX West Midlands
PO56RRU	Rotala	R220MSA	Rotala	R547XOB	NX West Midlands
PO56RRV	Rotala	R241XDA	NX West Midlands	R548XOB	NX West Midlands
PO56RRX	Rotala	R250PRH	EYMS Group	R549XOB	NX West Midlands
PO56RRY	Rotala	R252PRH	EYMS Group	R550XOB	NX West Midlands
PO56RRZ	Rotala	R283EKH	EYMS Group	R551XOB	NX West Midlands
PO56RSU	Rotala	R309NGM	Centrebus	R552UOT	Centrebus
PO56RSV	Rotala	R314NGM	Centrebus	R552XOB	NX West Midlands
PO56RSX	Rotala	R315NGM	Centrebus	R553XOB	NX West Midlands
PO56RSY	Rotala	R317NGM	Centrebus	R554XOB	NX West Midlands
PO56RSZ	Rotala	R319NGM	Centrebus	R556XOB	NX West Midlands
PO62LNF	Rotala	R322HCD	Centrebus	R557XOB	NX West Midlands
PO62LNN	Rotala	R401XFL	Rotala	R558XOB	NX West Midlands
PO62LNU	Rotala	R407FFC	Rotala	R559UOT	Centrebus
PR62TON	Rotala	R409FFC	EYMS Group	R568XDA	NX West Midlands
PRN909	Rotala	R417SOY	EYMS Group	R569XDA	NX West Midlands
R1NEG	NX West Midlands	R419SOY	EYMS Group	R572XDA	NX West Midlands
R2NEG	NX West Midlands	R420SOY	EYMS Group	R579XDA	NX West Midlands
R7TYB	RATP Group	R425AOR	NX Coaching	R581XDA	NX West Midlands
R8TYB	RATP Group	R426AOR	NX Coaching	R582YON	NX West Midlands
R9TYB	RATP Group	R455CCV	Rotala	R584YON	NX West Midlands
R10TYB	RATP Group	R457LGH	Rotala	R586YON	NX West Midlands
R11TYB	RATP Group	R459LGH	Centrebus	R591YON	NX West Midlands
R11WAL	Centrebus	R460LGH	Centrebus	R594YON	NX West Midlands
R12TYB	RATP Group	R461XDA	NX West Midlands	R595XOB	NX West Midlands
R13TYB	RATP Group	R462LGH	Centrebus	R595YON	NX West Midlands
R14TYB	RATP Group	R462XDA	NX West Midlands	R596XOB	NX West Midlands
R15TYB	RATP Group	R463XDA	NX West Midlands	R596YON	NX West Midlands
R16TYB	RATP Group	R464XDA	NX West Midlands	R597XOB	NX West Midlands
R17TYB	RATP Group	R465XDA	NX West Midlands	R598XOB	NX West Midlands
R32LHK	TrentBarton	R466XDA	NX West Midlands	R598YON	NX West Midlands
R59RAU	TrentBarton	R467XDA	NX West Midlands	R599XOB	NX West Midlands
R63RAU	TrentBarton	R468XDA	NX West Midlands	R601XOB	NX West Midlands
R84GNW	NX West Midlands	R470XDA	NX West Midlands	R601YON	NX West Midlands
R86GNW	NX West Midlands	R471XDA	NX West Midlands	R602XOB	NX West Midlands
R91XNE	Rotala	R472XDA	NX West Midlands	R603XOB	NX West Midlands
R93LHK	TrentBarton	R473XDA	NX West Midlands	R604XOB	NX West Midlands
R94LHK	TrentBarton	R474XDA	NX West Midlands	R606NFX	Centrebus
R95LHK	Transdev	R475CAH	Rotala	R606XOB	NX West Midlands
R120XOB	NX West Midlands	R475NPR	RATP Group	R606YON	NX West Midlands
R123XOB	NX West Midlands	R475XDA	NX West Midlands	R607NFX	Centrebus
R125XOB	NX West Midlands	R476NPR	RATP Group	R608NFX	Centrebus
R128XOB	NX West Midlands	R476XDA	NX West Midlands	R610YCR	Rotala

R613NFX	Centrebus	S566VUK	NX West Midlands	S642VOA	NX West Midlands
R780SOY	EYMS Group	S568VUK	NX West Midlands	S643VOA	NX West Midlands
R781SOY	EYMS Group	S569VUK	NX West Midlands	S648VOA	NX West Midlands
R782SOY	EYMS Group	S570VUK	NX West Midlands	S649VOA	NX West Midlands
R812NUD	TrentBarton	S571VUK	NX West Midlands	S650VOA	NX West Midlands
R813NUD	TrentBarton	S572VUK	NX West Midlands	S651VOA	NX West Midlands
R935RAU	TrentBarton	S573VUK	NX West Midlands	S654VOA	NX West Midlands
R974KAR	TrentBarton	S574VUK	NX West Midlands	S655VOA	NX West Midlands
R977KAR	TrentBarton	S576VUK	NX West Midlands	S658VOA	NX West Midlands
RCE510	EYMS Group	S577VUK	NX West Midlands	S660VOA	NX West Midlands
RUI2116	EYMS Group	S578VUK	NX West Midlands	S661VOA	NX West Midlands
RYV77	EYMS Group	S579VUK	NX West Midlands	S662VOA	NX West Midlands
S1TWM	NX West Midlands	S580VUK	NX West Midlands	S664VOA	NX West Midlands
S20PJC	Centrebus	S581VUK	NX West Midlands	S665VOA	NX West Midlands
S53VNM	Transdev	S582VUK	NX West Midlands	S669VOA	NX West Midlands
S54VNM	Transdev	S585VUK	NX West Midlands	S671VOA	NX West Midlands
S56VNM	Transdev	S586VUK	NX West Midlands	S672VOA	NX West Midlands
S57VNM	Transdev	S589VUK	NX West Midlands	S673VOA	NX West Midlands
S63WNM	Transdev	S58VNM	Transdev	S674VOA	NX West Midlands
S64WNM	Transdev	S590VUK	NX West Midlands	S675VOA	NX West Midlands
S81DOX	Rotala	S591VUK	NX West Midlands	S677VOA	NX West Midlands
S160VUK	NX West Midlands	S592VUK	NX West Midlands	S680VOA	NX West Midlands
S231EWU	NX West Midlands	S593VUK	NX West Midlands	S681VOA	NX West Midlands
S233EWU	NX West Midlands	S594VUK	NX West Midlands	S684YOL	NX West Midlands
S237EWU	NX West Midlands	S59VNM	Transdev	S687YOL	NX West Midlands
S276AOX	Centrebus	S607VUK	NX West Midlands	S693YOL	NX West Midlands
S277AOX	NX West Midlands	S608VUK	NX West Midlands	S708YOL	NX West Midlands
S281AOX	NX West Midlands	S609VUK	NX West Midlands	S711YOL	NX West Midlands
S285NRB	Centrebus	S610VUK	NX West Midlands	S758RNE	Rotala
S286AOX	NX West Midlands	S611VUK	NX West Midlands	S759RNE	Rotala
S287AOX	NX West Midlands	S612VUK	NX West Midlands	S789NRV	EYMS Group
S287RAG	EYMS Group	S613VUK	NX West Midlands	S793RRL	Rotala
S288RAG	EYMS Group	S614VUK	NX West Midlands	S937UAL	TrentBarton
S290RAG	EYMS Group	S616VOA	NX West Midlands	S939UAL	Centrebus
S292RAG	EYMS Group	S616VUK	NX West Midlands	SEL23	RATP Group
S293RAG	EYMS Group	S618VUK	NX West Midlands	SEL36	RATP Group
S294RAG	EYMS Group	S619VOA	NX West Midlands	SEL73	RATP Group
S295RAG	EYMS Group	S619VUK	NX West Midlands	SEL133	RATP Group
S296RAG	EYMS Group	S620VOA	NX West Midlands	SEL392	RATP Group
S298PKH	EYMS Group	S620VUK	NX West Midlands	SEL702	RATP Group
S299PKH	EYMS Group	S621VUK	NX West Midlands	SEL853	RATP Group
S305MKH	Rotala	S622MKH	EYMS Group	SF07VOB	Rotala
S330PKH	EYMS Group	S622VUK	NX West Midlands	SF10EBN	Rotala
S343MOJ	NX West Midlands	S623MKH	EYMS Group	SF54HWG	Rotala
S377TMB	Rotala	S624JRU	Centrebus	SF54ORC	Rotala
S378TMB	Rotala	S624MKH	EYMS Group	SF54ORK	Rotala
S393HVV	Rotala	S624VUK	NX West Midlands	SF54ORL	Rotala
S395HVV	Rotala	S625JRU	Centrebus	SF57FZK	Rotala
S396HVV	Rotala	S625MKH	EYMS Group	SH51MHU	RATP Group
S397HVV	Rotala	S625VUK	NX West Midlands	SJ04DVH	Yourbus
S399HVV	RATP Group	S626JRU	Centrebus	SJ04DVK	Yourbus
S401HVV	RATP Group	S626MKH	EYMS Group	SJ04DVL	Yourbus
S403NVP	NX West Midlands	S626VOA	NX West Midlands	SJ04DVM	Yourbus
S404JUA	Rotala	S626VUK	NX West Midlands	SJ56GBY	RATP Group
S404NVP	NX West Midlands	S627JRU	Centrebus	SJ56GCF	RATP Group
S405JUA	Rotala	S627MKH	EYMS Group	SK02XGW	Transdev
S405NVP	NX West Midlands	S627VUK	NX West Midlands	SK02XGX	Transdev
S405TMB	Rotala	S628MKH	EYMS Group	SK02XHD	Transdev
S406NVP	NX West Midlands	S629JRU	Centrebus	SK02XHE	Transdev
S407NVP	NX West Midlands	S629MKH	EYMS Group	SK02XHG	Transdev
S408NVP	NX West Midlands	S630JRU	Centrebus	SK02XHH	Transdev
S409NVP	NX West Midlands	S630MKH	EYMS Group	SK02XHJ	Transdev
S410NVP	NX West Midlands	S630VOA	NX West Midlands	SK02XHL	Transdev
S411NVP	NX West Midlands	S631MKH	EYMS Group	SK02XHM	Transdev
S412NVP	NX West Midlands	S632MKH	EYMS Group	SK02XHN	Transdev
S462LGN	Centrebus	S632VOA	NX West Midlands	SK02XHO	Transdev
S464ATV	RATP Group	S633MKH	EYMS Group	SK02XHP	Transdev
S464ATV	RATP Group	S633VOA	NX West Midlands	SK02XHR	Transdev
S466LGN	Centrebus	S634MKH	EYMS Group	SK07DYB	RATP Group
S490MCC	Rotala	S634VOA	NX West Midlands	SK07DZA	RATP Group
S496MCC	Rotala	S635MKH	EYMS Group	SK07DZB	RATP Group
S502APP	Centrebus	S635VOA	NX West Midlands	SK07DZC	RATP Group
S522KFL	Centrebus	S636MKH	EYMS Group	SK07DZD	RATP Group
S561VUK	NX West Midlands	S636VOA	NX West Midlands	SK07DZE	RATP Group
S563VUK	NX West Midlands	S638VOA	NX West Midlands	SK07DZF	RATP Group
S564VUK	NX West Midlands	S639VOA	NX West Midlands	SK07DZG	RATP Group
S565VUK	NX West Midlands	S640VOA	NX West Midlands	SK07DZH	RATP Group

Reg	Operator	Reg	Operator	Reg	Operator
SK07DZJ	RATP Group	SP10CXJ	NX West Midlands	T124OAH	Transdev
SK07DZL	RATP Group	SP10CXK	NX West Midlands	T125OAH	Transdev
SK52URX	RATP Group	SP12DAA	NX West Midlands	T126OAH	Transdev
SK52URY	RATP Group	SP12DAO	NX West Midlands	T127OAH	Transdev
SK52USG	RATP Group	SP12DAU	NX West Midlands	T128OAH	Transdev
SK52USH	RATP Group	SP12DBO	NX West Midlands	T129OAH	Transdev
SK52USJ	RATP Group	SP12DBU	NX West Midlands	T130UOX	NX West Midlands
SN05FLR	Rotala	SP12DBV	NX West Midlands	T133AUA	RATP Group
SN05HDD	Rotala	SP13BRX	NX West Midlands	T134AST	Rotala
SN05HDE	Rotala	SP13BRZ	NX West Midlands	T148CLO	Centrebus
SN08AAU	NX Coaching	SP13BSO	NX West Midlands	T153OGC	Rotala
SN08AAV	NX Coaching	SP13BSU	NX West Midlands	T156OGC	Rotala
SN08AAX	NX Coaching	SP13BSV	NX West Midlands	T157OGC	Rotala
SN08AAY	NX Coaching	SP13BSX	NX West Midlands	T159OGC	Rotala
SN08AAZ	NX Coaching	SP13BSY	NX West Midlands	T163RMR	Centrebus
SN08ABF	NX Coaching	SP13BSZ	NX West Midlands	T164RMR	Centrebus
SN08ABK	NX Coaching	SP13BTE	NX West Midlands	T165RMR	Centrebus
SN08ABO	NX Coaching	SP54CGG	NX West Midlands	T266POC	NX West Midlands
SN08ABU	NX Coaching	SP54CGK	NX West Midlands	T270BPR	RATP Group
SN08ABV	NX Coaching	SP54CGO	NX West Midlands	T271BPR	RATP Group
SN08ABX	NX Coaching	SP54CGU	NX West Midlands	T272BPR	RATP Group
SN08ABZ	NX Coaching	SP54CGV	NX West Midlands	T273BPR	RATP Group
SN08ACF	NX Coaching	SP54CGX	NX West Midlands	T274BPR	RATP Group
SN08ACJ	NX Coaching	SP54CGY	NX West Midlands	T275BPR	RATP Group
SN08ACO	NX Coaching	SP54CGZ	NX West Midlands	T276BPR	RATP Group
SN08ACU	NX Coaching	SP54CHC	NX West Midlands	T277BPR	RATP Group
SN08ACV	NX Coaching	SP54CHD	NX West Midlands	T278BPR	RATP Group
SN08ACX	NX Coaching	SP54CHF	NX West Midlands	T284PVM	EYMS Group
SN08ACY	NX Coaching	SP54CHG	NX West Midlands	T292UOX	NX West Midlands
SN08ACZ	NX Coaching	SP54CHH	NX West Midlands	T293UOX	NX West Midlands
SN08ADO	NX Coaching	SP54CHJ	NX West Midlands	T295UOX	NX West Midlands
SN08ADU	NX Coaching	SP54CHK	NX West Midlands	T297BNN	Centrebus
SN08ADV	NX Coaching	SP54CHL	NX West Midlands	T298BNN	Centrebus
SN08ADX	NX Coaching	SP54CHN	NX West Midlands	T298UOX	NX West Midlands
SN08ADY	NX Coaching	SP54CHO	NX West Midlands	T303JRH	EYMS Group
SN08AEA	NX Coaching	SP61CSY	NX West Midlands	T303UOX	NX West Midlands
SN08AEB	NX Coaching	SP61CSZ	NX West Midlands	T304JRH	EYMS Group
SN08AEC	NX Coaching	SP61CTE	NX West Midlands	T306JRH	EYMS Group
SN08AED	NX Coaching	SP61CTF	NX West Midlands	T307JRH	EYMS Group
SN08AEE	NX Coaching	SP61CTK	NX West Midlands	T319UOX	NX West Midlands
SN08AEF	NX Coaching	SP61CTO	NX West Midlands	T320UOX	NX West Midlands
SN08AEG	NX Coaching	SP61CTU	NX West Midlands	T407SMV	Transdev
SN10CDE	Yourbus	SP61CTV	NX West Midlands	T408SMV	Transdev
SN10CDF	Yourbus	SP61CTX	NX West Midlands	T409SMV	Transdev
SN10CDK	Yourbus	SP61CTY	NX West Midlands	T411LGP	Centrebus
SN11BVG	RATP Group	SP61CTZ	NX West Midlands	T413UON	NX West Midlands
SN11BVH	RATP Group	SP61CUA	NX West Midlands	T415UON	NX West Midlands
SN51TBX	Transdev	SP61CUC	NX West Midlands	T416UON	NX West Midlands
SN51TBX	Transdev	SP61CUG	NX West Midlands	T417UON	NX West Midlands
SN51TCU	RATP Group	SP61CUH	NX West Midlands	T418MNH	Rotala
SN51TDO	RATP Group	SP61CUJ	NX West Midlands	T418UON	NX West Midlands
SN55DVC	Centrebus	SP61CUK	NX West Midlands	T419LGP	Centrebus
SN55DVH	RATP Group	SP61CUO	NX West Midlands	T419UON	NX West Midlands
SN55DVJ	RATP Group	SP61CUU	NX West Midlands	T419XVO	Centrebus
SN55DVK	RATP Group	SP61CUV	NX West Midlands	T420UON	NX West Midlands
SN55DVL	RATP Group	SP61CUW	NX West Midlands	T421UON	NX West Midlands
SN55DVM	RATP Group	ST02MZN	NX West Midlands	T421XVO	Centrebus
SN55DVO	RATP Group	ST02MZO	NX West Midlands	T422UON	NX West Midlands
SN55HSG	RATP Group	ST02MZP	NX West Midlands	T422XVO	Centrebus
SN55HSX	RATP Group	ST02MZU	NX West Midlands	T442EBD	Rotala
SN55HTD	RATP Group	ST02MZV	NX West Midlands	T443EBD	Rotala
SN55HTF	RATP Group	T1WET	Centrebus	T445EBD	Rotala
SN56AWZ	Rotala	T5EEV	Rotala	T447EBD	Rotala
SP04HRM	NX Coaching	T18TYB	RATP Group	T455PRH	RATP Group
SP10CWV	NX West Midlands	T19TYB	RATP Group	T464HNH	RATP Group
SP10CWW	NX West Midlands	T20TYB	RATP Group	T468HNH	Rotala
SP10CWX	NX West Midlands	T21TYB	RATP Group	T469HNH	Rotala
SP10CWY	NX West Midlands	T22TYB	RATP Group	T503TOL	NX Coaching
SP10CWZ	NX West Midlands	T23TYB	RATP Group	T540AUA	Transdev
SP10CXA	NX West Midlands	T24TYB	RATP Group	T541AUA	Transdev
SP10CXB	NX West Midlands	T25TYB	RATP Group	T542AUA	Transdev
SP10CXC	NX West Midlands	T26TYB	RATP Group	T543AUA	Transdev
SP10CXD	NX West Midlands	T27TYB	RATP Group	T544AUA	Transdev
SP10CXE	NX West Midlands	T28TYB	RATP Group	T546HNH	Rotala
SP10CXF	NX West Midlands	T71JBA	Rotala	T577ASN	NX West Midlands
SP10CXG	NX West Midlands	T112AUA	TrentBarton	T628FOB	NX West Midlands
SP10CXH	NX West Midlands	T122OAH	Transdev	T629FOB	NX West Midlands

T630FOB	NX West Midlands	V1PKF	NX Coaching	V172ESL	NX West Midlands
T631FOB	NX West Midlands	V4PKF	NX Coaching	V173ESL	NX West Midlands
T632FOB	NX West Midlands	V5PKF	NX Coaching	V174ESL	NX West Midlands
T633FOB	NX West Midlands	V9PKF	NX Coaching	V175ESL	NX West Midlands
T634FOB	NX West Midlands	V11PKF	NX Coaching	V176ESL	NX West Midlands
T635FOB	NX West Midlands	V32MOA	NX West Midlands	V177ESL	NX West Midlands
T636FOB	NX West Midlands	V34MOA	NX West Midlands	V177MOA	NX West Midlands
T637FOB	NX West Midlands	V35MOA	NX West Midlands	V179ESL	NX West Midlands
T638FOB	NX West Midlands	V36MOA	NX West Midlands	V189OOE	RATP Group
T638XNP	EYMS Group	V37MOA	NX West Midlands	V190EBV	Rotala
T639FOB	NX West Midlands	V38MOA	NX West Midlands	V191EBV	Rotala
T640FOB	NX West Midlands	V39MOA	NX West Midlands	V192EBV	Rotala
T641FOB	NX West Midlands	V41MOA	NX West Midlands	V193EBV	Rotala
T642FOB	NX West Midlands	V42MOA	NX West Midlands	V194EBV	Rotala
T643FOB	NX West Midlands	V43MOA	NX West Midlands	V195EBV	Rotala
T644FOB	NX West Midlands	V45MOA	NX West Midlands	V196EBV	Rotala
T645FOB	NX West Midlands	V46MOA	NX West Midlands	V202ENU	TrentBarton
T646FOB	NX West Midlands	V47MOA	NX West Midlands	V206EBV	Transdev
T647FOB	NX West Midlands	V48MOA	NX West Midlands	V207EBV	Transdev
T648FOB	NX West Midlands	V49MOA	NX West Midlands	V208EBV	Transdev
T648KPU	Centrebus	V51MOA	NX West Midlands	V209EBV	Transdev
T649FOB	NX West Midlands	V52MOA	NX West Midlands	V210EBV	Transdev
T650FOB	NX West Midlands	V53MOA	NX West Midlands	V261HEC	Centrebus
T651FOB	NX West Midlands	V54MOA	NX West Midlands	V262HEC	Centrebus
T652FOB	NX West Midlands	V56MOA	NX West Midlands	V264HEC	Centrebus
T653FOB	NX West Midlands	V57MOA	NX West Midlands	V265HEC	Centrebus
T654FOB	NX West Midlands	V58MOA	NX West Midlands	V266BNV	Rotala
T655FOB	NX West Midlands	V59MOA	NX West Midlands	V266HEC	Centrebus
T656FOB	NX West Midlands	V61MOA	NX West Midlands	V267BNV	Rotala
T657FOB	NX West Midlands	V62MOA	NX West Midlands	V313GLB	Centrebus
T658FOB	NX West Midlands	V63MOA	NX West Midlands	V315GLB	Centrebus
T659FOB	NX West Midlands	V64MOA	NX West Midlands	V317GLB	Centrebus
T660FOB	NX West Midlands	V65MOA	NX West Midlands	V355DLH	Centrebus
T661FOB	NX West Midlands	V67MOA	NX West Midlands	V377SVV	Rotala
T662FOB	NX West Midlands	V68MOA	NX West Midlands	V382SVV	Rotala
T663FOB	NX West Midlands	V69MOA	NX West Midlands	V383SVV	Rotala
T664FOB	NX West Midlands	V71MOA	NX West Midlands	V384SVV	Rotala
T665FOB	NX West Midlands	V72MOA	NX West Midlands	V386JWK	Rotala
T667FOB	NX West Midlands	V73MOA	NX West Midlands	V387SVV	Rotala
T668FOB	NX West Midlands	V74MOA	NX West Midlands	V388SVV	Rotala
T669FOB	NX West Midlands	V75MOA	NX West Midlands	V391SVV	Rotala
T670FOB	NX West Midlands	V76MOA	NX West Midlands	V400CBC	Centrebus
T671FOB	NX West Midlands	V78MOA	NX West Midlands	V401JTO	TrentBarton
T672FOB	NX West Midlands	V79MOA	NX West Midlands	V402JTO	TrentBarton
T673FOB	NX West Midlands	V81MOA	NX West Midlands	V403JTO	TrentBarton
T674FOB	NX West Midlands	V82MOA	NX West Midlands	V404JTO	TrentBarton
T675FOB	NX West Midlands	V83MOA	NX West Midlands	V405JTO	TrentBarton
T676FOB	NX West Midlands	V84MOA	NX West Midlands	V410MOA	NX West Midlands
T677FOB	NX West Midlands	V85MOA	NX West Midlands	V415KMY	Centrebus
T678FOB	NX West Midlands	V86MOA	NX West Midlands	V423MOA	NX West Midlands
T679FOB	NX West Midlands	V87MOA	NX West Midlands	V424MOA	NX West Midlands
T680FOB	NX West Midlands	V89MOA	NX West Midlands	V425MOA	NX West Midlands
T681FOB	NX West Midlands	V91MOA	NX West Midlands	V426MOA	NX West Midlands
T682FOB	NX West Midlands	V92MOA	NX West Midlands	V427MOA	NX West Midlands
T683FOB	NX West Midlands	V93MOA	NX West Midlands	V428DNB	EYMS Group
T684FOB	NX West Midlands	V94MOA	NX West Midlands	V428DRA	RATP Group
T685FOB	NX West Midlands	V95MOA	NX West Midlands	V428MOA	NX West Midlands
T686FOB	NX West Midlands	V96MOA	NX West Midlands	V429DNB	EYMS Group
T687FOB	NX West Midlands	V97MOA	NX West Midlands	V429MOA	NX West Midlands
T688FOB	NX West Midlands	V98MOA	NX West Midlands	V431MOA	NX West Midlands
T689FOB	NX West Midlands	V101MOA	NX West Midlands	V433MOA	NX West Midlands
T690FOB	NX West Midlands	V102MOA	NX West Midlands	V440MOA	NX West Midlands
T701APX	EYMS Group	V103MOA	NX West Midlands	V450MOA	NX West Midlands
T875HGT	Rotala	V104MOA	NX West Midlands	V455MOA	NX West Midlands
T876HGT	Rotala	V105MOA	NX West Midlands	V460MOA	NX West Midlands
T877HGT	Rotala	V106MOA	NX West Midlands	V466MOA	NX West Midlands
T881KLF	Rotala	V107MOA	NX West Midlands	V470MOA	NX West Midlands
T884KLF	Rotala	V109MOA	NX West Midlands	V477MOA	NX West Midlands
T885KLF	Rotala	V159EFS	Centrebus	V480MOA	NX West Midlands
T949BNN	Centrebus	V165ESL	NX West Midlands	V490MOA	NX West Midlands
TAZ4062	Centrebus	V166ESL	NX West Midlands	V499MOA	NX West Midlands
TAZ4063	Centrebus	V167ESL	NX West Midlands	V508EFR	Centrebus
TAZ4064	Centrebus	V168ESL	NX West Midlands	V509NOF	Rotala
TIL4051	Centrebus	V169ESL	NX West Midlands	V540ESC	Rotala
TJI6925	RATP Group	V170ESL	NX West Midlands	V541ESC	Rotala
TM52BUS	TrentBarton	V170MOA	NX West Midlands	V542ESC	Rotala
UYF463	Centrebus	V171ESL	NX West Midlands	V542JBH	Transdev

V543ESC	Rotala	W80EYM	EYMS Group	W439WGH	EYMS Group
V543JBH	Transdev	W112DOP	NX West Midlands	W446DOP	Rotala
V544ESC	Rotala	W113DOP	NX West Midlands	W448WGH	EYMS Group
V544MOA	NX West Midlands	W114DOP	NX West Midlands	W461UAG	EYMS Group
V545JBH	Transdev	W116DOP	NX West Midlands	W462UAG	EYMS Group
V546JBH	Transdev	W117DOP	NX West Midlands	W464UAG	EYMS Group
V548JBH	Transdev	W118DOP	NX West Midlands	W466UAG	EYMS Group
V550JBH	Transdev	W119DOP	NX West Midlands	W467BCW	TrentBarton
V559JBH	Centrebus	W119PNP	EYMS Group	W468UAG	EYMS Group
V652HEC	Rotala	W122DOP	NX West Midlands	W469UAG	EYMS Group
V653HEC	Rotala	W124DOP	NX West Midlands	W471RTO	TrentBarton
V654HEC	Rotala	W139XRO	Transdev	W471UAG	EYMS Group
V656HEC	Rotala	W142WGT	Rotala	W474BCW	TrentBarton
V657HEC	Rotala	W178CDN	Centrebus	W475BCW	TrentBarton
V658HEC	Rotala	W181DNO	Rotala	W476UAG	EYMS Group
V660HEC	Rotala	W201EAG	RATP Group	W477BCW	TrentBarton
V691MOA	NX West Midlands	W204DNO	Rotala	W477UAG	EYMS Group
V692MOA	NX West Midlands	W207DNO	Rotala	W478UAG	EYMS Group
V694MOA	NX West Midlands	W208DNO	Rotala	W481UAG	EYMS Group
V695MOA	NX West Midlands	W209DNO	Rotala	W499WGH	EYMS Group
V696MOA	NX West Midlands	W211DNO	Rotala	W523DOP	NX West Midlands
V697MOA	NX West Midlands	W213PRB	TrentBarton	W544WGH	EYMS Group
V698MOA	NX West Midlands	W214PRB	TrentBarton	W561CWX	Transdev
V699MOA	NX West Midlands	W221PRB	TrentBarton	W566XRO	Centrebus
V701MOA	NX West Midlands	W223DNO	Rotala	W567JVV	Rotala
V702MOA	NX West Midlands	W224PRB	Centrebus	W571JVV	Rotala
V703MOA	NX West Midlands	W229DNO	Rotala	W572JVV	Rotala
V704MOA	NX West Midlands	W232DNO	Rotala	W573JVV	Rotala
V705MOA	NX West Midlands	W233DNO	Rotala	W601CWX	Transdev
V706MOA	NX West Midlands	W261EWU	TrentBarton	W601MWJ	NX West Midlands
V844FSG	Transdev	W284EYG	TrentBarton	W602MWJ	NX West Midlands
V857HBY	Rotala	W285EYG	TrentBarton	W603MWJ	NX West Midlands
V860HBY	Rotala	W286EYG	TrentBarton	W604MWJ	NX West Midlands
V862HBY	Rotala	W288EYG	TrentBarton	W605CWX	Transdev
V877HBY	Rotala	W289EYG	TrentBarton	W605MWJ	NX West Midlands
V882HBY	Rotala	W291PFS	TrentBarton	W606MWJ	NX West Midlands
V886HBY	Rotala	W292EYG	TrentBarton	W606PTO	Centrebus
V894HLH	Rotala	W292PFS	TrentBarton	W607CWX	Transdev
V899DNB	Rotala	W293PFS	TrentBarton	W607MWJ	NX West Midlands
V901FEC	RATP Group	W294PFS	TrentBarton	W607PTO	Centrebus
V902FEC	RATP Group	W295PFS	TrentBarton	W608CWX	Transdev
V903FEC	RATP Group	W296PFS	TrentBarton	W608MWJ	NX West Midlands
V903FEC	RATP Group	W301EYG	Centrebus	W608PTO	Centrebus
V906FEC	Centrebus	W302PRB	TrentBarton	W609CWX	Transdev
V907FEC	Centrebus	W335VGX	Rotala	W609MWJ	NX West Midlands
V929FMS	Centrebus	W336VGX	Rotala	W611CWX	Transdev
V941DNB	Rotala	W337VGX	Rotala	W611MWJ	NX West Midlands
V942DNB	Rotala	W361ABD	Rotala	W612CWX	Transdev
VDV138S	EYMS Group	W366ABD	Rotala	W612MWJ	NX West Midlands
VDZ8001	RATP Group	W401JAT	EYMS Group	W613CWX	Transdev
VDZ8002	RATP Group	W408JAT	EYMS Group	W613MWJ	NX West Midlands
VDZ8003	RATP Group	W409JAT	EYMS Group	W614CWX	Transdev
VDZ8004	RATP Group	W411DOE	NX West Midlands	W614MWJ	NX West Midlands
VDZ8005	RATP Group	W411DOP	NX West Midlands	W615CWX	Transdev
VDZ8006	RATP Group	W411JAT	EYMS Group	W616CWX	Transdev
VDZ8007	RATP Group	W411YAL	TrentBarton	W617CWX	Transdev
VDZ8008	RATP Group	W412DOE	NX West Midlands	W617YNB	Centrebus
VU02TSV	Centrebus	W412JAT	EYMS Group	W618CWX	Transdev
VU02TSX	Centrebus	W412YAL	TrentBarton	W618YNB	Centrebus
VU02TSY	RATP Group	W413JAT	EYMS Group	W619CWX	Transdev
VU52UEA	Centrebus	W413YAL	TrentBarton	W659WKH	EYMS Group
VU52UEC	Centrebus	W414JAT	EYMS Group	W681TNV	RATP Group
VU52UEK	Centrebus	W414YAL	TrentBarton	W689TNV	RATP Group
VX05LKM	EYMS Group	W415BOV	NX West Midlands	W694EOP	EYMS Group
VX08HZS	Rotala	W415JAT	EYMS Group	W767URP	Rotala
VX54MSU	Rotala	W415YAL	TrentBarton	W817UAG	EYMS Group
VX54MSY	Rotala	W416JAT	EYMS Group	W901JNF	Rotala
VX54MTE	Rotala	W416YAL	TrentBarton	W902JNF	Rotala
VX54MUC	Rotala	W417JAT	EYMS Group	W903JNF	Rotala
VX54MUO	Rotala	W417YAL	TrentBarton	W904JNF	Rotala
VX54MUP	Rotala	W418YAL	TrentBarton	W905JNF	Rotala
W6JPT	Centrebus	W421DOP	NX West Midlands	W906JNF	Rotala
W30PJC	Centrebus	W421RTO	TrentBarton	W922JNF	Centrebus
W40PJC	Centrebus	W422RTO	TrentBarton	W985WDS	Centrebus
W50PJC	Centrebus	W423RTO	TrentBarton	WA57CYX	Rotala
W60PJC	Centrebus	W424RTO	TrentBarton	WET1K	Centrebus
W70EYM	EYMS Group	W425RTO	TrentBarton	WLT307	RATP Group

Reg	Operator	Reg	Operator	Reg	Operator
WU51LBE	EYMS Group	X584XKH	EYMS Group	Y157HRN	Transdev
WX07UOB	Rotala	X585XKH	EYMS Group	Y158HRN	Transdev
WX58FRR	Rotala	X592EGK	EYMS Group	Y159HRN	Transdev
WX58FRU	Rotala	X603EGK	Rotala	Y161HRN	Transdev
WX58FRV	Rotala	X606EGK	Rotala	Y162HRN	Transdev
WX58FRZ	Rotala	X607EGK	Rotala	Y163HRN	Transdev
WX58FSA	Rotala	X608EGK	Rotala	Y164HRN	Transdev
WX58FSC	Rotala	X609EGK	Rotala	Y165HRN	Transdev
WX58FSD	Rotala	X612ERB	TrentBarton	Y166HRN	Transdev
WX58FSE	Rotala	X627ERB	TrentBarton	Y167HRN	Transdev
X1VTD	Transdev	X628ERB	TrentBarton	Y168HRN	Transdev
X2VTD	Transdev	X629ERB	TrentBarton	Y169HRN	Transdev
X3VTD	Transdev	X631ERB	TrentBarton	Y171HRN	Transdev
X4VTD	Transdev	X636AKW	Rotala	Y172HRN	Transdev
X5VTD	Transdev	X637AKW	Rotala	Y173HRN	Transdev
X6VTD	Transdev	X683RDA	TrentBarton	Y174HRN	Transdev
X7VTD	Transdev	X685REC	TrentBarton	Y176HRN	Transdev
X8VTD	Transdev	X701EGK	Rotala	Y177HRN	Transdev
X9VTD	Transdev	X704UKS	Rotala	Y178HRN	Transdev
X10VTD	Transdev	X732FPO	TrentBarton	Y198KNB	TrentBarton
X11VTD	Transdev	X761ABU	EYMS Group	Y211HWJ	Rotala
X12VTD	Transdev	X762ABU	EYMS Group	Y212HWJ	Rotala
X14VTD	Transdev	X763ABU	EYMS Group	Y213HWJ	EYMS Group
X147JWP	EYMS Group	X764ABU	EYMS Group	Y214HWJ	EYMS Group
X182RRN	Rotala	X808NWX	Rotala	Y242FJN	Centrebus
X183BNH	Rotala	X831NWX	NX Coaching	Y246FJN	Centrebus
X183RRN	Rotala	X832NWX	NX Coaching	Y247FJN	Centrebus
X184BNH	Rotala	X833NWX	NX Coaching	Y251KNB	Rotala
X184RRN	Rotala	X834NWX	NX Coaching	Y252KNB	Rotala
X185RRN	Rotala	X835NWX	NX Coaching	Y253KNB	Rotala
X186RRN	Rotala	X836NWX	NX Coaching	Y254DRC	TrentBarton
X187RRN	Rotala	X837NWX	NX Coaching	Y254FJN	Centrebus
X188RRN	Rotala	X838NWX	NX Coaching	Y254KNB	Rotala
X189RRN	Rotala	X839NWX	NX Coaching	Y256FJN	Centrebus
X194FOR	Centrebus	X840NWX	NX Coaching	Y256NLK	Centrebus
X197RRN	Rotala	X841NWX	NX Coaching	Y257DRC	TrentBarton
X198RRN	Rotala	X842NWX	NX Coaching	Y257FJN	Centrebus
X199RRN	Rotala	X843NWX	NX Coaching	Y257NLK	Centrebus
X201UMS	RATP Group	X844NWX	NX Coaching	Y258DRC	TrentBarton
X202UMS	RATP Group	X845NWX	NX Coaching	Y258FJN	Centrebus
X203UMS	RATP Group	X846NWX	NX Coaching	Y259DRC	TrentBarton
X211HHE	Centrebus	X847NWX	NX Coaching	Y259FJN	Centrebus
X212HHE	Centrebus	X938NUB	Centrebus	Y259NLK	Centrebus
X213HHE	Centrebus	X941NUB	TrentBarton	Y261DRC	TrentBarton
X214HHE	Centrebus	X998WRA	TrentBarton	Y261FJN	Centrebus
X215HHE	Centrebus	XIL6081	Centrebus	Y263DRC	TrentBarton
X227WRA	Centrebus	XIL6082	Centrebus	Y263FJN	Centrebus
X231WRA	Centrebus	XKH455	EYMS Group	Y263KNB	Rotala
X232MBJ	Centrebus	Y1CHT	NX Coaching	Y264DRC	TrentBarton
X232WRA	Centrebus	Y2DRM	Centrebus	Y264FJN	Centrebus
X233MBJ	Centrebus	Y2JPT	Rotala	Y265DRC	TrentBarton
X233WRA	Centrebus	Y2NBB	Rotala	Y266DRC	TrentBarton
X234WRA	TrentBarton	Y3JPT	Rotala	Y271DRC	TrentBarton
X235MBJ	Centrebus	Y3NBB	Rotala	Y272DRC	TrentBarton
X235WRA	TrentBarton	Y20CHT	NX Coaching	Y274FJN	Rotala
X236MBJ	Centrebus	Y20HMC	Rotala	Y276FJN	Centrebus
X236WRA	TrentBarton	Y30HMC	Rotala	Y283HUA	Rotala
X267NNO	Centrebus	Y32YVV	Rotala	Y284HUA	Centrebus
X372CUY	Rotala	Y36YVV	Rotala	Y297FJN	Centrebus
X385NNO	Rotala	Y37SVV	Rotala	Y298FJN	Centrebus
X385VVY	TrentBarton	Y38HBT	Centrebus	Y299FJN	Centrebus
X388NNO	Rotala	Y39HBT	Centrebus	Y301FJN	Centrebus
X441YUB	Transdev	Y40HMC	Rotala	Y301HUA	NX Coaching
X508EGK	EYMS Group	Y49VRH	EYMS Group	Y302FJN	Centrebus
X557YUG	Transdev	Y50HMC	Rotala	Y303HUA	NX Coaching
X562YUG	Transdev	Y60HMC	Rotala	Y351DAB	EYMS Group
X563YUG	Transdev	Y142HRN	Transdev	Y352DAB	EYMS Group
X564YUG	Transdev	Y143HRN	Transdev	Y352FJN	Centrebus
X566YUG	Transdev	Y144HRN	Transdev	Y366GKR	Centrebus
X567YUG	Transdev	Y146HRN	Transdev	Y411CFX	RATP Group
X569YUG	Transdev	Y147HRN	Transdev	Y412CFX	RATP Group
X573YUG	Transdev	Y148HRN	Transdev	Y413CFX	RATP Group
X574YUG	Transdev	Y149HRN	Transdev	Y414CFX	RATP Group
X575YUG	Transdev	Y151HRN	Transdev	Y415CFX	RATP Group
X576YUG	Transdev	Y152HRN	Transdev	Y416CFX	RATP Group
X577YUG	Transdev	Y153HRN	Transdev	Y417CFX	RATP Group
X584EGK	EYMS Group	Y154HRN	Transdev	Y418CFX	RATP Group

Y431PBD	RATP Group	Y776TOH	NX West Midlands	YD02UMU	Transdev
Y432PBD	RATP Group	Y778TOH	NX West Midlands	YD02UMV	Transdev
Y451TBF	Centrebus	Y779TOH	NX West Midlands	YD02UMW	Transdev
Y482VRH	EYMS Group	Y781TOH	NX West Midlands	YD02UMX	Transdev
Y483VRH	EYMS Group	Y782TOH	NX West Midlands	YD02UMY	Transdev
Y485VRH	EYMS Group	Y783TOH	NX West Midlands	YD02UMZ	Transdev
Y486VRH	EYMS Group	Y784TOH	NX West Midlands	YD02UNB	Transdev
Y487VRH	EYMS Group	Y785TOH	NX West Midlands	YE52FGU	RATP Group
Y489VRH	EYMS Group	Y787TOH	NX West Midlands	YE52FHL	RATP Group
Y534XAG	Centrebus	Y788TOH	NX West Midlands	YE52FHM	RATP Group
Y539XAG	RATP Group	Y789TOH	NX West Midlands	YE52FHN	RATP Group
Y701HRN	Transdev	Y791TOH	NX West Midlands	YE52FHO	RATP Group
Y702HRN	Transdev	Y792TOH	NX West Midlands	YE52FHP	RATP Group
Y703HRN	Transdev	Y793TOH	NX West Midlands	YE52FHR	RATP Group
Y704HRN	Transdev	Y794TOH	NX West Midlands	YE52FHS	RATP Group
Y705HRN	Transdev	Y795TOH	NX West Midlands	YG02DJZ	Rotala
Y705TGH	Rotala	Y796TOH	NX West Midlands	YG02FVZ	Centrebus
Y707HRN	Transdev	Y797TOH	NX West Midlands	YG52DFX	Centrebus
Y708HRN	Transdev	Y798TOH	NX West Midlands	YG52DHC	TrentBarton
Y709HRN	Transdev	Y799TOH	NX West Midlands	YG52GDJ	Transdev
Y711HRN	Transdev	Y801TOH	NX West Midlands	YG52GDK	Transdev
Y712HRN	Transdev	Y802TOH	NX West Midlands	YG52GDO	Transdev
Y713HRN	Transdev	Y803TOH	NX West Midlands	YJ04BJF	RATP Group
Y714HRN	Transdev	Y804TOH	NX West Midlands	YJ04BMV	Centrebus
Y715HRN	Transdev	Y805TOH	NX West Midlands	YJ04BOV	RATP Group
Y716HRN	Transdev	Y806TOH	NX West Midlands	YJ04BYH	RATP Group
Y716TOH	NX West Midlands	Y807TOH	NX West Midlands	YJ04HHY	RATP Group
Y717TOH	NX West Midlands	Y808TOH	NX West Midlands	YJ04HHZ	RATP Group
Y718TOH	NX West Midlands	Y809TOH	NX West Midlands	YJ04HVS	NX Coaching
Y719TOH	NX West Midlands	Y811TOH	NX West Midlands	YJ04HVU	NX Coaching
Y721TOH	NX West Midlands	Y812TOH	NX West Midlands	YJ04LXN	Transdev
Y722CJW	NX West Midlands	Y813TOH	NX West Midlands	YJ04LXP	Transdev
Y722TOH	NX West Midlands	Y814BOJ	Transdev	YJ04LXR	Transdev
Y723TOH	NX West Midlands	Y814TOH	NX West Midlands	YJ04LXS	Transdev
Y724TOH	NX West Midlands	Y815TOH	NX West Midlands	YJ04LXT	Transdev
Y726TOH	NX West Midlands	Y816TOH	NX West Midlands	YJ04LXU	Transdev
Y727TOH	NX West Midlands	Y817TOH	NX West Midlands	YJ04LXV	Transdev
Y728TOH	NX West Midlands	Y818TOH	NX West Midlands	YJ04LXW	Transdev
Y729TOH	NX West Midlands	Y819TOH	NX West Midlands	YJ04LXX	Transdev
Y731TOH	NX West Midlands	Y821TOH	NX West Midlands	YJ04LXY	Transdev
Y732TOH	NX West Midlands	Y822TOH	NX West Midlands	YJ04LXZ	Transdev
Y733TOH	NX West Midlands	Y823TOH	NX West Midlands	YJ04LYA	Transdev
Y734TOH	NX West Midlands	Y824TOH	NX West Midlands	YJ04LYC	Transdev
Y735TOH	NX West Midlands	Y825TOH	NX West Midlands	YJ04LYD	Transdev
Y736TOH	NX West Midlands	Y826TOH	NX West Midlands	YJ04LYF	Transdev
Y737TOH	NX West Midlands	Y827TOH	NX West Midlands	YJ04LYG	Transdev
Y738TOH	NX West Midlands	Y828TOH	NX West Midlands	YJ04LYH	Transdev
Y739TOH	NX West Midlands	Y829TOH	NX West Midlands	YJ04LYK	Transdev
Y741TOH	NX West Midlands	Y831TOH	NX West Midlands	YJ04LYP	Transdev
Y742TOH	NX West Midlands	Y833TOH	NX West Midlands	YJ05FNH	Transdev
Y743TOH	NX West Midlands	Y834TOH	NX West Midlands	YJ05FNK	Transdev
Y744TOH	NX West Midlands	Y867PWT	TrentBarton	YJ05FNL	Transdev
Y745TOH	NX West Midlands	Y968TGH	Centrebus	YJ05FNM	Transdev
Y746TOH	NX West Midlands	Y972GPN	Rotala	YJ05FNN	Transdev
Y747TOH	NX West Midlands	Y972TGH	Centrebus	YJ05FNO	Transdev
Y748TOH	NX West Midlands	Y973GPN	Rotala	YJ05FNP	Transdev
Y749TOH	NX West Midlands	Y976TGH	Centrebus	YJ05FNR	Transdev
Y751TOH	NX West Midlands	Y978TGH	Centrebus	YJ05FNS	Transdev
Y752TOH	NX West Midlands	YAZ4142	Centrebus	YJ05FNT	Transdev
Y753TOH	NX West Midlands	YAZ4143	Centrebus	YJ05KHC	Transdev
Y754TOH	NX West Midlands	YAZ8773	Centrebus	YJ05KHD	Transdev
Y756TOH	NX West Midlands	YAZ8774	Centrebus	YJ05KHE	Transdev
Y757TOH	NX West Midlands	YAZ8827	Centrebus	YJ05KHF	Transdev
Y758TOH	NX West Midlands	YC51HAA	Centrebus	YJ05KHG	Transdev
Y759TOH	NX West Midlands	YC51LXX	Transdev	YJ05KHH	Transdev
Y761TOH	NX West Midlands	YC51LXY	Transdev	YJ05KHK	Transdev
Y762TOH	NX West Midlands	YC51LXZ	Transdev	YJ05KHL	Transdev
Y763TOH	NX West Midlands	YC51LYA	Transdev	YJ05KHM	Transdev
Y764TOH	NX West Midlands	YC51LYD	Transdev	YJ05KHO	Transdev
Y766TOH	NX West Midlands	YD02PZJ	Rotala	YJ05PVO	Centrebus
Y767TOH	NX West Midlands	YD02PZK	Rotala	YJ05PWE	RATP Group
Y768TOH	NX West Midlands	YD02PZL	Rotala	YJ05PWF	RATP Group
Y769TOH	NX West Midlands	YD02PZM	Rotala	YJ05PXF	RATP Group
Y771TOH	NX West Midlands	YD02PZN	Rotala	YJ05WDA	Centrebus
Y772TOH	NX West Midlands	YD02PZO	Rotala	YJ05WDD	Centrebus
Y773TOH	NX West Midlands	YD02RBX	Centrebus	YJ05WDE	Centrebus
Y774TOH	NX West Midlands	YD02RBZ	Centrebus	YJ05XMU	Centrebus

Reg	Operator	Reg	Operator	Reg	Operator
YJ05XMZ	Centrebus	YJ08DGY	RATP Group	YJ12GWD	TrentBarton
YJ05XOO	Centrebus	YJ08DHF	RATP Group	YJ12GWE	TrentBarton
YJ06FXP	Centrebus	YJ08DWK	Centrebus	YJ12GWF	TrentBarton
YJ06FXR	Centrebus	YJ08DWL	Centrebus	YJ12GWG	TrentBarton
YJ06HRX	Centrebus	YJ08DWM	Centrebus	YJ12GWK	TrentBarton
YJ06LFO	Centrebus	YJ08DWN	Centrebus	YJ12GWL	TrentBarton
YJ06LFV	RATP Group	YJ08DWO	Centrebus	YJ12GWM	TrentBarton
YJ06WTY	Transdev	YJ08DWP	Centrebus	YJ12GWN	TrentBarton
YJ06YPP	Rotala	YJ08EFL	TrentBarton	YJ12GWO	TrentBarton
YJ06YPR	Rotala	YJ08PFN	TrentBarton	YJ12GWP	TrentBarton
YJ06YRX	Centrebus	YJ08PKK	Rotala	YJ12GWU	TrentBarton
YJ07EFR	TrentBarton	YJ08PKN	Rotala	YJ12MZM	Transdev
YJ07EFS	TrentBarton	YJ08PKO	Rotala	YJ12MZN	Transdev
YJ07EFT	TrentBarton	YJ08PKX	Transdev	YJ12MZO	Transdev
YJ07EFU	TrentBarton	YJ08PKY	Transdev	YJ12MZP	Transdev
YJ07EFV	TrentBarton	YJ08PKZ	Transdev	YJ12MZU	Transdev
YJ07EFW	TrentBarton	YJ09MHK	RATP Group	YJ12MZV	Transdev
YJ07EFX	TrentBarton	YJ09MHL	RATP Group	YJ12MZW	Transdev
YJ07EFY	Centrebus	YJ09MHM	RATP Group	YJ12MZY	Transdev
YJ07EFZ	Centrebus	YJ09MHN	RATP Group	YJ12MZZ	Transdev
YJ07JJO	Rotala	YJ09MHO	RATP Group	YJ12NAE	TrentBarton
YJ07JJU	Rotala	YJ09MHU	RATP Group	YJ12NAO	TrentBarton
YJ07JLU	Centrebus	YJ09MHV	RATP Group	YJ12NAU	TrentBarton
YJ07JNN	TrentBarton	YJ09MHX	RATP Group	YJ12NBA	TrentBarton
YJ07JRO	Rotala	YJ09MJO	Centrebus	YJ12NBB	TrentBarton
YJ07JRU	Rotala	YJ09MJU	Centrebus	YJ12NBD	TrentBarton
YJ07JRV	Rotala	YJ10DFA	Centrebus	YJ12NBE	TrentBarton
YJ07JSZ	Centrebus	YJ10DFC	Centrebus	YJ12NBF	TrentBarton
YJ07JVE	TrentBarton	YJ10EYO	Centrebus	YJ12PHU	TrentBarton
YJ07JVL	Centrebus	YJ10EYP	Centrebus	YJ12PHV	TrentBarton
YJ07JVM	Centrebus	YJ10EZC	Centrebus	YJ12PHX	TrentBarton
YJ07JWA	TrentBarton	YJ10EZD	Centrebus	YJ12PHY	TrentBarton
YJ07JWC	Centrebus	YJ10EZE	Centrebus	YJ12PHZ	TrentBarton
YJ07JWU	TrentBarton	YJ10EZF	Centrebus	YJ12PJO	TrentBarton
YJ07JWW	TrentBarton	YJ10EZG	Centrebus	YJ12PJU	TrentBarton
YJ07OZU	Transdev	YJ10EZH	Centrebus	YJ12PJV	TrentBarton
YJ07OZV	Transdev	YJ10EZK	Centrebus	YJ12PJX	TrentBarton
YJ07OZW	Transdev	YJ10MDE	RATP Group	YJ12PJY	TrentBarton
YJ07OZX	Transdev	YJ10MDF	RATP Group	YJ12PKA	TrentBarton
YJ07PAO	Transdev	YJ10MDK	RATP Group	YJ12PKD	TrentBarton
YJ07PBF	Transdev	YJ10MDN	RATP Group	YJ12PKE	TrentBarton
YJ07PBO	Transdev	YJ10MDO	RATP Group	YJ12PKF	TrentBarton
YJ07PBU	Transdev	YJ10MDU	RATP Group	YJ12PKK	TrentBarton
YJ07PBV	Transdev	YJ10MDV	RATP Group	YJ12PKN	TrentBarton
YJ07PBX	Transdev	YJ10MFV	Rotala	YJ12PKO	TrentBarton
YJ07PBY	Transdev	YJ10MFX	Rotala	YJ12PKU	TrentBarton
YJ07PBZ	Transdev	YJ10MFY	Rotala	YJ12PKV	RATP Group
YJ07PCF	Transdev	YJ10MFZ	Rotala	YJ12PKX	RATP Group
YJ07PCO	Transdev	YJ11EJA	RATP Group	YJ12PKY	RATP Group
YJ07PCU	Transdev	YJ11EJC	RATP Group	YJ12PKZ	RATP Group
YJ07PCV	Transdev	YJ11EJD	RATP Group	YJ12PLF	RATP Group
YJ07PCX	Transdev	YJ11EKT	TrentBarton	YJ51EKB	Rotala
YJ07PCY	Transdev	YJ11EKU	TrentBarton	YJ51EKD	Rotala
YJ07PCZ	Transdev	YJ11ENC	TrentBarton	YJ51EKE	Rotala
YJ07PDK	Transdev	YJ11ENE	TrentBarton	YJ51EKF	Rotala
YJ07PDO	Transdev	YJ11ENF	TrentBarton	YJ51EKG	Rotala
YJ07PDU	Transdev	YJ11ENH	TrentBarton	YJ51EKM	Rotala
YJ07PDV	Transdev	YJ11ENK	TrentBarton	YJ51ELX	RATP Group
YJ07PDX	Transdev	YJ11ENL	TrentBarton	YJ51XSH	Centrebus
YJ07VRV	Centrebus	YJ11ENM	TrentBarton	YJ51XSL	Centrebus
YJ07VRW	Centrebus	YJ11ENN	TrentBarton	YJ51XSO	Centrebus
YJ07VSA	TrentBarton	YJ11ENO	TrentBarton	YJ51ZVX	Centrebus
YJ07VSC	TrentBarton	YJ12GTY	Rotala	YJ51ZVZ	Centrebus
YJ07VSD	TrentBarton	YJ12GTZ	Rotala	YJ54BTV	Centrebus
YJ07VSE	TrentBarton	YJ12GUA	Rotala	YJ54BUA	Rotala
YJ07VSF	TrentBarton	YJ12GUC	Rotala	YJ54BUE	Rotala
YJ07VSG	TrentBarton	YJ12GUD	Rotala	YJ54BUF	Rotala
YJ07VSK	TrentBarton	YJ12GUE	Rotala	YJ54BUH	Rotala
YJ07VSL	TrentBarton	YJ12GUF	Rotala	YJ54BUO	Rotala
YJ07VSM	TrentBarton	YJ12GUG	Rotala	YJ54CFD	RATP Group
YJ07VSN	TrentBarton	YJ12GUH	Rotala	YJ54UBH	Centrebus
YJ07VSO	TrentBarton	YJ12GVD	TrentBarton	YJ54UBR	NX West Midlands
YJ07VSP	TrentBarton	YJ12GVE	TrentBarton	YJ55KZZ	Centrebus
YJ07VST	TrentBarton	YJ12GVF	TrentBarton	YJ55WRA	Rotala
YJ07VSV	TrentBarton	YJ12GVG	TrentBarton	YJ55WTD	Centrebus
YJ07VSX	TrentBarton	YJ12GWA	TrentBarton	YJ56AUA	Rotala
YJ07VSY	TrentBarton	YJ12GWC	TrentBarton		

YJ56AUC	Rotala	YJ60GFY	Centrebus	YK55AVE	Transdev
YJ56AUH	Rotala	YJ60GGP	Centrebus	YK55AVL	Transdev
YJ56AUN	Centrebus	YJ60GGU	Centrebus	YK55ZZY	Transdev
YJ56AUO	Centrebus	YJ60KAA	Transdev	YL02FKU	TrentBarton
YJ56JYA	TrentBarton	YJ60KAE	Transdev	YL02FKV	TrentBarton
YJ56JYB	Centrebus	YJ60KAK	Transdev	YN03NDU	Centrebus
YJ56KAO	TrentBarton	YJ60KAO	Transdev	YN03UVS	Centrebus
YJ56KBF	TrentBarton	YJ60KAU	Transdev	YN03UVW	Centrebus
YJ56LJZ	Transdev	YJ60KAX	Transdev	YN03UVZ	Centrebus
YJ56LKA	Transdev	YJ60KBE	Transdev	YN03UWA	Centrebus
YJ56WFH	Centrebus	YJ60KBF	Transdev	YN03UWP	Centrebus
YJ56WFK	Centrebus	YJ60KFK	Yourbus	YN03UWR	Centrebus
YJ56WGC	Transdev	YJ60KFL	Yourbus	YN03UWS	Centrebus
YJ56WUT	Transdev	YJ60KFN	Yourbus	YN03UWT	Centrebus
YJ56WUU	Transdev	YJ60KFP	Yourbus	YN03WRA	TrentBarton
YJ56WUV	Transdev	YJ60KGA	RATP Group	YN03ZXA	Centrebus
YJ56WUW	Transdev	YJ60KGE	RATP Group	YN03ZXB	Centrebus
YJ56WVN	TrentBarton	YJ60KGF	RATP Group	YN03ZXC	Centrebus
YJ56WVO	Centrebus	YJ60KGG	RATP Group	YN03ZXD	Centrebus
YJ56YDO	Transdev	YJ60KGK	RATP Group	YN03ZXE	TrentBarton
YJ57BBE	RATP Group	YJ60KGN	RATP Group	YN03ZXF	RATP Group
YJ57BNB	RATP Group	YJ60KGO	RATP Group	YN04AGY	TrentBarton
YJ57BSU	Centrebus	YJ60KGP	RATP Group	YN04GMY	Centrebus
YJ57EHB	TrentBarton	YJ60LPY	Centrebus	YN04GMZ	Centrebus
YJ57EHC	TrentBarton	YJ60LPZ	Centrebus	YN04LWT	Centrebus
YJ57EHU	TrentBarton	YJ60LRA	Centrebus	YN04LWU	Centrebus
YJ57EYL	Rotala	YJ60LRE	Centrebus	YN04LXS	Rotala
YJ57UFH	Centrebus	YJ61CHD	Rotala	YN04XZC	TrentBarton
YJ57XVN	Transdev	YJ61CHF	Rotala	YN05GZB	TrentBarton
YJ57XVO	Transdev	YJ61CHG	Rotala	YN06CJE	Centrebus
YJ57XVP	Transdev	YJ61CHH	Rotala	YN06CYO	TrentBarton
YJ57XVR	Transdev	YJ61CHK	Rotala	YN06TFY	RATP Group
YJ57XVS	Transdev	YJ61JJE	Rotala	YN07EXP	Centrebus
YJ57XVT	Transdev	YJ61JJF	Rotala	YN07LDC	Centrebus
YJ57XVU	Transdev	YJ61JJK	Rotala	YN07LDD	Centrebus
YJ57XVV	Transdev	YJ61JJL	Rotala	YN07LDE	Centrebus
YJ57XVW	Transdev	YJ61JJO	Rotala	YN07LHT	Centrebus
YJ57XVX	Transdev	YJ61JJU	Rotala	YN07LHW	Centrebus
YJ57XVY	Transdev	YJ62FFZ	Rotala	YN07LHZ	Centrebus
YJ57XVZ	Transdev	YJ62FGF	Rotala	YN07SYS	TrentBarton
YJ57XWA	Transdev	YJ62FGP	Rotala	YN08CWT	TrentBarton
YJ57XWB	Transdev	YJ62FHR	Rotala	YN08CWU	TrentBarton
YJ57XWC	Transdev	YJ62FHV	Rotala	YN08CWV	TrentBarton
YJ57XWD	Transdev	YJ62FHZ	Rotala	YN08CWW	TrentBarton
YJ57XWE	Transdev	YJ62FUD	RATP Group	YN08CWX	TrentBarton
YJ57XWF	Transdev	YJ62FUG	RATP Group	YN08CWY	TrentBarton
YJ57XWG	Transdev	YJ62FVN	RATP Group	YN08DMV	RATP Group
YJ57XWK	Transdev	YJ62FVT	RATP Group	YN08DMX	RATP Group
YJ57XWV	Transdev	YJ62FWB	RATP Group	YN08DNU	TrentBarton
YJ57XWW	Transdev	YJ62FXA	RATP Group	YN08FEO	Rotala
YJ57YCG	Rotala	YJ62FXG	RATP Group	YN08JWC	TrentBarton
YJ57YCH	Rotala	YJ62FXK	RATP Group	YN08JWD	TrentBarton
YJ57YCK	Rotala	YK04JYG	Transdev	YN08JWE	TrentBarton
YJ58CFF	Centrebus	YK04JYH	Transdev	YN08MOF	Rotala
YJ58FFE	Centrebus	YK04JYJ	Transdev	YN08MRO	Centrebus
YJ58FFH	Centrebus	YK04JYL	Transdev	YN08NKH	RATP Group
YJ58FFK	Centrebus	YK04JYN	Transdev	YN08NKW	TrentBarton
YJ58FFP	Centrebus	YK04JYP	Transdev	YN08NLG	RATP Group
YJ59NPA	Centrebus	YK06DNO	Transdev	YN08NLJ	RATP Group
YJ59NPC	Centrebus	YK06EHL	Transdev	YN08OAJ	Centrebus
YJ59NPD	Centrebus	YK06EHM	Transdev	YN09AOS	TrentBarton
YJ59NPE	Centrebus	YK11EKW	Rotala	YN09KHO	RATP Group
YJ59NPF	Centrebus	YK55AAE	Transdev	YN09KHP	RATP Group
YJ59NPG	Centrebus	YK55AAF	Transdev	YN10FKM	RATP Group
YJ59NPK	Centrebus	YK55ATN	Transdev	YN10FKO	RATP Group
YJ59NPN	Centrebus	YK55ATO	Transdev	YN10FKP	RATP Group
YJ59NPO	Centrebus	YK55ATU	Transdev	YN10FKR	RATP Group
YJ59NPP	Centrebus	YK55ATV	Transdev	YN10FKS	RATP Group
YJ59NPU	Centrebus	YK55ATX	Transdev	YN10FKT	RATP Group
YJ59NPV	Centrebus	YK55ATY	Transdev	YN10FKV	RATP Group
YJ60ADU	Transdev	YK55AUA	Transdev	YN11AYA	RATP Group
YJ60ADV	Transdev	YK55AUC	Transdev	YN11AYB	RATP Group
YJ60GFE	Centrebus	YK55AUN	Transdev	YN11AYC	RATP Group
YJ60GFO	Centrebus	YK55AUO	Transdev	YN11AYD	RATP Group
YJ60GFU	Centrebus	YK55AVB	Transdev	YN11FTU	RATP Group
YJ60GFV	Centrebus	YK55AVC	Transdev	YN11FTV	RATP Group
YJ60GFX	Centrebus	YK55AVD	Transdev	YN51MJE	Centrebus

Reg	Operator	Reg	Operator	Reg	Operator
YN51MKZ	Transdev	YT09FME	Centrebus	YX06HVO	EYMS Group
YN53CHC	Centrebus	YT09FMF	Centrebus	YX07HJE	EYMS Group
YN53CHD	Centrebus	YT11LPX	NX Coaching	YX07HJF	EYMS Group
YN53ENL	Centrebus	YT12RLV	NX Coaching	YX07HJG	EYMS Group
YN53SUF	RATP Group	YT51EAO	Rotala	YX07HJJ	EYMS Group
YN53SVE	Centrebus	YT51EBC	NX West Midlands	YX07HJK	EYMS Group
YN53SVK	RATP Group	YT51EBD	NX West Midlands	YX07HKA	EYMS Group
YN53SVL	RATP Group	YT55TMT	TrentBarton	YX07HKB	EYMS Group
YN53SVO	RATP Group	YT59NZZ	NX Coaching	YX07HKC	EYMS Group
YN53SVP	RATP Group	YT59RXR	Transdev	YX07HKD	EYMS Group
YN53SVR	RATP Group	YT59RXS	Transdev	YX07HKE	EYMS Group
YN53SWF	RATP Group	YT59RXU	Transdev	YX07HKF	EYMS Group
YN53ZXA	RATP Group	YT59RXV	Transdev	YX07HKG	EYMS Group
YN53ZXB	RATP Group	YT59RXW	Transdev	YX07HKJ	EYMS Group
YN54DCL	Centrebus	YT59RXX	Transdev	YX07HKK	EYMS Group
YN54OAA	Transdev	YT59RXY	Transdev	YX07HKL	EYMS Group
YN54OAB	Transdev	YT59RXZ	Transdev	YX07HKM	EYMS Group
YN54OAC	Transdev	YT59RYA	Transdev	YX08FWE	EYMS Group
YN54OAE	Transdev	YT59RYB	Transdev	YX08FWF	EYMS Group
YN54OAG	Transdev	YT59RYC	Transdev	YX08FWG	EYMS Group
YN54OAH	Transdev	YT59RYD	Transdev	YX08FWH	EYMS Group
YN54SYG	TrentBarton	YT59RYF	Transdev	YX08FXA	EYMS Group
YN54WCO	Centrebus	YT59RYG	Transdev	YX08FXB	EYMS Group
YN54WCP	Centrebus	YT59RYH	Transdev	YX08FXC	EYMS Group
YN54WCY	Centrebus	YT59RYJ	Transdev	YX08FXD	EYMS Group
YN54WCZ	Centrebus	YT59RYK	Transdev	YX08FXE	EYMS Group
YN55NDZ	NX Coaching	YT59RYM	Transdev	YX08FXF	EYMS Group
YN55NHT	Transdev	YT59RYN	Transdev	YX08FXG	EYMS Group
YN55NHU	Transdev	YT59RYO	Transdev	YX08FXH	EYMS Group
YN55NHV	Transdev	YT60OSO	NX Coaching	YX08FYA	EYMS Group
YN55NHX	Transdev	YT60YYM	Centrebus	YX08FYB	EYMS Group
YN55NHY	Transdev	YT60YYN	Centrebus	YX08FYC	EYMS Group
YN55NHZ	Transdev	YT60YYO	Centrebus	YX08FYD	EYMS Group
YN55NJE	Transdev	YT61FEM	Rotala	YX08FYE	EYMS Group
YN55NJF	Transdev	YT61FEO	Rotala	YX08FYF	EYMS Group
YN55NJK	Transdev	YT61FEP	Rotala	YX08FYG	EYMS Group
YN55NJU	Transdev	YT61FEU	Rotala	YX08FYH	EYMS Group
YN55NJV	Transdev	YT61FEV	Rotala	YX08FYJ	EYMS Group
YN55NKA	Transdev	YT61FEX	Rotala	YX08FYK	EYMS Group
YN55NKC	Transdev	YT61GRF	NX Coaching	YX08FYL	EYMS Group
YN55NKD	Transdev	YT61GRU	NX Coaching	YX08FYM	EYMS Group
YN55NKE	Transdev	YT61GRX	NX Coaching	YX08FYP	EYMS Group
YN55NKF	Transdev	YU04XHY	Centrebus	YX09BKA	EYMS Group
YN55NKG	Transdev	YX02JFY	EYMS Group	YX09BKD	EYMS Group
YN55NKH	Transdev	YX02LFK	EYMS Group	YX09BKE	EYMS Group
YN55NKJ	Transdev	YX02LFL	EYMS Group	YX09BKF	EYMS Group
YN55NKK	Transdev	YX02LFM	EYMS Group	YX09BKG	EYMS Group
YN55NKL	Transdev	YX02LFN	EYMS Group	YX09BKJ	EYMS Group
YN55NKM	Transdev	YX02LFO	EYMS Group	YX09BKK	EYMS Group
YN55NKZ	RATP Group	YX02LFP	EYMS Group	YX09BKL	EYMS Group
YN55NKZ	RATP Group	YX02LFR	EYMS Group	YX09BKN	EYMS Group
YN55PXB	NX West Midlands	YX02LFS	EYMS Group	YX09BKO	EYMS Group
YN55UTA	Centrebus	YX02LFT	EYMS Group	YX09GWA	EYMS Group
YN55WSO	RATP Group	YX02LFU	EYMS Group	YX09GWC	EYMS Group
YN55WTP	EYMS Group	YX03MWG	EYMS Group	YX09GWD	EYMS Group
YN55YSG	Centrebus	YX03MWJ	EYMS Group	YX09GWE	EYMS Group
YN55YSH	Centrebus	YX03MWK	EYMS Group	YX09GWF	EYMS Group
YN56AHY	TrentBarton	YX04JVW	EYMS Group	YX09GWG	EYMS Group
YN56OSG	RATP Group	YX04JVY	EYMS Group	YX09GWJ	EYMS Group
YN56OSJ	RATP Group	YX05EOP	EYMS Group	YX09GWK	EYMS Group
YN56OWP	TrentBarton	YX05EOR	EYMS Group	YX09GWL	EYMS Group
YN57BXG	TrentBarton	YX05EOS	EYMS Group	YX09GWM	EYMS Group
YN57KFE	TrentBarton	YX05EOT	EYMS Group	YX09HYW	Rotala
YN58NDV	TrentBarton	YX05EOU	EYMS Group	YX09HYY	Rotala
YN60FLR	EYMS Group	YX05FFY	Centrebus	YX09HYZ	Rotala
YN60FMO	RATP Group	YX05FNT	Centrebus	YX09HZB	Rotala
YP02LCA	NX West Midlands	YX06CXJ	EYMS Group	YX09HZC	Rotala
YP02LCE	NX West Midlands	YX06CXK	EYMS Group	YX09HZD	Rotala
YP52CUU	NX Coaching	YX06CXL	EYMS Group	YX09HZE	Rotala
YR52VFE	NX Coaching	YX06CXM	EYMS Group	YX09HZF	RATP Group
YR59NNT	Centrebus	YX06CXN	EYMS Group	YX09HZG	Rotala
YR59NNU	Centrebus	YX06CXO	EYMS Group	YX10EYS	EYMS Group
YR59NNV	Centrebus	YX06HVJ	EYMS Group	YX10EYT	EYMS Group
YRC180	TrentBarton	YX06HVK	EYMS Group	YX10EYU	EYMS Group
YRC181	TrentBarton	YX06HVL	EYMS Group	YX10EYV	EYMS Group
YRC182	TrentBarton	YX06HVM	EYMS Group	YX10EYW	EYMS Group
YS10XBO	Rotala	YX06HVN	EYMS Group	YX10EYY	EYMS Group

YX11CNJ	Transdev	YX51AYB	EYMS Group	YX57BXA	EYMS Group
YX11COH	Transdev	YX51AYC	EYMS Group	YX57BXB	EYMS Group
YX11COJ	Transdev	YX51AYD	EYMS Group	YX57BXC	EYMS Group
YX11DVJ	EYMS Group	YX51AYE	EYMS Group	YX57BXD	EYMS Group
YX11DVK	EYMS Group	YX51AYF	EYMS Group	YX57BXE	EYMS Group
YX11DVL	EYMS Group	YX51AYG	EYMS Group	YX57BXF	EYMS Group
YX11DVM	EYMS Group	YX51AYH	EYMS Group	YX57BXG	EYMS Group
YX11DVN	EYMS Group	YX51MUO	EYMS Group	YX57BXH	EYMS Group
YX11DVO	EYMS Group	YX51MUP	EYMS Group	YX58CWA	EYMS Group
YX11DVP	EYMS Group	YX51MUU	EYMS Group	YX58CWC	EYMS Group
YX11DVV	EYMS Group	YX53AOD	EYMS Group	YX58CWD	EYMS Group
YX11DVW	EYMS Group	YX53AOE	EYMS Group	YX58CWE	EYMS Group
YX11FZA	Transdev	YX53AOF	EYMS Group	YX58DCE	EYMS Group
YX11FZB	Transdev	YX53AOG	EYMS Group	YX58DCF	EYMS Group
YX11FZC	Transdev	YX53AOH	EYMS Group	YX59BYA	Transdev
YX11FZD	Transdev	YX53AOJ	EYMS Group	YX59BYB	Transdev
YX11FZE	Transdev	YX53AOK	EYMS Group	YX59BYC	Transdev
YX11FZF	Transdev	YX53AOL	EYMS Group	YX59BYD	Transdev
YX11FZG	Transdev	YX53AOM	EYMS Group	YX59BYF	Transdev
YX11FZH	Transdev	YX53AON	EYMS Group	YX59BYG	Transdev
YX11FZJ	Transdev	YX53AOO	EYMS Group	YX59BYH	Transdev
YX11FZK	Transdev	YX53AOP	EYMS Group	YX59FGM	EYMS Group
YX11FZL	Transdev	YX54FWL	EYMS Group	YX59FGN	EYMS Group
YX11FZM	Transdev	YX54FWM	EYMS Group	YX59FGO	EYMS Group
YX11FZN	Transdev	YX54FWN	EYMS Group	YX59FGP	EYMS Group
YX11FZO	Transdev	YX54FWO	EYMS Group	YX59FGU	EYMS Group
YX11FZP	Transdev	YX54FWP	EYMS Group	YX59FGV	EYMS Group
YX11FZR	Transdev	YX55DHJ	EYMS Group	YX59FGZ	EYMS Group
YX11FZS	Transdev	YX55DHK	EYMS Group	YX59FHA	EYMS Group
YX11FZT	Transdev	YX55DHL	EYMS Group	YX59FHB	EYMS Group
YX11FZU	Transdev	YX55DHM	EYMS Group	YX59FHC	EYMS Group
YX11FZV	Transdev	YX55DHN	EYMS Group	YX59FUO	EYMS Group
YX11FZW	Transdev	YX55DHO	EYMS Group	YX60BZA	Transdev
YX11FZY	Transdev	YX56DZJ	EYMS Group	YX60BZB	Transdev
YX11FZZ	Transdev	YX56DZK	EYMS Group	YX60BZC	Transdev
YX11GBE	Transdev	YX56DZL	EYMS Group	YX60BZD	Transdev
YX11GBF	Transdev	YX56DZM	EYMS Group	YX60BZE	Transdev
YX11GBO	Transdev	YX56DZO	EYMS Group	YX60BZF	Transdev
YX11GBU	Transdev	YX56FHL	EYMS Group	YX60BZG	Transdev
YX11GBV	Transdev	YX56FHM	EYMS Group	YX60BZG	Transdev
YX11GBY	Transdev	YX56FHN	EYMS Group	YX60DWK	EYMS Group
YX11GBZ	Transdev	YX56FHO	EYMS Group	YX60DWW	Transdev
YX11GCF	Transdev	YX56FHP	EYMS Group	YX61EMV	RATP Group
YX11GCK	Transdev	YX56FHR	EYMS Group	YX61FYR	RATP Group
YX11GCO	Transdev	YX56HVF	EYMS Group	YX62FLC	EYMS Group
YX11GCU	Transdev	YX56HVG	EYMS Group	YX62FLL	EYMS Group
YX11GCV	Transdev	YX56HVH	EYMS Group	YY52KXJ	EYMS Group
YX11GCY	Transdev	YX56HVJ	EYMS Group	YY52KXK	EYMS Group
YX11GCZ	Transdev	YX56HYM	EYMS Group	YY52KXL	EYMS Group
YX11GDA	Transdev	YX56JUC	Rotala	YY52KXM	EYMS Group
YX11GDE	Transdev	YX56JUE	Rotala	YY52LCL	EYMS Group
YX11GDF	Transdev	YX57BWD	EYMS Group	YY52LCM	EYMS Group
YX12CGV	Centrebus	YX57BWE	EYMS Group	YY52LCN	EYMS Group
YX12CGY	Centrebus	YX57BWF	EYMS Group	YY52LCO	EYMS Group
YX12CGZ	Centrebus	YX57BWG	EYMS Group	YY52LCT	EYMS Group
YX51AYA	EYMS Group	YX57BWH	EYMS Group	YY52LCU	EYMS Group

ISBN 9781904875 72 7 © Published by British Bus Publishing Ltd, September 2013

British Bus Publishing Ltd, 16 St Margaret's Drive, Telford, TF1 3PH

Telephone: 01952 255669

web; www.britishbuspublishing.co.uk
e-mail: sales@britishbuspublishing.co.uk